Return to the Father

Wisdom from God and His Saints

Given to the Heavenly Grace Prayer Group

Introduction

God is Love.

The words from God and His saints in this book were meant for you. I believe they are a gift from the Holy Spirit that reveals the love that is God. His love for you is greater than any love you have ever known. The love that He has for you at this *very moment*, wherever you are in your life and whatever you've done, is total, perfect, and unconditional. There is nothing you can do to lose His love. God exists, and He loves you absolutely.

That message is the heart of this book which records almost thirty years of grace that impacted every aspect of my life. In 1996, something unusual happened to me. Sometimes when I was in quiet prayer, I would hear the melodic voice of Mary, the mother of Jesus, speaking to me internally. My prayer life improved and I was growing in my Catholic faith as her wisdom led me closer to Jesus. I never expected or wanted my experiences to be more than that. Yet after several months of this private guidance, Mary asked me to begin a journal. "I would like for you to spend several minutes each day in quiet meditation," she requested. "Because the Lord has allowed it to be so, I will give you each day a teaching for the good of the world." Every day after that, she gave me a lesson to write down. These daily teachings were simple and concise. They invite us to live the joy of the Gospel. They speak of peace, patience, mercy, love, and forgiveness. Mary illuminated a way of living in union with God that will bring us true joy.

Mary's daily lessons continued until May 1997. That summer was a time of spiritual rest for me. In August, I was given an interior vision of Mary. The light that exuded from her is the whitest, purest light. It is the same light that I have seen coming forth from everything in Heaven. This light shines in a way that is the opposite of the light on earth. Here, we see objects because a light shines on them and reflects off them, making them visible to us. The things of Heaven produce their own radiant light because they exist perfectly and solely for the glory of God. Glory gleams *through* them!

I was told by Mary that God would send her once per month, each time with a saint. Her daily lessons had reminded us of the scriptural truths we had forgotten and implored us to live them out. The messages of the saints of Heaven would demonstrate that with God's help, this was possible for us. I saw these saints the same way I saw Mary. I discovered that I was able to describe them to others who were present in the room. Each time they spoke, their words came through me to family and friends who were praying with me and listening. We began to audio record the messages so those who were not present could hear them. By the end of the year, a group of people were meeting each month to pray together, learn from Heaven, and support one another in faith. This was the beginning of the Heavenly Grace Prayer Group that Mary has guided to the present day.

We learned that saints are not the ancient, stoic, and unrelatable people that we presumed they are. They are gloriously different and so wonderfully human! They had their natural talents and their weaknesses as we do. They struggled and failed at times in their mission. By trusting God and following Him, they were transformed into beautiful examples of holiness. The hopeful possibility in their stories is that we can choose to become more by living in friendship with God.

I received the last message from a saint in August 1998. Mary asked that our prayer group continue to meet each month. She would teach, encourage, and admonish us when necessary. Occasionally, Jesus chose to speak. In one such message, the Lord explained his purpose for sending Mary,

> "My children, she goes to you as a messenger. I have sent her that you would know that I Am with you, that I shall never leave My people, that My hand works in your lives, that I lead you, that I call you, that I reach into you to bless you, to purify you, to fill you with My Spirit, that you might be filled with love, and joy, and mercy, for it is these gifts that I extend to you. It is these gifts that pour forth from My heart as blood and water, to purify and renew you, as I shall renew the face of the earth."

Encounters with Jesus are astonishingly different than with Mary and the saints. When I see Him, I know I am in the presence of absolute truth and supreme authority, but I am not afraid. I am certain that I am entirely known and perfectly loved. A life lived in intimacy with Jesus is His desire for all of us. His love destroys fear. Being with Jesus helps me understand why sin is so damaging. In the presence of perfect holiness, I want to run from sin which looks so ugly in comparison. I want to be like Jesus! Sin is so much less than the splendor God created us for.

In November 2004, Mary announced that she would no longer impart a message each month. She would return once per year, on the 24th of October. This pattern continues as the words from Heaven still come. In recent years, Jesus has chosen to address the prayer group, and all those across the world who will hear his voice and respond. I see consistency in the messages, but also increased urgency. Our Lord pleaded,

> "I have given this grace to the world because My church, My people, are in need of conversion. They have forgotten

> My love. They do not know their value, their tremendous worth! The Adversary has sown seeds of division and despair where I desire unity and hope. He has sown seeds of hatred and anger where I desire love and forgiveness. He has told you every deceit about who you are. Why can you not hear the Word of your Lord crying out to you from the silence of your own hearts, speaking to you, 'You are loved for all ages?'"

Most of the time I received this grace from God, I was walking in a deep valley. Many difficulties befell my family in a brief time. I was shrouded in grief, confusion, questioning desperation, and even anger at times. There were times when I felt close to God and other times that I did not. My faith was challenged. Yet precisely in the misery, I have met God. He has painstakingly mended my wounds. He helped me emerge with greater wisdom and more resilient faith. I understand that God is present with me at every moment, just as he is even now with you. He sees your suffering. He will respond to your need. You are never left alone. I pray this book offers you hope, comfort, and peace as I close with the words of God,

> "Every heart I see is a broken heart. How much pain have you endured? How much sorrow? How many injuries? How weak have you become under the weight of your own sin? Do you look for reprieve? Do you look for rest? Are you weary of the burdens of this life? Do you cry out for something else? Do you sense in the depths of your soul that this is not as it was always meant to be? That is the image of My love there, for there is no heart that has not been impressed with My love.
>
> If you lived in the misery of this world without the image of My love in your soul, you would not know that you were in misery. You would not seek to look up to find something greater. You would not raise your eyes to Heaven to say, "Father, where have you gone?" It is a mark of your fidelity that you seek me, that you cry out for something else and

rebel against the present darkness in which you live, the present misery that oppresses you, for you were created to be so much more! You were each created to be sons and daughters of the King of Heaven! That is the gift I offer you, that is the truth I speak to you. You are loved beyond your wildest imaginings with a passionate, intimate, love!

Does this surprise you? Do you look to your own failings, and faults, and sins, and think, "How, Lord, could I possibly do your will or accept your love, as weak as I am?" Do you not yet know that My power is perfected in weakness, for where you are weak, I Am strong. Where you are broken, I will heal. Where you are lost, I will find you. Where you grieve, I will give you joy. Where you sorrow, I will bring peace. Where you despair, I will bring hope. Where you die, I will bring life eternal.

Therefore, little ones, step toward Me. Make a motion. Move toward Me. Think of Me. Breathe a sigh of desire toward Me. All that I need to work in you is one moment when you give your will to Me. That is the depth, and the breadth, and the width, and the height of the love and the mercy I extend to you. Reach out to Me, then. Permit Me to save you. Permit Me to love you, to bring you out of the misery and brokenness in which you live and create a new life in you, a new heart, a new soul, a beautiful and infinitely precious creation of My Own heart. Each of you is infinitely precious. For each of you, I give My all. Respond to Me in love and let Me hold you fast to My heart."

The Daily Lessons of Mary

December 1, 1996

My dear daughter, I would like for you to spend several minutes each day in quiet meditation. Because the Lord has allowed it to be so, I will give to you each day a teaching for the good of this world. I would like for you to keep a journal of my words, that it may reach as many of my children as possible, for time is short and the end of the age is drawing near. Do not worry, nor have any doubt in your Lord, for it will be given to you what I wish for you to write. This, the first of my teachings, will be on love. I would like for you to begin your book with that word, for it is most important.

Daughter, even when I walked upon this earth two thousand years ago, in as much humility as I desired to offer the Lord, I could not understand the love and grace of God. He is pure and true love. Love abounds in Him, and He wants nothing more than the love of His children. It is something unfathomable to humankind and only in His kingdom is it possible to understand His goodness. Go now and write what you have been given. You may share news of this, your mission, with others. I love you so much, my daughter, and draw you ever nearer to my Immaculate Heart. May the peace of Christ be with you.

December 2, 1996

My dear daughter, the gift of forgiveness is an essential part of loving your brother as God loves. To truly forgive, you must open your heart to the love and grace of the Father in your own lives. Only then can His infinite mercy fill you and can the coldness of your hearts give way to His compassion. Forgiveness is the first preparation in loving as the Father loves; forgiveness for yourselves and your neighbors. My children who have closed their hearts to the ability to forgive can never find their way from darkness. May the peace of Christ be with you.

December 3, 1996

My little ones, today I would like to speak to you in detail on the virtue of charity, for it is a gift from God so little practiced in this world. Charity is the genuine love and concern for your brother. A person whose heart is filled with charity is able to see Christ in all of God's children. Those who practice charity have great respect for all life, simply because it has been given through the goodness of God. The virtue of charity purifies the heart as the grace, hope, and love of the Father enters your lives. I desire for all my children to understand this gift and seek to bring charity to their lives. May the peace of Christ be with you.

December 4, 1996

My daughter, the Lord is a God of faith. He knows each of His children. As His little ones turn away from Him and choose a path of darkness, He is with them ever faithful, truly believing that His love can pierce their hearts and cause in them a great love and joy. In the same way, He offers to His little ones the gift of faith, that they may choose to see with eyes of love and have peace in their lives. The Lord is a merciful and loving God. He seeks to know His precious little ones and desires for His children to know Him. This, my daughter, can be accomplished only through faith. The great gift of faith encompasses all that is good and holy. Faith is the heart of love and peace, and faith brings great joy to all hearts it touches. Strive, little ones, for an increase in faith. Seek out your Lord in prayer. Know Him. Strive to hear His voice, for He has never left you. His faith in you is unshaken. May the peace of Christ be with you.

December 5, 1996

My dear daughter, today I wish for all my children to hear my plea for holiness. Live, dear ones, a life of holiness. Be pure in mind, heart, and body. Do not allow the passing temptations of Satan to discourage you in your life in God. Reflect on your lives. Do those around you see that you are a disciple of Christ by the example you set in your lives? Does your love for Him radiate from your being? Little ones, the road to holiness is long and there are many places at which to stumble. Continue to pray, children, for the loving guidance of the Father that He may lead you to holiness and renew your hearts. May the peace of Christ be with you.

December 6, 1996

My dear one, as you have considered the promise of marriage in your life, I see fit to speak to you today concerning this most holy sacrament. As your mother, I have offered to you my blessing and raised you to the Father in prayer. Many now enter into Holy Matrimony without fully understanding it's significance in the eyes of God. This is a sacrament in which, like the reception of the Holy Eucharist, two become one. At the moment when God in His glory joins these two, this becomes an indissoluble bond. Marriage does not bind only the two, my daughter, but also binds those children to the Father by their solemn vows, and so it is that a trinity is formed, a sacrament shared by God and His little ones.

Everything created in God is holy. The sanctity of marriage is without measure. Breaking faith with your spouse is a grave matter. This is a sin against your spouse, against yourself, and the dignity of the Church. All married people must follow strictly a discipline of fidelity and respect. God has offered to His children this great gift, union with one another and a covenant with Him. In this age, when so many marriages have been broken by the work of the Evil One, I ask, dear one, for continued prayers for those living this sacrament. May the peace of Christ be with you.

December 7, 1996

Dear little ones, in this age, when so many of God's children walk in darkness, sin is ever increasing. The ugliness of sin is beyond your comprehension. Sin can be likened to putrid mud, staining a clean washed robe. As it destroys the garment, so too is your soul tainted and marred by the sin in your lives. Do not let sin separate you from the Father. When you live in sin, you choose to turn away from Him. Receive often the sacrament of Reconciliation. Ask forgiveness from your God. In doing so, you shall make white your robes and be reconciled in the Lord. May the peace of Christ be with you.

December 8, 1996

My dear daughter, the Lord looks upon the world with great mercy. In the same way, let mercy flood your heart as you look upon all His children. During this season, a time of preparation for the Child Jesus, the greatest gift of the Father, let mercy flow from within you as a gift to your God. Make sacrifices, little one, that through your mercy, many can come to know God. To be merciful, dear one, is to truly be as Jesus is. Let compassion move you, that the Holy Spirit may fill you and do good works through you. May the peace of Christ be with you.

December 9, 1996

My dear daughter, children, may the grace of God be with you. Today I invite you to turn your lives toward holiness. God desires from you perfect love, His love, and true faith. My little ones, holiness is living perfectly God's will for you. Holiness is loving your brother as God loves. Holiness is hearing the call of the Holy Spirit and answering. My little ones, pray always that you would strive to be holy. Pray that you might model the holiness of Christ in all of your work. Dear ones, pray that the holiness of God might unite you with Him.

December 10, 1996

Dear daughter, prayer is the means through which a relationship with God is built. Through prayer many souls can be saved. Prayer benefits not only he who speaks to the Lord, but also those remembered in prayer to the Lord, and allows graces for the whole world. When you pray, bring to your God all the burdens of your life. Lay them at the foot of the cross. Allow Christ to carry them as He carried the great burden of sin upon the cross. Offer also to the Lord your joys. Thank Him for His great blessings and praise Him for His goodness. When you pray, do not merely repeat words, but strive to understand your prayer more fully. Listen too, dear one. Listen for the voice of God in your heart, for He speaks His will in the silence there. I urge you, pray! You cannot understand the importance of prayer. Let not only your words be a testament to your God, but your actions. Live your life as a prayer, a song of praise without end. May the peace of Christ be with you.

December 11, 1996

Dear little ones, so many today parade through life full of pride. In doing so, people often make idols of themselves. It is necessary to realize, my little ones, that nothing is possible without God. Recognize the gifts He has given you. Praise and thank Him, and go out as those given an inheritance and make those gifts multiply among others. Offer back to your Lord all that He has given you by using them for His glory. As an earthly father provides for his children, so too has your Heavenly Father given you all that you need. May the peace of Christ be with you.

December 12, 1996

Dear little ones, you cannot possibly understand how precious you are to the Lord. You are as rare diamonds and gems. For you, the Lord saw fit to send His only Son that He might become flesh born of a simple woman. In humility, He came into this world to bring God's love to His children, to teach them each the way to salvation. For your sake too, He was mocked and scorned, spat upon, and humiliated. Because of His great love for you, He was placed on a cross of wood. There, He suffered many hours until His life left Him. Most importantly, dear ones, for His love of you, He rested in a tomb three days before overcoming the power of sin and death by resurrecting to a new life. For you, His precious children, He ascended into the kingdom and is seated at the right hand of the Father and, for His great love of you, He shall return again in glory. This, dear ones, is the fulfillment of all prophesy from the beginning of the ages. You are more loved by God than all of creation. Why then, children, will you not love one another as your Lord loves each of you? Why do you continue to turn your backs to Him? Daughter, may the peace of Christ be with you.

December 13, 1996

Dear daughter, the most Holy Spirit of God, third person of the Blessed Trinity, is so often misunderstood. The Holy Spirit is the giver of all gifts. It is through the Holy Spirit that God's mercy pours from His heart. The true heart of God, the Holy Spirit, is knowledge and love. The Holy Spirit is the root of faith. Through the Holy Spirit, the work of God is accomplished. My dear one, pray that the Holy Spirit may work through you as He did through the first disciples of

Christ. Pray that you may be used for the glory of God. May the peace of Christ be with you.

December 14, 1996

My dear daughter, praise and give thanks to the Lord God, for He is mighty and has blessed you in so many ways. Those of my children who live in worldly ways do not recognize the great blessings God has given them. So often they ask, "Why Lord?", yet they do not open their hearts to see His will. In good times they are children of God, but when trials fall upon them, they resent the Father. "How", they ask, "could God allow this to be so?" Little ones, know this. The Father in Heaven sees all things beyond your ability to understand, for He is mighty and His love for you is great. Do not dwell on the trials you endure. Do not become frustrated. Instead, trust that God knows your heart and will care for you. Praise Him and offer Him thanks and glory for the gifts He has given. May the peace of Christ be with you.

December 15, 1996

Dear little one, peace is imperative. Your world suffers greatly for lack of peace. The Lord God brings peace to the hearts of men. I desire for all my children to look with trusting eyes to the Father and ask for peace to fill their lives. In this age, when violence erupts so rapidly, the only way is peace. Little ones, if you are truly filled with the gift of faith and with all your hearts love the Lord, begin now to live your faith. In being an example to your brother, in doing as Christ would do, you serve your Lord and your brother. A life in God brings great joy and great peace. You shall overflow with His goodness and love. May the peace of Christ be with you.

December 16, 1996

My dear one, I would like to explain further how to live your life as Christ. Do not live a life as the Pharisees who made a great show of the good deeds they did. Instead, do your good works for the eyes of God only. Instead of boasting about your accomplishments, live humbly. Recognize that all you accomplish is done through the mercy of the Lord. Dear ones, love! To love is to give freely of yourself. Offer all your gifts and your talents for the glorification of the Lord. Work to be an example of charity. Strive to be an instrument of peace. Do not resent your brother, but forgive with unconditional love. Show mercy to all you encounter. Let your life be as a light in the darkness. Dear little children, it is necessary that you pray fervently, for through prayer you are strengthened and filled with the Holy Spirit. Let the light of Christ shine in you. Dear ones, I ask that you increase your devotion to His Sacred Heart, the way to salvation. Remember His great love for you. Know that I pray for you without ceasing as your loving mother. May the peace of Christ be with you.

December 17, 1996

Dear daughter, trust in the Lord, for He works great things in the hearts of men. Know that He cares for you in all things, and His love is beyond your understanding. Each day, let there be a conversion of your heart. Try with all your will to better do what the Lord has asked of you. Do not become frustrated in your journey of conversion. Ask the Father continually for His guidance and mercy. Know that He is ever with you. Be firm of faith. Let no one dispel your hope in God. Dear ones, I wish only for you to become closer to Him, that you might feel His love and joy in your lives in a greater way. May the peace of Christ be with you.

December 18, 1996

My dear daughter, alleluia! Let us, this day, praise God for His goodness! My dear ones, I would like to instruct you on prayer.

Prayer is most important, the most necessary of daily tasks. When you pray, address the Lord as your father, as you have been taught in the scriptures. Offer to Him your daily needs and burdens. Thank Him for the blessings you have received. Dear ones, ask always to be filled with the Holy Spirit that you may speak the word of God and act as He would have it. Pray that His will becomes your will. Allow Him to touch your hearts, to turn hearts of stone to His love. Bring to the Father all people in your prayers, especially those who do not yet know His love. Dear ones, sing a glad song unto Him, for His mercy and love is abundant! May the peace of Christ be with you.

December 19, 1996

My dear daughter, I cannot emphasize enough the importance of conversion! My little ones must turn their hearts back to God. So many today stumble in darkness, lacking the light of God. Dear ones, conversion is a journey that begins in the heart. Pray that you may become more open to God's love. Offer to Him your whole lives. Let Him change your hearts. Pray little ones! Know God and love Him. He so desperately desires for you to return to Him. Truly, as a shepherd welcomes a lost sheep, so too will your Heavenly Father receive you with open arms. May the peace of Christ be with you.

December 20, 1996

My dear daughter, blessed are all people, for they have experienced the mercy of God! Dear ones, this is a time in which God's mercy flows from His hands as honey. Praise and give thanks, for you are all blessed. My little ones, continue to seek the will of God in your lives, for His will is perfect. The Father's will can be likened to the work of a fine carpenter, gently built with loving hands. For each of you, He desires many graces. Pray, dear ones, that you might come to recognize His work in your lives. He is ever guiding His precious little ones. Dear children, all confusion and destruction of the souls of men is caused by the Evil One. Do not allow him to destroy your relationship with God, for in turning your lives over to God's hands, an abundance of joy and peace shall fill you. May the peace of Christ be with you.

December 21, 1996

My little one, all of God's children must learn to be pure in spirit. To be pure in spirit is to practice the virtues of charity, honesty, faith, hope, and love. Remember that you are the dwelling place of the Lord. Offer all you do with your bodies, hearts, and minds to Him. Be as a gentle lamb, reserving your works for the will of God. Know that His love for you is great and you will be given all you need to accomplish His work. May the peace of Christ be with you.

December 22, 1996

My dear daughter, all of God's children are called to live in humility. Recognize, dear ones, that all that is mighty is done through God. See that all people are precious to the Lord, and He has blessed each with His special graces. In every person, God has breathed His life and His love. Live simply, dear ones. Do not allow the worldly attraction of materialism to cloud your vision. Do not allow the vices of greed, pride, and selfishness to cause you to lose your way. The Father in Heaven wishes you to live in humility. Be an example of goodness among your brothers. Work many deeds of great compassion and mercy. Seek out the will of the Lord and desire to be fulfilled in Him. Dear little ones, pray fervently that you may be gifted with the spirit of humility. Study the scriptures and follow the example of Christ, Who so humbled Himself to walk among His people in such a simple way. May the peace of Christ be with you.

December 23, 1996

My dear daughter, I would like for all my little ones to learn the virtue of patience. All things in God's will occur according to His time. When you pray, do not be troubled if it seems your prayers go unanswered. God answers all prayers fully, in His time and by the means which He deems best. You, my children, cannot possibly see all that God sees. In God, the possibilities are endless. What is a lifetime to you, is but a blink of the eyes for the Father. He is eternal and knows what is in your heart. He seeks to give you all that you need. He provides all good things. Do not be lonely or feel abandoned. Your God hears and answers you. May the peace of Christ be with you.

December 24, 1996

My dear daughter, on this eve of my Son's birth, my heart is heavy. Many among you forget my Son. All around your world there will be many celebrations in the morning, yet how many of my children will understand the true gift they have been given? Your world has crumbled under the foot of materialism, even in your own country, where my little ones scramble about in preparation for this event, harboring ill will and selfishness. In many homes gifts will be given, and a celebration had, but Jesus will not be welcome there. It pains my heart, dear ones, to see this. Remember that on this day, God gave Himself completely to you. So much does He love you that He came as one of us, to teach us the way of salvation. Dear ones, rejoice in His love for you. Celebrate His goodness and mercy. Praise Him for His glory. May the peace of Christ be with you.

December 25, 1996

My dear daughter, rejoice! The Lord has done great things for the sake of the world! Upon this day His Son is given, the Redeemer of the world. Let your hearts sing, as the Angels, glad songs unto the Father, Whose infinite mercy and great love is endless. Welcome, my children, the Christ Child into your hearts this day and each day you are given. Let His peace fill you. May His light shine through you, that you become a beacon to guide the lost. Yes, dear ones, you are as lights guiding ships upon a violent storm. As you journey on the road to the kingdom Christ has prepared for you, strive, dear ones, to guide many souls into safe harbor. Dear ones, alleluia! Christ is born! May the peace of Christ be with you!

December 26, 1996

My dear daughter, from each of my children, I desire a commitment; a commitment to prayer, to fasting, to conversion, and spreading the light of Christ. How easily you commit to tasks in your daily lives, to your jobs, to your friends, to your families. Will you not commit your time to God? The time He has given you is short. Your lifetimes are as fleeting as the wind. Use what you are given. Commit yourselves to the work of the will of God. Allow God to be a priority in your lives. This, dear ones, this is truth, anyone who lives their life with God at the center and heart of all their activities, shall live a life of peace and joy. Can you not do this? A life lived in God is not easy. The road of Christ is littered with thorns. Yet, the most narrow of paths is the most rewarding, and will show you to the Father's kingdom. May the peace of Christ be with you.

December 27, 1996

My dear little one, there are many who would say that Satan does not exist. My little ones, I say to you, the presence of the Evil One is a grave reality. The Scripture teaches that the Angel, Lucifer, was cast out of Heaven with his cohorts because of his terrible sin of pride. Little ones, his greatest weapon is ignorance. The Evil One feeds upon the pride of my children. His way is the way of confusion and darkness. To deny his existence is to fall prey to his subtle trickery. Do not be deceived. Know that he does seek out the ruin of your souls! Your greatest weapon against this adversary is prayer. Enrich your lives in God through prayer. Become ever closer to God. Have no fear, my children. Let those who would walk in the Lord, trust in His goodness, and be assured of His divine guidance. May the peace of the Lord be with you.

December 28, 1996

My dear daughter, why do you find this task so difficult? Do you not know that you need only to open your heart with great trust to the Lord and innumerable graces will flow forth into you? Truly, the Lord cares for His dear children. Let all my little ones learn to reveal themselves to the Lord, as He has given Himself to you. Search your hearts, dear ones. See as God sees. The Lord knows your strengths and weaknesses. As all loving fathers do, He supports and forgives His children with love and mercy. Dear little ones, open your hearts to the Lord. Make for Him there a sanctuary, that He might be ever present in your thoughts, words, and actions. There is no darkness that the light of the Lord cannot pierce. Trust in Him fully, for His love for you is great. May the peace of Christ be with you.

December 29, 1996

My dear daughter, just as the small mustard seed becomes a flowering plant, so too must your faith grow to a new understanding of God's love. Dear ones, to truly love God, you must first love your brother. Forgive your brother and you shall be forgiven. Show others mercy and the fruits of the vine of mercy shall be given unto you. Love also yourselves, as you are a creation of the Lord. Let your body be pure, as your thoughts, words, and actions. Learn to trust, dear ones, with the entirety of your hearts. Truly believe what I have said. You are most precious to the Lord.

Your prayers are heard. He seeks to do what is best for His children. Strengthen your faith, little ones. Pray that you might be moved by the Holy Spirit to a deeper understanding of prayer, faith, and your Heavenly Father. May the peace of Christ be with you.

December 30, 1996

My dear one, the greatest of fears among men is that of death. Little children, I come today to console your hearts and, as your mother, to reassure you in your times of sadness. As your earthly body is left upon this world, know that God will gather each of your souls in His arms. How glad He is to see the coming of His faithful into the great kingdom He has prepared for you. Oh, how great His joy, as He is united with His children, as He embraces them with great love and tenderness! It is written, dear ones, that the Lord shall wipe away every tear from your eyes and you shall live with only joy in your hearts. The splendor of His kingdom is beyond imagination. Be strong in your faith. Know that you shall not be abandoned- not in life, nor in death. May the peace of Christ be with you.

December 31, 1996

My little one, do not judge the Church by the actions of the people. So many now would turn away from their faith because of human conditions. Dear ones, the Church is not only a place of worship. The Church is the completeness of each person, united in faith through Christ. Do not pass judgment on your priests. My sons have much to suffer in these times of great temptation and trial. In the same way, do not judge your brothers. Only God knows the hearts of men. Look to caring for your soul, that you might be an example of the love and mercy of Christ. Dear ones, pray for the Church. In this age, many of my children fall far from faith. Let your churches be purified through your prayers and participation in the sacraments. It is necessary that you learn the law of the Church.

How can one be part of a faith community without knowing what it is he professes to believe? Little ones, guide one another. God has established the Universal Church, the community of the faithful, that through one another, you might remain close to Him. Carry one another through difficult times. Be a source of love and courage. Above all else, be a fountain of faith. Dear little ones, remember God is with you. May the peace of Christ be with you.

January 1, 1997

Dear little one, the Lord in His greatness has created each of His precious children. Each little child of God is an emerald, a fine jewel. Because you are so precious to the Father, live your life with great dignity. Dear ones, all life is to be respected, for man is the masterpiece of God. Your souls are created in His image, placed in your bodies to glorify Him. Just as the Lord is great and merciful, so too are those in His image. Sadly, the wickedness of sin taints your souls. God designed you to be pure and holy, full of dignity, a mirror of Himself. The more you immerse yourself in prayer, little ones, the closer to the Lord you shall become, and you shall truly live as He has intended. May the peace of Christ be with you.

January 2, 1997

My dear daughter, it is important that God's children have hope in Him. Even in the days of Noah, he and his kinsmen survived hoping in the Lord. As the Israelites, led into Sinai, relied completely on their Lord for the manna they ate, so too should you rely on the Lord for all good things. Many of His little ones are so lost. They wander in the darkness without a light to guide them. My dear children, let the Lord be your hope and salvation. Through His mercy, you are saved from the darkness. You, dear ones, have a guide: the cross. Follow the way of the cross. Walk in the footsteps of Christ. Then, dear ones, you will never walk astray. May the peace of Christ be with you.

January 3, 1997

My dear daughter, daily my Jesus is abandoned and left alone in your tabernacles. My dear children, the Most Holy Eucharist, given to you as a symbol of the new covenant between God and His people, is the true body and blood of Christ. Within this most holy sacrament lies your Lord. Dear ones, as in reconciliation with the Lord, this sacrament unites you with the Lord. Understand that, though concealed in the humble bread you offer, God truly comes to you. Each day my Son waits in His eucharistic form for His dear ones to come before Him to worship and adore Him. He waits for the children of God to bring before Him their joys and sorrows, but how He is left abandoned! Many times, I have come to Him with the Angels, in sanctuaries and churches everywhere, to console Him in His loneliness. Dearest little ones, would you not console your Jesus? Would you not stay with Him a short while, as His followers did in Gethsemane? Dearest little ones, how He desires your company! Go to your churches and recognize the mighty power of God in the Holy Eucharist. Look with eyes of faith and see your Savior and Lord, Jesus the Christ. May the peace of Christ be with you.

January 4, 1997

My little one, be as little children, dear ones, and look upon your Father with trusting eyes. I would like for all my dear children to place their trust in God. The Lord knows all things and His will is perfect. Trust that He will guide and aid His children. Know that He loves each of you. You are so precious that He would forsake even His Son for you. You are so precious that He would offer Himself to you in the Eucharist. You are so loved that He would come to you in the sacraments. Trust in your Lord. Allow His strength to carry you and comfort you in all things. My dear children, pray that you might learn to trust with the fullness of your hearts. May the peace of Christ be with you.

January 5, 1997

My dear daughter, there are many of my children who claim to be children of God, yet they have hate for their brother in their hearts. There are those who call themselves followers of Christ, yet they cloud their souls with terrible sins. Even still, there are some who say they are believers, but they walk past the hurt and spit on the lame. Dear little ones, now is the time to decide. If you are not for God, you stand against Him. There is no room to stand between. My dear children, choose to walk the road of God. Live in His light and love. Do not be mastered by the temptations and material idols of this world, but instead allow the Lord to be the king of your heart. Live each day, each moment, for the Lord. Offer to Him all you have to give. Truly, you shall be rewarded one-hundredfold for the deeds you have done for the glory of God. May the peace of Christ be with you.

January 6, 1997

My dear daughter, it is good, dear children, to study the Scripture daily. Read and meditate on the words and actions of the Lord. God has provided for you, through His divine will, the Gospels, that you might be further inspired by the life and works of Christ. Dear little ones, let the Scripture guide you to a better understanding of your God and His covenant with His people. See His love for you in His words. Let the Scripture be a guide for you to teach you the way of life. Live, dear ones, as you have been taught, with the love and mercy of God in your hearts. God speaks to each of His children in the Holy Bible. Read, meditate, and believe! Most importantly, live the way of God. Let His lessons and instruction guide you. May the peace of Christ be with you.

January 7, 1997

My dear daughter, children are so dear to God. Their hearts are light and pure. They look upon the Father with trusting eyes and full faith. Dear ones, I pray that your children may always be a treasure in your hearts. Each little one is a blessing sent by God in His great love. My dear children, teach your little ones the way of faith. Plant in them the roots of love and compassion. The Lord has entrusted to you these precious little ones. As Jesus calls for all children to come unto Him, so I call that I may truly be your mother. Dear ones, as you love and care for your children, so God does for you. Strive to be teachers. Live a life of goodness that your children will see your works and believe. The Heavenly Father, Whose children are numerous throughout this world, desires from you not only your good works, but also your prayers. Pray, dear ones, that the youth might find the way of the Lord through your love, faith, and example. May the peace of Christ be with you.

January 8, 1997

My dear daughter, let peace be in your heart. My little ones, do not hold grievances against your brother. Forgive all wrong done unto you. My little ones, pray for those who have done harm to you. Fast and offer sacrifices for their good. Little ones, it is easy for you to love your friend. A much greater deed is it to show mercy to your enemy. As Christ forgave His persecutors from the cross, asking the Father to pardon them from their wrongdoing, forgive without conditions. Be an example of unconditional love. Do unto your brother as you would treat your Lord, for He is truly in the hearts of all men who invite Him there. Do not judge if you wish not to be judged. Do not persecute if you desire not to be persecuted. Instead, let God's great mercy be with you, that you might show compassion to your brother. May the peace of Christ be with you.

January 9, 1997

My little one, blessed are the meek of the earth, for they shall be glorified in the Father's kingdom. Dear ones, learn to be meek and humble, that the love of God might shine from within you. If you are persecuted and mocked for your faith, recall that Christ too was persecuted. If you are wronged by your brother, recognize that you too have sinned and do not judge him. No one is fit to judge the heart of a man but the Father. My little ones, it is through the humble that the Most Holy Spirit works great things. Your humility before the greatness of the Lord is a great sign to those who do not believe in the strength of your faith. Therefore, dear ones, look to your God in humility and pray that through your simpleness, you might serve Him. Pray that His will be done in all things, that you might be filled with peace and joy. May the peace of Christ be with you.

January 10, 1997

My dear daughter, I would like for all my children to understand what it means to have faith. Dear ones, to be faithful is to believe with all of your heart in God's great love for you. To have faith is to love the Lord so much that you would offer to Him your whole life as He has done for you. Faith, little ones, is striving to live in the way of Christ, for He has come to show you the way to His kingdom. My little ones, if you had faith within you, you would speak the truth to all you meet, for you would be so overjoyed you could not be still. My dear ones, I only wish that you would pray for the gift of faith. If you had true faith in your hearts, you would have nothing to fear, trusting in the Lord completely for all you need. My dear little ones, welcome faith in your hearts. Nurture and strengthen your faith. Live your faith. May the peace of Christ be with you.

January 11, 1997

My little daughter, it is very important for all my children to practice obedience. The Lord has given you His commandments to teach you to live righteously. Obedience to His law and His will is necessary. Your Father in Heaven loves you greatly and desires for you to obey Him. Husbands and wives, be obedient to the vows you have made before God. My dear ones, I assure you, these vows are most solemn and of great importance to God. Dear children, obey your parents. Through His servant, Moses, the Lord has given this commandment. Little ones, obey the laws of the Church. Division and lawlessness can only bear bad fruit. Churches united with one another in God shall stand while the divided fall. In this time of turmoil, I ask especially for your obedience to the papal authority of the Church. So much rebellion stirs against Christ's vicar on earth. Dear little children, pray that God blesses you with the patience and perseverance to be obedient. May the peace of Christ be with you.

January 12, 1997

My dear daughter, the cross has always been a symbol of God's love for you, the means by which He died for you. The cross is a symbol of His ultimate act of mercy. My dear children, today I ask that you see the symbol of the cross in a new way. Just as the narrow boughs of the cross intersect to make the four directions, so too does your life hold many decisions, many directions for you to follow. Just as for the cross, each direction leads to an end. There is only one place that is eternal: the center. The heart of the cross is like the heart of man. It is where what is eternal can be found, the love of God. Dear ones, invite Christ to fill your hearts. Let Him bring you His goodness and peace. Seek Him out, for you shall never be left abandoned. My dear ones, meditate on the significance of the cross and you will, through the grace of God, begin to understand more fully His love. May the peace of Christ be with you.

January 13, 1997

My dear daughter, God has designed each of His children by hand. My little ones, you are certainly created unique and special in the eyes of the Lord. To each of you, He has given many talents and gifts hoping that you would use them to serve Him through serving your brother. Dear children, each of you is blessed. Use the talents God has given you. To some the gift of teaching, to others He gives healing, and yet others receive wisdom. His gifts are more numerous than the stars, yet none is more precious to Him than another. Together, His spiritual gifts and the faith of His children make a most beautiful offering. Do not envy another, dear ones, for what the Lord has given him. To each He gives the gifts best suited to his heart, which can be seen by God alone. Trust that your service to Him through your gifts and talents is made possible through His divine will for each of you. Dear little ones, pray that you might be open to the works of God in your lives and be willing to serve Him in His ways. May the peace of Christ be with you.

January 14, 1997

My dear daughter, so much division exists in your world. The Heavenly Father created all mankind that you might love one another as your brother. Dear children, instead of uniting yourselves together in God, you break that unity. A body cannot exist if the feet separate from the hands. You, little ones, are the true followers of Christ on this earth, commissioned to be His hands and feet. How then, can you complete the work God has prepared for you without one another? Many divisions have been made in your church, in your countries, and even in your homes. Do not see yourselves as better than another. Remember the Pharisee who thanked God he was not as a tax collector, but how much more blessed are the worst of sinners when they view themselves with the greatest humility. Dear children, do not fall divided, but instead be united in God's love for each of you. May the peace of Christ be with you.

January 15, 1997

My little one, blessed are those who work for peace. My dear children, let the light of God be in you, that you would be as a torch to light the way from darkness. Little ones, when so much violence spreads its errors across the world, I would ask you to be bearers of peace. Let peace be your sword and love your shield, as you do the work of the Lord. My little ones, I love you so very much and desire for you to be closer to my Jesus. By imitating Him and living as He teaches, you grow closer to the Father in Heaven. Jesus was the true example of living in peace. Even in His last moments He did not utter words of anger against His enemies but asked that His Father show unto them the face of mercy. My dear children, live in love and in the peace that the Lord desires for all of His children. Truly, may the peace of Christ be with you.

January 16, 1997

My little one, God has created a multitude of angels to give Him glory. In the beginning, the Lord loved His angels, but He desired something more. My dear children, then from His hand came forth all of mankind, created that they would be given the free will to choose the ways of God. Many of His little children chose righteous paths and this brought our Father great joy, yet there remained many who would turn their backs to Him. My dear children, the gift of free will is of the greatest God has given to you, and one that pains His heart deeply. In promising to man the option to choose the course of his life, many were lost. My dear ones, if you could see the great sadness in the heart of the Lord over the loss of His precious ones, you would most certainly die from grief. My little ones, the loving Lord, Who wants all good things for His children, so wishes to deliver His lost ones! And so, He has sent you, that through His faithful a great harvest can be reaped for the Lord. My little ones, offer yourselves to Him, that through you His work can be done, for the Lord is mighty and all things can be done through Him, in Him, and with Him. May the peace of Christ be with you.

January 17, 1997

My dear daughter, the world has been corrupted by the power of selfishness. My little ones, the Evil One has taught you the ways of greed and pride. Idolatry is the faith of the people, their money to be worshiped. I desire generous hearts. I wish for all mankind to learn the ways of compassion and charity. Dear children, if you see your brother in need, provide for him, for the Lord has never left you in want. If your eyes find one who is lonely, embrace him. Your Lord has not abandoned you in your time of need. If you befriend one who shakes with grief, comfort him. Your Lord has sent His most holy Son to be your comforter. Just as the Lord has provided for you, so do I wish for you to give to your brother. Dear little ones, Christ has said that the world shall know His followers by the works that they do. Give freely of yourselves to your brothers. Offer all you have to give, and the Lord shall give you His kingdom in return. My children, this is a most wonderful gift to the Lord, a generous heart. May the peace of Christ be with you.

January 18, 1997

My dear daughter, I would like to remind each of you, with a joyful heart, that I am truly your mother. From His cross, my most holy Son turned to His beloved brother and placed me in his care. His words to me were most precious, "Woman, this is your son". In this, dear ones, my Jesus gave to me the great honor of becoming the mother of all mankind. From the day the Lord first selected this most unworthy woman, He has blessed me. I, this woman who has been given the great gift of becoming the mother of the Christ, not even I am worthy of such honor! Dear ones, I desire so much to be your mother. I love you so dearly! If you only knew how dear you are to my heart. Little ones, I long to guide you to my Lord Jesus. I want with all of my heart for each of you to find your way home to His arms. I am your protectress. Daily, I pray that you might become stronger in your faith. As all mothers look on with great joy as their little children take their first steps, so I am filled with joy as you walk towards God. My little ones, do not fall away to the darkness. How sad I am at the loss of each little one! How I weep for love of them! Dearest children, I desire most, as your mother, for you to love God with all the strength of your hearts, to learn to pray fervently, and to love. I will always intercede on your behalf at the throne of our Father. May the peace of Christ be with you.

January 19, 1997

My dear daughter, the most precious of all bonds are those that exist in a family. My dear ones, God created families that each person would support, love, and learn from each other. The family unit is so very important. Even when the Son of God walked upon this earth, He came as a child in a family. My little ones, so many families are wrenched apart by the evils of this world. We all need to belong with those who love and support us. My dear little ones, pray for all families, that the strength of their faith and love for one another would carry them in difficult times. I would ask that all families come together in prayer, for this is a special time when you are united in God. My dear children, love and support one another. Through each other, grow closer to God. May the peace of Christ be with you.

January 20, 1997

My dear daughter, I would ask for all my children to increase their devotion to the Sacred Heart of Jesus, for it is through this special devotion that His pains are consoled. My dear little ones, when you venerate images of the Sacred Heart of Jesus and meditate on this mystery, God pours down great blessings and graces upon you. It is pleasing to Him that you desire to console

Him in His suffering. Deep love for the Sacred Heart of Jesus is the gateway to God's mercy. How can the Father hold back His mercy and love from His devoted little ones? My dear ones, truly when you pray in honor of the great suffering of the Christ, your prayers make reparation for the sins of the world. There is so much sin and so few who would offer themselves to God. Daily, my children, I call upon the mercy of my Son and intercede on your behalf. In loving the Sacred Heart of Jesus, the pains of His passion are lessened by the warmth of your love. Continue, dear ones, to pray in this way. May the peace of Christ be with you.

January 21, 1997

My dear daughter, may the Lord make of each of us true servants. Dear little ones, now is the time to serve God! Let there be great joy in your hearts as you pray, that He might make His will your will. Dear ones, ask the Lord to change your hearts, that you will be open to the wisdom and guidance of the Holy Spirit and be directed in your lives. Let each precious child of God serve Him, each in their own ways, offering all their works for His glory. Serve in humility. Never is the servant greater than His master. Just as Jesus washed the feet of His disciples, you too are called to wash the feet of your brother. In serving one another, you serve Jesus who reigns over all hearts. My dear children, a life of servitude is difficult. The promise of eternal life with our Heavenly Father has been given to you. Imitate Christ. Use your time to strengthen love and devotion to Him in all your brothers through a life of service. May the peace of Christ be with you.

January 22, 1997

My dear daughter, do not be afraid of the trials and obstacles in your life. Little ones, your hardships are not too heavy for the Lord to bear. Again, dear ones, I encourage you to give up your difficulties to the hands of God. The Lord wants to walk with you on your journey of growth and change. The greatest changes are produced in the midst of the hardest trials. Let God carry you through these times. In doing this, you will grow stronger in your faith and trust in God. My dear children, learn to be holy in all aspects of your lives. In difficult times, learn to rely on the mercy and love of God. Practice the virtue of forgiveness. To forgive your enemy with love in your heart is to be as God is. Continue to strive towards becoming more and more like Christ. My dear children, pray that God will give you the courage to face your trials with Him. As Jesus spoke to His disciples, let any who wish to follow Him take up their crosses. The Lord, Who has conquered the most difficult of crosses, will carry yours for you. May the peace of Christ be with you.

January 23, 1997

My dear daughter, praise and give thanks to the Lord! My dear ones, the Lord gives you so many blessings, and how often do His children forget to give Him thanks! Dear little children, each day, praise the Lord and celebrate the gifts you have been given, the simple gifts that mean so much: food to eat, shelter, love. My children, when you ask the Lord for His blessings and beseech Him to hear your prayers, thank Him, even if it seems your prayers have gone unanswered. No prayer is unanswered, dear ones. God cannot deny His precious ones. Many times, the answer to your prayers does not come in a way that you can understand. My little ones, most importantly, each time you celebrate the Holy Mass and you look upon the sacred body and blood of Christ, fall to your knees in thanksgiving for His sacrifice. It is through His death and resurrection, the true sacrifice and final sacrifice, that you are cleansed from your sins. Through Him you are made holy in the eyes of God. Only through the passion of Christ are you made worthy to inherit the Father's kingdom. Give thanks, dear ones, for God's goodness. May the peace of Christ be with you.

January 24, 1997

My dear daughter, I ask that all my children fill their hearts with compassion. So many of God's little children suffer ills of the body, mind, and spirit. Many, who are young and old, need your mercy, your kindness. Dear children, much is required for a person to be whole and complete. It is not wellness of body, for that is passing. It is not so much wellness of the mind, for no one can comprehend God's works. Dear children, it is wellness of spirit that so many seek out and need so desperately. Each precious little one needs the love of God, and His love radiates in all His blessings. You, dear ones, can be bearers of His love. Find compassion for all children of God. The Lord loves them all tremendously. Show them His love for them. Let it pour forth from an ocean of compassion in your hearts, made possible by the power of the Holy Spirit. May the peace of Christ be with you.

January 25, 1997

My dear one, remember that the Lord sees all you do. He knows the innermost secrets of your heart. He knows your words before they pass your lips. My dear children, do not hide behind shame or regret and distance yourself from the Father. This is not what He desires. Do not feel that you cannot be forgiven for your wrongdoings. What father would not forgive his child? Instead, look with trusting eyes to the Father and ask for forgiveness. Dear little ones, be honest. Search your hearts. Your loving Lord knows your sins. Dear children, make reparation for your sins. Pray and offer sacrifices to amend your wrongs. Dear little one, you must trust that God has forgiven you fully and that His love for you will never cease. May the peace of Christ be with you.

January 26, 1997

My dear daughter, love is greater than all other emotions. Love is the answer to every question, and the truth. My dear children, God is love, and love is His greatest gift to you. There are many now who would exploit the sanctity of Godly love. In this world, love has become trivial and conditional. My little ones, I long for you to know love as God intended it to be. In its purest and most delicate way, love lifts your heart ever closer to God and frees you. Love is a great weapon against the wickedness of sin. My dear children, resolve to live a life of love and peace. Accept this gift from the Father with gratitude and cherish it. Experience love and have God in your hearts. My dear children, as ever, I your mother love each of you. May the peace of Christ be with you.

January 27, 1997

My dear daughter, when you pray, do not allow yourself to be distracted by the world around you, but rather let your heart and mind be completely focused on the words you speak. Understand the meaning of what you pray. Know that God is closer to you than you can possibly comprehend. My dear children, your prayers are the foundation of your relationship with God. Just as Jesus called Peter, "the Rock" of His church, I say that your prayer is the rock of your love for Him. Make your prayer solid, that your faith can withstand the trials of this life. My little ones, God truly is your father. He longs for you to bring to Him all your joys and sufferings. It is important also, dear ones, to remember your brother in prayer, for this serves a two-fold purpose. Your life is blessed for your selflessness and love, and the Lord shall pour His mercy down on all that are brought to Him in prayer. My little children, do not cease to pray, but instead, live your lives as a prayer, giving glory to our Father in Heaven. May the peace of Christ be with you.

January 28, 1997

My dear daughter, there are many of my children who look for signs and miracles to nurture their faith. It is true that God creates miracles and signs so that His little ones might believe, but truly blessed are those who have not seen and yet believe. Blessed are all of you, dear ones, for although you have not seen the face of Jesus, you believe He is Lord, and though you have not touched His cross, you know that He died for each of you. Even though you have not placed your hands in His wounds, you have faith in His resurrection to glory. My dear children, do not seek out wondrous signs and miracles, but seek to deepen your faith and trust in God. Look with the eyes of your soul and see that He is with you and loves you. Know that His protection is upon you, and His love is eternal. My dear little children, trust in the goodness of the Lord. May the peace of Christ be with you.

January 29, 1997

My dear daughter, many do not understand the importance of fasting. Although God's people have offered up fasts to Him many times since He first breathed life into man, many now neglect this sacred act. Dear little ones, in fasting you purify yourselves by denying the pleasures of the flesh. Your mind, body, and heart are freed from the cares of this world and made wondrous for the Lord. In purifying yourselves, you become ever closer to the Lord. When fasting, dear children, offer your small sufferings to console the sorrow of the Lord. Many blessings and great mercy are made possible through your small sacrifices. The Lord accepts your gifts joyfully. Finally, dear ones, when you fast, while depriving yourselves of worldliness, immerse yourselves in prayer. Pray that the Lord will make you strong in the times that a sacrifice is asked of you. Pray that you might have the wisdom and courage to be bold in your faith, while having a most humble heart. May the peace of Christ be with you.

January 30, 1997

My dear one, tonight, I pray that you might be blessed with the spirit of boldness, that you might teach the ways of Christ. Dear ones, there is a great difference between having the courage to stand with God and being too proud not to. Blessed little ones, any man that is filled with the courage and boldness of the Holy Spirit is a holy man. Although strong in faith, he has a meek and humble heart, seeking only to use his gifts for the glory of God. Many men stand with God because of their pride. To be a child of God is to be great in their eyes. These proud little ones take great joy in believing that they are more blessed than their brother. My little ones, truly I tell you, any man who has no love in his heart for God cannot be for the Lord, and any man who has not a meek and humble heart will find no place at the Father's table. The Lord is the shepherd of the humble, those who would give themselves up so that He might be glorified. These little ones shall find that they are given all of God's mercy, while the proud do not know Him. May the peace of Christ be with you.

January 31, 1997

My dear daughter, recall that Jesus has said that a tree might be judged by the fruit it bears. In the same way, I ask you to judge your actions. My little children, as the disciples of Christ, we all strive to do the works of God. Look at your lives, dear ones, as God sees. See the times when your actions have caused pain and sorrow. Also, recognize the times when you have brought the light of God to the darkness that this world offers. Work to act in a way that would always bring the love of God. Remember that you are each a teacher by example, that many who search for God find their way by your compassion and love for all people. My dear children, I desire for all my little ones to walk with the Lord. Be a true example of this light, that you would be a beacon in the darkness. May the peace of Christ be with you.

February 1, 1997

My dear daughter, many times in life, each one of God's little children experiences sorrow and failure. My little ones, when you fail to walk the path of God and stray far, you are not even then abandoned, for God is always with you, calling to you. My dear little children, everyone stumbles, makes mistakes. It is so very important that when you fall from the path of goodness, you pray to God to lead you back to a faithful life. My precious children, remember that Jesus too stumbled on His way to Calvary. Your sins are the weight that the Christ stumbled under, the weight that He took upon His cross, and died for, but in doing so, He made it possible for your soul to be wiped clean of all wrong doings. In dying so you might live eternally, Jesus offered the final sacrifice and the new covenant between God and His people so that forevermore, your sins may be forgiven through the mercy of God. Do not despair in your failings, my little ones, but rejoice in your repentance and forgiveness. May the peace of Christ be with you.

February 2, 1997

My dear daughter, be merciful to all who suffer. My dear ones, a most holy gift is to be shown compassion. Daily there are opportunities for you to show compassion to your brother. Practice the virtue of patience. Listen to the least of my children, and your God will most certainly hear your prayers and answer them. Wipe away the tears from the eyes of a child, and the Lord shall wipe away the greatest sorrows of your heart. Offer love to a hurting stranger, and you will know love. Whatever is given, is received one hundredfold. My little ones, if you give the goodness of your works to the Lord by serving all His children with compassion, the great mercy and compassion of the Lord shall fill you. If you exude His graces, my children, you will receive them one-hundredfold. May the peace of Christ be with you.

February 3, 1997

My dear daughter, I am pleased by the willingness of many of my children to dedicate themselves to God. Remember that it is necessary to reflect Him in all that you do, so that others might see His love in you. My dear little ones, it is never right to slander your brother. Many of my little ones suffer because of the persecutions they endure by words and actions of their brothers. Do not insult another for his actions or talk harshly about him. In doing this, you judge him, and only the Lord has such power. Instead, reach out with the love of God and offer your friendship to him. Do not allow vicious words to be spoken about another, but hold your tongue and pray for blessing upon that peace. My dear children, it is a greater grace to pray for these little ones, and a grave wrong to promote persecution. May the peace of Christ be with you.

February 4, 1997

My dear daughter, the Rosary is a most powerful prayer. I have asked all of my little ones to recite it daily. Dear children, as you meditate upon the life and works of Christ, let the Holy Spirit inspire you to understand, more fully, the Christ. The power of the Rosary is its ability to change the hearts of men. Though all prayers are holy, this is a most special prayer because through it, my little ones come to understand the greatest gift of our Lord, His Son, in a much deeper way. I ask that when you pray the Rosary, you contemplate each mystery. See the Lord's love for you in His sorrowful passion. Know the power of God by the glorious resurrection of Jesus. My little ones, I ask you to pray the Rosary often. Know that I accompany you with the Angels of Heaven in offering this prayer to our Lord. Through the Rosary, God's mercy will embrace the whole world. May the peace of Christ be with you.

February 5, 1997

My dear daughter, while on earth, it is not possible to imagine the splendor of God's kingdom of Heaven. My dear children, the place which the Lord has prepared for you resounds with His glory. In His heavenly kingdom, we meet our Father as He embraces us with joy at our arrival. My little ones, it is as if the Prodigal Son returns to his father, and all the heavens sing out with joy! My dear children, nothing on earth can compare to the kingdom of God. The beauty and love there is beyond this world. I assure you, dear ones, a man can spend one-thousand years looking into the loving face of his Father and his joy will not be quenched. My dear little children, I cannot possibly tell you my joy as I returned home to my Son, to our Lord! I long for each of you to be in Heaven with me. With my Son, we look to the day that we will embrace you and welcome you to the place He has prepared for you, and with my Son, I will joyfully present you to the Father, that you might gaze lovingly on one another, creature and creator. My dear ones, the rapture of that moment, the purity of God's love, is truly wondrous! Pray, dear children, that God will deliver you safely home. May the peace of Christ be with you.

February 6, 1997

My dear daughter, to each of His children, God gives a special call. My dear ones, hear and answer Him! We are all called to the service of the Lord, each in our own way. The Lord has given each of His children gifts and graces. Each is called to a life in God, some to marriage and family, others to the priesthood, others yet to missions of charity. Each one of you, dear ones, has been called in a special and unique way. Many times, the greatest glory can be given to God through the smallest of tasks. My dear children, I challenge you to respond to the Lord's call to you with the fullness of your heart. His path is the true path, and the way to eternal joy. My dear ones, pray that you might recognize the hand of the Lord in your life, and devote your heart to Him fully. May the peace of Christ be with you.

February 7, 1997

My little one, the Lord has planted the seed of His word in the hearts of all men through the Scripture, through His prophets, and by way of all those who serve Him. By His mercy, He has sent me to you that I might teach and instruct you. My dear ones, you have been shown the way to honor the Lord and serve Him. You have been taught how to pray and to love. My little ones, I encourage each of you to resolve to put into action all you have been taught in a greater way in your lives. Each day, strive to love more than the last, drawing ever closer to the Lord. My precious little ones, you are the children of God, His beloved. Let us all give Him glory and praise His name! He desires so much your love, and wishes for each of His children to live in His goodness. May the peace of Christ be with you.

February 8, 1997

My dear daughter, I am saddened by the loss of faith among my children. Dear little ones, do you not know that your God loves you more than all creation? Children, hear me as I assure you that you are so loved. Your Father in Heaven will not forsake you. My precious ones, place your trust in Him. Daily ask Him to guide your lives, that you might follow the road to eternal joy. Be certain that your God hears you and provides for you. Do not lose faith, dear ones. Although many would fall around you, maintain your convictions and dedication to the Lord. It is not an easy journey. Follow the way of the cross, for your Lord and Christ came to free you from your sins and show you the way to the Father's kingdom. May the peace of Christ be with you.

February 9, 1997

My dear daughter, I love all of my children very much. I pray that all of my little ones would come to trust in the Lord. My dear little ones, be examples of the goodness in your hearts. My precious ones, let your souls sing praise to God Almighty for the good works

He has done through you! The Lord will reward you in Heaven, for the way to Heaven is service. Let God bless you with all of His graces so that He might work in you to accomplish His tasks. He desires for all His dear children to reign with Him in Heaven. May the peace of Christ be with you.

February 10, 1997

My dear daughter, daily in your churches you hear the word of God read to you from the Scriptures. My dear children, tonight I ask you to really listen to what it is that God teaches you through His word. The Scripture is a fine treasure, for in it is contained God's new covenant with His people. My little ones, listen to your God, for He speaks to all your hearts. Come to understand His goodness and mercy, His great love for each of you. The Lord has given you the way to salvation through His word. Listen to His call. May the peace of Christ be with you.

February 11, 1997

My little one, during this life there are many decisions to be made and much uncertainty. My little children become lost in fear and anxiety about what is to come. My little ones, do not live in your futures, but in each moment you are blessed with. Why do you worry so? Remember, as Jesus said, the Father cares so dearly for each little sparrow, will He not care for you, His precious children? Do not be anxious or concerned, but live each moment with full faith and trust in God. Remember that your Father in Heaven sees all that you have been, all that you are, and all that you will be. Trust in His loving guidance for your lives. Pray that you will always be drawn closer to Him, especially in times of uncertainty. May the peace of Christ be with you.

February 12, 1997

My dear daughter, Jesus Christ is the king of Heaven and Earth. My dear children, how differently you define a king than the Father! An earthly king bears treasures of gold, while the Christ brought the treasure of life. Your rulers live royally with much splendor. The Christ came into this world in a place fit for a livery. Great monarchs of your time dress in shining garments with gemstone crowns. The Lord wore only rags, gathered from among scraps of stitching wool, without even a cloth to adorn His head. Your kings die celebrated deaths, surrounded by servants and handmaids. My Jesus died as a criminal, with only a few to comfort Him. My dear little ones, as the difference in lives is great, so is the promise of each. From the worldly kings, an abundance from the earth is given. From the Heavenly King, an abundance from Heaven is given. My little ones, he who is meek, is mighty, he who is small, is great, and God shall give you eternal life in His perfect kingdom. May the peace of Christ be with you.

February 13, 1997

My dear daughter, the Heavenly Father created each little child with His own hands. Dear ones, with love He gave you life, filled you with His love, and placed in you a shining soul. My little children, do not become frustrated by the things of this world, for God has counted each of your days until your world passes away. Do not cry out, "injustice", when terrible happenings occur in your lives. Your worries and anger will not add one day to your lives. Do not envy that of another, for all that you have has been given by the Father. Instead, dear ones, use your time wisely. Learn to trust in God's ways and strengthen your faith in times of trial. Sing and praise Him for the life He gave you. Take what you have been given and multiply the goodness of your gifts, for it is true that from him to whom much has been given, much must be reaped. May the peace of Christ be with you.

February 14, 1997

My dear daughter, do not strive to be great among men, dear children, but rather great in the kingdom of God. To be great in His kingdom is to be humble and selfless. Seek not to glorify yourselves, but the God Who loves you so dearly. Strive to be honest, for honesty keeps your hearts pure. The Father in Heaven has given you His holy commandments. Live your lives by their words. My blessed little ones, be great in God's kingdom. Ready yourselves. Do not think that there will be tomorrow to love and serve Him, for you do not know when you shall be called home to Heaven. Serve God with each day you are given, even in the smallest of daily tasks. May the peace of Christ be with you.

February 15, 1997

My dear daughter, the greatest sin of this world is the sin of anger. My dear ones, you fill yourselves with darkness when you give in to the temptations of anger. Anger is the weapon of Satan, for it is the root of hate and injustice, and can only destroy love. My little ones, when you find yourselves filled with anger, ask God to free your hearts, that you might be open to the healing goodness of love. To be angry is to destroy yourself. My dear children, I love you so very much, and wish that you would be filled with joy. Invite peace into your hearts. Where there is the darkness of anger, there is no room for the light of God. I only wish for you to be filled with His love. May the peace of Christ be with you.

February 16, 1997

My dear daughter, today I would like to speak to you on purity and beauty of the soul. So many of my little ones concern themselves with physical beauty. Your bodies are holy temples created by the Master's hands and they are most beautiful. Your beauty, dear ones, shines from within the great gift of your soul. The Heavenly Father has created you lovingly, and the Holy Spirit of God dwells in His creation. Therefore, little ones, have great respect for the bodies God has given you, for they are the creation of His hands and, ultimately, belong to Him. Concern yourselves not with adorning yourselves with jewelry and fine clothing, but develop the rich beauty that is within each of you. Many have made their bodies an idol. They live to serve the pleasures of their earthly bodies. My dear children, as God created man from the dirt of the earth, so you shall return to it. Your eternal soul radiates your true beauty. Through faith, love, and trust in God, your souls will shine as the sun, and be most pleasing to the Father. May the peace of Christ be with you.

February 17, 1997

My dear daughter, praised be Jesus! I am most joyful to be with you. My dear ones, be glad, for the Lord is good and His love is unending. My little ones, I would like to encourage you, once again, to take time to adore our Lord in a special way in the Eucharist. During this time of preparation, when we remember the great suffering that the Christ endured to free the world from sin, recognize with great devotion, His second sacrifice, the Eucharistic Sacrifice. Daily our Lord offers His body, that His precious ones may be united in Him. Pray, dear ones, before His holy body, and all of the graces and mercy of the Father will be given to you. It is before the most blessed Eucharist that the mercy of God can be given most freely to His people. The Lord is greatly pleased by this holy devotion, and your loving attention to His holy body. During this time of preparation, may the realization of the true Christ of the Eucharist bring you closer to the heart of God. May the peace of Christ be with you.

February 18, 1997

My dear daughter, my prayer is that you will persevere in all ways, despite difficulties you may face. My dear children, this life is littered with stumbling blocks, times in your lives when it is easy to stray from the path of righteousness. For many, this occurs in times of great sorrow and loss when they begin to question the way of God. For others, the fall from God's way comes in times of bitter loneliness. Still others stray in the midst of daily trials. My little children, I encourage you to persevere through trial, and continue your walk with God through this life. Strive daily to better answer His call to you through your families, your friends, your careers. Every person is precious to the Father, and each is called to be among His beloved. Give thanks to the Lord for His great mercy, and seek to serve Him. It is in giving your lives to the will of God that you receive true life, a life of love and joy. May the peace of Christ be with you.

February 19, 1997

My dear daughter, it is sad to see how much anger and hatred exists between my little ones. Dear children, you have divided yourselves into many communities of faith. How often those who call themselves "Christians" fight against one another because their faith is not the same, and each serves God differently. Do not be divided, little ones, for the Father of Sin is the cause of division. The Evil One so desires the collapse of the true Church, the Church that God has given you through the way and example of Christ. Do not persecute those who do not profess your beliefs. What right have you to judge their faith, that which only God can see? You are all, dear ones, branches on the same fig tree, though different in many ways. Together you grow in harmony as a complete gift to God and, like the fig tree, if the branches are divided and torn from the tree, it will surely collapse and die. My dear ones, trust that the Lord will strengthen you, that you might grow strong in Him. May the peace of Christ be with you.

February 20, 1997

My dear daughter, God desires pure hearts. Only a heart that is free from the bondage of sin can truly know God. My dear children, that is why it is so important to receive the sacrament of Reconciliation often. This most perfect gift of God unites the Lord and His people through His mercy. Allow the Lord to touch your heart and purify it. God loves the world so dearly! The Christ was sent to take away the sin of the world. You need only to confess and repent. My little children, I wish for you to live holy lives dedicated to the Lord. Pray that you might always be pure of heart, that you might serve God with all of your heart. May the peace of Christ be with you.

February 21, 1997

My little one, I ask, dear children, that you would spend less time making vows and promises to your God and spend more time living your intentions. To give your words will not benefit you, for you are not perfect and will make mistakes. The Lord has lovingly created you this way and understands each of your weaknesses. My dear ones, instead of promising change, live it! Each day become more and more the person God intends for you to be: joyful, peaceful, and radiant with His love. The Lord is a God of forgiveness, and He knows that you will fall. I desire that when you stumble, you faithfully continue to walk closer to Jesus. My little ones, pray that you will begin to fully live in the true example and way of Jesus Christ. May the peace of Christ be with you.

February 22, 1997

My dear daughter, so many of my little ones try so hard to journey through life alone. They struggle through hardships and find that they have no root to hold them to safety. My dear little ones, why do you try so hard to live your lives without God? I ask each of you to examine your hearts. Ask yourselves why it is that you do not depend on God. The sin of pride keeps many from trusting in His ways. My little ones, the Lord wants only to guide you, to carry you through the difficulties and joys of this life. Do not distance yourselves from Him, but rather, embrace His love as He embraces each of you. Pray, dear ones, that you will be given the strength to ask for His guidance. May the peace of Christ be with you.

February 23, 1997

My dear daughter, hate comes easy to the hearts of men. The Evil One infects my dear ones with fear and hatred. My little children, it is because you trust so little that you fall so easily. The Lord is love. All love comes by His grace. He has designed you to be instruments of His love. You, His children, are so precious to Him. He offers to you the gift of love. My dear children, do not allow your weaknesses to trap your hearts in hatred, fear, and anger. Instead, be freed by the love of God. Accept the great love your Lord offers to each of you, and love Him with all your hearts. Love too, your brothers in whom Christ dwells. To honor your neighbor is to love the Lord Who created each of you. I pray that you will be filled with the love of God, and receive the wisdom to overcome the anger, fear, and hatred that is in your lives. May the peace of Christ be with you.

February 24, 1997

My dear daughter, often I have told you of the importance of speaking the Word of God. Today I wish for you to understand the importance of listening. My dear children, when you listen, you begin to experience the peace of God. It is good to spend time talking and laughing together, but it is in the times of silence that your hearts are still and peaceful. Little ones, strive to listen more often, not only to the Lord who whispers in the silence of your hearts, but also to your brother. How many times a lonesome heart can be consoled by a friend! Try each day to take time to listen to your brothers and sisters in God, the world around you, and the silence of your hearts. I pray that in this way you will find greater peace. May the peace of Christ be with you.

February 25, 1997

My dear daughter, your world is so desperately in need of prayer. God has been replaced by money and material. I wish I could show you, dear children, the sorrow, the horrible grief, that the Lord feels when He is rejected by His people. It is unimaginable! How sad it is to see the loss of one of His children to the darkness of the world. My dear children, please pray for those who struggle with faith, for there are so many. Pray that all of God's children will turn to Him for love, mercy, forgiveness, and guidance. Pray that the world will learn to serve and glorify God. In your prayer, you will be strengthened by the love of God and come to understand His ways. My little ones, remember that prayer is so very important. Your prayer unites you with the Father and is a channel of His peace and mercy for all people. Continue to pray, my dear children. May the peace of Christ be with you.

February 26, 1997

My dear daughter, I would like for all of you to reflect on the true meaning of forgiveness. When you forgive, do not allow your heart to continue to be angry with those who have wronged you. Forgive completely, letting the grace of God fill you. My little ones, one of the most difficult of virtues for man to live is the ability to forgive. It is not easy to love those who have hurt you. By your love for them, you are an example of the unconditional forgiveness of God. You cannot imagine the great forgiveness that God blesses the world with. So many turn away from Him, sin against Him, and hate Him, but for those who cry out for His mercy, His love is poured out and He embraces them. My dear ones, in learning to forgive with love, you begin to understand the healing forgiveness of God and move closer to learning to forgive yourselves for your mistakes. May the peace of Christ be with you.

February 27, 1997

My dear daughter, how wonderful it is that tonight you would come to me in this special way. My dear children, I desire for all of you to come before God in prayer. Present your love before the throne of God as you pray with love in your hearts. There are so many who desperately need your prayers! You cannot possibly understand the strength of true prayer. Truly, the faith and trust of a true prayer could move the hearts of all men. When you pray, my little ones, pray with your hearts. Do not recite your prayers, but feel each word in your hearts. Be consciously aware of God's presence with you, as He is always with His people, especially during prayer. My little children, you cannot have a strong bond between two people without talking, sharing, laughing, and crying together. It is the same way with our Lord. Bring to Him all things in prayer, that He will bless you. May the peace of Christ be with you.

February 28, 1997

My dear daughter, the Lord created the Angels, and they love Him dearly. Each of you has a special angel charged to care for you from the moment God breathed life into you. These angels are your spiritual companions, who pray for you without ceasing. In giving each of you a guardian, the Lord has provided for your spiritual guidance. Thank the Lord for the help that His angels offer to you in your daily lives. So often they whisper to your hearts words of comfort or direction, always seeking to glorify God. My dear little children, love these special angels. Be glad that the Lord who loves you so dearly would provide such a companion for you. Pray that you may be united with all people and the heavenly court, in singing praises and glory to God. May the peace of Christ be with you.

March 1, 1997

My little one, I gather together all of my children and protect each with my love for them. Dear children, each of you is so special to God! Each of you have so much purpose. God works in His children. My dear ones, the Lord touches the hearts of those He loves through His little children. If you would only make your hearts open to His love, He would fill you with the greatest of graces. My dear children, the Lord wants to touch you. You cannot possibly know how He desires for you to follow His way, the way of peace and life. My dear children, pray that you might be spiritually strong and filled with love, so that you might be instruments of God's will. May the peace of Christ be with you.

March 2, 1997

My dear daughter, you do not know how important it is that you be willing to do God's work. The Christ calls together His disciples in His churches, and inspires each to serve Him in a special way. My dear children, even in the smallest of daily events, look for the work of the Lord, for truly He works in awesome ways. My little ones, you can be instruments of God's work. Open your hearts to hear His call and pray fervently. It is through prayer that we begin to understand the Father's will. Truly, the Father desires to comfort all of His people. When you serve the meek of the earth, comfort the sick, and befriend the broken, you are doing as He would have it, following the example of the Christ. This is so very pleasing to our Father! Children, pray that you might always seek to serve the Lord throughout your lives. May the peace of Christ be with you.

March 3, 1997

My dear daughter, be determined in your efforts to follow the way of God. Though you may fall, do not become lost. My dear children, look not to your failings to judge your lives, but to what you have accomplished through God for His glory. When our Father carved you out from the dirt of the earth and gave you life, He knew every one of your failings. When He gently placed you in your mother's womb, He felt the pain of each of your sins. Yet, He has such great love for you, that He looks upon you and is pleased by the good works you do. It is human to fail, my little ones, but only by the strength of God is it possible to continue to love through it all. Look not to your faults and weaknesses, but raise up your gifts of love to the Father. May the peace of Christ be with you.

March 4, 1997

My dear daughter, you are all blessed when you practice the virtue of humility. My dear ones, this is so difficult for you in your material world. Surrounded by your possessions and earthly riches, it is difficult for you to be small and easy to lose your way on the path of life. My little ones, truly, you may open your eyes one morning and find that you have wandered far from the Master. It is easy to lose sight of His way. Pray each day that you might come to see your lives as God sees them, and to cherish your eternal lives, while renouncing your lives of material pleasures. This is not to say that all my dear ones must leave their homes, possessions, and families to serve the Christ as His apostles did. Instead, seek to serve the Lord in the midst of your daily lives and earthly goods. Use your gifts, both material and spiritual, to help your brother. My dear children, in serving your brothers and sisters in the family of God, you do serve the Master who created each of them. May the peace of Christ be with you.

March 5, 1997

My dear daughter, greed is a terrible sin that destroys the souls of so many of my children. My dear children, do not have greed in your hearts, but be filled with generosity. Be willing to give of yourselves for the glory of God. All good works done in His name give Him glory, for all of the Angels of Heaven sing out with joy to serve Him. My little ones, share what you have with your brothers and sisters. In the same way, when two are married, your gifts should be given to one another, and God shall let all graces fall upon each. In your families, share your talents and you will all reap rewards. My dear children, in your churches, let no one be denied the gifts you have been given as a whole from your Lord, the gifts of community, of faith, and of companionship. Have generous hearts, my little ones, and the Lord shall generously bless you. May the peace of Christ be with you.

March 6, 1997

My dear daughter, you do not realize how much the Holy Spirit of God directs your life. It is through the third person of God that His will is realized, and His children lift up their voices in song and praise to Him. My little ones, be certain, only through the power of the Holy Spirit can a man utter glorious words unto the Lord. To confess before your brothers that you are a servant of Christ is possible through His graces. My dear children, invite the Holy Spirit of God to come to your hearts each day, that you might be filled with the wisdom and love of God. Through the grace that the Holy Spirit brings, that which is unfathomable can be understood, and that which is difficult becomes a light burden. My dear children, to be filled with the joy and peace of God, His Holy Spirit must dwell within you. Make yourselves pure, that His light might shine through you to light the dark road. May the peace of Christ be with you.

March 7, 1997

My dear daughter, I am quite saddened by the evils of the world. Your world, especially your own country, has become desensitized to the horrible acts of violence that my little ones do to each other. My dear children, I love you so much, as God loves you. Can you not love one another, if only because you love the Lord? A terrible toll does this violence take upon your nation. Each day, you watch such sin in your lives and through your technology. Many of my little children have forgotten God. My dear children, pray that all of God's precious ones will come to understand the importance and beauty of all life He has created. Pray that you all might grow to love and respect all people. You have no right to judge those who hurt you, for only the Father in Heaven shall judge the hearts of men. Pray, my little ones, that those who suffer from the sickness of violence may be healed by the mercy of God. May the peace of Christ be with you.

March 8, 1997

My dear daughter, I love you so very much! Tonight, I urge you, my little ones, to be spiritual support for one another. God sent His beloved Son, our Christ, onto this earth to be the new covenant with His people. Our Lord chose those who would be His apostles, those who would support and care for Him. In the same way, our Lord desires for you to share in a community of faith with your brothers and sisters. My dear children, alone the journey with God can be difficult. The Lord has provided you with your families, your loved ones, and your churches, that you might not travel alone, but united. Strengthen one another and lift each other up when you stumble. Remember, my little ones, as Jesus came together with His beloved, so you too should gather together to strengthen your faith, love one another, and glorify the Father in Heaven. May the peace of Christ be with you.

March 9, 1997

My dear daughter, I wish for all my children to live with joyful hearts. My little ones, so often you are plagued with the worries and disappointments of this life, and you forget to live joyfully! In all times, especially during hardships, pray that you might always be glad for the gifts you have been given and have a grateful heart. Pray that although you might suffer from confusion and turmoil, God will place in your hearts His everlasting peace. Seek to find His peace through your faith in Him. My dear children, I do not want you to suffer. As your mother, I want all good things for you. The way to live joyfully is to decide to live for God. When you place your life in His hands, He will direct you and shape you in ways you cannot imagine. My dear children, accept the trials of this life with faith and take joy in the gifts you have been given. May the peace of Christ be with you.

March 10, 1997

My dear daughter, the most precious of bonds are those of the family. Dear children, be grateful and give thanks to the Lord for His gift of family. Little ones, in the age of capitalism, when a greater emphasis has been placed on earthly wealth, the family has been lost. This most holy bond that God has designed is so often broken. Parents, take great joy in your children. They are the greatest of gifts that the Father desires for you. Spouses, care for one another physically, emotionally, and spiritually. So often in the hurried pace of your lives, the sanctity of marriage is forgotten, and this holy covenant destroyed. Grow in faith together. My dear children, may all families be strengthened through prayer together. I desire for each of you to love your family as purely as God loves you, with much patience and forgiveness. Dear ones, pray that your families may be the rock of your faith, and that all children of God may truly become brothers and sisters in Christ and a part of the family of God. May the peace of Christ be with you.

March 11, 1997

My dear daughter, the Lord shall shield you and hold you close to His heart always. My dear children, the loving Father cradles each of you in His arms. You are His true children. Like an earthly parent who knows what is good for the child, your God gently molds you as He walks with you throughout your lives. My dear ones, how can you not see His presence in your lives, nor understand the graces He gives you? My little ones, rely on the Holy Spirit of God to strengthen you. Pray that you will be given the wisdom to understand His will. My dear children, I ask that you would trust in your Heavenly Father with all of your heart, especially in times of uncertainty. Know also, that because of His great love for you, He has allowed you to be with me. Cherish these precious gifts and begin to live the way God has intended, full of peace and love. May the peace of Christ be with you.

March 12, 1997

My dear daughter, tonight I wish to speak to you on the virtue of living a pure and chaste life. My dear children, the Lord has given you law concerning chastity, asking you to use your bodies only to glorify Him within the sacrament of Matrimony. I wish to speak to you on chastity of the heart. To have a chaste heart is to desire purity. When you wish to do God's will and reject the temptation in your lives, your hearts are light, but many of you would fall beneath temptation and cloud your hearts with sin. Do not allow yourselves to be tempted into weakness in body and mind. To think an ill wish against your brother is no less hurtful to God than to commit that act. My little ones, you are all God's children! He desires for you to love one another with the same love He has for you. Let your minds and hearts be filled with His presence, that your lives will glorify the Lord. My children, live each moment for the Lord, and you shall constantly praise and glorify Him. Pray that He might bless you with purity, for only a heart that is pure can understand His will. May the peace of Christ be with you.

March 13, 1997

My dear daughter, I am so pleased that there are many faithful children who devote themselves to our Lord. My little ones, though you trust in God, though you adore Him, there is still much growth for you to do. No one here on earth can have perfect faith. My little children, each of you has much to learn. Your lives are a journey of love. Each day, you must love more than the last. This is the only purpose, to serve the Lord God, and glorify Him through your love for Him, your brother, and yourselves. My dear children, I encourage you to understand your faith. Meditate on your beliefs. In this way, your trust in God shall deepen and your faith in Him will grow tremendously. Dear children, most importantly, you must pray! Prayer is the way to strong faith and trust in our Heavenly Father. Prayer is a light that guides our hearts towards Him. Prayer lifts each one of God's children up to His loving arms, and unites each one of you in Him. May the peace of Christ be with you.

March 14, 1997

My dear daughter, though our Lord is a God of mercy and love, He is also a God of judgement. To Him, we are accountable for all actions, words, and thoughts. My dear little ones, know that the Lord sees what you do, and knows the will of your heart. From Him, nothing can be hidden. He has created you with His own hands, and can trace every emotion, thought, and deed in your soul with His hands. My dear children, when you come before He Who is mighty, what will you have done with the gifts you have been given? No man knows the hour of his death. My little children, live the will of God while you are here on this earth, that you might have eternal life with Him. You must be responsible for what you have done. Remember, my children, if you live the example of love and gentleness, so shall your Father in Heaven give unto you. A hard heart, and soul without compassion, cannot expect the mercy of God. Pray that you will live as His children, that your meeting will find you at peace in Him. May the peace of Christ be with you.

March 15, 1997

My dear daughter, let joy fill your heart this day and be at peace! My little ones, I come this day to encourage you to recognize the presence of God in your lives, for truly He is there! As a king walks among His people, so too is the Lord in your midst. My dear children, recognize each day all that is from Him, and thank Him for His goodness, for His gifts. Praise Him for your lives, for this most glorious gift. My dear ones, see God in all of those you meet, for the Master dwells in His creation. Be moved by the power of the Holy Spirit to inspire your brother through your lives. May the peace of Christ be with you.

March 16, 1997

My little one, there are many who are called to suffer. They do not know how much the Lord loves them, and they despair. My little children, when you suffer, do not doubt the love of your Lord, nor His presence in your lives. Be assured that in times of suffering, He is with you most lovingly. My dear children, when you suffer, do so with a pure and loving heart. Do not curse the Father in Heaven for what He has done. Instead, offer your suffering to Him as a great sacrifice for those souls who are unable to reach salvation, through their own actions. Yes, my little ones, there are many who would not accept God, and lose the salvation that the Christ has promised to His people. Through your sacrifices, the mercy of God can pour down upon these little lost children, and their hearts might be converted. Pray, dear ones, that in your times of suffering, you will be strengthened by the Holy Spirit and offer it to the Lord for the sake of your brothers and to console the crucified Christ. Dear ones, truly your loving sacrifices are a great comfort to Him, for upon the cross, He did look at the hearts of His people, at those who would mock and hate Him, and at those who would live to love Him. What a great consolation your gifts of love are to our Lord Jesus! Your good deeds are so pleasing, especially the sacrifices you make for your God. May the peace of Christ be with you.

March 17, 1997

My dear daughter, often in times of hardship, many of my little ones would curse the Lord for what has happened in their lives. My dear children, I would like to explain to you that our Lord is not a punishing God. He shall not condemn any soul to a life of misery on earth. My little ones, He is, however, a Lord of justice. Every man will reap the harvest he has sown, just as a farmer must reap from his fields. If he is careful and plants only good seeds in fertile ground, the day of harvest shall be a celebration in his home, but the one who sows weeds among his crops by his wicked deeds and hurtful words will have no reward at that time. The Lord is not a punishing God. His love for you is tremendous. He wishes only to see you home with Him, safely through the trials of life. Remember, my dear children, each day, this story. What will your harvest yield? Pray for the guidance of the Holy Spirit, that you might multiply your gifts one hundredfold for the glory of God. May the peace of Christ be with you.

March 18, 1997

My dear daughter, look at the world around you. See the hurt that all of my children have caused one another. See how your actions, dear children, have offended God. My little ones, tonight I ask that you would pray for the gift of right judgement. So many of my children are foolishly caught up in the evils of this world. My dear children, listen to your hearts, to the conscience the Lord has given you. I desire for you to make good and holy decisions for the way of God. You, my little ones, are not all without faith. There are those among you who are most devoted, and that is pleasing to me and to the Father in Heaven, but even the most faithful fall into the corruption that this world offers. My little ones, a wise man, a fool will never be. You are most blessed with the presence and power of the Holy Spirit of God in your lives. It is through Him that you will receive the graces of wisdom and judgement. Pray, my children, that the world will see God's mercy, and turn its face to His shining love. May the peace of Christ be with you.

March 19, 1997

My dear daughter, I would like to explain to you what it is to be the light of the world. My children, often I have asked you to be the light of God in the darkness. My little ones, be an example of the wisdom and love of God. To be wise is to live your lives according to His will. Your neighbors will look upon you and see His wisdom within you. My little ones, be joyful! Hearts that are given to the Lord are light. Be glad in the knowledge of the love, mercy, and forgiveness of God. Also, be at peace. No one can be filled with the Holy Spirit of God with the turmoil of this life in their heart. Instead, pray that you will receive the strength to accept all things, the joyful and the difficult, with a peace that only God can give. Dear ones, to be the light of God is to be His instrument, whom He works through to embrace His people. Know that this can only be obtained through prayer and sacrifice. Pray, dear ones, that with the strength of God, each of you may be a light so bright that you lead the way to the Father's kingdom. You have been told in Scripture the story of the foolish women who burned all of their lamp oil before the arrival of the groom. In the same way, many of God's children are lost without His light. Through the mercy of God, He shall make His disciples the lamp that will never be lost. May the peace of Christ be with you.

March 20, 1997

My dear daughter, remember how God loves you. Without knowing this, it is not possible to be at peace. You are worth so very much to Him, my children. Dear ones, you are worth the life of His Son! How great is His love! Little children, examine your lives. What is of value to you? What do you find worthy? My little ones who love the Lord, it is easy to forget what is truly valuable. Do not lose sight of that, for you can only suffer the loss of your treasures by stifling them. Remember, my children, do not store up your treasures here on earth where they may be lost or stolen by thieves, but in Heaven, where they shall be offered to the Lord eternally. May the peace of Christ be with you.

March 21, 1997

My dear daughter, grace is a beautiful gift of the Father. My children, to have the grace of God is to be strong in your faith, for it is through His power that you are strengthened. His grace is wisdom, the wisdom to understand the way of God. Little ones, pray that the Holy Spirit of God would fill your hearts, for wherever He is, there too is the grace of God. My dear children, His grace brings peace to the hearts of those it touches. Be at peace! Place your burdens in the arms of the Father, that He might carry them. My dear children, pray that God would bless you with His living grace. May the peace of Christ be with you.

March 22, 1997

My dear daughter, Jesus is our Lord. Let us praise Him! My children, the Christ is the Word incarnate, God made man. So often my faithful ones forget the lessons that Jesus taught you, His beloved, while on earth. Though truly our Lord, my Jesus laughed and wept as you and I. He loved His family and His friends. He learned. He grew. Our Lord came to earth as man to live the way that He desires for each of His children to know. My little ones, in His human life even the Christ was not spared trial and suffering. Oh, the pain of seeing Him crucified. My heart bled that day! The Lord God understands your trials and your hardships. He understands that the road is difficult. My dear ones, the Almighty Father sent to you His Son to be a savior for the world and a testament to the life in God. Follow His example! He will not abandon you on your journey. Have faith in Him. May the peace of Christ be with you.

March 23, 1997

My dear daughter, I wish that all of my children would learn to trust in God fully. Little ones, it is so difficult for you to trust. In your lives, those you trust have failed you. No man can love perfectly, without any faults, and so it is in your families and among those you love that you have been discouraged from trusting. My dear children, God loves perfectly and unconditionally. His love is eternal, and He is unfailing. Place your trust in Him and you shall not fall astray, for He will guide you ever nearer to His heart by means of the Holy Spirit. My dear ones, strive to trust that you might be an instrument of God's will and an example of His love. May the peace of Christ be with you.

March 24, 1997

My dear daughter, it is most important that all of God's children respect one another. It is never right to criticize your neighbor. My dear children, remember that Jesus has taught you this through the Scripture. He has given you the story of a woman caught in the act of adultery. The Lord has said to you through this teaching, "Let the man without sin cast the first stone against her". Dear ones, never has this teaching had more meaning than in these times when there is so much hatred in the hearts of my children. Little ones, the Lord calls you to respect your brother. You, as followers of Christ, are called to be examples of His unconditional love for all of God's children. Remember what you have been taught. The creator dwells in His creation. Just as Jesus asked Saul, why do you persecute Him? When you have no love for God's children, you offend His love for them. My dear ones, I desire most for you to live in the way of God's love, perfect and unconditional love. May the peace of Christ be with you.

March 25, 1997

My dear daughter, there are many who do not understand the reality of sin. Especially in these times of materialism, the world is plagued with sin. My dear children, I love you so dearly and desire that each of you would come to love God with the fullness of your hearts. Little ones, sin keeps you from God, for it is the trap of the evil one. Sin hardens your hearts, making it easier to sin and weakening your consciences. My dear children, to be fully with God you must have a pure heart as He does. The Lord has saved you from this impurity by taking it upon Himself on the cross. Through His death, all men were freed. Little ones, receive often the sacrament of Reconciliation, for this sacrament is a means for God's love, mercy, and healing to your lives. May the peace of Christ be with you.

March 26, 1997

My dear daughter, I wish for all my little ones to practice the gift of generosity. My heart is heavy, for there are so many with so much, who give so little. Even in your own country, where there are many blessings, few of my children would share their graces with their neighbor. My dear children, generosity is a gift that is most precious to those who are in need. My little ones, care for one another. If you have been given much, offer your gifts back to the Lord through His people. Truly, your gifts are given to the Father, for when you feed the hungry and console the broken, you care for our Lord who dwells in all of His people. Dear ones, I assure you, whenever you relieve the suffering of your brother, you have eased the suffering of the Christ. Remember, you are all one family under God. I desire for you to care for and love one another as your Lord loves each of you. May the peace of Christ be with you.

March 27, 1997

My dear daughter, I bless and thank all of my children for your increased prayer. Those who have responded to my call for the glory of God are so very pleasing to Him. My dear children, continue always to pray, for this is so important in your relationship with God. It is easy to drift away from Him in the midst of the worldliness and materialism that you experience daily. Prayer is the bond that holds God's children fast to Him. My little ones, pray often and with the fullness of your hearts. Meditate on your prayer. Let it truly be from your heart. Dear ones, it is so pleasing to me when you come together to share your faith in prayer groups. This is quite important. The Lord placed each of His children here to help and strengthen one another. My dear children, by coming together in His name, you strengthen your community of faith and are strengthened by the Father in Heaven, and the power of His Holy Spirit. May the peace of Christ be with you.

March 28, 1997

My dear daughter, conversion is a journey of inner healing. All is possible through God. His love can convert the hardest of hearts. My dear children, I would like to explain to you the meaning of true conversion. The Lord God touches the hearts of all of His children each day. Those who know Him recognize His love in their lives. Along the journey of conversion, His great love for you becomes a strong rock on which you, little children, might build your faith. My dear ones, the Father in Heaven constantly reaches out to His children. The beginning of conversion is recognizing His love for you and turning all your trust to Him. Go to Him in prayer, dear ones, with your strengths and your weaknesses. Pray that He would inspire you, change you, mold you to His perfect will. My dear little children, conversion takes a lifetime of the power, mercy, and love of God. May the peace of Christ be with you.

March 29, 1997

My dear daughter, tonight I ask you to truly pray that you would come to understand God's love. Dear little ones, it is with His love that I wish for you to care for one another. My dear children, God's love is pure and without conditions. His love does not judge harshly or criticize. The love of God flows freely and is the root of compassion, the way by which you become strong in faith. My dear ones, love one another as He loves you. This is truly the way to be great in the kingdom of God. Love the Lord with all of your strength and you will be blessed with the grace of sharing His love with one another. May the peace of Christ be with you.

March 30, 1997

My dear daughter, alleluia! This is the day that the mighty Lord has risen! Dear children, on this day, the Angels of Heaven sing praise to our loving God. On this day in Heaven, Jesus Christ is the reigning king of all hearts. My dear little ones, on this day, your salvation has been earned by the glorious resurrection of the Great Sacrifice, the Christ. My little ones, I call you to reflect on the mystery of the Resurrection. Truly know in your hearts that the Father in Heaven has done all this, for love of you. It is because of His tremendous love for you that Jesus died and began life anew, that your sins would die with Him. So great is God's love for you, that He has allowed His terrible passion and resurrection into glory. Alleluia! May the peace of Christ be with you.

March 31, 1997

My dear daughter, I would like to reaffirm that I am truly your mother. The Lord has blessed me with the honor of becoming the heavenly mother of all His children. My dear ones, as I cared for Jesus upon the earth, so too do I care for you. I love each of you so very much. I only desire that you love one another and our Lord with all of your hearts. How much peace would this world know if all of my little ones would do so! The Lord is a loving God Whose heart spills over with mercy. He sees that His precious ones have gone astray and as a shepherd, desires to gather them back in His arms. My little ones, He has sent me to gather His sheep, just as He sends you. I come to you and bring His love and glory to my little children. Dear ones, you must now take His light to others, that all might know His goodness. May the peace of Christ be with you.

April 1, 1997

My dear daughter, this is a time of great turmoil in your world. My little children stumble far away from God. My dear children, this is the time when you must be courageous in faith! My little ones, begin to live the lessons I have given you. Have the wisdom to be humble and the knowledge to follow the way of God. He is the light in the darkness of this world. Let those around you know that you are a disciple of Christ in your actions. When you look upon the least of God's people with love in your eyes, the world will know who your master is. My dear children, now is the time to serve. In this difficult time, serve one another! In doing this, you lighten the burden of your brother and serve the Almighty Creator. Dear ones, bow your heads and recognize the deep strength and love of God. In His eternal mercy, find the courage to be bold in your faith. May the peace of Christ be with you.

April 2, 1997

My little one, I call all of my children to reflect in prayer on their lives. Do you live your faith fully? It is so very important that my little children reflect their faith in their lives. You have been taught that faith is a grace that can be spread by example. My little ones, as your mother, I desire for you to be perfectly united with our loving God. I wish for you to know His presence in your lives and to understand His will. My dear ones, I am saddened by how often God's precious children forget Him. Let your daily lives be a prayer with all of your actions mindful of God. Live life to give Him glory. In this way, you will experience His lasting peace. May the peace of Christ be with you.

April 3, 1997

My dear daughter, I bless you and thank you for your prayers for my intentions. My dear children, so many of you struggle with guilt. Your hearts are heavy with this burden. My little ones, when you sin, you offend God. When you ask Him for His forgiveness, He is overjoyed and forgives completely. A repentant heart will never be turned away. My dear ones, the Lord loves each of you just the way you are, even in your sins. How much it pleases Him to see a heart that truly desires His forgiveness! My little children, when you ask His forgiveness with a true heart, know that you have received this grace. The Lord does not want you to suffer from guilt, but to accept His gift of forgiveness with joy. My dear children, place all of your guilt in the hands of Jesus, for He will carry your burden and make your heart light, as He carried the burden of sin upon the cross. Let God's healing forgiveness enter your lives, for guilt can only keep you from Him. Let nothing stand between you and the Father. Trust always in Him. May the peace of Christ be with you.

April 4, 1997

My dear daughter, today I wish to thank my little ones for continuing to pray and learn to live your faith. My dear children, when you chose your professions, you have a great opportunity to live your faith. At this time, pray that God will direct you in His ways. My dear children, every one of God's children has a special call. To some the Priesthood, to others, to teach. Some are called to be healers and care takers. In every vocation, there is the road of God. Be certain that you glorify Him when you chose to do His work. My dear ones, I tell you this is all part of living for God. I have told you that you live for God through your faith, your families, your daily activities, and in all ways that God calls you. Pray that you might begin to live fully in Him. May the peace of Christ be with you.

April 5, 1997

My dear daughter, my little ones place their faith in their earthly goods. Dear ones, these things are passing! What good are all of the riches of the world compared to the kingdom of God? My dear children, I ask that you not seek wealth in the world, but store your treasures in our Father's kingdom. This life is but an instant, a brief moment in eternity. Ah, the joy of living eternally in God! His lasting peace fills your soul. His joy encompasses His dear ones. Little children, His kingdom is greater than the riches of this world. By loving the Lord with all of your heart and in loving your brother as God loves, you will come before Him in His kingdom to be with Him forever. Little children, pray that your hearts would desire only Him. May the peace of Christ be with you.

April 6, 1997

My dear daughter, at the moment when God breathed His life into your body in your mother's womb, your body became the dwelling place of your soul. Little ones, I ask you to respect the bodies that you have been given. They are holy because they have been formed by the Father's hands and are a reflection of Him. His work is always good. Dear children, do not poison your bodies with the pleasures that are offered by this world, but use them to glorify God. Let your hands do the work of Christ and your feet walk the road of God. May your arms embrace His children and your eyes be raised to the heavens as you praise Him. My little children, strive always to be holy in your actions. In this way, your bodies, minds, and souls might be forever united with the Father. May the peace of Christ be with you.

April 7, 1997

My dear daughter, my little children have scattered themselves among many churches. Still, you remain divided. My little ones, you each have come to worship in your own ways, yet do not forget that you are all children of the one Lord who has created you with His love. You must stand unified in Him. My little ones, division can lead only to destruction, for even within each church, the people stand divided. My dear children, as your mother, I ask you to examine your faith. The One Lord is the master of all of His churches and every kind of faith. He is the One in Whom you trust, He Whom you love. When you confront the worldliness and wickedness that threaten your communities of faith and your churches, be united in the Christ. My dear children, it is man who has divided the Church. The Lord is pleased with all of His faithful. Love one another as you would love your Lord. May the peace of Christ be with you.

April 8, 1997

My dear daughter, I call you to reflect today on the Parable of the Sower that has been given to you by Jesus through the Scriptures. Dear little ones, are you living as good, strong seed that grows on the fertile ground of faith, or seed that has fallen on the rocky earth to be scorched by the sun and eaten by birds? The former, dear children, is what I as your mother desire for you. I wish for you to take the Word of God into your hearts and devote yourselves to living as your faith has taught you. How sad it is, little ones, to be as the latter, to reject the Word and life that the Lord offers to you for the sake of worldly pleasure. My little children, I know that this is difficult, to reject the ways of the world. I do not ask you to sell your possessions and remove yourselves from the world, but to live your faith in the midst of it. In your daily lives, let God direct your activities. In this way, you might be His instrument to bring the world back to Him. May the peace of Christ be with you.

April 9, 1997

My dear daughter, I wish to remind you, little children, that your actions impact the lives of those around you. A kind word from a strong, faithful friend can do such wonders in a hurting heart. Your faith can heal the lost. Your love can shelter the suffering. My dear children, you must also remember that each hurtful word you speak against your brother is not only a deep pain for him, but a sin against the Father Who created him. My little ones, my purpose in coming to you is to teach you how to love one another and your God with the fullness of your hearts. Only by doing this will you live with joy always. There is a great peace that enters the hearts of those who know God's love. I wish, as your mother, that you would strive to extend that peace to one another. This is a most important lesson. Pray that you will love more each day until you are called home to the Father's kingdom. May the peace of Christ be with you.

April 10, 1997

My dear daughter, today I wish to urge you once again to work for peace. My dear children, this is a time during which much unrest has come upon the world. Many of my children have become lost and are far from God because they have chosen to reject Him. They no longer have His peace in their hearts, and they suffer from frustration and anxiety. This frustration spills out among their brothers and sisters in the form of anger and violence. The peace of God is necessary to calm the turmoil of this world. My little ones, first I ask that you work for peace in your own hearts. By spending time in prayer and in the presence of the Lord, He will heal your brokenness and extend to you His peace. I ask that you work for peace in your families. Love one another. Your families are a gift from God. Practice the virtues of patience and forgiveness. Finally, I ask that you work for peace in your communities, allowing the light of Christ to shine through each of you, the instrument of

His will, that His peace may come to this earth. May the peace of Christ be with you.

April 11, 1997

My dear daughter, God does not wish for His children to feel ashamed of their sins. He does not demand guilt and anxiety. My dear children, when you have sinned, be repentant. True repentance is twofold. First is the regret of causing sin to enter your heart. Second, little ones, is the desire to change your heart from a sinful state to a state of true union with God in His love. A repentant soul strives for purity. My little ones, God does not wish for you to live in the sins of your past. He does not wish for you to be anxious about your future. Instead, my dear children, live in His forgiveness for today, each day at a time. His mercy and love are so great, He forgives His little ones and carries their sins upon the cross. My dear children, when in your lives you find occasion to sin, pray! Prayer will keep you near to the Lord and hold you fast to His way. May the peace of Christ be with you.

April 12, 1997

My dear daughter, tonight I wish to urge all of my little children to forgive those who have injured them. My little ones, I have spoken to you on the meaning of forgiveness. I wish for you to put this in practice in your daily lives. Little children, anger is a grave sin. This world has been corrupted by the anger that comes only from the Evil One. He is the root of all anger, fear, and confusion. Many of my dear ones fall away to His road of anger. Forgiveness is the greatest weapon against anger, for forgiveness is an act of love. When you forgive your brother for his misdeeds, you are blessed with the grace of God. Continue to forgive one another as God forgives, with a pure and loving heart. My dear children, to forgive is a perfect reflection of God's mercy. If you desire mercy, be merciful! Just as God forgives you your sins, so too must you forgive each other. May the peace of Christ be with you.

April 13, 1997

My dear daughter, I wish for you to ponder the mystery of the resurrection of Christ. My little ones, through His resurrection, our Lord overcame even death. In the same way, you, His children, can overcome all obstacles in life. By dying and rising, Jesus taught His disciples that true life awaited them in His Father's kingdom. My little ones, through His resurrection, He has shown you the way to the Father's kingdom where you will live eternally. My dear children, call to mind often His passion, death, and resurrection. See the great love He has for you, that He would take upon Himself the sins of the world, that you might dwell with Him forever. May the peace of Christ be with you.

April 14, 1997

My dear daughter, there are many whose hearts remain hard and who have turned away from God our Father. My little children, is it so difficult to have trust? In your world where you are so often abandoned by those whom you love, where you suffer the disappointment of human failings, you have not learned how to trust with your hearts. My dear children, God is the greatest of fathers, the greatest of friends. Truly, you will never be abandoned, nor failed by Him. His will is perfect, as is His love for you. My little children, open your hearts. Do not fear the pain of failure or disappointment, but open your hearts and lives to the grace of God. Be as children again! Look with loving eyes to your Father in Heaven and trust in His providence. He will care for you. May the peace of Christ be with you.

April 15, 1997

My dear daughter, remember to live humility. My dear children, do not be concerned with your goods and clothing. These things are passing. My little ones, live a simple life. How much easier it is to remain humble when you live simply. Dear ones, simplify your lives. Dear little children, God desires humility. Know that He has created you so very special and unique. He has a purpose for you. Instead of rushing about and worrying much over your material goods, it is good to spend more time in His presence through prayer. It is in kneeling down in prayer when you learn to have the gift of humility. May the peace of Christ be with you.

April 16, 1997

My dear daughter, seek freedom from sin in the Lord, dear ones. My little children, be reconciled with God. Through Him and in Him, temptation has no hold on you. The most powerful gifts of God are His love, mercy, and forgiveness. Confess your sins and do penance, for a remorseful heart is embraced by the Father. My little children, the kingdom of God is in your hearts. Here on this earth, you can begin to understand eternal life in His kingdom, if you allow Him to reign over your hearts. My little ones, I ask of you as your mother, choose God now, for if you do not stand with Him, you stand against Him. His love for you is so great, He wishes only to be with His people. Dear ones, fall to your knees and choose God! He is the Way, the Truth, and the Life! May the peace of Christ be with you.

April 17, 1997

My dear daughter, come before the Lord in the Eucharist, for this is the time when His mercy and love pour down from the heavens. My little ones, in the form of the Eternal Sacrifice, the Lord comes in body to your churches and into your hearts. When you receive Him, you become united in Him. My dear children, I pray that you would practice great reverence and respect during the

Holy Mass. It is during this time when the Spirit of the Lord descends upon His people. My priestly sons, I ask of you, strive to lead your people in the move towards a deep love and devotion to the Eucharistic Christ. At the time of consecration, fall to your knees and beseech the guidance of the Holy Spirit. My little ones, it is through this holy sacrament that the Lord prepares the hearts of His children for His kingdom. May the peace of Christ be with you.

April 18, 1997

My dear daughter, today I call each of you to be teachers. Long have I taught you how to love, how to pray, to live the virtues of your faith. There are many of my little ones who do not have the opportunity to read my word or hear the Word of God taught each day through the Scripture in your churches. As Christ sent His first apostles, I send you, my faithful. Just as the founders of the Church, you are charged with the responsibility of teaching the ways of God. Little ones, be bearers of my love, bearers of the love of God. Teach by your example how to serve. Pray, dear ones, that all of God's people will come to give Him glory. May the peace of Christ be with you.

April 19, 1997

My dear daughter, pray, dear children, that you might not become concerned with your worldly possessions, but that you might store your treasures in heaven. My little ones, you do not realize how little time you are on earth. An instant after your creation you grow, learn, teach, serve, and return home to the family, to the God of eternity. Your lifetime is but a blink of the eyes. Use the time you have been given by Him fully. Each day, seek to serve Him in a new way. My dear children, be not concerned with your material goods, for they will do you no good in the next life. Instead, be steadfast in your efforts to learn to love, for in the end, it is only love that lasts in the kingdom of God. May the peace of Christ be with you.

April 20, 1997

My dear daughter, praise the Lord this day for His goodness! Dear little ones, I come today to encourage you to gain a deeper reverence for the Holy Eucharist through prayer. My little children, if only you could see with eyes of faith! If only you could know the true presence of Christ in the Eucharist. Oh, how the Angels of Heaven praise Him, surrounding His altars and tabernacles in worship! My little ones, as the Angels adore the Great Sacrifice, so too should you worship and adore Him. My little ones, be filled with the Holy Spirit, that your eyes might be open to the presence of your Lord in the Eucharist. May the peace of Christ be with you.

April 21, 1997

My dear daughter, I bless you and love you so dearly. This day, I would like to encourage each of my little children to desire a life of mercy. My little ones, you have been taught that the Lord is a God of mercy. To His people, He gives the light of life and salvation. Though they would mock, crucify, and kill Him, Jesus forgave each of His persecutors through the mercy of the Holy Spirit. Though no man is worthy, the Lord comes to you each day in the Eucharist, because He is merciful. My dear children, be merciful as God has shown you mercy. May your hearts be gentle and filled with love. Pray that the Holy Spirit will guide you in the way of humble mercy. May the peace of Christ be with you.

April 22, 1997

My dear daughter, in this lifetime, you, my children, suffer much loss and grief. Know that in your times of sadness, your

Father in Heaven holds you ever closer to His heart. My little ones, when you experience loss in your life, do not be overcome by mourning. This is the way of those who have little faith. My dear children, as followers of Christ, you know of His tremendous love for you. In times of grief, let Him be your hope. Be strengthened in the knowledge that God cares for you and guides you through your trials. My dear children, trust in Him and pray that your loss might be offered up to Him, that He who freely lost everything that this earthly life promised will gain for you the graces of peace. May the peace of Christ be with you.

April 23, 1997

My dear daughter, fidelity is so very important, especially in this age of sinfulness. My dear children, be faithful to your God. Trust and follow His word. Stand firm against those who would mock and ridicule Him. Be the foundation of the Church, its strength and love. My little ones, be faithful to one another. Husbands, be devoted to your wives. Children, be loyal to your parents. My dear children, practice honesty. Do not say one thing and do another, but fulfill your word. There are many who would speak out in praise of fidelity, but few who would practice it. Dear ones, pray that God may place in your hearts the virtues of patience and love, that you may remain faithful always to His way. May the peace of Christ be with you.

April 24, 1997

My dear daughter, Jesus is the Healer of the heart, soul, and body. Little ones, just as when He walked among His people on this earth, curing the sick and granting sight to the blind, His presence is with you, His beloved. Jesus the Healer wants only to mend the brokenness of His people. My dear children, give to God your wounds and your scars. Allow Him to smooth them away with the touch of His hand. Truly, He will fill you with His graces. The Lord heals the broken hearted and suffering. His love is the strength on which you, His dear children, can build a fortress of trust. Follow His way. Pray that the Christ might enliven your hearts and heal your wounds, that you might be made whole in Him. May the peace of Christ be with you.

April 25, 1997

My dear daughter, tonight I call each of you once again to conversion of the heart. Dear children, do you know how much your Father in Heaven loves you? Do you not yet see His presence in your lives? My little ones, as your heavenly mother, I will call you always to Jesus. Receive the sacrament of Reconciliation and be forgiven for your offenses to God. Little ones, in this way will your heart begin the journey of conversion. Conversion truly is a journey. You are all called to be converted to the love of God each day. My little children, in this time when the world is trapped in darkness, darkness that is caused by sin, I call you to begin anew. Devote your hearts to God, that He might do mighty works within you. May the peace of Christ be with you.

April 26, 1997

My dear children, tonight, I call you again to prayer. My dear children, prayer is the greatest weapon against the Evil One. Prayer is your protection from temptation. In prayer, you come to know the love of God fully. Dear ones, in all things pray! Live your lives as a prayer to be offered up to your Lord. There are no obstacles in this life too great to be overcome through the wisdom that God gives through diligent and fervent prayer. Strengthen your hearts and your love for Him. Be ready for His call. Cleanse yourselves. Let Him fill you. In prayer you become His perfect instruments of love. May the peace of Christ be with you.

April 27, 1997

My dear daughter, I love you so dearly! My little ones, as I love you as your heavenly mother, so much more does your Heavenly Father love you, His children. He reaches out to you, my little ones, to bring you from the brink of death into the light of eternal life, for this is what He has promised you, what He died to give you, and the place that He has prepared for you. My little ones, I come as His daughter and as your mother. I come to show you the way back to God, to lead you to my Jesus. My dear children, receive His gifts. Pray that He will fill you with faith, for this is the first step in coming to know and love Him completely. My dear children, do not forget to pray! This is so very important. Pray and let your hearts be filled with the light of His love. May the peace of Christ be with you.

April 28, 1997

My dear daughter, peace be with you. Dear little children, I ask that you devote yourselves to a life of faith. You have been given the tools of faith: prayer, peace, love, and forgiveness. My dear children, only from a life of faith can much joy abound. Dear little ones, the Lord desires those who would do His work as His instrument, that He might truly work through you to gather His fallen sheep. Dear children, you are so precious to Him! When just one little child is lost, He goes in search of him. Little ones, be as pillars of faith. May your lives always reflect God. Let those around you know that you belong to Him by your words, your deeds, and your faith in God. May the peace of Christ be with you.

April 29, 1997

My dear children, I call you, dear ones, to become more aware of Jesus' presence in your lives. See Him in each child whose eyes shine brightly with the love of God. See Him in the faces of the aged and wise, who are blessed with the wisdom of the Holy Spirit.

See the face of Jesus reflected throughout all of creation. My dear children, wherever it is that you see Him, serve Him there. In serving the poor and the weak, you serve Him. In loving the old and the young, you have loved Him. In having dignity for all that the Lord in His goodness has created, you give dignity and respect to your Savior. My dear children, I call you today into the service of the Lord, for there is no greater calling. May the peace of Christ be with you.

April 30, 1997

My dear daughter, my children lose their hope in God so easily. The Evil One seeks out the destruction of hope, for a man who does not hope in the Lord does not live in Him. Little children, God has sent me to you to teach you that the greatest of all things are love of God, love of neighbor, and love for yourselves. Through me, His humble messenger, He has promised that through prayer, your faith in Him becomes strong, and that faith is the root of love. My dear children, now I say to you, in prayer, faith, and love, you, little ones, can truly hope in God. To hope in Him is to trust, to love, to be at peace, and to understand His mercy and love. This is what I wish for you, dear children, that you would be full of hope. May the peace of Christ be with you.

May 1, 1997

My dear daughter, may the Lord bless you with His grace. My dear children, I wish for you to find joy. I desire for your hearts to be full of love. My little ones, if you pray, the Lord will guide you. Through your love for Him and perseverance in all of life's difficulties, you will learn to trust and hope in Him. My little ones, only a heart that is strong in faith and full of hope can be filled with joy. My dear ones, I call you to bring the Father's kingdom to earth. Begin to live in His eternal love and joy at this moment. Let His light shine forth from you to light every place of darkness. Pray, dear ones, that the fire of love, joy, and hope within you might spark faith in the hearts of those who are lost. May the peace of Christ be with you.

May 2, 1997

My dear daughter, I have called each of you to the Father through the Holy Spirit. My little children, now is the time to choose for God. Now is the time to dedicate yourselves to Him. My little ones, I love you so dearly and want you to choose to walk with Him. His way, the way of light, will bring you peace. It is difficult to follow with all of your heart what you have been taught. Remember, the Lord has given you the way of salvation through His Word, the Holy Scripture. My dear children, choose to follow Him! I thank you for your prayers. Continue to pray, that you might always be guided by the Holy Spirit. May the peace of Christ be with you.

May 3, 1997

My dear daughter, I wish to thank you for committing yourself to this task that has been given to you by the Father in Heaven. Dear children, I as your mother, thank you for your prayer and sacrifice. Truly, your faith has made many graces of God possible! In this age of darkness, your faith brings light to the world. My little ones, when your faith is tested, remain strong in God, for He shall not fail you. Little ones, I thank you for your sacrifices. When you offer your sacrifices and sufferings to the Lord, many are blessed by your gift. The Lord shows His mercy to all, because of the love of a few. My dear ones, do not abandon prayer! Do not abandon your Father. He will carry you in His arms, always. May the peace of Christ be with you.

May 4, 1997

My dear daughter, I wish to reconfirm to all my children that, truly, I am your mother. My dear little ones, I love you so very much! I have come to you because of my great love for you, and the mercy and love of the Father. Dear children, know that I am always with you as your intercessor. I lift high all prayers to our God, that they may glorify Him alone. I am just a simple woman, chosen by God for a mighty task. I am the Woman Clothed in the Sun, she who brings forth the Christ; not in flesh as once before, but in Word as He is, and ever shall be. My beloved children, how I do love you! I thank you for hearing the call of our Lord and answering Him. May the peace of Christ be with you.

May 5, 1997

My dear daughter, I love you so dearly and I thank you for serving God in this way. Little children, as I began, so shall I end, with a reminder of God's great love. Through His grace, I have come to teach you the way of life, His forgiveness, His mercy. I have been but a messenger, telling of His joy for each of you. Most important of all words, the greatest of all gifts, is love! This is the message of the Scripture, the Word of God, for God is love, and all that are of God and for God, are filled with His love. Little children, as your mother I desire only to unite each of you together with God in His love. Love is the root of all virtue. From love grows hope, faith, and charity. Where there is love, goodness abounds, and a light that cannot be quenched by darkness. This light, the light of God, is His love, that love which created each of you, that love that shapes your souls, that love that unites you with the Father. Above all else, there must be love, or all is for naught.

My dear children, I offer to you my guidance as your heavenly mother. I bring to you the Word of God as His messenger. Know that it is only through His love that this has been possible. My dear children, my prayer is that each of you will come to love God with all of your hearts, to know and understand Him as He has intended, to be one in Him, creature and creator. My dear children, the greatest gift that you have been given and the true gift, this gift from which all else is brought forth in goodness, is love. My dear children, love one another as God has loved you. Be filled with His love. Live your lives joyfully, for you have been chosen as His people, His children. Thank Him! Praise Him! Alleluia! Be filled with joy. May the peace of Christ be with you.

The Saints of Heaven

St. Peter, November 25, 1997

Carolyn:

The Blessed Mother is dressed in pale blue. She is wearing a white veil with gold along the edges, and it falls around her and comes around her arms. She is kneeling. Her face is turned down toward her arms and she is smiling. At first, she had a lamb in her arms, a white lamb. Now it is a child, but I didn't notice it change.

St. Peter is with her. He is dressed in brown, and he too is kneeling. He looks older than the Blessed Mother. He has dark hair that is graying in some areas. He has a beard and a mustache. His eyes are dark brown, and he is looking toward the Blessed Mother. He has a book in his right hand that is closed. In the other, he is holding something like a menorah. There are seven torches on it, and each is lit, and they come to a common base. On each of them there is a word written: Faith, Hope, Love, Charity, Sacrifice, Martyrdom, Courage.)

Mary:

My dear children, it is good to be with you. I have called each of you here tonight because you are to be the recipients of this special grace from the Father. It is for His love of you that this is made possible, and it is for my love of you that I have made this request. My little children, I wish to teach you that God is so very near. I wish to show you His kingdom is without measure, that His goodness is beyond comprehension, and above all, His love for you is as vast as the sea. My children, I am so pleased that you have come today in faith, and I wish for you to receive this great blessing and this gift.

St. Peter:

Glory to the Son of Man, to the One who sits on high, to Him Who is all things, Who always was and ever shall be! His kingdom is without end. Brothers and sisters, brothers, sisters, I love you. Glorify the Lord in your hearts. Pay homage to His mother, Queen of the Heavens. Join your voices to the voices of the Angels, saying "Hosanna" and "Alleluia".

I wish to tell you about the Christ as He was on earth, for I was His brother. I ate with Him. I slept by His side. I saw His labors of His love. I witnessed His mercy. I experienced His goodness. I was there at His betrayal and ultimately, it was I with my brother, who discovered His tomb empty on that morn, and it was I who gazed upon the risen Lord, the fulfillment of all things, of all prophecy, from age to age, from beginning to end. Let me share with you my words, words from one who witnessed all this, from one who now shares in His glory, the glory of the Father, Son, and the Spirit united, perfect in all things and in all ways.

I am nothing without Christ. You know well of me. I was a fisherman, poor, hardworking, and lacking God in all ways. Yes, I was a Jew and I, in the synagogue, followed the Law. I knew nothing of God, He was not with me. I turned my face from Him as I would do after His betrayal three times. For most of my life, I wanted nothing of God, not His goodness, not His mercy, not His love. I had a family as you do. I had children and a wife, parents who loved me and taught me the ways of the Jewish Law. And my pride was my great weakness and oh, stubborn days did I see, but He changed all that! From the moment my eyes encountered His gaze, He changed me. He changed my heart. I was nothing before Him. I am nothing without Him.

What a sight it is to see the Son of Man standing, beckoning to you, for in my heart, I wanted nothing to do with God and yet, from the first time my eyes fell upon His face, I confess that I knew who He was. And be sure, it would have been better for me if I had not known, for I knew when I betrayed Him Who He was. And I chose to walk with Him, and to cast away my life to follow Him. You should have seen the things that were said about me, the way people looked at me. I was no stranger to persecution, and often I knew not why I followed Him, save for the way He looked at me, with such compassion and such understanding. He filled my soul!

And so, I left all things and I followed Him, and He became my master. I with my brothers, we ate with Him, drank with Him. We preached with Him. We learned. We taught with Him. So many things did He do! How many people did He touch! It is countless. I could not number them. How many of the sick He cured! His greatest miracles were the changes in the hearts of all those who knew Him. There would be none who would deny He was the Son of Man, were they to open their eyes and ears and hear His words.

The time I spent with Him was so joyous, and so sorrowful. There was much confusion, and oftentimes, I felt as if I should run, run far from Him, from all this, this life of traveling, of preaching, of trusting in One Who seemed to be no more than a simple man with great love in His heart, save for that mercy! I wish you could have been there. I wish you were able to see. You too would have followed, for you follow Him now and it is much more to your credit, for you have not seen nor heard His words.

The night that He was betrayed, there would be none other so dark for all time. Even then, all those who had pledged their lives to Him, deserted Him. What a frightening time it was for me! I had no courage then, and I fled. And after, when morning came, it was not over, for it got worse. The One Whom I had followed, Who I had given everything for, my Master, was beaten, was judged, was made to walk with a tree on His back, and was hung on that tree, where He remained three hours before He died.

Faith, faith, faith could do nothing for me then. My Master had been killed. For what did I give my life? We all, all of Jesus' brothers, we knew not what to do. And there were a few who had hope, but I confess, it was not I. I worried much more for my own life. Those were dark days without Him. And even after I, setting foot in His tomb, saw that He was not there, still my heart was hard. But on that day, when He in His glory came and was once again with us, when He showed us the wounds in His hands and in His side, when He shined like the stars of the night and had the countenance of a lion, with strength and courage, beauty so regal, it was then that my heart was pierced! What a splendid sight! What a splendid thing! Oh, and I was so afraid, and yet so peaceful. And He spoke! "Brothers, God be with you. I have been glorified!" I have been glorified! With these words, I felt God in my life! And even though He had been with me all along, it was not until then that I felt Him with my heart, with my soul, piercing me with His love! Then He departed from us, and He sent the Spirit to come among us to give us the strength and courage to teach all nations of His love, His sacrifice.

There is much you have not been told of His works and His miracles, for it would not be possible to make a list of all His doings, and there is much you have not been told of my life as well. Did you know that I am a coward, except for God's Spirit who dwells within me? Did you know that I am afraid, except for His boldness? Did you know we are nothing without Him, and all good works you do are possible only in Him? Now, I share in His goodness with His glory in His kingdom, as it is and always will be, and I have the great gift of looking upon His face each day, that face which I once saw mangled with tears and blood, now glorified. I shall pray for you each day, that you would join Him here.

Life, life is not as you know it, for it is but a blink of the eyes of God. You have not yet begun to live! My life was full of cowardice, and there was but one thing that I did for my Christ that gives me great pride: I gave up my life for Him as He had done for me. Oh, and I was so pleased at that moment, knowing that my sacrifice would never amount to His, but knowing too that I would soon be home to Him. Be blessed and be praised, God, forever!

Look forward with great anticipation to the life you will share with Him. Know that you will meet Him in that heavenly home. He will open His arms to you and embrace you as He embraced me, as He embraces all. May His love guide you. May the Holy Spirit descend upon you. May He give you all that you need, that you may be His instrument and, like me, may join Him in Heaven.

Give thanks to Him for allowing me to be with you this day. I will pray for you. Know that God is so close to you, as He was close to me those years, and I failed to recognize Him. Do not fail to recognize Him in your life. He is there. He is waiting for you to want Him, to love Him, to accept Him, to remember Him. May His peace follow you all the days of your life.

Mary:

My children, I impart to you my motherly blessing. I wish to remind you of my love for you. I thank you for coming together in prayer, for prayer is most important. Wherever my faithful are gathered, I and my Son are among them.

St. Joseph, December 23, 1997

Carolyn:

Mary is wearing a slate blue dress and a blue veil. There is a man with her. I saw Mary first and then suddenly, Joseph was there. He genuflected before her, and she reached her hands out to him. He is now standing next to her and is holding both of her hands.

St. Joseph is tall and older looking. He has a long face and dark brown eyes. He has a bushy beard that stands out quite far, and black and silver hair. There is a white sash around the back of his neck, and it comes over his head and the ends fall to just below his waist. It looks knitted. It is not a solid fabric and there is tasseling on the bottom of it. Joseph also has a gray cloak with sleeves over his shoulders. It doesn't come around to the front of him, but hangs straight down like an open robe.

Mary has moved back her veil and she has a baby in her arms. She and Joseph are both looking down at the child. The baby has a bald head, is very beautiful, and shines just like Mary does.

Mary:

My dear children, today I bring to you my spouse, he who brought me much joy while on earth and who is still a great joy and comfort to me in Heaven. Dear children, I wish for you to know him as you know me, for his love for you is great, and he is a great warrior of prayer and an intercessor on your behalf.

St. Joseph:

Brothers, sisters, I present to you the Son of God, given to my wife and to me, that we would care for Him and raise Him up to be great, to give glory to God. Be joyous, as this is the season of His birth, the season of the coming of the Lord, of His promise and the fulfilment of that promise, that promise made ages ago to our fathers. Be full of life, more alive than ever, as He is life and the love which you feel, as He is the greatest gift, the only gift. Bless and praise God for allowing me to be with you this day.

Sisters and brothers, I love and pray for you. You are truly sisters and brothers of mine in the family of God, in the Christ, He Who came to save even those to whom God had given Him, His mother and I. What an awesome responsibility! What an honor! I, myself, was not worthy. In that season and in that day, Mary, being with child, so joyous, so beautiful, and I so nervous, eagerly anticipating the birth of my Son; though He was not of my seed, God blessed me with His life to raise as mine. And traveling with her to the city of my fathers and of her kin, I worried so! Why had God chosen me? Why had God asked this of me? What fears!

On that night, the night of His birth, the stars shone so brightly, and the sky danced with angels that I and His mother were privileged to see. And as she held Him, such light, such wondrous light! And she and I gazed upon Him, our Son, the Savior, the promised King of Ages, and could not speak, and could not move, and could not breathe, for He was so beautiful and so perfect! And then I, knowing the prophesies, that which God had given to us, His people, cried. For it is written that the Son of Man would come to suffer, to be mocked and to be ridiculed, and that in His suffering, man would be redeemed. Knowing this, I still felt such joy as only a parent can, as he looks upon the life that God has given, even if it be for a short while, to raise, to love, to teach, to hold.

And I took my wife and my Son home and into my house. And as He grew, I taught Him many things. I taught Him the Law of our Fathers and the Jewish way, and I took Him to the synagogue where He was introduced to His true Father. And I taught Him the Scriptures, the words of the prophets, those words that were fulfilled as I stood on that crystal night and watched His miraculous birth. And I taught Him my trade and He was schooled, as all the young Jewish boys were at that time, and had many friends. And at the time, there would be no indication that He was the King of Ages, save for the knowledge in His mother's and my hearts. It was easy to forget. I would go about my business and she with hers, kept busy with all the responsibilities that parenting requires, and it was easy to forget that the Lord was in our home. Oftentimes, we looked upon our Son and when the realization touched our hearts that we were seeing God in our form, it was overwhelming!

It is not different for you. You, each of you, have had such an experience as you kneel before the Holy Eucharist. For as I forgot, so too do you, as all people will. As I carried on with my daily business, I forgot that I was in the presence of the Lord. There are so many who forget, as they enter their churches and go to worship and to pray, that they are in the presence of the Lord in His spirit and in His body as He is sacrificed upon your altars. It is no different for you than it was for I, and you and I are blessed! My Jesus, such a sweet child! Such a wondrous child! And He grew. And it was difficult.

And then came the time of my passing and I left this world, and I joined the Heavenly Father. What a joy, what an honor to be in Heaven with God, to know all that He knows, to see all creation from the beginning to the end! And it was only then that I could see the complete fulfilment of the promise given to God's people through my Son, and the ferocious beating of my heart ceased, for there were times when it raced as I thought of what must happen, of what would happen. He was so precious to us and the thought of His suffering, it broke our hearts. And yet, when I joined our Father, I saw the glory that was my Son, the glory that He gave to the Father in the redemption of all people, and I was so proud.

I did my best to raise Him to love God and to know God. And He, being divine, knew so much more than I, and yet, He was so obedient, for even in the Scriptures as you have them it is written of His loss in the temple. And you know how His mother and I worried, and how we sought Him out, and even though He did His Father's work there, at His mother's request and mine, He left to journey home with us, obedient. Unfathomable, that God would obey His creature!

The fullness of this lesson did not fill my heart until my passing from this earth, for in Christ, we were shown the way to live, to love, to die, and to glorify God. And in His obedience, we were taught the greatest lesson. Though we do not understand why it is that God does what He does, and in His time, we must obey, for He is a loving Father. And as Jesus obeyed me and learned- though He knew so much greater things than I- from me, a simple man, a tradesman, we must do the same, trusting that God knows what we cannot know, that the Father will reveal to us the truth in His time, and in His way. The greatest lesson of Jesus was His obedience, even until the time of His passion. "Take this cup from me", He prayed, full of fear and yet, He obeyed His Father.

Obedience. Trust. These things are great, but greater than these is love. Jesus Christ was the mark of God's love on this earth. He was the proof of His love, the fulfilment of His love, the root and the ends of His love, the beginning and end, the everything. Jesus, He taught His mother and I much of love. Oh, love through obedience, through submission to God's will, through giving of oneself! How difficult it was for I, to live in a home with the Son of God and the Virgin Mother chosen by God and free of sin! You might know well that anything that occurred in our home that caused division and strife, well, it was certainly not the fault of my Son nor my wife! But what joy! And what great things that God had done for me!

The love of a family is the greatest of love. The love that exists between husband and wife, parent and child, sister and brother, this is the model of God's love, and it is love as God truly intended it to be. Cherish one another, especially in these days, in this season. Your children, they are gifts, the greatest gifts to enter your lives, blessings to be cherished, treasured. Your spouses, gifts! Reflections of God. Reflections of His love. And this is why it is so important to free yourselves from pride, from anger, from jealousy, greed. These things are not of God and not part of His love, but it is only through the freedom that truth, generosity, peace, and joy bring, that you can experience God in your lives through those who love you, whom you love.

I am full of joy in this season, as now in my Father's kingdom, in our Father's kingdom, I can behold my baby Son once again, that gift that God gave to me, that responsibility, that treasure that He entrusted me with. With Mary His mother, the Queen of Heaven, and the Angels, I too will sing praises to Him and celebrate the coming of the Christ to the earth. He is the Redeemer of All, and the Bringer of Peace, King of Kings, and the Lamb. Worship and adore Him in your lives, in your churches, through your family. Know that He is with you, as He promised His first disciples, each day. I thank you for inviting me to speak with you this day.

Mary:

Dear children, may the Christ bless you this day and always, being ever at your side, close behind and walking before, as I your mother am, with my love, my guidance, and my intercession.

St. Paul, February 1, 1998

Carolyn:

Mary is dressed in slate gray with a long white veil. She has her hands folded in prayer. She is accompanied by two angels. The Angels are beside her and hover off the ground just a bit. One is dressed in gold and the other in green. She is also accompanied by St. Paul.

St. Paul is wearing a brown smock that comes down the front of him and sandals on his feet. He has short, sandy blond hair. He has a mustache and a beard that are also sandy blond. St. Paul has a medium build, and appears to be middle aged. In one hand there is a gray tablet. In the other there is a shield, the kind used for a coat of arms, and it has FAITH written across it. St. Paul genuflects before the Blessed Mother. She is still in prayer.

Mary:

Dear children, I am with you joyfully this day! I bring to you the Evangelizer, one who answered the call of my Son, who gave to all nations the gift of faith. He was a forebearer of you, one of the first disciples in many. I offer to you my motherly blessing. I pray for each one of you. I take your needs and your petitions to my Son.

St. Paul:

Brothers, sisters, I come to you bearing the peace of Christ, He who sent me. You are followers of Him, as I was and am, and now I have the privilege of serving Him in our heavenly home. Sisters and brothers, let me tell you, God asked me to go out to preach His Word, to teach. But as you well know, I was not always His servant, nor His friend, nor His disciple, but once I was His persecutor, His executioner. For it was my practice to travel from city to city, in Damascus and beyond, and bring suffering and torture to those who followed the Way. I was quite proud. What a service I was doing to my Jewish forefathers by destroying the lives of these who followed this newfangled religion, this cult, if you would. Imagine, exclaiming that the Messiah had come to this earth as a babe in a stable! It was an insult to all I had known and all I had been taught. And so, I went about my business, and was careful to report to the leaders of the synagogues about the tortures and the executions I had overseen. And I myself was responsible for the very martyrdom of Stephen, whom you venerate.

I did not have the gift of visiting with our Lord in His body as did His apostles, Peter, James, those who were near to Him, His beloved. But I was graced and blessed when one day on my travels, He came to me. His words shook my heart like thunder! The very earth could have swallowed me up in such light and such beauty!

And at that moment, I wanted nothing more than to hide my face in shame for what I had done, what I had allowed and condoned, the terror that I had brought to the lives of those who proclaimed the truth. I was not worthy to be in His presence. And He forgave me, and He sent me on with a mission.

It is the same now. There are many in the world today who sin and fall away from God, who have causes that are not the true cause of God, the cause of love, Christian charity, truth. And as I did see the truth, so too will all people one day see the truth, the Lamb who was led to the slaughter. And like me, they too will see their souls and feel the quaking of their hearts when they see how they have offended God. And like me, perhaps the most wretched of sinners, these too shall be forgiven and given the grace to go out, to love, to serve, to be an example of Christ.

It is such joyful, joyful news! For it is easy to become dismayed at the evils that inflict terrible suffering on this world, but fear not, and have joy! Maintain your love, your relationship with God. He does not abandon even the most wretched. He lifts up those who are lost. He comes to save the weak. I offer to you this as encouragement for days that are difficult. Know that He will lift you up as He lifted up His most lowly servants, and the most wretched of sinners.

On that day, my life became much different. Stricken and unable to see, I wallowed in my own pain, the pain of my soul. How is it that I had failed God? I was zealous for God! I thought that I knew what God wanted from me. In my own imaginings, I had decided what God wanted, and I had gone off on my own crusade in the name of God. This is not what He required of me. This is what my will had created and had decided that it was true. Everything I knew was turned upside down.

I changed my life on that day, and I was most privileged to come to know many of the good people who belonged to the Way, the Christian faith. At first, I was not accepted. "This is Saul, the persecutor! This is the one who killed our children and our fathers, and he, *he* should come to be a Christian?" Truly I tell you, there were many who did not believe that I had been converted in the heart. "This must be a trick, sorcery!" And yet, there were others who fell to their knees proclaiming, "God is alive, for what a miracle! He was the most wretched, and even he now calls Jesus, Lord."

I befriended a man who loved the Lord, who was the dearest, dearest friend to the Lord, His brother John, and he taught me Christian love and charity. He taught me the truth that God loves us, the God of my zealousness, of the old ways of the Pharisees, the God of justice, of anger, of punishment. What a terrible, terrible, terrible, limit to place on the O Holy One! He is a God of love, and of mercy, and of justice, and of goodness, and peace. And so, I came to know Christ as my Lord.

Led by the Spirit, I went out to proclaim these truths that had been revealed to me in a miraculous and wonderful way. And I shared with all peoples, traveling much, one truth. In all that I shared, in all of the Gospels, in all of the writings, in all of your Bible, there is but one truth: Jesus is Lord. He loves you. He died that you might be free, and He welcomes you. He wants you. He desires you. You are the children of God. You are the promised nation, the descendants of Abraham, they who would receive the Messiah. Blessed are you who believe! Blessed are you who have faith! It took a miracle for me to see God as He is. You have faith though you have not seen. You, truly, will be glorified much more than I in our Father's house.

In all of my travels, and in my journeys, and in the difficulties, I faced those who would mock me, both those in the Jewish community and those who belonged to the Way. In imprisonment and in freedom, I tried always, always, to say but one sentence each day, in each situation, for it was all that needed to be said: "Jesus, I give this to you." What a powerful, powerful, statement that was in my life! "Jesus, I give this to you." You trust that when you call upon the name of Jesus, He is with you, and it is so, and He receives your prayer and the gift that one little child would give, in every suffering and in every joy, is taken up into His arms, and becomes a great joy to Him.

And so, I encourage you in your times of struggle and strife: "Jesus, I give all this to you." Do not forget this. You will know great peace, if only you allow Him to work in you, to do His will through you. I did nothing in my years as a missionary. I simply allowed God to work through me and to do His will, what truly was His will, not what I thought He had willed for me, not what my friends told me He willed for me, not even what my closest loved ones told me He willed for me to do, but what He wanted, desired, needed, and asked of me.

All people are capable of knowing this. It is as simple as listening to the silence, the silence of your heart. For there, the secrets, the truths, the Word of God, is revealed. All people are capable of knowing His will, and if only you would give up your lives to it, you would find a peace, and a grace, and a mercy, that is greater than all things on earth, and is worth forsaking your very life for it.

I recall on one of my journeys, I was traveling with my companions, and I came into a city where I was known as a persecutor. I had visited that city many times to drag away the Christians there in chains. And I and my companions, we preached there, and there were many conversions by the grace of God, but there was nothing more influential in the entire course of my life than one conversation with one man that I met in this city.

Even after my conversion, I was a proud man and I struggled for my entire life against this pride. And one day while preaching, I cited the writings that a dear, dear friend of mine had kept in his journal about his relationship with God and with the Christ. He had written, "I dearly wish that my beloved children would know Christ as I know Him, would accept Him as the Messiah, in that they too would be saved. However, I trust that they will be saved because I believe and I know that Christ saves all, and He came to save those who know Him and who are distant, those who are far and who are near, the Jews and the Gentiles, all people, as He is King of Heaven and Earth for all time, for all people." And I used this for the basis of my sermon that day and I spoke about Jesus as the King and the Messiah that had been promised. And I cited well from the old scriptures, Isaiah, Jeremiah, these books that I had come to know as a scholar, and the beloved Torah, the Law, the Word, what I had known as a child to be the truth. And how proud of myself I was. "Truly," I thought, "many people will be converted because of me."

And then I met this man. He approached me after I had finished this sermon, and he looked into my eyes. And he spoke to me,

"Paul, what do you desire?"

"Well... my Lord!", I replied.

"Paul, what do you desire?"

"My Lord! My Christ!"

"Paul, what do you desire?"

And he turned, and he was gone. And I thought, "How foolish! The ramblings of an old man!" Of course, I desired my Christ!

And then, I realized, that I had not. In my pride and in my arrogance, I had designed a situation where I would be glorified, where all who would look to me as their teacher would say, "He is good. He is a follower. Certainly, he will be in Heaven!" Again, even after accepting my weaknesses, I had fallen prey to the very thing that had kept me from knowing Jesus to begin with, the pride of self-glorification and righteousness!

And I thought long and hard that day, and I believe that this is a good lesson for you, for the world as it is now. For as I see it, there are three kinds of people who follow Christ. One follows Christ with all of his heart, all of his soul, all of his mind, and gives up all things for the Beloved, for He who gave up His very life for him. And I believe that these are those who are most holy and most virtuous. The second preaches well as I did, speaks of his love for Christ, worships Christ, but alas, it is a show. For the truly devoted are humble and meek of heart and seek not glory for themselves, but the glory and graces of God. And then there is a third, those who proclaim their Christianity, their faith, but God slips away from them, for they have not the time to pray nor the time to worship. They haven't the time to think of God or matters of faith and the spiritual life, for there is so many things to do, a family, a job, a home to care for. Where is God?

"Paul, what do you desire?"

And so, I ask you, what do you desire? These words that meant so much to me in my life, made me realize that twice, twice-not once, I had not the mind to serve God. What do you desire?

I hope that my words are an encouragement to you. I wish only to tell you of His goodness, and His mercy, and His love, and above all else, His forgiveness. What do you desire in your lives? May it be Christ Jesus! May it be the Messiah. May it be the peace of God, the very heart of God. For in this way, you shall be fulfilled. You will know His grace and His love in a way that you cannot imagine, and the cares of your life will melt away, as you look forward to joining Him in the place He has prepared for you, and the struggles that you endure will be but joys, the thorns of a rose lifted up high to our crucified Lord. I assure you, there is no suffering too great for the precious treasure of Heaven! There is nothing that you could endure that is too terrible or too frightening for that reward! God calls each of us to a different mission. Whatever He calls you to do, whatever He asks of you, do it with love and with gratitude, for your reward is more precious than you can imagine.

Do all that you can for the Lord that you might join Him, and your brothers and sisters in the Church, in Heaven. It is a most, most beautiful place, a place of love and of goodness, of unending joy! And there you will come to know the Lord as He truly is, more beautiful than any of His creations, more holy than any imaginings.

There are no words I can offer to you to describe the true Lord. You know but a piece. How Christ must have hidden His glory! The very thought of Him existing on this earth as a Man-God, it baffles me! For He is so glorified in Heaven, I cannot lift my eyes to look upon His face! Do all that you can to serve Him. Do all that you can to join me here. Remember, you will be forgiven when you fall and loved unconditionally, and no price is too great for the pearl, the jewel, the treasure that God has in store for you.

I thank you for listening to me this day and it is my pleasure and my joy to be with you in this way. Give thanks to God, for He has allowed this. He has made this possible through His holy mother, who is our intercessor, who is our mother, who loves us dearly. I give to you my prayers and my aid as your Christian brother. Know that I pray for you, and I will recommend you to the Father as brothers and sisters of Christ.

St. Clement, February 17, 1998

Carolyn:

The Blessed Mother is dressed in white with a pale colored veil that is somewhat transparent. I can see her hair through it. She has her hands turned up toward Heaven and she is standing along the side of an altar. The altar has a shimmering gold cloth over it and on the front of the cloth there is a cross.

St. Clement is standing in front of the altar. He is older. He has white hair and a white beard, a long white beard, and he is dressed in a black robe. He is holding a tablet in his arm, close to his chest. It has "Father, Son, and Spirit" written on it.

Mary:

My dear children, I am so pleased to be with you. I am overjoyed at your response to my call. I have come as your mother, with love, to bear the gifts of the Father to you, that you would know His mercy and His grace, that you would know His infinite goodness and His love for you. He has allowed this wonderful grace because He wishes for you all good things. He wishes for you to know how dear you are to His heart, that He would give all things to you, to the very life of His Son.

I am overjoyed and filled with happiness that you have responded wholeheartedly to my call to prayer, to peace, to conversion! Seek the road of conversion every day in your lives. Walk nearer to my Son. As your mother, I wish only to bring to you His peace, His joy, the life that is Him, the life which He promises to each of you. I wish to share with you the hope of Heaven, of the place that our Father has prepared for you, the joy and the love through this grace that He has allowed.

I have brought many to you thus far and you have opened your arms and your hearts and your ears to hear their words, their words that are an echo of the Gospel given to you, the words of my Son, the words of God, the message of love, the message of forgiveness, the message of peace. Today, I bring to you another, he who suffered and struggled for the sake of the infant Church that Christ had established. He now shares in the glory of Christ, as you who persevere shall. You are the faithful Church.

I am most pleased to share with you this grace, this gift. You are my beloved children. I am with you always, ever near to your hearts, walking beside you. The Lord has permitted me to come among you, that you would not be left to the wolves, but cloaked in my mantle of grace and of love, of motherly comfort and consolation.

St. Clement:

People of God, praise His name! May the Lord have mercy on us. May Christ grant us peace. May the Lord lift us up. Brothers and sisters of the Church, you who are faithful, you who are the Body, the very heart of Christ, it is good to be with you.

You are so pleasing to God in your actions and in your faith and in the homage that you give to His mother. She is so exalted in Heaven! You cannot know how glorified we, the Church, is in Heaven. For when Christ established His church, He designed it for perfect glory, perfect purity, that it would be the Rock. Indestructible. Untarnished. Unending. That although the forces of Hell would thrust themselves upon it, it should not be broken nor marred, but kept pristine and holy. Our dear mother reflects this holiness and this purity, the immaculate, the very immaculate will of the Father. And so, we who join Him in Heaven, reflect His will. It is for you to strive toward this goal of perfection in the soul through action and faith.

Church of God, your lives are lived in a time of persecution much like the time when I was upon this earth. For in my day, those who followed the Christ were made to suffer atrocious, horrific crimes committed against God's faithful. Many gave up their very lives, as the Christ Himself gave His life for us. In my day, the Church was at its beginnings. The great teachers, the great evangelizers, Paul, James, Peter, they had taught to all nations, to Jews and to Gentiles, traveling, preaching, leaving behind the Church of God in Corinth, Laodicea, Smyrna, Philadelphia. All these places, I traveled to.

As a young man, I went among these early churches and I watched as the Holy Spirit came to all nations, just as He descended on those first apostles on Pentecost and inspired them. These little churches- so persecuted, so fought against by the legions of the Evil One- grew, spread, became alive in the Spirit, nurtured as seeds beneath the snow. And so, these little churches, communities of faithful, were brought up. Oh, the task of those first evangelizers, to keep the faith of these people alive! I recall my travels to Corinth. What a difficult church it was to establish! For the people there were trapped, trapped in their ways of sinfulness, in sins of the flesh, in eating and in drinking, and enjoying all things, but not God or His will. This was perhaps the most difficult church, and it caused my friends, the Evangelists, much grief. But through the grace of God, it persevered.

The age of Peter was over. A kind man he was, a good man, truly devoted to the Christ, a pillar of faith. And then it was my turn to take from him the staff of faith, as those before me had, and I watched over the flock, these churches so scattered. In my day, the law was "death to the Christians." These churches, so unstable as they were, began to fall, suffered. They laid in a state of disarray, and truly I say to you that without the Spirit, none of you would know Christ this day, for no church, no community, would have survived those days.

But because of the grace of God and the gift He gave to us in the Holy Spirit, these scattered churches began to unite under the persecutions. And though threatened with death, they emerged from their hiding places. And this was my task, to unite these communities, to make one, holy, church. How vulnerable this early church was! Many false teachers passed, many false beliefs. Idolatry was rampant. People fell into their old ways, as they so often have the habit of doing. The zeal for God was gone among much of His people. What was I to do? How could I unite these people who suffered so much under the heavy hand of opposition?

Faith in God, trust in God, is a powerful example to those who wish to suppress you. And this is the route that I chose, faith, unshakable faith, with good works and with the firm belief that God would guide us, as He had watched over and guided those who traveled in the Sinai for so very long, our forefathers. As He had told Abraham, as He had spoken to Moses His Law, I trusted that He would guide us, this new church, the Church of His new covenant. And through the example of many faithful, these churches were strengthened, and so many gave up their lives, that they would be a powerful example to the authority that opposed us.

It is not much different in your day. Once again, the Church is in a time of darkness, a time of opposition. There are many forces that wish to tear apart the unbreakable Church- materialism, communism, egoism. There is no room for God there, but faith, love, and hope open the door to God, and to His mercy and forgiveness. You too suffer under the persecutions, as your early forefathers did, and it is the same now for all of you as it was for those early churches that felt so very isolated, and so very alone, and so very abandoned. You gather together in groups and into communities, and how often do you feel as though you are alone, fighting against all of the world? I tell you, this is not so!

You are confined to the human state. In your humanity, you seek to praise God with your voices, your eyes, your ears, your hearts, and your very souls, but there is much that you do not know! Do you know that all of the Angels of God stand with you? Myriads! Do you know that we, the faithful who have passed before you, stand with you? Do you know that the Church of God, the unbreakable rock, far outnumbers those who wish to suppress and poison it? You must never feel alone, for it is not the case. Do you know that the very mother of God is with you, among you, and that God Himself- all power, all glory, and all mercy, is among you? How, my brothers and sisters, could you ever be alone? Nor are you isolated, but connected to your sister and brother communities on this earth, those who know Christ and who are in Christ as you are, to the church past, to the church to come. God is not restricted by time nor space. Language is no barrier for God. His family transcends time, transcends humanity itself.

For me, as the leader of the church, I suffered much, just as the vicar of Christ here on earth now suffers. Pray for him. Pray for all whom Mary, the Virgin Mother of Christ, has called, and Christ Himself has called, to the holy priesthood. These are your generals, your commanders in the army of God. Yes, in His very army! And how should an army of God behave? Truly, what is the army of God? Certainly, it is not an army as you would know it. No guns, no fighting, no violence would be here. I tell you to arm yourselves with prayer. Arm yourselves with hope. Shield yourselves with forgiveness. Ride upon mercy and go honorably into battle against evil with humility. It is only in this way that the Church can triumph. It is only in this way the Church will be what God has intended. Glorified! Powerful! Indestructible!

My life was so small, so very meaningless, and yet to God, I was everything. For when I met Him, He embraced me with such a love that I could imagine that His Son died for me alone! Many have come to His kingdom since, and I have seen that He shares this love for each and every one. A great mystery it is, that for each person He would have given the whole of Himself and yet, His death and His resurrection were enough to save all. You must always be certain that His love for you is greater than any suffering that you might endure, or any persecution. It is greater than death itself. You are not alone, nor abandoned, but you are loved. You are loved!

My death was a holy death. It was all that I could give to the Father. It was all that I had left, and I was honored to do as Jesus Himself had done. Each of you, each one of you, dies one thousand "deaths" a day. Each of you has the opportunity to offer these little "deaths to yourself" to the Father. Each time you sacrifice, each time you do penance, you offer your life to Him. Never can our sacrifices add up to, or be worthy of, the sacrifice that God made for us, but this is not what He wants from us. He is not a God who seeks from us that He has given. He does not require our sacrifices in order to give out His graces. He wants our love, our very best, our all in what we do and in what we say, in what we have done and what we will do, in all that we are, in all that He has made us, in our strengths and in our weaknesses. For if we give to Him everything we have, can He not do the same for us? His mercy and justice are for always. He will give to us manyfold what we give to Him. He gives to us more than we can imagine. This is His way. He is our Father. He loves us. He wants all good things for us.

And this is why He sends to you His mother, a guardian of faith, a general in God's army, a pillar in the unbreakable church. This is His most precious gift, the one whom He loved most on this earth, and He has given her to you. Accept her! Hear her words. Answer her call. Do as she asks, for as a mother, she wants for you all good things and wishes only for you to share in the glory of God. Know that the Church will prevail! The Angels in Heaven, the Angels shall present a glorified church to God and sing, "Alleluia," forever! The Church will prevail! It is your task to give all that you can to God, that His glory might be multiplied for always.

Sisters and brothers, people of God, take heart! Have hope in these words that I have given to you. Know that there is nothing that can crush what God has instituted, God's very heart. There is nothing, nothing worth giving up your share in His glory. Accept Him and His mother whom He sends. She is the pathway to the Son, the Son Who is the Way. He is every hope, is every love, is every mercy. Take heart! Be encouraged by this. Go out as the first evangelizers did and teach the young, the sick, those who thirst for God's love. Show them, as I showed those early Christians who looked to me for an example, the way to be Christlike in your action, in your faith. And it is in this way that the whole world would be converted to God and His church would be glorified on Earth, as it is in Heaven and shall forever be. I thank you for having heard me. Remember all that I have told you in the spirit of Christian love and in fellowship.

Mary:

My children, I thank you for gathering this day. I am with you as your mother. Praised be Jesus, Lord of Lords on High! Prayer, prayer is so essential. Do not forget to pray! Do not forget my Son! I have spoken to you that the greatest prayer is Holy Mass and again, I wish to repeat this to you. I thank you for the prayers that you have offered to me. Know that I lay them before my Son, and He has accepted them with joy. You are a great comfort and consolation to the Crucified Lord. I love you so very much and draw you ever nearer to my Immaculate Heart.

St. John, March 17, 1998

Carolyn:

The Blessed Mother is wearing a slate-gray dress that is tied at the waist by a sash and she has a white veil. She is standing with her hands placed together in prayer. There are pink and white roses, and little red roses, around her feet. She has a coral-colored rosary that is very long and does not have just five decades, but all fifteen. On the bottom is a gold crucifix that has little round bulbs at the ends of it.

St. John is standing beside the Blessed Mother. He is a short man. He and the Blessed Mother are about the same height. He is dressed in brown and wearing sandals. He has dark brown hair and is balding a bit on the back of his head. He has a very round face and dark eyes. He is smiling. He is clasping something small and shiny in his hands, but I cannot see what it is. I think it may be a rosary.

Mary:

Dear children, I am overjoyed that you have come here today in such great numbers, for you have heard my call and you have responded with the fullness of your hearts. It is for this very reason that the Father allows me to work many graces upon this earth. He loves His children and He desires all that is good for them. As you who are parents respond to a child who embraces you, who loves you, who desires you, so too does He respond when His children reach out to Him as you do. I have accepted your prayers, and I have taken them up and laid them before my Son. They are most beautiful roses. Thank you for your prayers. I am overjoyed!

I bring to you this day, John, he who was the most intimate friend of my Son, and who cared for me so very well after He ascended to glory. Thank God for this gift, for He has made it possible. I thank you for your response, for your great desire to know God's love and God's mercy.

St. John:

Children of God, I greet you in the name of the Word Made Flesh, the One Who sits on high, now and forever. It is good to be with you, to be able to teach you what I have known of our Lord, being with Him for so very long. I was greatly blessed! I shared many years with Him. I knew Him as a man and in His glory. This was an awesome thing, one that I was not worthy of. Now I wish to share this experience with you, that it might deepen your faith and open your hearts to God in a very special and new way.

Brothers and sisters, before I was blessed to see the Son of Man and walk with Him, I was a simple man. I had very little schooling and lived as many others did in my day. And one day, this man Whom I had heard much about, came calling to me. There were so many things that people were saying about Him! Some believed He was the Messiah, the Promised One, the One that God would send to free us from bondage, the One He had promised to Abraham, to David, to our forefathers, but these were few. They were the ones who followed Him closely, and listened to His words, and lived His message. And there were others who thought He was a false prophet, One Who came to deceive, the "Seed of Evil," as He was called. Many of these were devout Jews, those who knew the Law, who had studied it as the Pharisees and the Sadducees had. These were the ones who were set against Him from the very start, who mocked Him, who ridiculed Him, who tried every means to trick Him, and deceive Him, and those who followed Him. By the grace of God, these too were few.

Most people in my day, they knew not what to think. He was a wise man. Everyone agreed on that, for He could look deep into the soul of those whom He encountered and touch them in a way that no man could without the grace of God. He was special. There was something about Him. My own family, even they had heard these rumors. My parents were devoutly Jewish. They believed in the Messiah. They knew their Scripture well, and so they had little difficulty believing that Christ was the Messiah, for as Isaiah had written, the Messiah would come and would not be recognized. The Shepherd would walk among the lambs and not be seen nor heard, and the lambs would turn upon him, and he would suffer.

I knew not what to think, but I knew I must follow Him, for when He beckoned to me, there was nothing like it. And so, I put down my work and set aside my life, and I traveled with Him. And soon, He became my master, and I knew Him as the Lord.

Jesus, He was what we all must be! He was goodness and mercy, love. How many have passed those in need and done nothing? And why? Perhaps because you thought there was nothing you could give, or perhaps you knew that someone else would come along and give assistance to this person? Ah, but Jesus, when He saw those who ailed, those who suffered, there was nothing else in the world but that person for Him. And when He touched them and looked upon them, the love in His eyes, it was tremendous! Never did He turn any away, but He gathered all who loved Him near. He told stories, magnificent stories! And He taught us without us ever realizing it. He was wise and He was humble. He did not discriminate. He ate among the rich and the poor, the sick and the healthy, those who were noble and those who were lowly, and He loved each the same.

We must all strive to do this, for this is the greatest of God's laws: love one another. For each of you are made in the image of the Christ, of God the Father, the Spirit, O Holy. When you serve one another, you serve Him, He Who created you. I believe that this is the greatest calling: to be a servant. Truly, the richest are the poorest, the meekest are the wisest, and those who would forsake all of themselves for another, even to their very lives, they are the most holy.

Jesus, He was a divine person, the Son of God in body and soul, full of His divinity, and yet, He was a man. This is a mystery that is incomprehensible to our minds. He grew tired, as you do, and hungry. He knew pain and joy. He laughed and He wept. He was great fun to be with, for He always had a kind word and perfect compassion in times of trial. I found it to be most amazing that even when He was downtrodden and discouraged, as all people will be, even when He was hungry and tired and weak from travel, from speaking, still He did not lose that perfect love, that perfect empathy, that perfect compassion and understanding for those who called to Him. He never rested. You know this. Your Gospels tell the story. For three years He walked among His followers, and He converted, and He healed, and He ministered, and He taught. All these things, they are difficult work. And He relied much on us, those who were His brothers, who were His disciples.

I believe that this too is important, for this is when the Christian has the hardest time living the life, the very life of Christ: in times when you are hungry and cold, when you are uncomfortable and tired. You know, you know the times of your weakness. It is easy to be good and holy when things are well, and you are well. But ah! How difficult is it to be holy when you feel everything but! This is the challenge that all Christians face, and persevere through: to be holy always. Holiness is a way of life. Holiness is the way of God.

If you wish to be truly holy, you must follow Christ's example. And what is it that Christ taught us to do? Christ taught us to love, and He showed us love. He taught us to heal the sick, minister to the lonely, love the poor, the weak, those who are hated. He taught us that we are all children of God and equal in His eyes. And, even more so than all of creation, we are beautiful. There is no measure for the dignity of life. We are created in God's image. We are His children. To show respect and give dignity to life is to emulate Christ, Who is life itself. Death could not remain where Christ was. Many did He raise from a state of death. Even death could not keep Him! How could death harness life? Life overcomes!

Christ also taught us to be humble. As you know, He was born to a virgin, a holy woman in a very small town, in a stable, a place where animals dwelled. And He lived His whole life simply, the Son of a carpenter. And even when He ministered, He ministered simply. He did not ask for material things. He did not worry about His meals, His clothing, His day-to-day needs. No, He trusted that the Father would provide, and He did. He was perfect humility. Never, never did He seek to do anything but glorify God, and in doing so, glorify He Himself, that it would glorify the Father.

He was an example of perfect obedience, obedience to the Father, obedience even to His creation. Let me ask you, what was it that caused the death of our Lord? Was it His crucifixion and His executioners? The nails that they drove into His body and the spear they drove into His side? No! He is the Lord! He gave His life in obedience to the will of the Father. And the will of the Father was to redeem each one of you. Perfect obedience, even to His executioners.

Christ, He was perfect forgiveness, for from the cross He forgave even the penitent sinner and those who inflicted such suffering upon Him. What terrible suffering He endured! Never was there a more inhumane execution, for at that time the Evil One sought to destroy His very will and very spirit. The torments He suffered, they are unimaginable! And yet, in His heart was only forgiveness, and peace, and love. From His cross, He gave to you one of His greatest gifts, the love of a mother, of His mother, of your mother. The Blessed Mother, she is goodness and is the only one who is a perfect example of what God intended for all of us to be. Follow her way, for her way always leads to the Son.

I knew Christ well. Many things did He confide in me, many fears, His angst, His love, and His joy. Most miraculous of all things that I witnessed was His compassion, and His love, and His goodness, and it is for this reason that I have spoken to you on these things. It is essential for you to live in holiness, for in holiness is the very Spirit of God. This is well. And yet you might ask, "How is it that I begin to live in holiness, for there is so much?" It is not easy to love when you feel like hating, to give when you feel like holding, to smile when you feel like frowning, to be peaceful when you wish to fight. But you, you have a weapon! You have a weapon against the evil, the very Evil One who has set himself against you to prevent you from living in holiness. That weapon, it is prayer. Prayer!

Without prayer you would die. You shrivel and dry up like a seedling without water. There are many who walk, who live, who talk, who are but empty shells. This causes great distress to our Lord. Prayer, it is food for the soul. It is drink for the thirst that your soul has for life itself. It is comfort and rest. And so, I say to you, how is it that you be joyful in sorrow, patient when you are hungry and thirsty, strong when you are tired and weak, and bold in God's love? Satisfy your weakness with prayer, the perfect, perfect, perfect expression of love! The more that you pray and the more that you commit yourself to prayer, the easier it will be for you to live in holiness and goodness.

So, I urge you, pray! Pray frequently and with the heart. God will turn no one away in prayer when they pray with the true love that Christ has for His people. Pray, especially in these times when there is such evil in this world. Prayer is the remedy, the elixir, for the diseases of materialism, the disease of division in family, the disease of isolation from God. No one will truly understand the greatness of prayer until they arrive in our Father's home. My brothers and sisters, I have spoken to you about many things, many virtues that you should possess and that I am sure you desire to possess. And I have told you that the way to acquire such virtues is prayer, for prayer brings about the graces of God. This is what you must do above all else. For what good is it to do the work of God if you have not made yourself a temple for Him to dwell in, to work through you?

Each person has an altar in the depths of their heart, and on these altars are their gods, the gods that they worship and adore. For most, the god is power. For many more, it is pride, money. These are idols. These are false gods. These things are passing.

Place Jesus on your altar by living a life of holiness and prayer. God will not reject the sacrifice of His Son. It opens the very gates of His mercy. Come to the Father in the name of the Son and with gratitude for His sacrifice, and you shall find that you will be blessed abundantly.

All of what I have told you is true, and yet, there is more. For all that I have said that Christ is, He is still! While on earth, He was good and He suffered much for it, and you who are good, you too will suffer. This is inevitable. But Christ, He had His day of glory where He ascended to the Father in the company of minions of angels, who sang and praised, "Glory to God in the highest and peace to good people on earth!" He now sits at the right hand of the Father, and with the Father and the Holy Spirit, will rule for all of time and for all of eternity. He, a faithful servant of the Father, although God Himself, has been rewarded for His sacrifice.

Live a life of goodness and you too shall know these rewards. For at the hour of your death, when you are called home into the Father's care, you will know great joy! There is none like it! Have hope, then. Have hope in this reward, this great treasure that God desires to give to you. For as Christ was glorified, you shall know His glory. You shall know His true being. I have described to you but a small part of the Christ, that you would come to know Him in a deep way. I assure you, when you join the Father and experience Him, all things, all cares, all sorrows, all joys, and all trials will pass away, and you will know only perfect joy.

My brothers and sisters, have hope! Children of God, praise Him and thank Him. Live a life of goodness through prayer and you will come to know Christ our Lord as your redeemer, your love, your friend, your brother, and your life. I thank you for hearing me this day and allowing me to speak to you. Take what I have said to heart and meditate upon it.

Mary:

Dear children, I with my Son bless you. I am with you always. Rely on my intercession and my aid, and you will never be abandoned. Love God with all of your hearts, and you will know His peace. Trust in Him, and you will know His joy. Thank you for having responded in such great numbers to this gift from the Father. It is through such responses that graces, the very graces of God, have entered this world and brought light to the darkness.

St. James, April 14, 1998

Carolyn:

The Blessed Mother is wearing a rose-colored dress and a long white veil. She has her arms extended out and raised up, her palms upward. Her eyes are lifted, and she is praying. St. James is standing beside her.

St. James is much taller than the Blessed Mother. He has medium brown hair and a beard. He is wearing a gray-brown robe with a brown sash around his shoulders, and he has sandals on his feet. St. James has a candle in one hand that is lit. In the other, a staff, but it has no crook. It's like a walking stick. He is looking downward. He is also praying.

Mary:

My dear children, it is good to be among you again. I am overjoyed that you have responded to me in such great numbers. I thank you for coming to me in this way, for accepting the gift that the Father has given for His love of you. My dear ones, do pray! Do stay near to our Lord! This is a time of great celebration. It is the time of the Easter renewal, the very resurrection of our Lord! Pray, dear children, that all might know the great joy that I do know, and the hope that my Son, Jesus, brings to the world.

Today I have brought to you a faithful servant of the Father, he who was a leader of your early church, he who is now with the Father in glory. I thank you, my little ones, for accepting this grace, for your prayers and your sacrifices. They are most dear to my Immaculate Heart! Do continue in your good works, and keep your hearts open for the voice of God. He is with you, as I, your mother, am with you.

St. James:

My Christian friends, I greet you in the name of Christ, He Who was, Who is, and Who is to come. Let His peace fill you this day and always. Know always His will. Live always in His love, in the shadow of His mercy, and may your heart be filled with His graces. Brothers and sisters, friends of God, I walked with our Christ and I knew Him. Let me tell you about the early days, the days of trial and persecution, the days of great darkness.

Our Lord, after His ministries, He was taken and He was crucified, and so began the darkest day of all time. And I and my brothers, we fled. We ran far. Such fear was within us! We knew not what to do. We abandoned our Lord! And there He suffered, and He died, and He was laid in a tomb. Together with Peter, John, Matthew, I wept. I was so very afraid! We hid. We spoke only to those whom we could trust, to those who belonged to the Christian Way, the followers of Christ. We feared for our very lives, for if they had killed our master, what would become of us? None of us were brave. We did not yet have the courage that the Holy Spirit brings. And so, we stayed there locked up together, hidden away and afraid.

My sisters and brothers, we did not have hope. This is the gift of the resurrection: the gift of salvation, the gift of hope, the gift of joy. At this time, you do celebrate these things as you reflect on the great mystery of the resurrection of our Lord, but we had no hope in that time, knowing that we would be scattered, be broken, be killed. And so, we waited. There were some among us who remembered our Lord's words. There were some who remembered that He had said that the Son of Man would be led away to death, only to rise again and be glorified. Let me tell you, this was not what was in our hearts on that day, but only angst, and despair, and hopelessness.

Time passed, and a knock! And a woman approached. "I have seen the Lord," said she. Impossible! How could this be? We all saw our master bleed! We watched on as cowards in the distance as He died, with only His beloved and His mother beside Him. How could this be? Jesus, we ate with Him. We taught with Him. We knew Him. We knew He was the Lord, and yet, the very idea that He lived was beyond us. And then He came among us, showing us the wounds in His hands, and in His feet, and in His side, proclaiming the good news of the resurrection! This is the great gift that you now celebrate. You share in the joy and the hope of the resurrection, and are assured of your salvation in it.

Oh, on that day, how afraid we were! To think, we feared when He was not among us, but what greater fear did we know when He appeared within the room with the doors barred and windows closed! I shuddered and fell to the ground, falling to my knees, my face to the dirt, "Lord, Lord I am not worthy!" And He lifted us up, and He took my hands. "James," He spoke. "James, rise up." And He looked deep into my eyes, placed His hands on my shoulders. I feared no more then, but I knew great joy! I share this with you so you can hear the story as I saw it, as I know it to be, of our Lord's greatest gift. For three years, He taught and ministered and healed, and this was good, but His greatest gift for all time was accomplished in but three hours on a tree on Calvary.

Still today, that sacrifice is renewed in your churches on your altars. Daily your priests offer Mass, the greatest of prayers, and again the sacrifice of the Christ is renewed. You have within your midst the full person of Jesus, His body, His blood, His soul and divinity. Within your tabernacles is the same Christ that I fell down before. "I am not worthy," did I cry. It is most important to give this same homage to the Eucharistic Christ, for truly, Jesus loves you so very much that He renews His sacrifice, gives His life to you, each day. How humbling it is to think that the Lord of all creation would come to this earth, and hide Himself in bread and wine, only to be with you. What a testament to love!

In the days after the Christ returned and was among us, we had much joy and much anxiety. And He gifted us with the Holy Spirit, and sent us out to minister to all nations. The time came when He left us and ascended to the Father. We, His disciples, began the mission of preaching, of teaching our brothers and sisters, Jews and Gentiles, the Word, the Truth. Many of my brothers went out. Peter, John, they taught. They evangelized. I remained in Jerusalem, where I kept watch over the infant Church. What a difficult task this was for me, for in that day, the Church was weak and suffered much.

There are many now who say terrible, blasphemous things about the true Church of God. How often have you heard that the Church is corrupt, or evil, or wicked and oppressive? Brothers and sisters, you must not say such things! For the Church, it is not made up of buildings, nor of particular priests, nor of the ways of prayer or rituals. The Church is the Bride of Christ, the very being of Christ. To blaspheme her is to speak evil against Christ Himself. The Church is Christ's hands and feet, His rule on this earth. You, each of you, are members of the Body of Christ. You continue His work this day, as I and my brothers did in that early time. You too teach, and evangelize, and give hope to those who are hopeless, as we once were. In doing so, you continue the work that Jesus gave to us, "Go out and make disciples of all nations."

In your vocations, in your lives, you are all called to bring Christ, to be bearers of Christ. By your very name of "Christian," you are called to His ministry. There are many, many vocations. Some are called to priesthood, and this is holy and good. Others to married life. Yet others remain single to devote their time completely to the Lord. There are those who work as teachers, as healers, as listeners. Whatever you have been called to do, do it well, and do it for the Lord. For you must understand, all that you are able to do is possible only because of the graces and the gifts that He has given to you. For when He created you, when you were but a thought in His mind, He made you just as you are. He placed within you all of the gifts and the joys, the beauty that you possess, the dignity that you have as His children, that dignity that you received at your baptism.

You are the children of God. The hands and feet of Christ. This is an indelible mark, one that cannot be erased. Not even death can take away your life in God. You must persevere and do well to serve Him, to devote yourselves to Him, to devote all of your actions to Him. For what you do in the Lord, it will be good, as He is good.

My sisters and my brothers, the days in which I lived were difficult and there were many arduous tasks. And it is the same now. It is difficult to be a Christian. The way that Christ called us to is not easy. For even He Himself understood that the road to Heaven is small and narrow, and for most, it is the path not traveled. It is not easy, but it is not impossible, as I once believed. Nothing is impossible with God. For me to limit the Lord, for me to doubt the resurrection, what an injustice! What a terrible limitation!

Our God is a God of love and mercy, and a God Whose very existence is devoted to loving His children. Would our Father in Heaven not provide for us all good things? Would He not send His own Son to be sacrificed as the Eternal Lamb, the sacrifice that can never be erased, outdone, the sacrifice that would bring about the salvation of all of us? Would He not provide for you? Would He not give to you the strength and the courage that you need to be disciples of Christ? Let me tell you, as one who has experienced the love of God in His kingdom, you cannot comprehend how much He does love you!

One day, if you choose to walk His road, you will stand before Him and see Him in all His glory. And He will embrace you, and draw you near to Him, and you will know what only those who now reign with Him can understand. But until that time, I assure you, you are most precious! Do nothing in vain. Avoid sin, for it robs you of the very life that Christ has won for you. It is an insult to your own dignity, and to the gift of life that the Father gave to you in His Son. Live in holiness, and with prayer, and with peace. Most especially, let peace be between you.

There is much evil in the world, and the light of Christ, it is all that can bring hope to the many. You must be able to bear that light. You must be able to bear that joy to those yet lost in the darkness. As the hands and feet and the Body of Christ, you must be able to emulate Him, to bring Him to the sick and the ailing, to the lost and the lonely, to those who are far from Him. This cannot be accomplished if you cannot be at peace within yourselves. This problem of division and strife, it was a problem that we faced in our early church. For as you know, there were many who wished to impose the Jewish law on the Christian Gentiles, and others who said it should not be so. Division is never of God. Division is caused by the Evil One who seeks to destroy all that God gives.

Peace can be found through prayer. Peace is sorely needed in this day. There is much division in the Church of God, and this cannot be so. How can the hand of Christ be divided from the feet? How can the body be divided from the soul? Christ is indivisible, as the Church is indivisible. Be united with one another. Be at peace with one another. Do not allow strife or anger to divide you, but embrace the virtues of forgiveness, mercy, love, and tolerance. Be patient. Be kind. Serve one another as you would serve Christ Himself, for within you, within each of you, dwells the Lord in the Eucharistic form so beautiful! When you take Him into yourselves, truly, He resides then in your soul always, so you must treat one another with great dignity and respect, and have great respect for all life.

These things are good, and they are practical, and they are things that all Christians should strive to do. But most importantly, you must always, always listen to the silence of your hearts. The voice of God, it is there. His Holy Spirit whispers to you His will, His way. Abandon yourselves completely to Him. Trust completely in Him. You will not be left alone, nor led out astray, but you will be lifted up, raised up. And by serving one another and those who do not yet know the Lord, you share in the mysterious salvation of Christ, and will with Him one day, share in His glory.

My dear brothers and sisters, I thank you for listening to me this day, for allowing me to come to you in this way. Lift grateful hearts up to the Father, for it is through Him that all graces are made possible. Finally, I do say to you, of all things in life, your families, your friends, your work, there is but one thing that is eternal, and that is the love that God has placed in each of your hearts to give to one another and to Him. Remember this as you go about your daily duties, for many are lost in the trivialness of life, the things that are passing. Possessions, desires- all these things are for naught. Only love, only love will transcend even death.

I do hope that this was an encouragement for you. I do wish for you to know how near you are to God. And though we all are faulted, and walk away from Him at times, our Lord is One of such love that He does not let us go, but pursues us, embraces us, forgives us. Look forward with great anticipation to seeing Him as I do now, in your heavenly home. Let that be a prize, a reward, that you seek, and do so by loving one another.

Mary:

My dear children, I give to you this day my motherly blessing. I ask you to continue in your prayers. Do pray especially for my priests who struggle, for those who have gone before you and are in Purgatory. Pray that God might continue to allow great graces to pour forth upon this earth, that all might know my Son as their redeemer and their Lord. I bless you in the name of the Father, and of the Son, and of the Spirit Who dwells within you. May the peace of Christ be with you.

St. Anne, May 17, 1998

Carolyn:

The Blessed Mother appears as a young woman. She is wearing a slate-gray dress with a mantle and a short white veil. She has dark black hair. Her hands are extended and she is smiling.

St. Anne is with her. She looks older than the Blessed Mother. She is also wearing a mantle and a long gown that is tied about the waist with a sash. Her veil is folded over and pulled back away from her face, and she has very dark hair and blue eyes. St. Anne has her hands on the Blessed Mother's shoulder and left arm.

Mary:

My dear little one, thank you for responding to my call and gathering again here tonight. You have come to receive these graces of God because you love the Son and the Father Who sent Him, and you have loved me as your mother and honored me. Thank you for your prayers and for your sacrifices. I thank you for all of the gifts that you have offered for my intentions, for those gifts which you have offered to console my wounded Son. They are a great joy to our Father in Heaven, He Who loves us and Who is so merciful that He has allowed you, His little children, to know me and the saints of the heavens in the most miraculous way. Again, I thank you for gathering here, and for offering your prayers. Continue always, always to place Jesus in the center of your lives, to emulate Him always, for He is the Way, and the Light of the World.

St. Anne:

Good people of God, it is good to be among you. Let us always praise Him, for He has made great things for us, His people, His chosen ones. Good people, I have been asked to come among you this day and to speak to you, that you might know in a most personal way that God does work among you, that the kingdom that He has prepared for you is not far, but so very near to you. God, He is with you! He lives among you, in your prayer, in your worship, in your church. We, those who have served Him and gone on to receive our reward with Him and in Him, we have the joy of eternal unity with Him, with the Blessed Trinity. This is a joy that you have yet to know, a most beautiful thing! I wish to impart to you some of that joy in the knowledge of the Trinity, some of the wondrous awe in the knowledge of the Son, He Who was made man and came upon this earth, and dwelt among us to show us the way to the kingdom that has been prepared.

I lived in a time when I grew up and worked simply, as a wife and a mother. I tended to my husband's animals. I tended to the house. I tended to his needs, as a good wife must. We loved the Lord. We kept the Law. We honored the Sabbath. We loved God, and yet, for so very long, He sent us no children. You must understand that in this day, to be barren, this was seen as a horrible thing. It meant that you had offended God, that He had withheld the very life that is Him, from you. Nevertheless, I persevered in faith, and I prayed that God would send me a child, a little one of my very own, that I might protect, and guard, and love. Often, I found my consolation in the tales of our fathers, of Abraham, of Sarah, of those who struggled, of those who too were barren, and I resigned myself to the fact that the life of a mother was not for me.

One should not limit God in such a way! For He did see fit to send me a child, a beautiful little girl, and I named her Miriam. She was a holy child, holy indeed, and from her first steps, learned to love the Lord, to walk with Him, to obey Him. When she was presented at the Temple, she knew then that God loved her as her father and I did, and she rejoiced, even though so very young. My husband and I, we brought her up to know the Law. We taught her by our example what it is to serve one another in a family and, though young, what a perceptive child!

As you know, children learn by watching those around them. This is why it is of great importance that your families be virtuous! It is the very cradle of God's arms, the very heart of life itself! The family is the place that the great gift of faith is nurtured and guided. Mutual service, charity- these things are important in family life. You must serve one another, as Christ served you. If you cannot do this among your families, how then, could you go out and do it for those whom you do not know? I urge you, strive for a special holiness in your families, and pray often in the name of the Holy Family, that God would strengthen your families in faith, hope, and love.

Wives, be true to your husbands. Obey them and serve them, for they are as Christ. Husbands, do honor your wives, for they are as His Body, the temple of life through which life, life, the very presence of God, is brought forth into this world. Children, do obey your parents, for God has commanded this as He gave His law to Moses in the Sinai. Honor your parents and your elders. Love them. Obey them.

My Miriam was a special child. And as you well know, God chose her for a special mission, that she would receive a grace so wonderful, so holy, that no other woman from age to age would share in the special honor that she had received. My Miriam was to become the Mother of God, the Savior that had been promised to our people for always.

Jesus, a special child, a beautiful one, God-Made-Man, though hidden, hidden quietly in a small child Who was like many others in our village. Jesus ran, and He played, and He laughed, and He cried, and His mother carefully nursed His wounds, watched Him pray, and helped Him grow. And she taught Him, with her husband, to love God and to serve God. Dear ones, these were the times, these were the times of God's greatest gift, the time when the Christ Child was brought forth into this world to bring light to the darkness, the Savior, the Lord! I do tell you, should you have seen Him playing, laughing with His friends, or in His schooling, one might not have guessed the great gift He would give to the world.

Dear ones, it is imperative that you, all of you, give the gift of faith, the faith that has been passed down from age to age, to your children. Just as the Christ Child was placed by the Father into a family, so too has the Father placed children into your care, that you would nurture them and bring them up for God alone. Ultimately, your children are not your own, but they are the children of God, given to you for but a while, to be taught and instructed. And so then, emulate goodness, and purity, and humility for them that, like the Christ Child, they would grow to serve God in whatever mission they have been called to do.

My message to you is one of trust. It was difficult for me to trust God. I endured many trials in my life. At a very young age, I found myself without parents. I trusted God as my father, that He would father me, and that He would take the place of my family, my cradle of love. I endured many illnesses, and a long period of trusting in God's grace and goodness, as I prayed for a child of my own. My husband, he too was a holy man and served God each day.

You know that we both share in God's glory as part of the Church Glorified in Heaven. I tell you, it is not that difficult to join the Father here. You must choose to serve, to serve in your families, to serve your spouses and your children, to serve your parents, your neighbors. You must choose to love God. It is not something that can be thought about, that can be decided with the mind, but something that must be chosen with the soul, an act of the will, of the mind, of the heart, and the soul together. A conscious choice to love. Once you have done this, it is not difficult, for God gives many graces to those who are persistent in their efforts. He has created each of you. He knows your strengths and your weaknesses, as He knows His own hands. He has molded you, and shaped you to be who you are, and called you to receive many graces to strengthen you.

Do choose to love Him, and discipline yourself to do so. My husband and I, we did no great things in our lives other than serve one another, and our children, and those around us. This is all that is required of you. You need not go out and perform great miracles, though there are many who are called to such a vocation. You need not become a priest or religious, though this is a holy sign of God's love and of Christ on earth. You need not do great things, only simple acts of love, and charity, and humility.

Each day start anew, for there will be many times when you will fail to love as you have decided to do. Each day, rise with the words upon your lips, "Jesus, grant me the grace to serve you this day in the little things in my life, in the times of disappointments and trials, and in joys." I assure you, were you to ask for His guidance and grace, it shall not be denied to you.

Each day, serve in little ways, with little sacrifices. In this way, you truly will become holy, and you will find yourself drawing nearer to God. Keep Him always in your mind and in your heart, and throughout the day, offer to Him your sacrifices, offer to Him your joys. Share your life with Him, as He has shared His with you, His eternal life, and you will find yourself growing very near to Him. You will find a love of prayer grow in your heart. You will find a love of peace where there was not peace before. You will find a perfect joy where there was bitterness and regret, and the true desire to love better, more perfectly, and more diligently, than you had the day before.

Simple acts of service, this is the way to the Kingdom of God. This is the way to be near to God, He whose very incarnation was a vast grace, an ocean of love, and the greatest service that ever has been, and ever shall be, performed upon this earth. Emulate His life. He did not go out and proclaim the Way of the Lord in a way that was large, in a way that was loud. He did not shout it out from the mountain tops, but through His service, through the laying of His hands upon the sick, through the touch of love, through eating with the poor and the lame. Sharing, laughing, loving, did He live His life, and gave all glory to God. Even in His death, it was not grand, but a simple act of service, as He died upon a tree with criminals. There is no more humble an act.

Many did not gather there. There was no one there to sing out praises to God, though many there knew He was the Messiah. There was no one there to proclaim the great gift that was being offered at that moment but a few who were faithful to Him, and those who were His executioners. In simplicity did He live, and in simplicity did He die. Even in His resurrection, He came again, and dwelt among His followers, and ate with them, and taught them, and embraced them. He touched them, and He allowed them to touch the very wounds that were their salvation.

The simple ways, good people, are the ways of God. Christ, He is Humility, born to my daughter, Miriam, a Jewish girl of no esteem. She did not stand out apart from her peers except for her joyful love of God. Christ grew up as every Jewish boy. He played, and He laughed, and He loved. He went out and answered the call of God, served in simplicity, and died a humble death.

You are asked to do the very same thing. None of you were born with esteem. Your parents and families could not be distinguished from the others, nor could you as children be distinguished from your peers, except that like Christ, you bear a mark, the mark that was placed upon your soul at your very baptism, the mark that defines you as a child of God.

You too, have a vocation and a mission. Follow Christ's example to grow and to serve in your mission, simply and with great love, that you would live a holy life and die a humble death, giving all things that you do, that you say, that you feel, for the glory of God. In this way, by placing all of your trust in Him, by allowing Him to guide you and Him alone, you will come to join us here, those who do now experience His great glory.

Good people of God, I thank you for having listened to what I have taught you this day, and I urge you to place your trust completely in the Lord. He is the Master of Humility. He is such love that He gives His whole self to you. If you would only throw yourself before Him in great trust and simplicity, as a child does in his family, you will be guided and led to a life of holiness, virtue, and love.

Mary:

Dear children, praise God for the gift He has allowed this day and for all gifts He has given. He is a generous God, and gives His grace to His children in a miraculous way. Dear little ones, as ever I am with you as a mother and an intercessor. May I extend to you my blessing, in the name of the Father, and the Son, and the Holy Spirit, that you would be strengthened and renewed in your trust and love for God, and filled with faith and the Holy Spirit. My little ones, be at peace this day and always.

St. John the Baptist, June 8, 1998

Carolyn:

The Blessed Mother is wearing a gray dress and a long white veil. Her hands are folded near her waist, and she has a coral-colored rosary draped over her arm. St. John the Baptist is with her.

St. John is wearing a brown robe that is tied at the waist with a cord. He is short and a little stocky. He looks older. He has short, gray-black, very curly hair and a beard and a mustache. He has a staff in his hand, and he is standing beside the Blessed Mother, looking toward her. She has now extended her arms.

Mary:

My dear little ones. It is good to be with you again in this way. Know that I am with you now as ever, and always as your mother. Praise God and thank Him for this gift He has allowed this day, for you have been chosen to receive a great gift. Through His mercy He allows His son, the Evangelizer, the Baptizer, the one who came before Him to announce His way, to speak to you this day.

Praise God! This is such a gift! I do wish for you to know that I am glad that you have gathered here, that I have called each of you here, that you might receive with open ears and open hearts these words. Know that each of these children, each of these little ones who now share in the glory of Christ, was as you are. Learn from them. Allow them to teach you. Hear their words and listen, for they can tell you many things of the goodness of God our Father. Know that as always, I extend to you my blessing and my prayers of intercession.

St. John:

People of God, my brothers and sisters in the Lord, I come to you with a message of the goodness of our Lord. He is so very good that He created man in His image and placed him upon this earth. He attended to his every need, gave to him all things, and man fell away and walked far from Him. But our Father in Heaven, He would not allow this to be so. He created us, each of us, uniquely like Him, to be with Him, to love Him, to serve Him. And so, He promised our forefathers that there would come a savior, One who would take upon Himself the sin of mankind, and that through His suffering and death, we might be restored to life.

To Abraham, He made the promise that he would be the father of the children of God. To David, that he might be the father of the Messiah, that from his lineage this Chosen One would come forth into the world. To Mary, our queen, He gave the promise of a new life, a beautiful life growing miraculously within her womb, a life conceived in spirit alone, a life more holy, more pure, than any life that this earth could sustain.

And the Son of God was born into this world to do as the Scriptures had prophesied, to grow up in humility, to learn from His creation, to be obedient to His executioners, to shed His blood upon this earth that His very hand molded, to wipe away our sins, and cleanse us, and free us. We are wretched creatures without God! He alone makes us beautiful. Within us He places our souls. He offers to us His own life, should we wish to take it. He has given us the cleansing waters of our baptism.

Do recall that it was water that poured forth from His heart, mingled with His blood. These are the gifts that our Savior gives to us: His blood to fill us with life, for blood itself is the very life of man, water to wipe away the sin that tarnishes the soul that God has painstakingly created to be beautiful, to be perfect, to be with Him. And so, in this great gift we received the very life of God, eternal life, true immortality, should we desire it. And forgiveness, perfect forgiveness, for the sins of our fathers and our own sin as the waters that poured forth from His heart do cleanse us, should we desire it. And so, I advise you, do make it your will to desire Him. A fool would turn away such a gift, and yet many in this day do.

Our God, the God of Noah, of Abraham, of Isaac and Jacob, the God of David, the God that helped armies march to great victories, the God that gave to Moses the tablets with the Law, that God loves us so very much that He sent His Son to die for us, this is a merciful God! This is love! For as Christ Himself has said, there is no greater love than for a man to lay down his life for another. What great love our Lord has for us!

People of God, do extend that same love to Him, for it is all that He desires. It is all that He has wanted. He has given to you all that you need. Could your lives be more fulfilled? Could you imagine another thing that you have not, that you need? He has given you a beautiful, beautiful life. He has provided food for you and shelter. He has provided for you all things that you need. There are many who are wrapped up in the materialism of this world, who desire this thing, or that, or another, who need to go there, or see this, or do this, and obtain that, but I tell you, you have all that you need within you. You have all that you need from our Father.

Water, that gift that washes away your sins, that sustains your life, He has provided. Shelter, your work, that you might provide for your families, none of you have gone without. In your homes you have warmth, and comfort, and the love of one another,

Christian friends to support you, the Church to comfort, and console you, and welcome you. You have all that you need. The Church is a gift! The sacraments, they alone are worth more than anything upon this earth, for even in them He has given you all that you need. He has baptized you to a new life.

Do you understand what it is to be a child of God? Do you know the gift you have been given? You cannot see what we who share in His kingdom can see. What a tremendous thing! He has taken the life from His own heart and placed it in you. He has given you His body as your food and His blood as your drink, His forgiveness when you are weak. He has given you the love of one another. He has given you the priesthood for guidance and consolation. He has given you His own mother, that she would intercede for you, that each day she would kneel before the cross and recommend you to Him. He has given all to you. Will you not do the same? Do know that you are blessed! You are so blessed, for not only has He provided all good things for you, but He has given to you such a gift as this- the wisdom that one can obtain only once he looks upon the face of the Messiah, and experiences that love in His embrace. You have been given a gift of wisdom that far surpasses the wisdom of many, many holy people. It is all a gift, a gift!

Our God is merciful, and He is loving. You should not be in the company of anyone who would tell you otherwise. Do not allow them to slander our God. Know your faith. Let your faith be your rock. As Jesus has built the Church upon the rock of Peter, stay true to your church, to the rock of your faith. You know our God is a loving God, and a merciful God, and a God of forgiveness, and of truth, and of life. Should anyone come to tell you that He is not this, but a God of anger, and strife, and hatred, you will know that this is a falsehood. You must not be persuaded by the times. You must not be persuaded by those around you. You must not be persuaded by your own doubts. You know the truth. You have been given all that you need. You know our Lord. As Christ has said, His lambs know the Shepherd and He knows them.

Watch for Him. See Him each day in your churches on your altars, in your prayer, in one another. Do not walk blindly past, as so many do, to seek out all that you need, that you want, that you must obtain, but look for Him, want Him, desire Him, seek Him out. You will find that He is there waiting for you. A God Who has given you so much, to His very life, will never be near to those who do not want Him, for they push Him away. But this same God who has given to you all things will not be far from those who call out to Him. He desires you so very much. You need only call upon Him, and He is with you. You need only cry out to Him, and you are forgiven. Be at peace, and be consoled in this. Find faith in this, and new life.

What is all this that you desire here? It is nothing! It passes away! And as my life on this earth passed, so will yours. And all these things that men collect will pass away too, all but faith, all but love. In all things, in all situations, you always have faith. You always have the love of God. And because you are a Christian, and you know your Lord, and He knows you, you have hope! You have a hope in the Resurrection, in the day when Christ will return and resurrect all of those who have suffered here to new life, in the day of your own death, when you meet your Lord and you are welcomed into eternal life, into the banquet hall that He has prepared for you. We are all called to die many times, to ourselves, to our desires, to our needs. But for as many "deaths" as we experience, there are as many "life's", new life, conversion, hope, peace, reconciliation, life in God. This is what feeds your soul! This is what God has provided for you. God is good. You are all blessed, as all of His children are.

Take to heart these things and remember them always, especially in the times of greatest struggle and strife. Allow no one to tell you anything different than that you are loved more than all things, that you have hope even when everything else is gone, that your faith is strong, and real, and alive in you, because Christ is alive in you every day, at every Mass, when you receive Him. You need fear nothing, for with God at your side, walking always behind you and before you, leading you to your heavenly home, you cannot go astray. Remain with Him. Be vigilant. Be constant. Call out to Him. He has given you His mother as a guide, His Son as a Messiah, and His life for all eternity. Be at peace. Live your lives for Him. Offer to Him all things. See Him. Seek Him out. Desire Him. And with grateful hearts praise Him, for He is good.

Mary:

My dear ones. I do pray that you would always have peace in your homes, and in your hearts, and among one another. Continue to pray fervently for your Christian brothers and sisters and those who are in Purgatory, for my young people and my priests, for those who are desperately in need of conversion. Continue to pray. The benefits, the graces of prayer, you cannot comprehend! I thank you for gathering this night, for hearing me, for hearing the one whom I have brought to you. Do praise God and thank Him. Do offer your love to Him in service each day. I bless you in the name of the Father, the Son, and the Spirit Who dwells within us.

St. Stephen, June 29, 1998

Carolyn:

The Blessed Mother is wearing a long, gray gown. She has a blue mantle and a white veil, and a sash around her waist. She has a coral-colored rosary in her hands, which are folded in front of her. There are red and pink roses around the bottom of her gown, and over her feet.

St. Stephen is with her. He is a rather small man. He has bright blue eyes and long, brown, curly hair, with a beard. He is dressed in brown, in the same kind of gown that the Blessed

Mother is wearing, and he has a burgundy sash around his waist. St. Stephen has a rock in his hand that he holds out in front of him.

Mary:

My dear little ones, it is good to be with you this day. As your mother, I am overjoyed that you have come in such great numbers to receive this gift of the Father. Praise Him, dear children, for it is through His mercy and His goodness that He has allowed such a grace as this. My little ones, I am as ever with you. I come to guide you, to advise you, to counsel you as a mother, to show you the way to our Father's home.

My dear ones, I bring this day to you a servant of God who has suffered much for Him. I wish for you to listen intently, to learn from the wisdom he has now gained, to listen for God's call to you through his message, to open your hearts, that Christ might be alive there and welcome there, that He might truly rule your hearts, and your souls, your minds, and your bodies, and that you, like this son and servant, will one day come to share in His glory. May His peace fill you.

St. Stephen:

Sisters and brothers in the Lord, may His name be exalted for always! Let me share with you some of who I am, that you might know how it is that God is alive in our lives and present with us at all times, even when we do not see His hands, nor sense His presence with us. When we know not Who He is, He fathers us yet.

I grew up a Jew, and was taught in the ways of the Law. Regrettably, I was not an obedient child. When still a young man, I took to the street and left my home. I left my father and all he had, all that would have become mine. I left my family and my friends. I left the Law of God. I left the Temple, I desired not to go there again. I went to build my life, to gather things, to be someone.

Many people did I meet, and many friends did I have. What a good time it was for me then, parties, friends, work! This was the darkest time in my life.

I worked and I toiled for many years on my own, far from God, far from the Law, from the teachings I had known. And then a day came, when I felt within my heart the loneliness from the life I had chosen, and a desire to return to God. But first, I had to make peace with my father. This, perhaps, was more difficult. And so, I went home, and there I remained for some time. But again, the restlessness of youth set in, and, after many good months of faith, and strength, and family unity, again I forced the wedge of division in my household to break open my family, and took off to be my own man. Many years I was away. Many things did I do and see, but none of this is important. None of this matters.

Again, as a young man taking a wife, I found God in the Temple. And as my child was born, I saw the goodness of God in him. These things brought me near to God and made me feel that the God of my father's fathers was alive! Three times I fell away. This newfound love for God did not last. I was a wretched person. I mistreated those I loved. Many times in my life, many times did I find God, only to lose Him by my own will again.

And then, when finally I felt as though I had established myself as an upstanding man in my community, and had begun to attend those rituals in the Temple that I had sorely missed, I heard of someone, a man from a very small town who had come claiming he was the Messiah, the Chosen One for the people of God, the sons of Abraham. My heart was still restless. Nothing had changed in those years of falling away from God and returning. Still, I yearned for something, something I did not find in my family and this life I had created of misery, of things that meant nothing, in my job, in work, in friends. And so, through those who belonged to the Way, I came to know of this man. I came to know the Lord.

Throughout my life I had known Him, and lost Him, and known Him, and lost Him, but I realize that I never did know Him until the day I heard of our Christ and of His great love. I believe that I could not accept the God of our fathers, for I felt that He was cold. I was taught that He was a vengeful God. I was taught that He was a God of anger. My heart, my very soul, could not accept this to be true, for as I looked at my children, I knew no God of anger could create such beauty! I loved my family, and I knew how faulted I was. God must be so much greater! In this Christ, this Messiah, I found God, and I became zealous for Him!

First, to my family the news, the Good News of the Messiah! Many of them scoffed and ridiculed. Know that this was a time of great persecutions for those who belonged to the Way. Many, many were killed. And yet, no one knew! There was no outcry in the government. There was no outcry from the people, from these people of God. Those who belonged to the Way simply vanished, were gone! How frightened I was! How terribly frightened to know not what had happened to those whom I had come to love. What would become of me if I followed this man? Would I too disappear? Gone, leaving a wife and children? What would happen to me? Did I truly trust this Messiah? What reason did I have to trust that this was truly the Son of God, for so many times in my life I had felt so near to a God, that I then abandoned?

At this point in my life, I knew I must make the decision to find myself in God. I was so wayward, and so lost, and so without meaning and purpose. And so, despite these fears, I began to teach. I began to teach not only my family and friends, but all those I met, that the Messiah had come, that truly He had come to save the children of Abraham. For the first time in all of my life, through the many falls, through the many terrible injuries inflicted upon my soul by my own hand, I felt fulfilled! I felt the grace of God! And as this grace multiplied in my soul, I began to become more fervent, and more bold in the Spirit, and I spoke freely of my beliefs in this Messiah, and freely of His love, His forgiveness, His ultimate sacrifice. Even then, in those times I had moments of doubt in my life and in my heart. Oh, and such fear! I simply relied on God, the God I had come to know through my Messiah, to give me the strength that I needed to do whatever it was that He would ask of me. Whatever fate I would share with my brothers and sisters, I would do so for God, if it was the only good thing I had ever done.

For several years I taught and spoke. And during those years, I felt within me something I had never known- peace, tremendous peace! Grace! Love! No longer did I mistreat my family, but I knew how to love them as God must have loved me. So many, so many injuries did I inflict upon my own soul through those times when I fell away from God! By my own hand I had bruised and battered my very own soul. For just as a body falls and is injured, so too does the soul become tarnished and bloodied, when fallen from God. This I knew must be true. Oh how I feared that God would see me as nothing but wretched! Still, I persevered, and it was difficult. By no means do I wish to say that it was an easy road. There were many times when I fell, and many times when I felt I could not get up but to pull myself up on the cross.

One day, as I spoke to a crowd of people, many men who were known to persecute those who belong to the Way came and surrounded me. This moment was the defining moment of my life. All the things that had happened to me, I do believe, had the purpose of preparing me for this moment. All those years of searching for God and searching for purpose. Did I have the courage now to face what I did not know, to walk blindly into a fate I could only hope that God would deliver me from, or give me peace with? By His grace alone, I stood tall, and as my soul had been battered and bloodied so many times in my life, my body was then battered and broken, and I left this earth with my body in the very state that my soul had been in so many years.

I found myself then in a place I could not have imagined, I could not have comprehended. I was so afraid. I was so afraid! I could scarcely look down, nor up, nor anywhere! And a light- a bright light! And I looked away. How strange it is that at this moment, when I was about to meet He Who had created me from the dust and the sky, all I could think about is how wretched I must look, how terrible. And I glanced down to see myself then. Oh, and I was astounded! All my life I had been convinced that my soul must be ugly for all of those injuries I had inflicted thereon, but it was beautiful! I could scarcely believe it was me. How could this be? I did not understand, and in my shock and amazement, I looked up, and my eyes filled with tears of terrible sorrow.

Then, at that moment, I saw the Lamb of God! And I looked down at myself- beautiful! And I saw Him. He wore my bruises, my cuts, those injuries that I had inflicted with my sin, with my disbelief. He wore my stripes upon His back, my lacerations on His head. His blood spilled from Him, that my blood, the very life of a soul, might be preserved. I fell before Him, wishing only that I could go, go back and do what I ought to have done.

I carried with me, though, a stone, the stone that had taken my life, and it was all I had so I gave it to Him. And as He took it, a tremendous thing happened! I dared to raise my eyes and I know not why, but suddenly, a light overcame me that was so bright, I had to turn my face from it. And as He took that stone that held my life, all that I had to give, He became not a beaten lamb, offered as a sacrifice, slaughtered by my injuries, but a lion with such power and such light, that I was more afraid then than I had been before! He reached out to me and when He touched me, that light overcame me, and He Who bore my scars, Who bore my injuries, Who spilt the blood that I should have spilt from my very soul, gave to me a share in His glory. Oh, what a tremendous thing! Nothing I had seen on this earth, nor experienced, nor loved, nor hated, nothing could be in my mind, but that moment, that moment when I met my Messiah!

Just as He bore my scars, He bears yours. But as the Good Shepherd, He wishes not for you to know Him as One who desires to punish you, nor be angry with you, nor resent you for these wounds inflicted upon Him, but as He gave me this vision of glory, He promises to you this same glory, this same eternal life. This is a tremendous thing! Something that you, too, will know.

Many times, people speak of life changing events. Life changing. May your life be always changing! May your life be always, always precious, in that it was created by God to be perfected in Him. Do not do as I have done, but instead, stand before Him with balms and oils for His wounds of service and love, to sooth and comfort Him in His distress. I had a rock to give to Him, a rock that took my life. And without it, I know not what I would have done there. What do you have to give to Him? I tell you this, there is nothing you can give Him that will match what He will give to you in return, not even your lives, as even mine was not worthy. But He is so good and is such love that He cares not, but wishes to give to you all things.

Pray that you might receive the grace to live your lives with the strength of faith and the courage of the Spirit, that you might have an armload of flowers to present to Him, that you might have your very self to give to Him as a gift, that even if it is a rock, you might have something. Your lives are precious. They are dear. Do not live them flamboyantly, without thought for cause, or reason, or purpose, but give every moment and every day meaning in God, and you will see yourself stand before Him bathed in His light, and you might reach out and comfort Him in His distress, share in His glory, and be with Him in His kingdom for always.

My friends, my sisters and brothers in the Lord, I thank you for having heard me. Do as I have told you, for yourselves, for the Lord. You cannot know what that moment will be like until you are there, until you have your eyes unveiled, until your vision is renewed, and your soul renewed, and you see in that way that God sees. I tell you this that you might know a piece of what is to come for all of you. And I tell you this that you might have hope, for you know what I knew not. You know that He waits for you, that He stands at the gates of His kingdom and waits for you. Join Him there! May you be filled with His love, and serve Him always in your thoughts, in your words, and in your deeds.

Mary:

My little children, I offer to you this day my motherly blessing. I give to you my prayers of intercession, and I ask the Saints in Heaven and all the Angels that God has created, to care for you and love you, to pray with me for you, that you might receive His grace, that you might know Him always, that you might join Him in Heaven. Do pray. Do serve Him. Do love Him. It is in His name that I bless you. Remember that I am with you in all things, and that I love you as your mother.

St. Andrew, July 27, 1998

Carolyn:

The Blessed Mother is dressed in a gray gown and a blue mantle. Her hands are folded, and her head is bowed. Her eyes are closed, and she is praying. She is surrounded by roses. St. Andrew is kneeling before her. He is a plump man. He has curly, gray hair and a long beard. He has one hand extended in front of him and slightly up. In the other he holds a crucifix.

Mary:

My dear little ones, I bless you and I thank you for gathering here today in such a great number. It is because of your response that God does allow such graces to enter this world, to touch His little ones, to renew their hearts and their spirits, that they might come to know Him in a more glorious, more intimate way. I wish to tell you of His love for you, for each of you, and how greatly pleased I am that you have offered prayer with such fervent hearts for my intentions.

My dear little ones, pray always! For through prayer your hearts are changed, nourished, and brought nearer to my Son, He

Who is the Light on the road to the kingdom our Father has prepared for you. Follow Him. Emulate Him. Walk His way. You shall not be left. You shall not be abandoned, for I will accompany you as your mother, always.

Today, I bring to you one who has much to tell of both suffering and life. He has much to tell of his walk with our Lord. He received a gift that many, many of my Son's children would desire with all their hearts, to be with Him on this earth as He taught and healed, as He loved each and every one of His little children who came to Him. There is much you can learn from him. I thank you for hearing me this day, for responding with the fullness of your hearts, and for praying with joy and love for God.

St. Andrew:

Brothers and sisters, lambs of God, peace be with you! It is a great joy to be able to share with you this day the Good News that our Lord is with you and has blessed you tremendously. Do thank Him and praise Him. Recognize Him in your lives. Know that He is among you.

My brothers and sisters, our God, He does nothing arbitrarily, for in every action is such great purpose, such reason as we cannot comprehend. It was not by chance that the Master selected me to follow, for I was in such need of leadership and guidance, as all of us were. My life, before He came into it, was as many of the Jewish men in that day. I worked very hard. I provided for my family. With my brothers, I worked and toiled and offered thanks to our God, our Yahweh, who had provided all good things for us. I knew the prophesies of old, that a Messiah would come and deliver us. Many in that day believed that He would come and sit on a throne as an earthly king, to rule over all of the tribes of Israel, to rule the world. As you know, it was not that way that God worked on this earth, but in a much grander way, a way that was so simple, one who did not know Him, who could not recognize the

Shepherd Who came to gather the sheep, might very well have missed Him.

My brothers and sisters, my life was empty. As much as I worked, I disobeyed and did all that I should not do. And on the Sabbath day, I would go to Temple and I would give alms, and I would thank our Lord Who had provided such great, great things for my family, and yet, I felt alone.

I would like to tell you that our Christ, His love was so beautiful that truly, He did not choose those who were most suited to follow Him to go out and be great teachers, great prophets, great healers. This has never been our Lord's way. You know well how He has chosen the simple, those who are fallen, those who are weak, and through His Holy Spirit, has made them strong. It was the same with us, with all of us who followed Him. We were not great men. We accomplished nothing on our own. All that we did, we did because the Spirit of God moved within us. It was His Spirit, truly, that founded the Church, the very body of Christ. It was His Spirit that moved in the Martyrs, those who, like myself, gave their lives up to follow Christ in the most perfect and most complete act of self-sacrifice. We were not strong. We were like you. We had times of great faith and times of great disbelief, times of great fervor and times when God, we felt, He was not with us.

I wish to tell you this that you might know that all is possible in the Spirit of God, that it is through Him that great things are accomplished. No man can accomplish what God can do. No man can work the great miracles of the heart that God can. In your times of despair, when you desire so much to change yourselves, to change those whom you love, to make a difference in the world, to do God's work, seek not to do it on your own, but seek to make yourselves a vessel for the Spirit, that He might work through you. Open yourselves. Be prepared to accept the mission, the gifts He gives to you, even if they are not what you had prayed for, nor what you expected. For truly, let me tell you, I never, never, never expected that my life would come to following a son of a carpenter, a man Who was a healer and a gentle teacher, following Him all the way to my own death. God works in mysterious ways.

Brothers and sisters, Jesus our Lord, He chose me I believe, because of my weakness. God chooses those who can do much good for others with His Spirit, but who desperately need the power of His Spirit within themselves. When He came into my life, there were profound changes in my very heart, and I began to pray and to love God as I never thought I could, as I always desired to do. He taught us great things. He taught us obedience and humility. He taught us to love one another. It was His passion that taught us the greatest lesson, the lesson of perfect love, perfect forgiveness, of reconciliation, as God is reconciled to His people. Salvation! Our God desires for each and every one of you to be with Him. He has designed you, and created you for this alone. He loves you so tremendously that He sent His Son to die for you, that you might know His glory, as I and those who have gone before, do now.

As you have reflected this evening on the Sorrowful Mysteries of the most beautiful Rosary, a prayer that is dear to our Blessed Mother's heart, she who does intercede so tremendously before her Son for each one of you, I wish to speak about each of these events that you have reflected on, to share with you how it is that Christ has fulfilled all prophesy, has forgiven all sins through His own death, and has redeemed the whole world.

You know how our Lord agonized. Before His death He prayed, "Father, take this from Me, if it be Your will." But it was not His will, as oftentimes life holds such suffering and, as confusing and troubling as it is, it is good to thank God for the sufferings that you endure. For God, He can make beauty out of all things, and cause great change, and great fervor in a heart that was once cold. Our Lord, He agonized, suffered, and this took place that those who have sinned in the mind might receive forgiveness and salvation. His agony, His mental anguish, forgave those poor souls who do in their mind turn from God, who seek their own will, who do not do as God has done, our Lord and our Master, and say, "Father, Your will be done and not Mine." It is all right to pray that your sufferings might be taken from you. It is good, for our Father has spoken, our Lord has spoken. "Ask! Seek!" Our God, He is ready and willing to give to us all that we need, but you must always pray that His will would become yours, as our Lord did in His time of anguish.

You have reflected also on His scourging, when His flesh was striped and He suffered so tremendously, that salvation might come to those who sin in the body. My little ones, His blood redeemed the whole of the world. Through His sufferings, those who are trapped are freed! This fulfilled the prophesies. This, the shedding of His blood, this lamb that was led to the slaughter, it was as our forefathers had said it would be. And in His anguish and in His suffering, our Lord had only love in His heart for those who would come to see the face of God through the conversions possible through grace, great grace, that our Lord merited through His suffering, that our Lord gave to the whole world as a beautiful gift. There were no people, no people there who could do what He did. There was no one there to shed holy blood! And so, our Lord, He came to touch, and to heal, and to love, and to die, that we would die no more, but live always.

Our Lord was humiliated, and stripped, and crowned with thorns. And through this humiliation, salvation was gained for those whose pride, and arrogance, and lack of humility has led them wayward. Our Lord, He was born in a humble place, a place where animals fed, in the dark, with no heat and no light, save for the stars and the moon that shown above. He lived with a mother and a father. He learned a trade, as all Jewish boys did then. He was schooled. He lived a humble life to teach us humility. This humiliation, this terrible cruelty He suffered at this time, was the ultimate lesson in being humble before God. For God, He loves a humble heart, a heart without pride, and arrogance, and disobedience, but ready to embrace all that God gives for His glory alone.

Our Lord was taken and given a cross of wood, and made to carry that cross. With this tree upon His back, He walked and made the journey to the place of His execution. Three times He fell, and continued on. This act of such love made possible the salvation of those who do not believe, who refuse to walk the way of God, who will not take up their cross and follow the Lord to Golgotha, but for one or two moments in their life, when they are given the grace to see the truth and they pray, "Please, Father, do not reject me! Though I have lived my life as a sinner, accept me! Though I have not walked the road to life, change me!" I assure you, any man who speaks such words, even in the last moment of his life, will know salvation because our Lord walked this most painful journey for each one of us.

Finally, He was hung from that tree, and His side was lanced, and His heart pierced, as His blood once again was shed upon the earth. In this action, salvation was gained for those who sin in the heart, who do not desire to love God or their neighbor, for those who do not act with love. This is a great sin that prevails in the world today, lack of love. This is a primary sin, for when you do not love yourself, your God, and your neighbor as you should, it is easy to become prideful and disobedient, selfish, lukewarm, or cold in faith, undisciplined. Lack of love, it is a great sin against the very Spirit of God Who is love! To refuse to love is to refuse God. It is a most private sin, a sin of the heart. It is the sin that Christ, He took upon Himself in the piercing of His own heart.

My brothers and sisters, the story of Christ's passion is not one of sole suffering, and death, and tragedy. For you do recall that with the blood, water- renewing, purifying water- flowed, came forth, that we might be baptized in it into life. Through the water and the blood that poured forth from His side, our Christ gave to us the great gift of salvation and renewal. Truly, this is what life must be: to accept God, to be baptized into His life, to receive salvation through His blood. It is the greatest gift that God has given to us. But on our journey, when we like Christ, fall and stumble, and perhaps we even walk wayward, when we come to know that we have gone far from God Who seeks us out with such fervency that no father could ever seek a son more diligently, when we come to see how we have fallen, there is water to purify, to renew, to give new life.

We must seek resolution and peace in our lives. Peace is so sorely needed today. Make peace with God. He has come to you in so many ways, reached out to you, called to you. He has instituted for you His sacraments, His holy body and blood, that He sheds for you again on your altars, His forgiveness and reconciliation, the renewal of the water, the new life of the Spirit, His church to guide and direct you, and your brothers and sisters to strengthen you in your faith and walk with you on your journey, whether it be a time when you are strong in God, or feel wayward. Rely on one another. Help one another. Know that we who are in Heaven do pray for you. Pray for one another and for those who are in Purgatory.

The Church, the Body of Christ, beckons to you as Christ Himself called each one of us, His disciples, from lowly places. Our God has purpose and reason. Such great reason, you cannot even imagine! As He called to me, and renewed me, and gave me new life, He beckons to you, that He would do the same for you. He seeks you. Find Him and answer Him! Ask for His peace and His love. And each time you fall away, each time, flee to Him! Run to Him, for He will deliver you. He will caress you as a father loves his son. You will know peace and joy when you are with Him.

I thank you for having heard me this day, and I do ask that you reflect on what I have said, and do remember that God seeks you out, desires you, to share in His glory. Do not turn from Him, but accept Him with the fullness of your hearts, that you might know perfect joy.

Mary:

My dear little ones, again I thank you for your prayers, and I do wish to offer to you my motherly blessing. Know peace in your lives and joy in your hearts, in God. Continue to pray. Pray always for my priests and young people, those who are in Purgatory, and those who do not yet know my Son as their Lord. Continue to pray that the world may be renewed in God's love. I bless you in His name, the name of the Father, and Son, and Spirit on high. Be at peace. May Christ always be with you.

St. Mary Magdalene, August 24, 1998

Carolyn:

The Blessed Mother is wearing a white gown that is quite beautiful. She also has a white mantle. Along the bottom of the gown and along the sides of the mantle is a tiny gold trim. She has a gold crown on her head. Her eyes are looking toward Heaven, and her hands are folded in prayer. There is a coral-colored rosary with a gold crucifix draped over her hand.

St. Mary Magdalene is standing near the Blessed Mother. She appears quite young, just as the Blessed Mother does. She is wearing a gray gown and a deep blue mantle. She has long, very thick, black hair. It is pulled back and held by a pin. She is looking toward the Blessed Mother. Near their feet are flowers and there is a small tin bowl near the feet of St. Mary Magdalene.

Mary:

My dear little children, how good it is for me to be with you in this way this evening. I come to you tonight as Queen of the Hearts of All Mankind. As my Son has given you to me to be my children from His cross, I am with you as your mother. I am so pleased that so many have come to receive this grace from God, Who gives it to you out of love of you. Do thank Him and praise Him for this glorious opportunity to truly know Him through those who have loved Him and served Him in their own lives.

During this past year, so many of you have been so faithful in living the messages that these children of God have brought to you. And it is this devotion, the graces that have come forth through this gift, that has made such things as this possible. Our God is so good. He desires to multiply grace, multiply gifts. It is for this reason that I ask you to continue to pray that He will bless the world, and all of His children, with His goodness and mercy forever.

My dear ones, truly, I love you and I invite you tonight to share in the mystery of our God's, our beloved Lord's, gift of Himself. In His crucifixion, death, and resurrection, in His glorious ascension to the right hand of the Father, He has made possible a wonderful reconciliation for us with God, a beautiful salvation, the great gift of conversion, a gift that would not be possible were it not for reconciliation, merited for you by the Christ. Be grateful. See how God loves you! I bless you in His name, my little ones.

Mary Magdalene:

Servants of God, I greet you in His name, in the name of the Father Who has loved us, and the Son Who is our redeemer, and the Spirit Who dwells among us. I have much to tell you, but first I wish to tell you that God is with you, that you receive such blessings as the world has never known. I too was blessed in my life, and I will tell you a bit of myself. I scarcely remember the time before I served our Lord. Were it not for this beautiful opportunity to teach, and to share, and to bring a sense of unity to His people here on earth through this gift, I would not speak of it, for it pains my heart to remember those days.

A young girl, I was orphaned very young. The same illness that claimed my parents afflicted me for many years. I knew nothing of God, of this Yahweh, and I lived a life that was not befitting a servant of His. From an age of fourteen years, I lived here or there or another place, without the guidance that a father and mother would teach me, and so fell into many things, many wayward things.

I befriended a woman in one place which is most dear to my heart now. This woman would come to be a dear friend, and the person who I loved most on earth. Why God allowed me even to be in her presence I know not, for she was His mother, and a righteous woman. I did not know this at the time, nor did I know her well enough to see her virtues. She simply lived near me and spoke kindly to me when many others would not.

She had a son. He had grown up as a carpenter, as an apprentice of His father. And He went out and worked such miracles, and did such things that all of those who were in His presence could say nothing more than that He was the Son, the Messiah, the Promised One. And so, from the very beginning, this man had many followers, and many who hated Him.

Sometimes I would go, and I would sit in the fields where He taught, and I would listen. And the things that He said, I could not, I could not comprehend,

"Love your neighbors and your enemies and those who hurt you." I was to love those who threw stones and sticks at me and taunted me? How could I do this?

"Love God with all of your heart and soul and mind." I did not even know Him. I could not love Him.

"Be kind to the poor. Be generous with what you have." I had nothing to give. I scarcely could keep myself alive.

"Go out among the sick, the uneducated, and teach and heal through a ministry of love." Who was I to presume to know anything of this?

But still, I listened. And each day, I came and I heard, and I listened, and I saw that there were those who were so dear to Him, brothers who traveled with Him, and I befriended them as well. But still, I suffered from great illness of both body and soul and, as much as I tried, I could not free myself from such affliction.

And then came a day when I found myself face to face with Him, He Whom I had watched from afar for so very long, my heart aching to do as He said and my mind knowing that I could not, that I was not able, that I did not have the will to do so, that I would not. And in an instant, this man of such mercy and such goodness made real what He had taught to me, and freed me from that which had suffocated me for so very long, that which had drawn the very life from my soul, that which had weakened my body and my will to be with God. And through His goodness and mercy, my body and soul were healed, and I was renewed.

I began to think again about my decision not to do as He taught, about my decision not to try. Whether I was able or not, I knew not, but I… I would try. At the very least I owed Him this. I knew not whether I could be a worthy servant to the Messiah, the Master, the Teacher, but from that moment on, I decided that is what I would do each day. And I was so privileged, so blessed with the opportunity to come to know Him and His mother so intimately, and oftentimes, He spoke so casual to me I could scarcely believe that it was the Lord who looked at me through His eyes.

"Mary," He would say to me. And I would go to Him with all of my troubles and all of my concerns. And each time I was tempted, and each time I fought against the darkness that had consumed me, I ran to Him. "Mary." He spoke only that, and I was renewed, and I was strengthened, and had the courage to go on again. But it was not easy. When one lives life in a certain manner, miracles performed even by the Son of Man do not change that human nature that draws one back into that which made them prisoner. And so, I fought hard against my own self, and my prayer each day was, "Lord, save me from myself! Save me from myself!"

I do believe that the Lord heard and had mercy on me, for the more I prayed, the more He changed my heart, and the less I needed to say such words. For I found that it was not a prayer of desperation any longer, but a prayer of hope,

"Lord, save me from myself, that I might be only what you would have me be, that you alone might dwell within me, and make me pure, and make me good, and all those things that my heart longs to be, but I cannot be alone!"

This is what the teacher gave to me, the gift of prayer, of a second try, and a third, and a fourth, and a fifth, and a sixth, and a ten thousandth! It is never easy, is it?

Those who followed Him, the men who were with Him, were so good. Though I'm sure that they too struggled as I struggled, as all men struggle, they tried so desperately to do all that the Master had commanded, to love one another and be patient, and be kind and generous, and gentle and humble, and there was so much to learn, and how difficult it was! They were a constant source of hope and joy for me, since I believed that if these fishermen, and tax collector, and poor men, with wives and children that bickered and squabbled just as any other family, could do such great things, and go with this savior to heal the sick, to cure those whose souls were as mine once was, then truly, with the help of God, I could do the same.

But it was His mother, His gentle mother, who was most important to me. Oftentimes I would sit, and I would watch her with Him. I do believe there was never a more perfect mother upon this earth than she. And sometimes, I wondered what it would be like to be her, to be so blessed by God and so favored by God that He would plant the seed of Himself within you. What, what an unimaginable thing! And it was so frightening!

Her manner was so gentle. She was never harsh. She was patient always, for just as there were many, many who came to her Son requesting that He pray, save, heal them, so too many came to her believing, I suppose, that if they could not reach Him, she must be able to do the same for them. Never did she do anything more but invite them in, and serve them, and talk to them of God and His goodness, and speak to them that which had been written so long ago, that which we held so dear in His Word, and spoke to them of the Prophets and of the hope that was promised there. And strangely, many who left her presence, though they were not healed of their afflictions, though perhaps they may have returned to their old ways of life, they came away with such a peace, such a joy, I cannot explain it.

I tried so very hard to be as she was and, let me tell you now, I was not! But I learned a great deal from her, especially in the time of her greatest trial, in a place that I was not worthy to be in, but that for some reason, whether it was only to be a witness to it that I might come and speak of it to you, God placed me there- at the foot of His cross. This is where I learned most of what it is to love and serve God. On that day, I followed our Lord as He bore a tree upon His back through the streets. And His mother was there also. I wept many, many tears, for He was so dear to me as a Lord, as a teacher, and as a friend and brother. And I was so afraid as I've never been afraid in my life. And in that time when I could find no comfort and no solace, she, she was so peaceful that it seemed horrible. She did not scream out as I did. She did not run and flee as I often turned to do, but she walked in silence, as near to her Son as she could be. And what a perfect, perfect trust in God she had, that she did not even cry out, for she knew that come what may, God was being served, and that was what she, and I, and her Son, and all on earth must do.

I was there when He spoke His last. There too, when His body was taken from that cross. This was the most difficult moment in my life, the time when the demons that had imprisoned me came back to me again and tempted me, "Mary, your Lord, your savior, your teacher, your God is dead!"

What should I do? I could not stay and stand with His brother and His mother who were so trusting in God when I had such anger inside me! And I could not go, for where would I go and what would I do, but go back to that which I hated? So, I did what my fear of loneliness alone had me do. I remained, though I never in my life was more tempted than at that moment, when all hope seemed to be gone, and there was nothing to comfort those who needed Him so much.

Trying my very best to be as His mother was, I put upon myself a brave face, though it was such a falsehood, for I was so torn within myself. And I left, once His body was laid in the tomb, to go. What a painful time it was for all of us, and we found joy and comfort only in each other. I do believe that all of us, those who traveled with Him, those whom He had commissioned to go out and to teach, to make disciples of all nations, those who would later be such great fathers of the church, they who were my company that night, we sat in dumbfounded angst. Still, His mother, so peaceful, so sad, but so peaceful. So firmly resolved to do what God had ordained from the beginning of time. She was our hope.

The time came when the Master's body was to be anointed. And I went, carrying with me nothing worthy to anoint our Lord, but the finest balm that I could possibly get, that I could possibly find. I searched and I despaired. What do you give to the Lord? How can you . . . my mind still swims! The Gospels that you have, that witness given to you by the command of the Lord Himself, tell you of what great grace I received. A man approached, "Woman, why do you weep?"

What? What words? What words at that moment! If I should have attempted to answer in the fullest truth, perhaps I would have said, "Because I am nothing, and I know nothing, and I can do nothing, and there is nothing for me anymore, and I am so alone!"

"Mary." It was our Lord! Hope reborn! And I ran to tell those who loved Him, He was alive in the time when we thought He was so far from us!

It is the same for you. In the times when you find yourself so far from Him, He is alive in your life, and real, and present. When you find yourselves in your churches and you are distracted by the things of life, as all of us are, He is there. When in your homes, and in your families, and caring for your children, and loving your spouses, and serving your families, He is there. In your work and in your prayer, He is there. Our Lord had never left us! Though His body was broken and His soul left Him, He was there!

Truly I tell you, if the Lord should see it fit to bless someone as myself with such a gift, you need never feel unworthy of His grace. For as He has taught, He came among His people not to save those who were well, but to find the lost, to heal the broken, to save the weak and the sinful. You must not feel that you cannot go to Him with all things, and throw yourself before His cross and beg His forgiveness, for truly I tell you, it is yours before you have even asked. Our God is so grand, He reads your hearts as you read words upon a page. He knows you better than you could know yourself in a thousand years of knowledge. Desire Him. Seek Him out in the sacraments He has given to you, in the prayers He has offered to you, in the gifts and the blessings He has given to you out of His mercy and true desire to have you with Him, as it was always, always meant to be.

After our Lord departed from us and went to the Father, those who had followed and loved Him, who were so weak, were strengthened by His Spirit. They went out, each of them, to all corners of the earth, and taught many things, and brought the Christ, brought that Christ that had dwelled with us, and ate with us, to the hearts of a thousand men. I remained with His mother and cared for her. And I did not do anything great in my life. I did not follow Peter and John, and go out and teach, and lead, and found churches, but I cared for His mother, which was the only thing I thought I could do, and what I truly believe the teacher would have asked me to do. This is all I did. Until an old woman, when He called me home to Him, I did nothing more than that each day, serving those whom He placed in my life, and running to Him when I found that hated darkness consuming me again.

You must do the same. God does not call all of His children to found churches and be priests, to religious life. He calls many of them to be mothers and fathers, teachers, healers, friends. In these things, do serve Him in all ways. Offer up all that you do for Him. There are many who seek out meaning in this life, who like me were lost, and see no hope, and ask, "What? Why?" This is something that I did learn:

"What?" The answer to "what" is the love of God.

"Why?" Because He wants us with Him, and will go to the ends of the earth to find us.

Hear Him, and answer Him, and follow Him, as I followed our Lord to His death, that just as He entered into the kingdom of God, that door might be open for you. It is this simple. Serve Him in all that you do. Offer all things to Him, your weaknesses and your strengths, your failings and your successes. Give it all to our Lord, and He will bless you and heal your bodies, and your souls, and your minds, and truly bring you home to Him as He has brought me home.

Children of God, thank Him, love Him, and serve Him through one another. I look to the day with joy when I can meet you here, for truly, truly, you are blessed and loved! Do remember what I have told you, for so many wander in such darkness, lacking such wisdom as this, this wisdom I only learned through what God had given me. Do remember.

Mary:

My dear children, I wish to remind you that ever I am with you, that I pray for your intentions, and I do wish to thank you for praying for those things that rest heavily on my heart. Continue to pray, my little ones, that all of my children will come to know the Christ, that all of my children would receive the strength through the Holy Spirit to be of strong faith and strong heart, that those who are in Purgatory might have relief and joy in the Father's kingdom, and that those who come to serve the Lord through all vocations in life would find peace and joy and a great desire to do the will of God. I do bless you in the name of the Father, and Son, and Spirit on high, and again I thank you for responding in such great numbers to such a grace.

The Monthly Lessons from Heaven

September 1998

Mary:

My dear little ones, praise God and thank Him, for He is good and gives all good things to you. Let us worship Him together in this way always. My dear little ones, I am most grateful for your prayers for my intentions. Through the prayers of many of my faithful ones, many graces are obtained from the Father Who wishes to bless the whole world with His love and mercy. I am most grateful for your prayers and ask you to continue to pray always, that your own soul might be strengthened, that your own heart might be strengthened, and that many graces might be obtained for your Christian brothers and sisters, for those whom you do not know, for your enemies, for the sick and ailing, and those who suffer in Purgatory; for those, my dear little ones there, who do desire with all their hearts to be with the Father, but rely on your prayers. Do pray also for my priests, and my young people, and for all married couples, for often in these days many of my little ones are tempted away from vows that they have made before God, are tempted away from the faith that God has placed in your hearts since your very conception.

My little ones, you have responded with such fervency and such desire to know our Lord, through myself, through the saints that I have brought to you, through the messages I have given to teach, to show you how to live the virtues of Christ, truly, how to emulate Him, how to be His disciple, how to live in holiness. Do follow these words and reflect on them often. Read them and meditate upon them. Read also, your Gospels, the Scripture, this Word of God, that you might always remain close to what God is calling you to do: to emulate Him, to be as He was, and to truly be His hands and feet on this earth.

In bringing these saints of Heaven to you, God has allowed me to give you such graces, such graces as the world has not known! I have brought many to you that they might tell you their stories, that they might speak of God's love and His mercy, that they may speak of Christ as a human, with a human soul and a human mind, in a divine spirit, that you would come to know Him, truly, as God-Made-Man, that you would come to understand how He was very much like you on this earth, that He had a mother and a father, family and friends, those who followed Him, and that they, most especially, were just as you are: weak and fallen, needing God's grace, God's love, and God's forgiveness, always being called to reconciliation on the journey of conversion.

My little ones, let this past year, the graces you have received, be a great joy to you, a great comfort, and a great source of encouragement and hope, for truly, as you have seen through the words of my children, my little ones who now enjoy the splendor of God's kingdom, God, He works many miracles! He truly is present in your lives, ever present. He touches you and changes you. He has called you all here that you might know Him in this special way.

I ask you to continue to come together in a group to pray for my intentions, for the conversion of the world, and for peace, which is most sorely needed in this world. Pray for the family, this bedrock of faith, that is so often assaulted by modernism and materialism. My dear ones, pray for one another and console one another in your times of sorrow. God has created you, not as individual beings to be kept alone within yourselves, to hide away, to be far from Him, and far from each other, but truly, as a community that together, one with another, hand in hand, you might worship Him and glorify Him, and help each other find the road of salvation.

My dear ones, as I have been in many, many ways, the precursor of our Lord, as I was the maid who brought Him into this world, as I do speak His words to you now, as I have given to you His message and announced Him to the world, and as truly I shall bring the good news of His love for you into this world through such graces that God has allowed, I do now come before Him again. Oftentimes, my little ones, you have heard my words, and you have yearned to know our God in the most personal and the most intimate way, to hear His words, to know His mind. I tell you this is a feat unimaginable, one that is incomprehensible, but God who is merciful and good, God who desires for His children to know Him, to love Him, and to serve Him in all things, to truly be with Him, united always, this God Who loves you so much that He has made all this possible, does desire to speak to you. And so, I do, my little ones, bless you with my motherly blessing, and I ask you to bow your heads and to pray, and know that God, the God of love, is with you.

God in His Trinity:

My sheep, your Shepherd calls to you. Gather and hear My Word, that I might speak to your hearts and to your souls. Children, I, in My Trinity, Am with you. In your prayer you invite Me in. You call Me to your very soul, and I do dwell there. Do you not know that though you turn your face from Me, I seek you out? I will not let you go, but always, always will seek you to the ends of the earth. My children, I know you as you cannot know yourselves, and truly, it is My fatherly love for you, My great love for you, that commands all that I do. You are My people! You, you have been given My very life.

From your very creation, from the very creation of time, I beheld each one of you, and knew you before you had yet come into being. As I held in My hands the form to become the earth on which you dwell, as I shaped the stars in the heavens, as I created all that you know, all that you are, I beheld you. I knew you. You were mine. For you, I brought light from dark, life from death, everything from nothing, for I desired to love! I created you to be loved and to love, to love Me as your Father and one another as your family in My house. I gave to you your earth and your sun to guide your days and your nights, the rain to renew your world, warmth to keep you, and food that you might eat and be sustained, but of all these things none was so important, none was so great, as My love. I could have given you nothing, nothing more than My love, for I have given you all of My heart!

It is because of My great love for you that I call to each of you, that I beckon to you. Many, many of My sheep have wandered, and have been lost to Me by their own will, that will that I created within them, that will that is such a gift, and such a pain to My heart, for it has taken many from Me. My little ones, I truly love you and seek you! In your lives, I Am with you. You cannot see what truly is. You do not know what I have created for you. Look beyond the horizon. See beyond yourselves. I Who conceal myself in a host and wine, I Who move silently as the wind, I Who whisper to you, Who calls to you, I Who inspire you with My Spirit to do great things in My name, I call to you.

I came to teach you in humility. I came to serve you as I desire to be served. I taught you all that you must know. I have provided all that you need. Know, know in your hearts that I shall never abandon you, nor reject you. Know that you are not alone, that you cannot be alone, for truly, should you climb to the highest heavens or sink beneath the sea, I Am there, speaking as loudly to you as I spoke to your forefathers, to those who have written the Scriptures that you know, to those who witnessed Me in My body on this earth, to those who now witness Me in My churches on My altars and find Me in reconciliation, who experience Me in the sacraments and in the service of one another. I speak to you loudly. I call to you.

I have given you each day and every moment of your life that, truly, you might live! So many have such time, but do not live. Let the life that I breathed within you at your very conception, the life that I knew before your existence, the life that I beheld upon the creation of your earth, and the stars, and the sun that warms you, let that life be one worth living! Let it be one of service, as I have served you, and above all let it be one of love, for if there is one truth that I have given to you in your souls, in your hearts, in My body and blood, in My Word, in one another, it is this: there is nothing but love! Nothing endures but love.

I truly Am love and life. To live in Me is to live in joy, to live in peace, to live in humility and obedience, and to live in a profound love in your heart! This is where you find Me. This is where I dwell. I Am never far from you, you who are more precious to Me than all of creation, for each one of you, I have given everything: My life which I breathed forth from My body, My Spirit that came to descend upon you and dwell with you, My body and blood to nourish you. All things are for you. Live according to My will. Live with great trust in Me, for your God Who is love, remains with you. Your God Who is love, seeks you out. Your God Who is love, desires you. You who are most precious to My heart. Hear Me.

October 1998

Mary:

My dear little children, it is with joy that.I am with you this evening, that I speak to you. I come before you, truly as your mother, as the Queen of the Hearts of all of Mankind, bringing to you the graces of peace and joy, that you might know them in your heart, and that you might live them each day. My dear ones, truly, you have been blessed! God has allowed such grace to pour forth from Him unto His people. It is unimaginable! You have received so much from God. Do thank Him and praise Him always, for it is only through Him, through His mercy, and out of His great love for you, that such things as this is possible.

My dear ones, I urge you as your mother, always to come before God in prayer, to make your life a prayer. Our Lord has taught you to pray in your scriptures. He has taught you that you should read and meditate upon them. He has taught you the words to say. I have come to teach you how to pray, to teach you what prayer of the heart truly means. Through my messages to you, through the prayers that you have offered with such fervency for my intentions, to our Father in Heaven that His mercy might continue to shine upon this world, and for your own intentions, you have learned to pray selflessly.

My little ones, when you pray, you need not pray in fancy words. You need not pray in a particular manner. You need not say a written prayer. God does not wish for you to come before Him with anything more than your heart, your simple heart. When you pray, it is good to pray the Rosary. It is good to pray those prayers that God has given to us in the Psalms, in His Word. It is also good to pray a prayer that is deep within the hearts of all of my little children, "God help me this day, for I alone can do nothing, and with you I can do all things". Let this be a prayer that you take into your hearts and that you speak each morning, for God, He is so grand, and He desires only the hearts of His children. that He might mold you, and shape you, and change you, not into what you are or into what you wish to be, but what is, truly, in His perfect will: an image, the perfect likeness of Himself. He has asked all of His little children to give to Him all of their joys, all of their sufferings, all of their needs, in prayer. When you pray, pray selflessly. Pray with joy and pray with gratitude! This is what our Father desires. He desires that His children come before Him with grateful hearts and give to Him all that is within them, for truly I assure you, if you decide to give all that you have to God, He will do the very same for you, and what a magnificent thing that is!

My dear children, in your lives, strive to live what our Lord has taught to you through His Word in the Scriptures, through His coming, and walking, and dwelling upon this earth, in His example, through His death and resurrection, and through the messengers He sends: His mother, the saints. Truly, these messages are given to you that you might know them, that you might live them, and they are of no purpose if they do not cause within you a great desire, a zealous desire, to love God, to serve Him, and to know Him.

This is my purpose in coming to you, and it is the purpose why the Father has sent me to you, why He sends me to many places, why He sends His saints and His angels, and why He has sent His very own Son, that you might come to know Him intimately as your father, truly as your teacher, as your friend, that you might come to know Him and love Him with all of your heart, all of your mind, all of your soul, and all of your strength. In serving one another, you do serve Him and love Him. That you might know Him, serve Him, and truly be joyful, this is what our Father has designed for you. Joy! Joy and peace in the Spirit. The world is so lacking these things! Such virtues as these are needed to combat the great evils in this world, the terrible sickness of loneliness, the terrible sickness of atheism and materialism.

And so I beg of you, teach your children. Teach those around you by your example, by your prayers, by your words. Teach them that God loves them tremendously, that they have value and worth because they are created as He is, and that God desires from them all that they can give, that He might return that same favor with all that He is. Each day, strive to live more like the Christ Who is the greatest teacher, Who is the ultimate teacher. In His example, in humility and obedience, in joy and peace, with the wisdom that the

Holy Spirit brings to His people, truly, you will be a pure vessel, that God might work through you, that He alone might be glorified, and that His will would be accomplished on this earth.

Finally, again I recommend to you, go, my little children, and visit Him often in the sacraments. You have such a gift in your Eucharist, in this most precious, most precious gift! God has given you Himself in His scripture. He has given you Himself in His messengers. He has given you Himself on a cross on Calvary, and He gives Himself to you again, on your altars each day. Find Him there and truly see Him! This is God's greatest gift in the world today, for truly, without His presence there, His real presence in the Eucharist, the world would be much darker. Visit Him there. Pray! Come before Him, for His love for you is so great that He remains veiled under the most humble species of bread and wine, made into true blood and true body! I tell you, if His faithful ones could but see what is truly there, they would die with joy!

My little ones, this is what I wish to bring to you today, peace and joy. And so, I bless you, and I pray that God's blessing would come upon you and your families, that you might have joy in your homes, joy in your hearts and in your lives, and that through prayer, peace would be with you always, the peace that Christ alone can bring to the world, and that each of you might be a true vessel for our Lord's will.

My dear ones, I thank you for gathering. It is most important that you continue to pray. I have asked my little ones everywhere to join cenacles of prayer, for God, He does not leave you alone in this world. He understands the difficulty there is in living His way, for it is not the easy road. He has given to you the gifts of the sacraments, His Word, and most especially in this group, friendship and comradery, that you might truly have Christian support and a love of one another to help you when you are weak. Rely on each other and continue to pray together. I am most grateful for your prayers, offered for my intentions. Continue always to pray. Pray that there may be true conversion in the world and that all of my little children might come to know my Son and our Lord as the

Christ, as the Redeemer, as the Teacher, and truly, as the salvation of the world.

Let His peace be with you, and I do bless you in His name, in the name of the Most Holy Trinity, Who reigns forever and ever.

November 1998

Mary:

My dear little ones, I greet you in the name of the Father Who is holy, and the Son, Redeemer, and the Holy Spirit, eternally espoused to the Church. My dearest little ones, just as Christ was the Word-Made-Flesh, so too must you live in the Word. Know that I come to you as a mother and as a teacher, always to lead my little ones closer to my Son, that our Lord might be glorified.

Dear ones, our God has loved you so dearly that He has sent His Son, He Who is, was, and always shall be, to become man, to be born of man, to grow as a man, to live as a man, and to die as a man, that you might know how it is that you must follow our Lord. Live in His way. Each day, my little ones, I invite you, strive to perfect yourself by imitating Him. In this way, you will come to know our Father in Heaven in a most intimate way. You will follow the steps of His very Son, He who came to teach, to guide, to lead. I invite you, each day to follow His way, a way of obedience and humility, a way of love and charity, a way of joy, and a way of peace. Meditate on the life and works of our Lord. Know Him, for He is the way, He is the truth, and all eternal life.

I invite you to know our Lord through the Gospels which He has given to you, your holy scriptures, given by the Father to guide you and direct you. Study them and know them. Absorb them into your very being, for they are the Word of God. Through His people, those inspired by His Most Holy Spirit, your Lord has spoken to you. He has given Himself a name: I Am. He has told you that He loves you. He has told you that you are good, for you are created in His image. He has promised to your fathers a savior when they fell from grace, that state which He does desire for His children to live in again. He, He Who gave you this Word sent His Son that the prophesies might be fulfilled. And this Son of Man walked upon the earth and did many things that were recorded, that you might see and believe. Learn! Learn from what you have been given! You have received such a gift in His Word, for truly, you know of Him, you read of Him. Absorb all that you have been given, that you might live as He did.

Finally, I call you to continue your walk of faith through the messages I have brought to you through our Father's goodness and mercy. Follow my Son! You have been given all that you need. You have been given, truly, such a gift in your scripture. You need never despair. You need never worry. Read and absorb what God has given to you. Meditate! All answers that you seek can be found in God, and He has given to you all that you require.

I have come as a servant of God, that He might be glorified forever and ever, and what I tell you is what He has told you for years, and generations, and ages. I tell you the message that you will find in His Word. I bring the message you will find in His Son, a message of love- love one another as God has loved you- a message of peace, the peace that only God can bring into your life and a sure-rooted faith can bring to your heart. I ask you to live in joy, for God has not created you for sadness, but He has created you to know His joy! I ask you to pray. Even our Lord, He Who was most holy, did pray, and God has seen fit to give you a record of this as He agonized in Gethsemane. This is so that you might know how truly essential prayer is, for the Son of Man did pray.

You too must do as He did. I ask you, my little ones, to pray for peace, to pray for conversion, to pray that my Son might be glorified, that His name might be spoken on every tongue, that our Lord, Three in One, would reign in the hearts of all mankind. Pray, my dear children, that you would be strengthened in your faith. I ask you also to pray in thanksgiving, for God has blessed you in such ways, such ways that you cannot imagine. He has given to you His Own heart, His Own life, His Own Son, and His Word, that you might be directed and guided, that you might have a light, a beacon, to guide you home.

My dear ones, be grateful, for He has sent His Most Beloved, His Most Precious to you. He has sent His Holy Spirit to you. He does send His mother to you now, that you might heed the call He has given to you from age to age, that you might know that He loves you, and that you might come to serve Him. that He alone might be glorified, forever.

My dear ones, I do invite you to serve with the fullness of your hearts, with the fullness of your lives. Live in the Word. Seek God in His Word, in the life of His Son, in that record which you have been given of it in your churches, in one another. Find Him and follow Him there. May His peace rest always with you, and may you be blessed by God's mercy, grace, and charity, always.

December 1998

Mary:

My dear little ones, know that I am with you, that I love you as your mother, that I come to you in the spirit of peace and joy, with much love. Glorify the Father in Heaven with all that you do. Sing His name as your praise. Teach your children of His love, for He alone is good, and He alone is Lord.

My dear ones, I speak to you in a season of great joy, in this Advent, this very dawn of hope. Know that I am with you most especially as the mother of Christ. This is the time of such joy for me, for it is the time when I fondly recall how I held my Son, and loved Him, and raised Him, and taught Him all that He needed to know. God sent Him to this earth, that He might become man and know His creation intimately. Know that it is again with such joy that I speak to you, and I urge you to do as I once did: hold Christ in your heart. Seek Him out in the world. Seek Him in yourselves and in one another. Just as the Magi came from the East to find a king, I invite you to look to find your King, for He is among you. He dwells within your hearts and this evening, as you have celebrated the most holy of prayers, the most holy of gifts, the Eucharist, He is within you in body, blood, soul, and divinity. Praise God, for such a gift this is! You will never know!

My dear little ones, know that I encourage you to find Him in the sacraments, find Him in the Eucharist where He waits for you, calls to you. Our Lord was so good, He sacrificed His Own body on Calvary that we all might be redeemed. Again, He sacrifices Himself on your altars that you might know salvation, hope, and joy. And so, it is as the time of His birth when I welcomed Him into this world. Again this eve, you welcome Him into the world, as the holy hands of your priest consecrate simple gifts of bread and wine that become His blood, His body, that same body that dwelled upon this earth so very long ago. And so, joined with me, Mother of Christ, I ask you to praise Him, and worship Him, and glorify Him always, for He comes again in glory to bring salvation to all people.

I give to you my motherly blessing. I pray that you might know joy and peace in this season, and that you might be blessed with the gift of wisdom to see Christ as He dwells in your life, in your home, in your heart.

January 1999

Mary:

My dear little ones, praise God always and forever! Know that He Who is grand, He Who is mighty, He Who is all things, is with you. Praise Him and thank Him, for He has sent me to speak with you that you might know that He hears and answers your prayers, that you might know He works in your lives, and that He is alive in your hearts. My dear little ones, truly, it is good to be with you in this way. Know that I come to you as your mother with love in my heart for each of my children, all of those whom the Lord has permitted me to mother, for from His cross He gave to me all of mankind, that I should not only bear the Son of God, Word Incarnate, but that I should mother, counsel, advise, teach, and intercede on behalf of all of the world.

My dear ones, there is much sickness in this world. Many people, they are sick with loneliness, they are sick with depression, they are ill from a lack of knowledge of the love of God. They are diseased by the corruption, by the materialism, by all those things which your society embraces that are not of God. Even in your own country that professes, 'In God We Trust', God is removed from your homes and your schools. He is taken from your government. He is taken from the people. These things I need not speak to you, for you know this to be true, for all time since Clement and Peter walked upon the earth, my little ones have known persecution.

My dear ones, I come today, not to remind you of all that is ill in the world, but to encourage you, truly to teach you, how to make the world bright and anew, shining for God, that He might look upon the world with joy and pleased eyes. My dear ones, you have been commissioned, truly commissioned, as the very first apostles who walked with Christ. From those twelve, He sent them out, that all of the churches of all of the world, from place to place, all of the peoples, might be converted to my Son, converted to our Lord, that all of these peoples might know that God is with them. He was called, "Emmanuel," when He came, that those who followed Him would know that God was with them. My dearest little ones, it is the same in this day, when evil and corruption have become the way of the world.

My dearest ones, go as those apostles commissioned by Christ! Go to all corners of the world and teach. Spread the news of Christ's love. A daunting task this seems, and when you read in your Scriptures about the travels and trials that the first founders of the Church encountered, oftentimes their difficulties are overlooked, and their accomplishments are recorded. At times, it must seem so difficult, and a task so unsuitable for a people who truly are faulted, but I tell you that those who founded your church, the Church of God, were just as you are. You have known this to be true. You have known through their messages brought to you through the mercies and love of God, that they were as you are, with their faults, with their weaknesses. They were as you are, with families to tend to, careers, work. They too needed a shelter, clothing, food in their stomachs. They were as you are- human, erred- but with God's grace, made into a great, great thing.

And so, I tell you, you have been commissioned, and each of you, each one of you, in your own way has much to give. Whether a priest or a teacher, a healer or keeper of peace, whether a mother or spouse, a friend or sister, you have much to give. My children are hurting. A mother's heart cries out for your help. My little ones, they are so in need. I do pray that you will go and that you will be as the first disciples, that you will tend to their needs, that you will go among those who are hurting, and bring the healing love of Christ. It is not a daunting task, and it is not difficult with the love of God as your strength and your courage. Pray, each day, that the Holy Spirit might work within you and inspire you, each day, in little ways, to bring Christ to the world.

God does not wish for His children to live in darkness. He desires that they know the light of His love, faith, and joy. In all that you do, in every task, in every moment, bring Christ into the world through your example, through your words, through your actions. Let all who know you, know that you are a follower of Christ. Let them know that, truly, the Lord is your Master, by who you are. There are many of my children who would say that they wish to follow. There are many of my children who would like to change the way of the world, but few who would take up the cause of God, who would truly devote themselves to bringing about a revolution of love. This is what I wish for. This is my prayer, that my little ones who I have come to, who I have spoken to, who I have brought messages of hope and encouragement to throughout the world, would go out as lambs among wolves, would go out as the first apostles of my Son did, and teach and spread the good news that God is alive, that God is with them.

My dear little ones, know that I am with you in this. Know that I do pray and intercede on your behalf each day in all things. Know that God is most pleased with you. He sends His Holy Spirit down upon you, that you might be strengthened, that you might know His will, and that you might have the courage and judgement to complete that which He asks of you. Do not strive to do big things, for our God speaks in silence, and He is humble and small among that which is great and built to be mighty in this world. Oftentimes, God cannot be seen in that which is grand, but most in that which is small, those things most overlooked, those words unheard, the silence that is often ignored. Seek His wisdom in the silence of your hearts. Pray that in a small way, each day you might be carriers of His will, you might truly serve Him in all that you do, and you might be blessed, continually blessed, to be called His children and in His favor.

My dear ones, it is with the love of a mother that I do say, may the peace of Christ be with you always, and may you know the joy and faith of God Who, with you, creature and Creator, loved and beloved, truly knows you and wishes to be part of your lives. Continue, my little ones, with love in your heart. Strive always to do what God asks of you, and know that I do pray with you and for you always.

Be at peace as I bless you in the name of He Who is mighty, in the name of the Son our Savior, and the Holy Spirit, Who dwells in the silence of your hearts.

February 1999

Mary:

My dear little ones, know that it is with great joy that I greet you this day. Know that I come to you as a mother, as your counselor, as your advisor. Know that I do love you, and bring you always before my Son as a gift and offering to Him. Praise and glorify God always. He alone is good, and through Him such graces are made possible. His love for you is so great that He pours out Himself upon this world, pours out His Spirit, that you might know Him, that He might know you, His little lambs.

My dearest little ones, I come today to speak to you about purpose, for when God lovingly created the world from the dust of the cosmos, He had purpose. There was reason in His creation, and goodness. For you, He formed a perfect world and breathed life upon it, that you might dwell in Him, that you might know Him, that you might love Him, that you might serve Him. His design for humankind was so grand! He desired that His little children would be forever in Him, perfect- Creator and creation.

My dearest little ones, it was through weakness that you fell. Your father's fathers, you yourselves, you have weaknesses. God does not despise your weaknesses, for He knows them, each of them. God desires for you to perfect yourselves in your weaknesses. One cannot perfect oneself if he does not realize that he is in such need of God. And so, I tell you, look to your lives. Know that God is with you. Recognize your great need for God, that He might perfect you.

In the weakness of humanity, the world has become a dark place. Never, never has the world been so far from God! Many of my little children choose to be far from Him. They turn their backs to Him, to His Word, to His people. Many of my children despise our Lord and hate Him. My dear ones, what a horrible thing this is! What a horrible thing, for our God loves you so much. He bursts with joy at our words of prayer. He delights in seeing your beautiful, shining souls when you come before Him in your masses, in your sacraments, in your prayer. All that our God wants is for you, His people, to be in love with Him.

I have told you that I will speak about purpose, and I have explained that God does all things with purpose. He designed you to be perfect, but humanity fell away from Him. His purpose in the world now is to bring humanity back into His arms, that He might cradle you as children and love you, that you might love Him as He loves you, and that creature and Creator, Father and child, might be united in a way that they once were. Dearest little ones, this is why He sends me. This is why He sends to you His saints, His angels, those who come as ambassadors of His will. Know that I do not come for any reason, save to glorify God alone, that His will might be done.

Dearest children, He sends to you all of His aid, all of His counsel. He gives to you your guardian angels, that they might watch and care for you, and direct you in goodness. He gives to you the saints, that they might be examples of walking His way. He gives to you His Own Son, that you might be fed and nourished by the body and blood of His love. And in sending to you His mother, He gives to you His most wondrous gift of joy, peace, and hope, for this is the message that He has told me to proclaim, a message of joy that His children might be joyful, for God is with them, a message of hope, for God loves His children so much that He will do all that He can to unite Himself with His children who are so lost, a message of peace, peace be with you. Live in peace. Let peace envelop you. Let peace fill you homes. Let it be in your heart, in your mind, and in your soul, for a heart in turmoil, a soul in darkness, a mind cluttered with things of this world, cannot see God.

Dear ones, my purpose is simple. I come to you that you would know God, that you might love and adore Him as He should be. He is so grand! Never could you comprehend while on this earth the love of our Lord. Certainly, you would die with joy! Dear ones, I have come to you that you might know His work, that you might know His will, that you might hear again that same message given to you in His scriptures, that message of love, peace, conversion, joy, gratitude. These are things you were taught by Jesus' humble, obedient example. I come to teach you as a mother, as a counselor, as an advocate for you before the Father, and I ask that you teach one another, that you take what I have given you, these messages that I have brought, and bring them to your homes. Give them to your families through your example, through your words, through your evangelization. Give them to your friends, to those whom you know, that the light of the Lord would permeate the darkness that covers the earth.

Dear children, my purpose for you is simple. Love one another. Teach those around you that they are loved by God. By all means, share this joy I have given to you, this great gift the Father has allowed for me to bring to you of His words, stated again through His humble servant. I come to you as a servant, not as a leader. I serve God Who loves you, Who desires to make you leaders, leaders of His church, His most beautiful church, that which is His hands, His feet, His body. It is the people who make the Church and Jesus Christ, He Who lived, died, resurrected, and ascended, that you might be saved, desires that you would go and lead His people, be shepherds of His flock, be stewards of His grace. Let Him work through you, that He might be alive on this earth. He has given to you Himself. He has given to you His mother. Again and again, He sacrifices Himself on your altars. He has given you His forgiveness in your sacraments, His joy, His love. Would you not give to your Lord the same? Would you not give Him all that you have?

Dearest ones, I know that in your hearts you desire to serve, and so this is why I come to you. This is my purpose, the purpose of God, to teach you to serve one another, to teach you to be good stewards of the graces you have received, to teach you to pray, pray without ceasing. And so, if you desire to know that which God wishes for you to do, follow these words: 'Pray! Pray always!' Make your life a prayer. Give all that you have to God, all of your joys, all of your sufferings, all that you endure, all that you must go through, all that is difficult, all that is joyful. Each day keep Him in your mind, and in your heart, and in your soul. Do not allow yourself to be separated from Him for an instant. Do not be distracted by that which is around you, for truly it is a distraction.

Secondly, I ask you to love one another. Love yourselves by respecting yourself and giving dignity to all life. Love your God by serving those who have no one to serve them, by teaching those who are uneducated, by helping those who are hurt and ailing, by being compassionate to those who are lonely, afraid, sick. Be merciful, and mercy shall be given to you. Be joyful, and you will know God's joy. Be workers of peace, and you will know the peace that Christ brings.

Finally, speak my words to those whom you know, the words that have been given to me by the Father to share with you. Tell them that God loves them so much that He breaks into this world to bring His sheep home to the Shepherd. God will never cease to call. He will never cease to call His sheep. Never will He leave you alone. Never shall you be abandoned. He breaks into this world through His body and blood, through the Holy Spirit that dwells upon each of you and within your homes and hearts, through the perfect sacrifice of the Lamb on the altar, through His sacraments- His Reconciliation, the marriage vows that He has given to you, that you might know truly what God's love is, the holy priesthood, the graces that you receive in anointings through the Church, that which is most holy. He gives Himself to you through His messengers, through His mother, through His saints, through His angels that guard you. Seek Him! You will not look far, for He is all around you, calling your name, knowing each one of your hearts. He is a God Who loves His people so very much that He goes to them, embraces them, draws them near, and invites them home to Him.

My dear ones, it is with great joy that I am with you. Know that the darkness of the world is great, and it is most, most saddening, but the light of Christ is eternal, and its brightness cannot be quenched. When in the hearts of His little children, our Lord works many miracles. Open yourselves to Him, that you might be a beacon in the darkness, and that this world, so dark and so alone, might come to know the love that God has intended for it since the beginning of time. He has created you for perfection. He has created you for love. Accept those gifts which He gives to you with a grateful heart, and know that He is with you.

March 1999

Mary:

My dear little children, praise God and glorify Him, for He alone is holy. He is all goodness and all joy. It is He who sends me, that you might know His peace. Dear little ones, be filled with grace. Open your hearts to grace, that it might fill you and free you from sin. Accept the grace that God offers to you through the many gifts He has placed in your lives.

In this time, when you prepare to remember our Lord's most precious gift of His passion, death, and resurrection, I urge you, find my Son and our Lord in the sacraments that He has given to you. Find Him as you reconcile with Him. Find Him as you commune with Him in the Holy Eucharist. Find Him in one another, as you are good stewards of His will. Practice the virtues you have been taught. Give with all of your heart to God, that He might give all in return.

Dear little ones, what a joyful task this is to give your hearts completely to our Lord, to give yourselves, the fullness of your heart and mind, the fullness of your body, for His work, that your hands might be His Own and your feet His Own, that you might speak His Word, that you might teach as He did, that you might be vessels for that mission which He calls you to. Our Lord has created you most marvelously! He has placed within your own hearts many gifts, many great gifts! Our Lord comes to you. He asks you to invite Him into your own life and into your heart, to pray, 'Lord, free me! Let me do your will!' He knocks, dear children. Will you answer Him? I tell you, what great joy you will know! Our God Who is love, Who loves you dearly, desires that you would do His will. Pray!

Open your hearts to Him through prayer. Give of yourself completely in prayer. In this way, you will know the Lord's will, as His Holy Spirit is with you and, in a small voice, a silent voice, He tells you that which He wills. Listen! This is something that is so often not done.

Dear children, how often my little ones will speak, and yet they do not open their ears to listen. They do not hear with their hearts. I ask you to hear with your heart. Open yourself to hear His Word in your church, in His gifts of the sacraments, in one another, in those whom you serve. Hear Him! See Him there, too, my little ones. See Him! He is with you. See with your heart and not your eyes, for they deceive you. Our Lord is alive, and He is with you. He walks ever beside you and ever before you. He leads you down the path of righteousness and goodness. He walks with you to holiness. See Him with your hearts in all that you do. Praise Him, for He is so good that He does not abandon His children, but as a gentle Father, leads them safely and joyfully to their eternal home, which He has prepared.

Dear ones, what a great Father our Lord is. How well He tends to our needs! What do we need that He has not given to us? What could we possibly desire that would not be ours, in God's will? Dear children, our God loves us so. He is so merciful and so good. He desires that you place yourself before Him. Place your hearts before His cross. Truly, give yourself to Him there. Lay yourself completely before His cross, that through His loving gaze, you might be filled and freed, you might be renewed in spirit, as you meditate and remember His passion, death, and resurrection. Dear children, know that in life, many times you are called to die to yourself. You are called to die to your own desires, to your own will. As Christ died for the sins of man, only to be raised up by the Father in Heaven to glory, so too will you be raised in glory, if you die to yourselves.

Dear children, God wants for you to live joyfully. He has given you life that you might live it abundantly. Do so with gratitude, and do so in a way which is self-sacrificing, that you might give to those who have less than you, that you might teach those who are uneducated, heal the sick, help the injured, comfort the lonely. Dear little ones, there is so much you can do. God has given to you such gifts, such grace! Open your hearts to His grace. None of you has no gift to offer. There is not one of you who could not touch the hearts of many. There is not one of you who is not essential in our God's plan of salvation for the world. He came into this world as a humble child. He taught. He learned. He laughed, and loved, and cried, and He showed us the way to eternal salvation through His cross, that resurrection into glory that our Lord has promised to those who are true to Him. In this same way, love your lives. Do love them, for they are a gift from God, but live them in a way in which they are a very gift to our Father in Heaven.

My dear little ones, when you reflect on our Lord's passion and death, remember that He has done all of this for love of you. Each one of you, your faces He beheld, your hearts He knew. Our Lord has created you so very special, so very special! You are more precious to Him than all things. Each heart, each soul is His Own doing, His Own creation, carved on the palm of His hand with the love of a Father, true love, unconditional love. So few of my little ones know how loved they are. No one person would deny the requests of the mother or father that loved them, raised them, and cherished them. No person would turn a cold shoulder to their parents, who brought them into the world and gave them life. I tell you, our Father in Heaven, Who brought you into this world and breathed His Own life into you, Who gave you His earthly life upon a cross on Calvary, He beckons to you. He beckons to you, and calls to you. He asks for you to give your life in service to Him by serving one another.

This is a task which is not difficult. Should you open your heart, God will fill you with the graces that you need to accomplish His will. He will send His Holy Spirit, that you, like His first apostles, might have the words to preach, might have the ears to listen, might have the eyes to see with the heart. Go as they did and teach, and pray, and live, and love, for God has given you many graces and much joy. Thank Him always, for He has blessed you abundantly.

Know that you have been given all things. Do give all that you have in return. In your own little ways this will please God tremendously, for He desires that you serve one another and lead one another to His heavenly home. This is the way He has established His church, that one man might take the hand of another and guide him, that one man might lead another. Christ came as that man, that God-Made-Man, to lead, to guide. He now asks you to do the same, to turn to your own brothers and sisters, and lead them, and guide them on the way to freedom, love, and joy.

I have spoken much to you on such things, and I have taught you that you are not alone, that you are so loved, that God is a good and merciful Lord, and that all that He desires is your own hearts. This is the message I wish to give to you again this evening, for I will say it to you again and again. It is most important. Do pray. Do love the Lord through service and good works. Do see Him in all that He has given to you. Do not turn a blind eye, nor deaf ear to Him, but see and hear with the heart. See that He is with you. Know that He loves you. See His goodness in your lives and praise Him. Glorify Him for all that He is, for He alone is deserving of all praise, and He alone is deserving of all glory.

Dear children, be joyful. Your Father in Heaven holds you near to Him. He beckons to you. He desires your own hearts. Hear and answer Him. Dear ones, I do bless you in His name, and I pray that His peace and His glory will be with you always.

April 1999

Mary:

My dear little ones, know that it is good for me to be here to speak among you. Do praise God and thank Him for all His goodness, for He is love, and has given to you such blessings, such tremendous blessings, you cannot imagine. He Who loves you like little children, is with you. He sends to you His angels and saints, His messengers and mother, that you might be pulled close to His heart, drawn ever nearer to Him, that each day you might walk closer, nearer, more beautifully and perfectly, in His light.

Dear ones, do all that you do for Him. Dedicate yourselves completely to God, for when God, Who is all powerful, is the center of your hearts and minds, spirit, soul, world, truly you will know great things. God has designed you for this, that you would give all that you have to Him. He has created you. He has given to you such gifts, such talents. He has made you masters over one another in that you are to truly lift up, support, and teach each other.

He sent His Son. You have celebrated this joyful season of His resurrection when you remember that it was the Son Who is the Redeemer and the Salvation. He sent His Son to teach you that to be a human being, to be a creation of God, is to live with compassion and mercy. There is nothing more than the Christ, Who is and always shall be compassion and mercy.

Emulate Him in all that you do. Live a compassionate life. It is one thing, my dear children, to give from your hearts. It is one thing to give freely all that you have, and then some. When you give, do not do it that you might be rewarded here. That is troubling, for God, He seeks to see that which no other sees, that which is hidden away, that which is contained in your own heart and in your own soul. In this way, you keep these treasures in your heart to present them to God when you stand before Him. Live a compassionate life. You have been charged with each other's care. Truly, it is your job to lead, and to guide, and to teach, and to learn, no matter who you are and what you do with your life.

There are so many, so many gifts given by the Father. To one, He gives the gift of prophecy and to another, the gift to hear and understand, to another the gift of wisdom, another right judgment and the discernment of all things good. Some are able to teach, others to speak, some but to listen. All are important and necessary, vital, truly essential! Jesus has set His church apart to be the Way, and the Truth, and the Life, as He was. He has made you the body, truly the hands and feet, of His church. The body has many parts but one mission, just as you all have been created in your individuality with one mission. Use those gifts that God has given to you to be an example of the compassion and mercy of Christ, for this is what motivated all that He did: love for His fellow human beings.

God has created you separate, distinct from all of creation, in that He has given to you the incredible gift of will. This is something that was given to no other creation. You retain will, a freedom, the ability to choose to reason, to think, to know, and to experience God in a way that no other creation from the beginning of time ever has, or ever will. You experience Him as Abba, as the Father, the One Who loves you tremendously and has sent His Own Son to be the Sacrificial Lamb. You experience Him as a teacher, as guidance in your life, in the quiet whisperings of the Holy Spirit, in the friends and comforters He sends to you. Rejoice, for you have known God in a way that no other creation has known Him!

He has created you in this way because He desires that you choose Him and choose His road. He desires that you choose to help one another. You know that there are many in the world who do not yet know that my Son is Lord, who do not yet know that they are loved by God. What a horrible thing this is! How terrible, for God has created you to be loved. He has created you to love. He has created you all as His children, more precious to Him than the stars of the night, than the oceans of the world. For each one of you, He would give His Own life. For each one of you, He gave His life, that you might receive life as well. Know this: if Christ had come but to save but one soul, He would have come. If there was only one who would have listened, He would have spoken. If only one would have been healed, He would have touched and reached out to His children. If there was but one who would open their eyes and see God, He would have come in all of His glory. Christ came to this earth for each one of you, uniquely, individually, for no other reason except that He loves you and desires that you choose Him.

Dear ones, you have been given such power of prayer! You do not know how beautiful your prayers are. You cannot imagine the joy in Heaven when my little ones pray. It is for this reason that I continue to tell you to pray. Pray always! Live your life as a prayer, for if you knew the joy of the heavens you would never cease to pray. Continue to build a life of holiness through compassion and mercy, through prayer and a love for the sacraments. Love my Jesus as you find Him in your churches, in your gifts, in that which you have to give to the world, and in those whom He has sent to you. Truly, I tell you, when God, He Who is all things, is in your presence, when God, Who loves you tremendously is with you, you will know that you have all strength, that you have all courage, that you have all things, because you are His. He does not abandon His children. Should you choose to walk with Him, He will be with you ever vigilant, ever protecting, as a father to a child.

Know this as well my little ones: when you stand before your God, there is nothing more important, no greater gift that you could give to Him, than to treat, each day of your life, your brothers and sisters in Christ, as you would treat our Lord, for truly they are the greatest creation of God. They are His children. God has placed His Own children in your care. He has asked you to be their teacher, their mentor, their friend, and their comforter. His Own dear little ones, would you not reach out with all of your heart to comfort those whom He loves so dearly? In all of the world there is no gift greater than to give yourself to another human being in friendship, in love, and in faith. It is in this way, and through strong prayer spoken with the true knowledge that God is with you, that you will come so very close to our Father's kingdom.

This was the life of Jesus, the life of He Who came to redeem, and to teach us how to find our own way home to our Father. He was compassion and mercy. He was prayer and obedience. He spent much time with those who were hurting, and He offered what He could, whether it was bread and fish, a healing touch, or words of great love and encouragement. Do the same in your lives. Reach out to those who are in need. Reach out to those who you can give much to, for know that you have been truly blessed. God will not forget you. He will not abandon you. How He seeks to serve the world through His people! How He desires those who give themselves to Him to be servants, that He might touch His Own children through them.

Dear ones, be encouraged and be filled with hope, for God is with you, and you are His children. He loves you as a father. He loves you in a way you will never be loved again. He knows you. He has created you all special, individual, and perfect in His eyes. When you have cause to fall from Him, when you walk a tempting road, lift up all that you are to God. Ask Him to see that which is most beautiful within you, your perfect shining soul, and ask Him through His mercy and compassion to help you, each day, to walk closer to Him. Find Him in your sacraments. Find Him in one another. My dear children, never cease to look, for He is there waiting for you.

Dear ones, be joyful and know that God is with you, as I your mother am with you. I offer to you my motherly blessing, and I pray that God might grant you peace, mercy, and compassion, all the days of your life. May He be with you, and may the Holy Spirit inspire you to go and to do that which you have been told to do: to teach, to assist, to comfort, to be Christ on earth.

My dear ones, may you be blessed in the name of He Who is holy, the Most Holy Trinity, Who is and ever shall be, forever. Amen.

May 1999

Mary:

My dear little ones, know that I am pleased to be among you, to worship our Lord with you. Thank Him and praise Him and know that you do please Him and give Him much glory when you honor His mother. Dear little ones, He Who is all goodness, is with you. He Who is all mercy and all compassion, is with you. Praise Him, for you are most blessed.

Dear little ones, today I invite you to a renewed sense of prayer within your homes, within your families, within your own hearts. I urge you to discover the peace and the beauty of prayer. God has given to you prayer as a most precious gift, a gift that is so often left by the wayside, gone unused, not multiplied, but hidden away. I tell you that prayer, it is so beautiful that all of the heavens rejoice when you lift your voices up to our Father in Heaven. You cannot know the power of your prayer, nor how one prayer multiplies into many, as you join your voices and your hearts together to pray for all of your needs, and to pray in thanksgiving for all you have been given.

I invite you to pray with the fullness of your hearts. In doing this, you must not concern yourself with those things that distract you. This is difficult, for there are many distractions in this world, but I invite you to find a place of quiet peace and rest to focus completely on your Lord, your God, to empty your heart of all that you do not wish to bring to Him. Thank Him. Praise Him. Give to Him your sorrows and also your joys. Remember the sick, the dying, the suffering to Him, for He Who is all mercy and compassion wishes to bestow such graces upon them. Bring your children before Him in prayer. Bring your spouse, your parents, your friends, and your enemies. All people who are remembered in prayer are blessed, for God does not let a prayer go unanswered, but He hears and answers with that which is in His will.

When you pray, do not be concerned if you are distracted. Instead, continue to pray and persevere in prayer. Do not become frustrated. Do not be anxious. Let peace fill your heart. The greatest fruit of prayer is peace- peace in your life, in your heart, in all that you do. Those who pray with the fullness of their heart and desire to find God there in prayer, know a peace that others cannot comprehend. God truly comes to you when you are with Him in prayer. He takes your heart, all of its cares, all of its sorrows, and blesses it and multiplies those graces, and carries those pains which you must bear.

Peace! Peace is so necessary in your lives, in your world today. Your world is so lacking peace, and it is so easy to attain. I urge you, find the peace that only Christ can bring, through prayer and a love for prayer. If you find prayer difficult, continue on, persevere, for God will give to you those graces necessary that you might love, truly cherish, those moments, hours, days spent in prayer. Each day, make it your true goal to spend more time with your Lord than you did the last. In this way, you will come to find such peace.

Prayer is not only spoken with the heart or recited with the mouth, but it is lived. Prayer is the Christian walk. It is the way which you are called to follow. When Jesus prayed, when He came before His people and He prayed to His Father in Heaven, He did so that they might know the words to speak to God, that they might know that He is their Father as He was our Lord's Father, that they might know that He is so grand that He has created each of you to call Him by that most precious and intimate name, for indeed you are His children. When Jesus prayed and taught His followers to pray, He did not worry about what others would think of Him. He did not consider the words He used, for words are so inadequate. Rather, He spoke that which was in His heart: "Father, you Who are glorious…". Do address our Father with such love, for He does love you tremendously, and deserves all of your worship and praise. Jesus asked the Father to send all that He needed, to supply each day the needs for Himself. In the same way, never fear to ask God to fulfill your needs- your health, your home, shelter, and food. He will provide for you, as He has provided for all of creation. "Preserve me from evil". Christ, even our Lord, did ask our Father to preserve Him from evil. In the same way, do pray this prayer, for it is powerful. Would you know the Angels that God sends to you when you pray these words, you would marvel! "Amen". A most precious word. Believe in God! Praise Him. Express your love and belief in Him.

Faith is something that is lived each day. It is a road and a conversion. It is a journey. Each day, you walk your trip of faith. Each day, you move closer to our Lord. He has planted within your hearts the seed of faith, that you might know Him and see Him as your Lord, your Master, and your Redeemer. He has given each one of you that grace, that tremendous grace, that is of the most beautiful and most wondrous man can receive. It is up to you to decide whether that faith that has been given to you will be nurtured and tenderly cared for, and grown until strong, stronger than the cornerstone, or if that faith shall be left unused, hidden away.

Our Lord invites you to pray. He invites you to a growing faith, a faith that changes each day as you become more and more in love with Him. He invites you to a life of prayer, to living your prayer through your actions, through your words, through your thoughts, through all that you are and all that you hope to be. Abandon yourself to God. I cannot tell you how wondrous this is, for there are no better hands in which to place yourself, no better care than the care of our Father in Heaven. Continue to pray. I am most grateful for your prayers said for my intentions and know that I do lift up you and all of your intentions to our Father, before the cross of the Almighty Son, and the Holy Spirit, where He reigns in Heaven.

Dear little children, know that you are most loved. Know that God desires an intimate walk with you. He desires to know your hearts, to love you, to serve you, His people, as He served you when He came upon this earth to teach you to pray. Do thank Him. Do praise Him. Do give Him all that He is deserving of: all that you have, all that you are, and all that you ever shall be through a life of building faith and a strong prayer from the heart.

My dear little ones, may you be blessed in the name of Christ who is and always shall be. Know that I am with you in a special way, that I do give to you my motherly blessing, that I lift you up before the Father and pray that you might know His peace. May the peace of Christ be with all of you each day. Each day, may you know God's grace, may you feel His presence, and may blessings abound in your life.

June 1999

Mary:

My dear little ones, know that I come to you and I bring to you my motherly blessing. Know that I join with you in praising God. Continue to be grateful and praise Him, for all that you have has been given to you through His goodness. All that you are has been formed by Him. All that you will be, will be accomplished through His Most Holy Spirit. Dear ones, know you are His most blessed. Know you are His children. Know you are most loved.

My little ones, I call you to be bearers of hope in the world. I call you to bring the joy of Christ- His peace, His love, and His forgiveness. This world is so in want for hope. There are many, many of my little ones who are desolate, who are afraid, who seek out our Lord, and yet their fear blinds them and they cannot see Him. My little ones, be bearers of hope! Christ has sent you as He sent His first disciples among many that you might be witnesses to Him through your lives, through your words, through all that you are. You are His hands and His feet upon this earth. You are truly the Church of God. He does His work through those who will lend themselves completely to Him, abandon themselves to Him, to His will. I invite you to give yourselves completely to God. Do not seek that which your own will desires, but rather, abandon yourself to Him that He might free you from all that binds you to this earth, and that He might give you purpose and meaning in His own will.

Dear ones, the will of God is always hope. It is always joy. It is always love. Know that as you bear the light of Christ in this world, you also bring the hope of God. The people of God are set apart by the mere fact that they do hope in Him, for God will not abandon you, and you know that you are your Father's children. You are protected and guided and inspired by His Most Holy Spirit. Flee to His comfort and to His aid! He will be with you, ever nearer to you. Run to Him! Let Him be your sole salvation, for He alone is the Redeemer and the Lord. There are many, many gods that people in this world would worship, but I tell you, none will bring salvation but the One True Lord. Be a people of hope in how you live. Live your lives joyfully.

Gratitude is such a gift of the Holy Spirit, gratitude for all that you have and all you have been given. I desire for my children to recognize the blessings in their lives and to thank God for them, for so often they are unnoticed. Be grateful! See how He has provided you the very things that you have, the very things that you own, that which you eat, and that which shelters you. See how He has provided companionship in family, blessings of love, and forgiveness, and friendship. See how He has given to you the greatest of gifts, His Own life, His Own Son, faith that is unshakable. Thank Him. Praise Him, for from gratitude stems hope.

When you are grateful for all that you have, you will see God most clearly in your life. You will see that He is real and alive and with you, so very present, more present than many of the things that are held to be gods in this world. I tell you this and it is true, though many do not see it, for God who is unseen and unheard, He is the most real, most beautiful, and most present gift in your life. He is with you through all things. Through times of happiness and trial, through joys and sorrows, He is with you.

Live a life of hope through prayer. It is only a hopeful people who pray, because those who believe that prayer changes the hearts of men have hope in God's mercy, His generosity, and His compassion. I assure you that prayer does change the hearts of many. Prayer is a great grace and makes possible such grace from

God, you cannot imagine. Pray with fervency and love. Pray with a desire to be nearer to our Lord, to know Him intimately, as you would know a friend. Pray with the desire to love Him and to serve Him. Bring before Him all of your faults in prayer and ask that He might heal you, for our Lord came upon this earth to teach, to heal, to minister in so many ways. He desires to heal you as a whole person- body, mind, spirit, soul. He is a God of goodness. Bring all things to Him and lay them before Him. Abandon all of your cares to Him. Know that He will truly provide all that you need, and during times of trial, will provide the strength for you to endure.

My little ones, be a people of hope through your families. Love one another. Share with one another your time, your talents, your gifts, your friendship, your faith. Show your family that you serve them as you serve God, with the fullness of your hearts. Be a people of hope in your church, in your community, in your world. Do not be despairing. Do not be discouraged. Do not allow the distractions and hardships of life to encompass you, but rather flee to God. Flee to your life, to your salvation, and know that God will give to you all graces necessary to endure all things, and He will multiply the blessings you receive many, many fold.

Dear ones, when you learn to live as a people of hope, you will be joyful, for the Holy Spirit brings hope and joy. This is what I have come to offer to you, the peace of Christ, a joyful peace, a peace that is without end, and a peace that is hope. I bring to you a message of holiness, for holiness is achieved through a life lived with God, in God, and through God. Only when you recognize Him in your life through gratitude, only when you see Him as He works ever vigilantly by your side, only when you see Him through the hearts of one another in hopeful peace, will you know, truly know, that God is with you, and you will be joyful.

My little ones, I have taught you many things, and you have learned much. I continue to teach you, that you might be evermore the people that God has created you to be, His most perfect disciples. Dear ones, know that you are loved above all else. Know that you are most precious of all creation. For this reason alone, have great joy. Take courage from this and be encouraged in your faith. Know that God has sent me to you to be a messenger of hope and a bearer of hope. He now sends you to be a messenger of hope to others that the darkness of this world might be lit by His love, His life, and His enduring love for all people. Whether they see Him and recognize Him, or turn their heads from Him, He is with all people. He will not forsake His children. He will not abandon them. He is an ever-vigilant Father, waiting and calling to His little ones.

Do help Him. Do show Him that you do desire to serve in your life by emulating Christ. Do pray with the fulness of your hearts, that you might reap the benefits of living a life of grace. Do ask Him to come into your lives to forgive all that is wrong, all that is sinful, and to heal all that is hurt, for I assure you, God will bring to you all mercies and all goodness, if only you would ask. Do be a people of hope. Live the Christian life, a life led in emulation of Christ. Know that it is not an easy life, but it is one that brings much joy. Place your heart, your whole heart, and all that you are, on the altar of God. Offer yourself completely to Him and you will find joy even in your sorrows, even in your trials, even in your weaknesses.

Do not despair nor be discouraged, but rather rejoice, for you are God's chosen people! He has called you by name and He has heard your prayers. You have answered His call, and you are most favored by God. Know that He has given you so many things. See Him and answer Him, each day, in your own ways, in your lives, that He might forever more be glorified, that the Holy Trinity of God- Father, Son, and Spirit, may reign in the hearts of all mankind.

My dear ones, I give to you my motherly blessing, and I pray that you might always know the hope that is of God, through God, and from God. My dear ones, be encouraged. Be at peace. Know that you are loved, and know that I am with you as a mother, protectress, and intercessor.

July 1999

Mary:

My dear little ones, how good it is for you to gather and praise the Lord together. May His name be blessed forever! Dear children, I lift up your prayers, your sacrifices, your joys, and your sorrows to our Father with the care of a mother. Know that I have interceded on your behalf, and I continue to do so. Know that I who come to guide you, sent by the Father, wish to remind you that you are loved, that you are cared for. For these things, be grateful.

More than any other gift you have been given, be grateful for the gift of faith, for truly this is what makes your life worth living. Without faith there is no hope, without hope, no love. Dear children, praise God each day for this gift He has given to you, for I tell you that faith truly is a gift. It is not something that is learned, nor is it something that can be earned. It is given freely by God, for He loves you tremendously.

You, as disciples of Christ, are called to serve, and yet you cannot teach the faith, you cannot give faith to those with whom you come in contact. You cannot let them share in such delights as God has given to you. Only the Lord can give the gift of faith. You are called not to impart this gift, but to ready the fields for the Father to plant. You are called to be the workers of His fields, the tenders of His vineyards. You are called to make ready the soil, that when the seed of faith is planted, it may not wither but grow strong and tall in the hearts of all men. I have called you to do this as the Father has instructed me, through a life of prayer, through a life of leadership by your Christian example, through a life of charity and obedience. And I tell you that it is not in the great, nor the powerful, that God exists most clearly in this world, but through the ordinary, and the mundane, and the trivial. Many great men have lived and done great things, but oftentimes, it is a small thing- one word, one action from an ordinary man, that makes all the difference.

Dear ones, I tell you that you are essential in our Father's plan, His plan of salvation for all mankind. He has sent to earth His Son to be the Shepherd, to be the Sower of the seeds, to tend to His lambs, to tend to His fields. The Son, our Lord, gave to you the Word. He gave to you, as to the first disciples, the gift of faith. He has sent you to become as the first disciples were- teachers, healers, ministers, friends. Through these actions you will impart charity, compassion, empathy, love, and all virtues to your fellow man. In this way you ready the fields, so the Father may plant the seed of hope, faith, and love in the hearts of mankind.

Dear children, do not cease to be grateful for this gift you have been given, for truly, truly you do not know what a gift you have! Many of my little ones live without faith in God. Many refuse to turn their face to His grace. How sad this is, and how difficult. It is for this reason that our Father in Heaven sends me, sends many messengers into this world, that it might become illuminated by His love and His light, by His joy and His peace, by His steadfast faithfulness. I ask you to continue in your missions, whatever the Lord has called you to, whatever vocation, whether it is as husband or wife, or priest, or friend, or sister, or brother, or daughter, or son. Continue in these vocations to be teachers of the faith, examples of the faith, for the gift of faith is freely given by God, but the hearts of men must be willing and ready to accept that gift.

Never cease to pray, my little ones, for prayer is so important. It strengthens your own soul and gives to you all graces necessary to endure hardships and rejoice in true joy. Know that the Lord provides for you all things, as He has provided for all creation. Trust completely in Him. He is unfailing. Dear little ones, I give to you, my blessing. I pray that the Lord will bless you with all graces, with all joys, with all wisdom, and all knowledge. I ask you to pray that the wisdom of God would fill your hearts, for it is in this way, through the Holy Spirit, through which you will be great teachers, great healers, great ministers of the truth.

Dear children, be encouraged in your faith. Be encouraged on your journey with God. Know that He is with you always, standing close behind and ever near, guiding you and guarding you, protecting you from harm. Dear little ones, praise His name. May He be glorified forever, and ever.

August 1999

(On this evening, the prayer group met in the church during Eucharistic Adoration.)

Mary:

My dear little ones, know how good it is for me to come to you in this way, before your most precious and holy gift, the greatest gift that the Father can give to you. Know that should I have not come and said a word to you, you would lack nothing, but without this gift in the Most Holy Eucharist, you lack everything. You have been witness to a greater thing this night than any sign and any miracle, than any words that I can supply to you, than any gifts of grace given to you elsewhere. You have been given the privilege of being in the true presence of our Lord, our Christ, He Who is one and the same, Who came forth from the power of the Holy Spirit and became man, Who walked upon this earth as teacher, master, friend, and healer, Who, through His own death and resurrection, has freed us, and saved us, and made our way clear, that we might join our Eternal Father in Heaven. Dear ones, know that you are so blessed. Contemplate the blessings you have been given. You do not know the grace, you do not know the glory that is hidden in the humility, in the obedience, in the perfect love, of our Eucharistic Lord.

My dear ones, on this night when you gather in this way, I ask you to consider these things. Often, I have called you to emulate our Lord, to do as He did, to go and to teach, to heal, to love, to forgive. It is in this way that you will become true followers of the Master, true servants of God, and it is in this way that you will teach the world that God is love, that He is mercy and that He is alive in this world, that He works through His people, for you are His hands and feet. You do His will. I ask you to contemplate this gift you have been given.

See how the Lord comes to you. See that He does not come with great splendor, with lights, with sound, with miraculous interventions. See that He comes to you in humility. See that He comes to you in silence. Emulate this. Live a life of silent prayer. Always be at prayer in your hearts. Let your hearts be filled with the Holy Spirit that every word you utter and every thought you think might be a prayer glorifying our God in Heaven. Live in humility. You have been given so much and you are so blessed, but do not allow yourself to be tempted in pride. Rather, live a life of gratitude, for humility does give gratitude.

Dear children, the Lord has given you so much. He is given to the world all that He is, poured out His Own Spirit, His Own blood, His Own body. Be grateful, for never ever will you see a finer gift. Never can you give to Him what He has given to you, for even should you give Him your entire life, your death, all that you are, you cannot give to Him eternal life, that most precious gift that He has given to you. Know that should you give all that you are to Him, He will give all that He has in return, and what a fine thing this is!

Dear ones, see that He comes peacefully. See that He does not come with airs. See that He does not come to teach in an arrogant manner. See that He does not come to yell, to fight in anger. I understand the difficulty in your daily lives, oftentimes with families, with homes, with spouses, with parents. There are so many things to overwhelm you, to pull you away from a prayerful peace. I tell you, do as Jesus does. No matter what insult is hurled at Him, and truly He is insulted in this world, He is peaceful, He is silent, and He is faithful. Ever can you find Him here in your church. Ever can you find Him in your tabernacles. He is unfailing. In the same way, my dear ones, be unfailing. When you are confronted with anger, be at peace. When you feel hostility, hurt, resentment, unforgiveness, pray that the Holy Spirit would fill you that you might know such virtues as forgiveness, joy, peace of your spirit, and a love for your neighbor, for your family, for those who have hurt you.

See how our Lord is so obedient, even that He follows your natural laws, this God of all power, of all glory, and of all might. He Who has created all that is in you, all that surrounds you, all that you ever shall be, He Who has created all that you know and all that you do, all that is true to you, He hides himself plainly without favor. He hides Himself in bread and wine, unseen to you, but glorified by the millions of Angels who surround Him. See that He was obedient even to His executioners. See that He died as a mortal man would die, that He laid in the tomb, He Who was King of all things, Who created the very rock that His tomb was made from.

In the same way, be obedient. Obey the Church and your priests. They are God's chosen ones to lead you. Obey your families, your parents and your spouses. Do that which you have vowed to do. Be faithful to those commitments you make. Obey the Lord. Do as He has called you to do with obedience, with love in your heart, with a true joy that comes only from serving Him. Be obedient when it is most difficult, and you will be rewarded. The Holy Spirit will give to you all that you need. You need not worry. You need not fret, for all that you need, all graces, all glories of God, are given to you as His children, for truly, you are His children.

Dear ones, worship our Lord always in all things. Do as He does, for He is the light of the world, and He shows you the way to the Father's kingdom. See how He is, how beautiful and how spectacular, how obedient, and how marvelous, how glorified! I wish that you could see how He is glorified in our Father's kingdom, for never would you turn your face from a church without genuflecting and bowing before Him. Never could you pass by without falling prostrate before His face, falling down before Him on your knees, crossing yourself, and thanking Him for His glory, for His mercy, for His compassion. If you could but see the Angels that surround Him, the Angels that come to Him to comfort Him in sorrows, to exalt Him, to glorify Him, never would you see with the same eyes again.

I encourage you, remove the veil from your eyes. See what you have not seen before. See what you cannot see unless you look with a heart of prayer, love, and joy. See the eternal sacrifice, the beginning, and the end, all that is and all that ever shall be. See your salvation, your very life, the love that you know in your homes, in your families, with your friends, the successes that you have had, the failures that you have shared with Him. See all that you can be with Him. See all that you can give up and happily so, for I tell you, how good it is to die to yourself and to inherit all that God has to give to you.

Each day consecrate yourself to Him. Come before Him. Pray that the Holy Spirit would make you not what you want to be, not what you desire to be, but rather, what God desires you to be, for it is a much greater thing. Truly, you will never know joy like you will know joy with God. He desires to give His children who are His very heart, who are His love, all things, all goodness, and all grace. Do not turn away from the love of a Father. It is before you as I speak. See the greatest gift, the gift of Himself, that He gives to you. He pours His heart out, His Own blood and His Own body, that He might be so intimately involved in your own lives, not only in your minds, not only in your souls, not only within your hearts, but part of your own flesh, as He came forth from my flesh in humility, that He might teach you the way to our Lord.

Dear ones, accept this incredible gift you have been given. Know that there are no words that I can say to you to describe the glory that He deserves, the glory that He is given in our Father's kingdom. I tell you this that you might be joyful and encouraged, for though many times it seems that all is lost, that there is much darkness in the world, I tell you, a much greater body of the Church, the Church glorified in our Father's kingdom, does honor Him and does worship Him. And it is for His love of all of you, those with Him in glory, those who, like you, still struggle on their faith journeys, and all people who ever shall come, it is for love of you that He comes to you in this way, that He allows me to come to speak to you, that He allows the small miracles in your life each day, the tiny things that often go unnoticed. Truly our God is love and His love for you is without measure. His love for you is greater than all things, and it is His greatest gift poured out upon your altars as His Own flesh.

Dear children, see this miracle before you. Never cease to praise God, for He is all goodness, and He is all joy. I offer to you this day, my motherly blessing. I pray that you might know the peace of God in your hearts, that in times of trouble, that in times of hardship, you might cling to Him as your salvation, and that you might follow Him on the walk to holiness through humility and obedience. May God be ever with you.

September 1999

Mary:

My dear little ones, glory be to God Who is and always shall be King of Kings, Lord of Lords. My dear ones, I bring to you my motherly blessing. I pray that you might be blessed with peace and joy without measure. I pray that you might be blessed by God in all things, that you might always walk in His light, and grow in faith each day.

Dear little ones, long have I come to you and spoken to you of many things. I have taught you that God is love, and that His love for you is unending. I have taught you that Christ is the Way. He is the Truth. He is the Life. I have taught you that to be as God desires you to be, you must follow Christ in carrying your crosses, in sharing your joys, in walking with one another to assist one another on your road to salvation. I have taught you that Christ was the teacher, that He was the Master, that He was all things good and continues to be all things good, as He reigns now in Heaven at the right hand of the Father Almighty. I have taught you that the Holy Spirit directs you and guides you, walks with you, speaks to you, whispers in the silence of your heart the will of God, that you might know it and love it. I have taught you to be charitable, to be obedient to God. Subject yourselves to God, to His will, to His most divine providence. Place yourselves entirely in His care. Turn your eyes trustingly toward Heaven and allow God to show you things unseen to all men.

My dear little ones, I have taught you of peace. I have asked you to bring peace to your hearts, peace to your homes, peace to your world. I have asked you to pray. I continue to ask you to pray. Prayer is essential. It is most, most necessary. Know that your prayers bring great grace to your life. Your prayers make light of the darkness. Your prayers, they are most precious.

My dear children, I have spoken to you of many things. Today, I come to you, and I ask you to dedicate yourselves to all that I have asked and to continue to pursue these things, these virtues that I have taught you. Learn to live all that you have been taught in a more full, in a deeper, in a more beautiful way. I invite you again to reflect on all you have been given, not only through my messages, but through the holy Scriptures, the Word of God, all that is necessary for your salvation. I invite you to reflect on your lives this day, to reflect on your life, your family, your home, your job, your needs, your graces, your blessings, all things given by God. I invite you, dear children, to strive to find new ways to serve Him, to go and to do all that has been asked of you with a fuller commitment, truly a deeper commitment.

I have asked many things of you, and I come, not with my own words and not by my own will but bearing the words of the Father in Heaven Who has sent me. It is by His will that I come. What a gift you have been given! What tremendous gifts you have. I come joyfully as your mother, as any earthly mother, to remind her children of what is right, of what is good, of what will help them to grow strong and sure.

Dear ones, this is my hope and my wish for you, this is my desire and my prayer: that each day you would walk nearer to our Father in Heaven, that each day you might see Him in all who surround you, that you might serve Him in all that you do, and you might know Him in your own lives. And so, I invite you, dear children, commit yourselves completely to God. Fill your heart with His joy, with His love, with His mercy. All that I have asked of you, I ask again from you, and I ask you to pursue it with a tremendous fervency, a love, a desire, a burning desire, to serve. I ask you to recommit yourselves to God, to dedicate yourselves to Him, to give to Him your lives, your homes, your families, all things.

Dear little ones, how easy it is for us to seek to serve God. How easy it is for us to desire to serve Him. I ask you to do what is most difficult, truly what is most difficult. Go out into the world and be lambs among wolves. Do what I have asked you to do, that which God has asked you to do. It is one thing to ask you to give up all things for God. Your hearts are filled with desire. Your hearts are filled with love and a desire to serve. You desire to serve God and to give all things to Him, but still, you find it difficult.

Know that I come to encourage you in this, to assure you that with God all things are possible. Alone you can do nothing for His glory. Alone you will stumble, and you will fall. That is the nature of man. It has been that way since man departed from God and will be that way until you see God reunited with man. I tell you though that God, Who has sent His only Son to be your savior, to be your light, to be your joy, to be your life, He has made it possible for you to be perfected in Him, if you seek His will, if you desire to do all that He desires, if you desire to do nothing for yourself but give all things to Him. Truly, the greatest things that you can do in your lives are to give all things to God, to give to Him all that you have and that you are, as He has given to you all that He is.

Dear ones, you do not know the power you have. You do not know how much God can do in this world. You do not know how He can be glorified through your simple, "yes". I invite you to say yes to God in your lives. I invite you to pray humbly, "Lord, may your will be done". I invite you to give your hearts to Him, to give your dreams to Him, to give your souls to Him, to give your heart, mind, body, spirit, will, all things that are most uniquely you, to Him.

Know He will purify you. He will build you up. He will strengthen you. He will bless you, and you will do great things in His name.

Dear ones, it is most beautiful that God has created you for this task. It is most beautiful! He desires for you to give up all things, that He might give you all things in return. Dear little ones, this is a very difficult thing. There are many things in this world that call your attention away. There are many things that are distractions. Some of these things that distract you from the work of God are good- your homes and your families, your pursuits of service. Others are not so good.

Dear little ones, I ask you to concentrate your efforts in your home. First and foremost, among all other things, the home is the bedrock of faith. It is the cradle of faith. It is the most beautiful and most perfect representation of the Trinity. In a home, in your families, you are bound together as one unit, not individuals, but as one. Serve one another as you would serve your own needs. Seek out all good things for one another. See God in the faces of your children, of your spouse, of your family, of your parents. See God there, and serve Him there. This world is in desperate need, my dear children, of family, of a loving family. Family is so tremendously important that God saw fit to send His Own Son, His Own divine Son, to an earthly mother and an earthly father, that He might be taught as you are taught, that He might grow as you grow, that He might learn to love in the family.

My dear children, in this way, this simple step will help you in your commitment to God, in your decision to dedicate all that you are to Him. If you can serve completely within your family, it will not be difficult to turn your efforts elsewhere, to your community, to your church, to those whom you come in contact with, in your work, in your friendships. It is the family that must be served as you serve God. You must serve selflessly. You must give all, that you might be given much in return. In this way, you will learn discipline. You will learn love. You will learn obedience. You will learn the beauty of humility. Dear children, serve your family members. Once you have completed these tasks, strive harder. Try harder, for never can you perfect yourself until the day that you stand in your Father's kingdom. There is always more you can do. There is much that can be done.

Pray! Pray! Pray! Prayer is the way that you will learn what is right. Prayer is the way that you will be strengthened. It is the way that you will know the will of God. Prayer is a most valuable gift. It is without measure. Dear children, through prayer God speaks to each one of you, to your hearts, to your minds. In the silence within you, He speaks to you. He whispers to you all that He desires of you. Pray always! Pray when you are joyful. Pray when you are sorrowful. Pray when you do not feel like praying and pray that God will place a love for prayer in your heart at these times. Know that the more you pray, the easier you will find it to be.

Serve your family. Serve your church and your community. Serve all those who come into your life, for they are reflections of God. God has placed His children in your care. He has reached out to you and offered to you a role in the most beautiful salvation of the world. Jesus Christ came that all might be redeemed, that all might be saved, that all might exist in the most beautiful place that God has prepared for us. He invites you, through His messenger, to go and to be truly His shepherds leading His sheep. Our Lord is present and alive in this world. He is more real and more present than many, many things.

Dear ones, it is good for you to do all that you do in your life. It is good for you to live a life that is abundant and joyful, but do not fail to see our Lord Who exists with you, Who walks with you, Who assists you, Who comforts you, Who loves and sorrows with you. Dear ones, this is the way to live a life that is worth living, to live it with the full memory that God is with you, to live it with full obedience to that which He has called you to do, and to live it with full gratitude for all He has blessed you with.

Dear children, I invite you to say yes to what God has asked of you. Though it may seem difficult, insurmountable, I tell this is not so. God has given to you the assistance of all of the heavens. He has sent to you His Most Holy Spirit that you might be filled with the gifts of courage, of wisdom, of knowledge and truth, a desire to do that which is right, and a reverence for all that is holy. You have been given all that you need. You have your homes and your families to provide love for you, that you might see the love of God and desire to emulate it. You have been given the Church to be your leader, your teacher, to be your master while here, for the Church is as Christ is. Dear children, you have been given all things good, the gifts of prayer, of your sacraments- the gift without measure that God pours into your life each day in simple ways, gifts so often overlooked.

Above all else, my dear children, desire to serve and continue to persevere in service. Do not fear failure, for God does not punish those who fail, but He desires that those who fail would turn to Him, ask for forgiveness, and be received with open arms. No father rejects a child. No mother turns away her little ones. Our Father in Heaven will never reject you. Our Father in Heaven will never turn you away. No matter how many times you fall, He is with you. He sends to you all assistance and all aid, that you might walk closer to Him.

Even in His passion on the road to Golgotha, our Lord did fall. He fell and He did not remain fallen but stood again, and continued on His road. In this, He has shown you that to fall is not to err. To fall, and to stay without desire to repent, without love in your heart, filled with anger and bitterness, this is a grave, grave error. Rather I tell you, when you do fail in this, pray to God. Pray fully with your heart. Beg Him to give you all mercies, and all graces, and all compassion, and know that it will be poured forth upon you more fully, more beautifully, more perfectly than you can imagine. Dear ones, our Lord does not expect perfection from you. He desires your obedience. He desires your love. He desires your commitment to serve Him.

Dear children, I too come as a servant. I come with the words of the Father upon my lips, that you might be taught, that you might be led, that you might be shown the way. I come to you pointing to the Christ, as I have done many times, as I shall always do. I lead you before His cross. I place you there in my own prayers and I place you before our Father in Heaven. I desire to serve God and I desire that you would serve as well, for He alone should be glorified among all things. He alone is goodness.

Dear ones, be encouraged. I tell you this again and again, for this world is filled with that which would discourage you. Know that Christ is alive. Know that He is risen. What a joy this is! If you were to mediate upon this each day, what joy you would have in your life! He is risen. He waits for you. He calls to you. He reaches out to you and invites you to participate fully in the great mystery of His love, the mystery of redemption.

Dear ones, serve God. Serve God that all might know what He has done for them. God came to save all people. He desires that all would know Him, that all would call Him, 'Lord'. Dear ones, with your commitment you make this possible, as you go, and you make ready the fields that He might sow the seeds of faith among the hearts of His people.

Dear children, know that I too, am with you. I am your mother, and I will continue to come to you so long as the Lord permits me to come. Know that this grace has made many, many, many blessings possible. Thank God for this grace you have received. I go before Him with all of your prayers, with all of your intentions, and I intercede on your behalf. I give to you the blessing of a mother who cares for you, who loves you as her own child, her own little ones. Dear children, united with our Lord, many, many great things are possible. Unite yourself to God. Bind yourself to His most beautiful Sacred Heart, that in all things and in all times, He might be glorified!

Dear children, I bless you and I pray that God will walk with you always, that you would know Him, love Him, and serve Him each day of your life. May His will become your will. May you lift all that you have to Him, and may you be grateful for the great blessings He has poured forth into your lives.

October 1999

Mary:

My dear little ones, may God be ever present with you. Know that I come bearing His graces, His blessings, the fruit of His goodness. Know that I come in His name as His messenger to bring to you a message of peace, a message of hope, and a message of love.

Dear little ones, you are so in need of peace. Your world, it hungers for peace. Peace is essential. There must be peace! In your world, peace is defined very differently than it is in the eyes of God. In your world, you seek peace that you might all strive to do that which you will with the freedom to seek your own desires, your own needs, all that you desire, without fear of violence, without fear of suppression. Peace, in this world, is a fragile thing. It is fleeting. It is imperfect. Peace, in this world, is a means to self love, a means to envy, a means to seeking that which one desires above all else, even at the expense of all others. When the world speaks of peace, it speaks of a time of selfishness, of freedom to choose what is good only for oneself.

I tell you that the peace of God, it is a much greater thing, for unlike the peace that you know in this world, the peace of God is a joy. It is a perfect joy! The peace that God desires to extend to you, to pour forth upon you and bless you with, is a peace that is also a freedom, but a greater freedom. It is the freedom for you, with your own will, with your own heart, with your own mind, created individually by God Who loves you more than all of creation, it is the freedom for you to use these things to choose to serve. It is the freedom to choose to put the will of God, the needs of others, above your own, above your desires, above your wants and your cares. The peace of God is a joy, for when you live in His peace you live with great humility and awe for the wonderful blessings He has put into your life, and a love for your fellow man. The peace of God is perfect. It is unfailing. The peace of God is most beautiful. When you live in the peace of God, you live to serve. You seek to know God through prayer. It is to know God through prayer, through the Church, through the Sacraments, through one another. When you live in His peace, you seek to obey. You live in humility. You live with a simple life, a simple desire to be an instrument of God. The peace that the world offers, it is not lasting. It is empty and it is shallow, but the peace that God extends to you, the peace that He brings, the peace that He sends me with, is a peace that, truly, will fill you and free you in ways that you have not known before.

The world enslaves my little children. The world teaches my children that they are not free, that they must follow their own desires, that they are no greater than that of the nature of an animal. I tell you, this is not so, for God has raised you up above all else. He has created you in His Own image. Into you, He has breathed His Own life, that you might have an eternal soul, a soul that will live and reside in His glory and in His love for always.

Dear little ones, do not believe that which the world has told you. Do not allow the world to discourage you, to take away your hope, to give to you false peace. I tell you, all that you know here is passing. All that you see, it is temporal. In God, all things exist in perfection. His only desire is to love His children, to be with His children, to lead and to guide His children, that they might join Him in the home He has prepared.

Dear little ones, strive to have His peace in your life. It is the peace that is acquired through prayer, through much prayer. Dear little ones, as you pray you intimately come into the presence of God. He fills your own heart and your own soul. He heals the wounds that you have acquired in this world. He breathes into you new life and new strength. He gives to you the power of the Holy Spirit that you might have wisdom, grace, courage, a boldness in your faith, and a deep gratitude for the beautiful gifts God has given to you. When you live in His peace and accept the gift of His peace, you will know tremendous joy, you will know tremendous love, and you will not have a day pass in which you do not see the hand of God working in your life.

I come to you often, extending the peace of Christ. I speak these words to you that you might hear and understand that this peace that I speak of is not a peace that is temporal. It is not a peace that will fail. Rather, it is the perfect expression of God's love for you, for it is enduring, it is eternal, and it will free you from all things that in your own individual hearts, in your own wills, in your own desires, with your own mind that God Himself shaped and molded, that you might have the freedom to choose to love.

To love is a choice. It is not something that comes easily. It is not something that comes without crosses to bear, but I tell you, if you should suffer your crosses with patience, if you desire to love in all things even when it is most difficult, God will be with you to strengthen you. He will not abandon you. He will not leave you. Rather, He will be glorified through your actions and He, in His perfect love, in His tremendous majesty, will glorify you.

Dear ones, know that God has lifted you up. He has raised you above all things. He has loved you to the point of dying and rising for your own salvation, that He might be eternally with you. The love that God has for you is without measure. The graces that He desires to pour upon you, they are unimaginable! Open your hearts to His peace, that you might receive this gift, that you might live a life of humility, obedience, and service, and that your eyes might be truly unveiled, you may not be blinded by the lies which the world has told you, but you might see that you are truly a most beautiful creation of God, destined to serve Him, to give Him glory, to know Him, to love Him, and to be loved by Him.

Dear little ones, I come to you extending my motherly blessing. I offer the peace of Christ to you. I bring to you the graces of God. Know that I continue to pray for you and intercede on your behalf. I thank you for the prayers that you have offered for my intentions. I ask you to continue to pray, for with prayer many graces are possible and the peace of God, not the peace of man, will fill this earth. God's peace will triumph and all of creation shall call Him Lord. Continue to pray. Know that your prayers are most beautiful. They are a great, great gift and they are most necessary.

Dear children, I bless you in the name of God and I offer to you the peace of Christ. May you live in His mercy and in His graces always. Know that I am with you.

November 1999

Mary:

My dear little children, peace be with you all. Know that I come to you as a mother, as a counselor, and an advocate. Know that I intercede on your behalf constantly before our Father in Heaven, offering to Him each of you as beautiful roses, as gifts, for His children are great in His eyes and He loves you without end.

Dear little ones, I invite you to accept God's love, His healing, and His forgiveness. Our Lord in Heaven loves you so dearly, He reaches out to you. At every turn, at every chance, every day, in every moment, He reaches out to you. Through the faith He has planted in your hearts, through the friends and family He has given to you to be your support, to be your friends, through the Church that is your strength and your life, and His sacraments that do give you life and help you to live each day with the Spirit of God, within you, around you, and pouring forth from you. Dear little ones, our Lord reaches out to you without ceasing. He pours forth all blessings and all graces, all things that are good, that you might embrace Him, that you might embrace His will, that you might do as He has asked you to do, that you might love Him, love your neighbor, and love yourself as He does love.

Dear little ones, our Lord will never tire of coming to you, to find you, to seek you out, to reach His hands out to you and offer to you the greatest of gifts, salvation, and life with Him. Dear little ones, He has poured many blessings upon you. He has given to you blessings of the spirit, of the mind, of the body, of the soul. Dear little ones, He provides all that you need. His providence is good. Oftentimes those things that are so good, that He has provided, do distract you. They become, for you, stumbling blocks in your faith, in your prayer, in your life with God. Oftentimes in life, when you find yourself disappointed, failed, hurt, and angry, you turn away from the God Who has provided to you such graces, such innumerable graces, and the ability to forgive, and to love, and to move, and grow with Him.

Dear ones, I invite you today, to place in God's hands all things that keep you from His love. Know that it is never God Who turns His love from His people. He will never turn His face from you. He will never reject you. He will never offer to you anything less than His warmest embrace, the embrace of a father to a child. It is in your pain and in your sufferings, in the hardships of your life, that oftentimes, you become distracted and lost. You turn your faces away from God and you find yourself struggling, struggling desperately with those things in life that are trials and tribulations. I ask you, this day, rather than go and live and do as you can do, struggling alone, embrace God. Invite Him to walk for you when you cannot walk, to talk for you when you have no words, to love for you when you cannot feel, to be your very hands and your feet, your eyes, and your ears, to be all that you are, for truly, by placing yourself so completely in the trust of God, you will find healing and strength. You will find in yourself the ability to forgive, the ability to love, the ability to live a life of joy even amidst troubles and trials.

Dear ones, the Lord is a God of healing. He came to this earth to teach, to heal, and to bless. How many He healed! How many sick, how many blind, how many poor and orphaned did He aid! Our Lord is a God Who loves you as you are. He is a God Who desires to provide all things for you. He concerns Himself with all that concerns you, from the smallest of worries to the greatest of trials. There is nothing that you can take to God that He will not accept and embrace. There is nothing He will not assist you with. Come before Him with all of your faults, with all of your needs, with all of your trials. Place in His hands your anger, your fears, your frustrations, and hurts, for it is these things that keep you from fully participating in the life of joy that God has given to you, that He has offered to you. Allow Him to take upon Himself your hurts and your pains as He took upon Himself the sins of the world. God did not design you to live a life of sorrow, of worry, of anxiety. He did not desire that you would live in a way that causes pain, in a way that causes you to be far from Him. Rather, He desires that you live in hope, live in joy, in His innumerable blessings.

Place yourself entirely in His care. Have the trust in your hearts that He will provide for you as any father provides for his children. He will not abandon you. He will not forsake you. He will lift you up and make you holy. He will raise you up. Just as He raised up His beloved Son, our Lord and Redeemer, the Father in Heaven raises you up too, for Christ took upon himself all that is unholy, all that is dark, all that is death, that you might live in life, in holiness, in joy, and in light.

Dear little ones, I recommend to you that you do this through prayer. I urge you to pray. The more you pray, the stronger you will become, for God gives His strength to His people. Dear little ones, when you cannot find the words, pray in silence, pray with your heart, pray with all that you feel and all that you know. Give to God all of your trials, all of your joys. Never cease to pray. Your prayers are great. Your prayers are most precious to our Lord. When you pray, the Lord, He communes with you. He instructs you. He inspires you. He leads you. Listen for His voice in your life through those He has sent to be leaders, through those He has sent to be friends, through the Church and your priests, through the sacraments He has given you, and the gifts of love He has placed in your life. He speaks to you loudly. He speaks to you plainly. Hear His words. Follow them, for they are a comfort and a joy to His people, an encouragement, a lifting up of the spirit and a source of great joy. Dear ones, entrust yourselves completely to God. Place in His hands all things and begin to live the life of hope and the life of joy He has designed for you.

My dear little ones, pray! Pray always without ceasing. Thank you for responding to my request for prayer. Continue to pray for you brothers and sisters in Christ, for prayer is such a gift and makes so many graces possible. Know that I bless you as your mother. Know that I come to you to deliver the good news that God is love and that you are His most precious children! Follow His way. Live in His light and know that He is with you.

December 1999

Mary:

My dear little ones, peace be with you. I greet you with joy, for this is a joyful season, a season of hope, a season of renewal, a season during which you remember the birth of our Savior. You celebrate this and remember that He came into the world as a meek child. He Who would be King of Kings and Lord of Lords, He Who would be the salvation of all, came to earth with such humility, such obedience, such beautiful, perfect love for you. Rejoice in this! Celebrate with the choirs of Angels and the Saints of Heaven. Know that I come to you in a special way with the blessings of the Infant Christ.

Dear ones, I see fit to remind you at this time of year, when you meditate upon His nativity, to be as little children when you come before your Father in Heaven. To be as little children is to be meek, to be humble, to be filled with a contrite heart and a desire to love, to know, and to grow. Do not come before God in fear, do not come before Him with anger, do not come before Him with anxiety- these things should not cross your mind. If you truly hoped in the Lord, you would not let these things stay in your mind for a moment but dismiss them as quickly as they come into your mind. Your heart would be filled with gladness and joy, for you would know that the Father in Heaven takes care of you as He cares for no other creation on earth. You would have no anxiety and no worry. You would have no fear, for not even death itself can overcome you. There would be no need for you to feel anything but a great peace and a great joy before Him. Come before Him, as little children come before their father, before their mother. With trusting eyes and a trusting heart, they reach out to them, imploring their love, desiring their assistance.

My little ones, children have the purest of hearts. They have no need, no desire, no want for material goods other than that which is provided to them by their mother and father, who are to them all of the world. I ask you to do the same. Have no need for material goods, for the wants of this world, for all of those things that can distract you here, but rather, have need for all that the Father provides to you. Look to Him as the Father Who is all good things. Look to Him as the One Who provides all that you need, trustingly, with the knowledge that He will give to you all that is good, that He will not abandon you, that He will not forsake you, but that He will lead you into a perfect peace and a perfect unity with Him.

Be as little children. Go out into the world with a desire to love, for what little child does not desire to do good, though oftentimes they are misguided? My dear ones, you who are parents know. You understand how it is to teach a little child what is right, to walk, to grow with that little child, to see in that child the spark of faith, the spark of hope, and the spark of joy. You know that in their eyes you can do no wrong. You are unfailing. It is the same with God. He is unfailing. He alone is perfection. Though you will make many mistakes in your life, God will never, ever, err. He is perfect love. All that He does comes from His love. All that He is, is love. All that shall ever be through Him, is love.

Dear little ones, reflect on the birth of Christ. Reflect on how it is that He came into this world as a helpless infant born to a simple woman, given to all of the world in a place unknown, at a time unknown. The King of All Nations came into the world, not crowned and clothed in royal garb, but swaddled in mere cloth, lying in a place where animals fed. Dear ones, He was born to parents who, like you, loved Him, love Him still, desire for Him all good things. I walked with Him, and I taught Him. I showed Him the love of God. I taught Him to obey, to be meek and to be humble, to follow the law of God and subject Himself to it, for God His Father, your Father, He is with you. He requires so very little of you, only that you turn to Him with love, that you continue to do all that you do with love, and that in your failures you come and reconcile before Him. I raised the Christ Child as my own little boy, with full knowledge that He was the Son of God, the Son of the Most High, and when I beheld my own infant Son, I looked into the eyes of my own Savior, my own Redeemer, and I worshiped and adored Him.

Dear ones, do worship and adore the Christ Child this day, and always, in your heart! Keep Him in your heart. Invite the Lord into your life. Be as He was, meek and humble, long-suffering and kind, patient among tribulations, desiring all that is good, coming in a way that is more beautiful than that of splendor, than that of riches, than that which is known to this world of materialism that is like a plague on this earth. Come in simplicity to the Lord. Do not bother, do not bother with anxieties. Do not let worries encompass you. Do not let all things, all things that trouble you, envelop your soul, depress your spirit, keep you from the Father in Heaven, but rejoice this day! Give all things to Him and let go of them. Place them in His care and let Him work through you, work in your life, change you and mold you into that which He desires you to be, His perfect creation, a model of His love, and an image of His Own heart.

Dear little ones, I ask you in a special way today, to pray for those who do not know my Son as you know Him, for those who have not seen His love and mercy in their life, who have turned their faces away, for they desire not to know Him as you have known Him, as you have been gifted to know Him. God has gifted you with faith. He has given to you the most precious of all things, for a life lived without faith, it is no life at all. This is a season for you of hope, but for many it is not a season of hope, for they do not know that the Christ Who is salvation, Who is redemption, awaits them, beckons to them, calls to them, and desires their love, for they are loved. All people of God are loved and nothing you can do, not by your own will, not by any deed, not by any word, can remove the love of God from you, for you will be loved until the end of time.

You will be loved for all ages, for God has created you as His own children. What father forsakes his son? What mother abandons a child? Know the Lord our God is goodness and truth and beauty, and He is with you all the days of your life. Praise Him. Glorify His name. Be as the Christ Child. Be an example and a light of holiness in this world. Be a beacon in the darkness, that those who have not had the gift of faith that you have received, the hope that you embrace in this season of joy, might see the light of Christ through you and might embrace Him with the fullness of their hearts.

January 2000

Mary:

My dear little children, it is good to be with you this day. I offer you up as perfect gifts to the Father that He might see you for what you are, His little children, who do love Him, who persevere in their trials and tribulations, who seek to know Him better and to serve Him more each day. Be as little children, my little ones. Be as little children. Find God in all that you are, and you will be blessed. Thank Him and praise Him, for He is with you.

My dear ones, often you have heard me tell you to live with joy. I have told you that God has designed you to live joyfully, to live peacefully, to live an abundant life in Him. Dear little ones, you have been given so much. You have been blessed, truly blessed, with the gifts of faith, of hope, of a life lived in God. These things are irreplaceable. They are great gifts. They cannot be forsaken, cannot be given up, for once you have faith in God, once you come to the realization that He is real, that He is alive in your heart and in your life, that He works, truly works, with you and in you, you cannot take back your ignorance. You cannot desire not to know, for once you have come to know Him, always you will see His face in your life, always you will see His works, always you will see His miracles, His graces, His mercies. Never can you turn your face to darkness once in light, when blinded by the goodness of His love, the Son of His love, the Son of His Own being Who came down from the heavens that He might become one of us, to live and to die for us, and to be resurrected for us. Once you have known the light of God, you cannot go back to your old ways. You cannot forsake this life.

My dear children, I invite you to embrace your Christian life. I invite you to embrace it with your entire being. Do not be afraid of what God calls you to do. Do not seek to know His will in matters that are not of Him. Do not think that you can figure in your own minds what it is that He desires for you, for I tell you that what He has designed for you is far beyond your imaginings, far beyond what you can know. Do not decide that you shall determine His will. Do not think that with all of the effort in the world, you can design a path better for yourselves, for God, Who is all goodness, desires great things for you, and He alone, Who is perfect and Who is all joy, can give you joy and freedom as you cannot know!

Dear little ones, know that alone you can accomplish only tiny, tiny, good things, but with God and in God, you can accomplish the greatest of miracles! God has been alive in His people. He has changed the world through His little ones who are humble, who are meek, who alone can accomplish the tiniest of things. My dear ones, God Who is with you has parted the greatest seas, has walked upon water, has cured all illnesses, and brought great joy and love to this world. Through His Son, our Lord, He has brought the mercies of mercy. He has brought freedom from the chains that bind you to this earth, from sin and from death. I invite you to open your hearts to Him, to ask Him to come and to reveal His will, to reveal all that He has to give to you.

Dear children, you can do nothing without God. You can do no good, for He is the source of goodness, and without Him you will falter, for it is the fallen nature of man that keeps him from perfection. My dear ones, God has designed you to be perfected and He desires to perfect you. Open your hearts to Him. Think nothing for yourselves, for you need not. Worry nothing for yourselves, for you need not. Do nothing on your own, for you need not. Simply, each day, offer your hearts and your minds, your bodies and your souls, your family, your work, your loves, to Him, your sorrows too, your trials. Give all to Him that is His, for He has given you all that you are. He has made you. Every one of you are His children. Each one of you has been called to a mission in Him. He alone knows your heart as no other. He alone knows what He has designed you for. Truly, all men are called to serve, for it is in this service that God is glorified. It is in His little ones that He moves in this world, that He changes it, that He forms it, that He makes bright what was dark, and good what was evil.

Dear children, be His messengers. Be His helpmates. Do all that you can do for Him. Ask Him to come into your hearts and into your lives. Ask Him to guide your hands, to lead your feet, to be in your heart, to be on your tongue, and in your ears, and in your eyes, and in all places in you, that you might see Him in your life and be joyful, that you might hear His words and learn the way to salvation, that you might think with the mind He has given to you of all good things He has given, that you might walk on His road and use your hands to reach out to your brothers and sisters in Christ.

Dear ones, God is with you. As truly as I say this to you now, as truly as I am present with you, God is with you. He remains veiled from you, behind the hidden cloth, behind all that you can see. Dear ones, I tell you, that which you see and that which you experience, it is not so real as the love of God is real in this world. What you see, it is simply a reflection of His goodness. It is but a reflection of the gifts He has in store for you. You cannot know what great things

God desires for you. You cannot know the depth of His love, nor the ends of His mercy, for He is all mercy and all love and all joy.

And so, I come to you today, my children, and I invite you, I implore you, to accept the Word of God, to accept what He has called you to do. I have often counseled you and I have taught you on His Word, and I have asked you to do nothing that is different from what you have already been told, what you have known since Jesus Christ, Himself, walked upon this earth, that which has been handed down from father to son for all these generations. Love God. Love your neighbor. Love through service. Love through giving. Love through sacrifice. Love through patience. Love through kindness. Love through peace. These are the words that Christ has given to you. This was His life, a life of obedience, a life of joy, a life of sacrifice, and ultimately a glorified life, as you too will be glorified. Jesus asks you to die to your own wills, to your own desires, to die to that which you have wanted for yourself, that He might enter into you, resurrect your heart and your soul and your will, and make in you a new creation, a creation designed in Him, perfected in Him.

Dear ones, this life I speak of is one of such promise, of such goodness. It is the way to truly know peace and joy. So many in this world reject the life that God offers to them, for they have found happiness elsewhere, but I tell you, you do not know happiness, until you know the Lord. You do not know joy, until you act in the Lord. You do not know hope, until you trust in the Lord. Place all that you are in His hands. Know that He loves you with such tremendous love as you shall not know, until you meet Him face to face and see the love of a father as to a son.

My children, I come to you these many months that you might know this, and still I remind you, for never can you be told enough, as a child cannot be told enough of the love of his parent. My little ones, God loves you! He desires you. He calls out to you, and He reaches to you. He invites you to do His will, to be His servants, to be His flock, to be leaders and teachers, to be healers and friends, ultimately, to lead all of the people of the world to His love that all might call Him, 'Lord' and every knee shall bend at His name.

Dear ones, this is what we, as His people, strive to accomplish through Him. Know that through Him such good things as this can come about. Know that through Him all things are possible. I invite you simply to let go of all that keeps you from Him, to reach out to Him and accept the graces He pours into you, and to act as He would have you act, in perfect obedience, in perfect love, and in perfect patience and joy. Dear ones, these virtues I speak of are great, and I do tell you that much good will be accomplished in this world, much good, if all of my children would come to heed this message, to take it into their hearts and to live it.

Live what I have told you! Each day, live what I have told you! I know the difficulties in this. I know it is difficult, as our Lord God in Heaven knows the difficulties you face. I ask you each day as your mother to try, to persevere, to persist in goodness, for this is what is asked of you. This is all that is required of you. God desires only that you persist, that when fallen you reconcile unto Him and try again, for never shall He give up on you, never shall He leave you abandoned. Do not abandon Him but come back to Him. Continue to come back to Him always!

Dear ones, be hopeful. I encourage you in your walk of faith. I ask you to continue each day, no matter what difficulties you face, no matter how hard it is, to follow the Lord, to seek Him out, to do as I have asked you to do, that which you have been asked to do through the life of Christ. My dear children, I bless you and I pray that God Who is holy, Who is all goodness and all mercy, will be with you, that He might show you the way, that He might lead you, that He might make you, truly, shepherds among His sheep. Dear ones, bow your heads and pray that He might bless you. Thank Him! Glorify Him! Know that He is with you and that He is love. His love for you is without end and He is ever with you, as I, your mother, am with you.

February 2000

Mary:

My dear little ones, peace be with you. May God bless you with all of His graces, with all of the love which He does desire to pour down upon you. Know that I am with you as your mother. Know that I come, and I bless you with my motherly blessing.

Dear ones, I ask you to examine your own hearts, to examine your faith, to examine your lives. Dear children, what is the nature of your faith? Little ones, know that your faith must be strong. It must be true. It must be unyielding. Jesus desires for you to have faith in Him, a full faith, a complete faith. You do not *think* that Jesus is your Lord and Savior, you *believe* that He is, so I ask you: what is the difference between your thought and your belief? Thought is arbitrary. It comes and goes. It is fleeting. Your thoughts change as with the wind, each day, a new thought, each experience, a new thought. Belief is steadfast. It does not change. It is expressed in your inmost being. It is expressed in all that you do, in all that you are, in all that you say. Faith is what you base your life upon. It is your rock. It is your truth. It is the very most precious thing that you possess! Faith cannot be separated from you. Faith cannot be forsaken. Faith cannot be given up once you have seen the great glory God has to give to you, for you cannot deny that He is there and that He loves you. That is faith, my children!

I ask you for a deepening of faith, for a faith of trust, for a faith of hope. Many of my children will acknowledge that our Lord is with them, and yet they do not believe He has the power to deliver them from their sorrows, from injustice, from trial, from illness, from all sufferings, both temporal and spiritual. Dear ones, I tell you, our Lord in Heaven has the power to do all these things. He has the power to change you, to move you, to mold you even as you are, even in your sinfulness.

My little ones, let your faith be expressed in your life in a new way, this day. Do not treat your faith as a thought, coming and going, to be expressed at some times and not at others, to change as the days change, but rather make it your life, your mission, your very heart. I ask you to express your faith in God, to worship and adore Him in the ordinariness of your lives. You do not need to do great things. You do not need to perform miracles and signs. God asks of you what He has given to you, gentleness and peace, mercy and compassion, kindness and love, truth, humility, obedience, and forgiveness. Dear ones, it is in your example, your example of simplicity, that you are a model of faith, and that faith is spread from person to person as lights in this world of darkness.

Dear children, not one of you has no hope, has nothing they can offer, has nothing to give. You have been gifted by God in ways you cannot fathom, you cannot understand. He has reached out to you. He has pulled you up from your despair. He has delivered you from your sorrows. He has healed you from all afflictions, and He desires your love, your obedience.

Dear ones, when Christ walked upon this earth, He commissioned disciples. He made fishermen, tax collectors, simple men, His followers, those who would spread the good news that He was risen, that He lives. From a simple man, the most holy and most humble and most obedient man, all of your faith, all of your gifts, are attributed. Dear little ones, know that this simple and humble man does call to you, does ask you too to follow Him, to be His disciples. As He called men from all stations of life, He does call you. He asks you to serve Him as they did serve, with the fullness of your hearts, each with your own talents, with your own abilities, with the graces God has given to you, and the gifts that He has given, that you might offer them to the world.

Dear ones, my Son told a story. He spoke of a man who was given much and hid that richness away so that it might be saved, and a man who was given little but He multiplied that manyfold. Which, my dear children, is the greater? I tell you, no matter what you have been given, if you live in humility, if you live in obedience, if you live with love in your hearts, you will multiply your gifts manyfold and the graces you will bring to this earth cannot be measured.

Dear children, Christ Who is our life and our love, Who is our savior and our redeemer, He calls to you. He calls from the right hand of the Father in His glory. He calls from His tabernacles, from His altars where He is consecrated, brought forth anew, where His most beautiful passion is renewed, is re-lived, that you might experience the healing salvation of His life and love, His body and blood. This is your meal of life, it is your ultimate, your greatest, your most holy, your most perfect, all joy, all goodness! I cannot tell you how blessed you are to have the Most Holy Eucharist as your spiritual food.

Dear children, know that God does feed you with His love and mercy. He nourishes you with His goodness and compassion. He encourages you with all that He gives to you. Turn then, all of your gifts, all of your talents, to Him. Turn then, your own lives, even in their ordinariness, to Him. Turn then, your hearts to Him, for what a gift it is to receive the heart of a child freely given to Him out of love, out of a knowledge that He alone is God. No greater thing can you do to worship Him than to give your life to Him, for you lay your life before Him as a servant to a master. Dear ones, know that God Himself lays all that has before you, even His Own life, His Own body, all that He is, and all that He ever shall be.

Dear ones, I ask you to join me in my mission to bring conversion to the entire world through the practices of love, faith, hope. Dear children, what great gifts these are. How you can be a light in the hearts of many! How you can be a joy in this world! Dear children, join me as I call all of my little ones home to God Who does desire them as a shepherd Who calls to His flock, as He Who goes to find the lost sheep, He Who is all goodness. My little children, join me, then! Pray often and fervently. Make your lives a prayer that not only your words, but your thoughts and your actions might be prayer, and that all this might be expressed through your steadfast faith. Build your lives upon faith. Do all things for God's glory and His goodness. Know that you will be most pleasing to Him and through your sacrifice. Through your gifts, many souls will come to know the mercy of God.

Dear children, be grateful. Know how God has blessed you, how He has touched you, how He has reached out to you with His own body and blood, with His church, with His gifts and graces. Know that He has come to you in a most precious way, and He calls to you to come to Him, to be with Him, to live in His love as His disciples, as His teachers, as His healers. Open your hearts then, and let Him pour His love into them. Let Him give to you all graces. Pray that you might know His will and that His will might be done through you. This is the greatest thing you can give, the fullness of your being.

Dear children, may God's will always be done through you. May you have every grace and every blessing, and may He find favor in you. I bless you with my motherly blessing and I ask you to pray. Continue to pray. Pray without ceasing, for it is so needed upon this earth. Dear children, be joyful! Praise God and thank Him and know that I am with you.

March 2000

Mary:

My dear little ones, know that I come, and I bless you in the name of the Father Who sends me, the Son Who is Redeemer, and the Holy Spirit Who works in this world through His children. Dear people, know that I am with you as your mother, for God has given me to you, to lead you to holiness, to lead you on His road of faith, a journey that is oftentimes difficult, but a journey that can be accomplished through the grace of God.

Dear ones, I speak to your hearts. I come to you and ask you to dedicate your lives and your hearts to God our Father in Heaven.

He has sent me that I might assist you, that I might give you good counsel, that I might advise you. Dear children, turn your hearts to Him. Live what He has commanded you. Live the truth that He has given to you. I ask this as your mother, as every good mother wants what is good for her children. My dear ones, know that I am as ever with you. Know that God gives His graces and mercies to you. Thank Him, for He is goodness, and He is love. He gives to you all that you have out of His mercy, out of His goodness. He is joy! Live life joyfully, for He has given it to you. Dear ones, have no fear, for He is with you.

I ask you, commit yourselves to the Lord this day. Our God in Heaven does not desire His people to do anything but give themselves to Him, that He might work through them and in them. He does not expect you to be without fault. He knows your every weakness as He knows all of your strengths. He knows every part of you, your innermost being, that which He has created. Dear ones, He does not expect you to be without fault, but He does desire from you your consecrated will. Give your will to Him that all that you might do might glorify Him. When you struggle, give to Him your sorrows and your troubles, give to Him your trials. In joy, give Him that too, for He is a God that rejoices in His people.

Dear Children, commit your wills to the Father. Give all that you have to Him and let Him work through you. You need not do His work alone, for He sends His Holy Spirit to be your guide and your shepherd, to be your inspiration and your knowledge, to give you wisdom and courage in faith, that you might lead all of His people to goodness and to light. Dear Children, all that I have asked of you is this: give all that you have to God in Heaven. Each day, dedicate your heart to Him. Ask Him to work in your life, to do His will through you. You need do nothing but allow Him to work through you. Place your trust fully in Him and know that much good can be accomplished through you.

Dear little ones, you are precious to God in Heaven. For you, He has given everything. For you, He has given His Own Son, His Own body, His death, His resurrection, His life eternal. For you, He has given all things. You are so precious to Him, so dear. You are His little children, and He is with you. As a father guides his children, so too does our Lord in Heaven guide you, so too does He shepherd you. Place your trust in Him. You need fear nothing, for with God you have no enemy. No power can stand against you, for God is love and He is truth, and He shall prevail above all.

Dear little ones, let me speak to you today, words of encouragement. Let me speak to you today, about the will of God. Know that His will perseveres. Know that His will prevails above all darkness, above all evil, above all sin. The will of God is perfect, and it is holy. The sanctity of His will is great. I ask you to unite your hearts to Him, to join your will to His, that He might work through you and in you, in the most perfected way. He has designed you, dear children, to be servants, to serve one another. By serving each one of you, He, our Lord, gave you everything. Upon the cross, He gave you His life. He calls you to serve your brothers and sisters, united always you are.

Dearest ones, see Him on the cross. See Him as a sign of resurrection, a sign of life, a sign of joy. Look to Him there for strength. Look to Him there, for He is with you. He comes to you as a resurrected Lord, as a suffering Lord, as a Lord Who takes upon Himself all of the sorrows and all of the joys, and life that He promises to you. Dear ones, our God in Heaven need not come to this earth for any reason but to show you that He, our Lord, loves you so tremendously that He would come and be His own creation, that He would show you the way home.

Dear children, what love and what joy is this! What goodness is this! What glory is this, that He would come and humble Himself down and be a man, a man Who walked upon the earth and taught you, showed you the way, showed you how to love. He humbled Himself to come, to be among you, to teach and to heal. He humbled Himself to be subject to your hand, to all of mankind, subject to the sins of man, to the punishments of man, to His Own crucifixion. Obedient our Lord was, even to His death. He comes now to you as a resurrected Lord as you celebrate this

Easter. I ask you during this time of Lent, when you prepare your hearts and your minds for the coming of the Lord in His glory, to reflect on the crucified Lord and unite your wills strongly to His. Only then will you know the will of God, when you give up all that is within you and offer everything to Him.

Your God in Heaven loves you. He gave to you all that He is, even to His Own life, even to His Own body. He has come to you in His most glorious Church. He has offered you Himself through the sacraments. Partake in these sacraments. Find the Lord there. Wait with Him as He struggled forty days. Spend this time in prayer. Spend this time with the Lord. Know that truly our God is glorified. His will shall prevail above all! Though you have times of darkness, also you look forward to the light. Though you will go through the darkness of death you have, to look forward, the resurrection. God is coming to you in the most miraculous and most mysterious way. He comes to you with the fullness of His being offering to you His life, His soul, His beautiful love. Accept Him during this time. Find Him in your hearts in a new way. Each day, devote your hearts to Him, devote your will to Him. Give to Him your mind, and your body, your spirit, and your soul, all that is of you, that He might give to you all in return.

Dear children, reflect on my words. See that I have come to you, bringing a message of hope and of joy. Know that God is with you, that He remains ever vigilant. Pray, dear children, pray always. I ask you to continue to pray for all of my intentions, especially for those children who do not know the mercies and the love of God. They go through the same times of darkness that you do suffer under, and yet for them, there is no light and there is no resurrection, for they fail to see the love that God gives to them. They fail to accept Jesus, the Savior and Redeemer of the world. It makes my heart sad, for I have come to lead all children to Jesus, that every name, every single child, shall be written in the Book of Life, that every tongue shall praise the Lord and every knee shall bend at the name of the Father. Dear ones, this is my prayer, and it is my hope. This is my mission upon this earth. I ask you to unite your prayers to mine, that this might become a reality.

My little ones, I give to you my motherly blessing. I pray that God will give you His peace and His joy and a beautiful sense of His love during this time when you prepare for His glorious resurrection. Dear ones, be at peace. Know that I am with you, that I intercede on your behalf to the Father, that I offer you up each day to Him, that I bring to Him all of your intentions, and I pray that His peace might be with you.

April 2000

Mary:

My dear little ones, praise be to Jesus, risen in glory! Alleluia! My dear children, I greet you this day with the blessings of a mother's heart. Know that I am with you, that I intercede on your behalf, that I protect you, that I am your advocate, that I love you most dearly. My children, worship God with all of your hearts. Praise Him with all that you do. Know that you are His dear children and His love for you is unceasing.

My little ones, I invite you this day to take on the role of instruments of God. I ask you to be His helpers, to be His little children, to be the ones who do His work, be the ones who do His will. Dear little ones, I ask you to take this into your hearts. Read the Scriptures. Dear little ones, pray. Be an example of goodness, that all of my children, all of the world, might see that God resides in you, that you are His.

My dearest children, as I have told you, you truly are the hands and the feet of Christ. You must pray. You must be an example of His goodness. Know that all look to you as His followers, that they might see God in you. Dearest little children, you are the Church of Christ. You are the ones who do His work upon the earth.

I come to ask you to increase your love for service, to increase your love for the sacraments, for the most Holy Mass and for our Lord Christ glorified in the Holy Eucharist. Dearest little ones, I ask you to increase your love for prayer, for prayer brings such graces into this world, such beautiful grace! My little ones, increase your love for one another. Serve one another as Christ served you and as He serves His Church. Increase your love for God. Worship Him. Adore Him. Give to Him all praise, all things due to Him. He alone is goodness. He is Creator. He is Lord of your hearts. Let Him be central in your life. Let all things revolve around His goodness. Know that His mercy pours forth upon you, that His goodness is ever with you, and that He desires for you a life of joy.

If you make Christ central in your life, you will find that things become much easier. Place Him in the center of your family. Consecrate yourselves to Him. Come together in family prayer. Worship together. Teach your little ones that Christ is alive and is with you. Make God central in your workplace. Do your work as Christ did His, obediently, humbly, with great joy, with a compassionate ear. Make Christ the center in your communities. Go and serve those who are in need. Pray for my children that many conversions would be made possible. Serve Christ in the world. Pray! Pray! Pray!

Dear little ones, when God is central in your heart, when He is central in all that you do, you will find that you see things through the eyes of faith. You will find that you see things as God sees them. You will see His little children as blessings, as precious gifts of the Father, all in need of His love. You can show them His love through your example, through what you do, through who you are, through what you say. Be an example of Christ upon this earth. Make God first in your life. You will know such joy! Such goodness awaits those who desire God, for He waits, waits patiently to lift up His arms to you, to raise you up, to bring you into His Own heart, to pour forth upon you all goodness, all grace. He offers to you His forgiveness, His joy, His peace, His love. He offers to you all that you would ever desire, should you desire to take Him into your heart. Turn your face toward Him. See Him as He suffered for you on the cross, as He died, as He was resurrected in glory and ascended to the Father where He reigns over the hearts of all mankind.

Dear children, know that the Lord is a Lord of love. I come to tell you that God loves you, that He desires you, He desires all of you. Consecrate your families to Him. Consecrate your heart to Him. Make Him central in your life and you will see many graces flow forth through you by the power of God. Entrust yourself to the Holy Spirit, that He might lead you and guide you on your journey.

Dear children, know that I do love you. Know that I ask you to continue to pray. Pray for all of those who do not yet know my Son as Lord, for they suffer from a great loneliness, a great loneliness that they have chosen for themselves, but that God does not wish for them to dwell in. Pray for those in need of conversion, for truly all people are in need of conversion each day. All people have times of doubt. All people have trials of faith. Pray for conversion that all of my children might call Jesus 'Lord', and that every knee shall bend at His name.

Dear little ones, I bless you this day with my motherly blessing. Know that I am with you. Know that I pray for you. Know that I guide you and I lead you on the path of holiness. I lead you to my Son. Dearest children, praise God, for He is with you!

May 2000

Mary:

My dear children, it is good to be with you. Know that I come to you with the blessings of the Father in Heaven, that I give to you the grace which He offers to you, if you desire to take it. Dear little children, praise Him! He is with you. He loves His people tremendously. He does not abandon you, but as a father, He shepherds you and comforts you, He cares for you and guides you.

He is your Father. He hears your prayers, and He answers them. Know that He is with you.

Dear little ones, I ask you today to recommit your lives to God, to His will. Many of my children have heard my words and they have gone, and they have tried with all of their might to do as I have asked, that which God sends me to tell you. They become discouraged. They see their efforts as futile, for they feel they have not accomplished anything. They see themselves slipping back into old habits and into old ways. Each day is the same struggle, never easier. Dear children, I tell you, there is a way to make your road easier. It is through prayer.

Through prayer God strengthens your heart. He strengthens your soul to make you a willing vessel of His will. He makes you a new creation. He fills you with His love, with His courage. The Holy Spirit descends upon you and makes you a new creation in Him. You are able to accomplish great things in His name. Pray always, dear children, especially in times of trial. When it seems you do not progress in your spiritual journey, when it seems you cannot get anything done alone, do all with God's help. Do all with God's assistance. This is how you should do all things. Entrust your needs to the Father. Entrust all of your acts to the Holy Spirit. Pray that His will might be always in your heart that He might always guide you, blessing your eyes that you might see His will, blessing your ears to hear His voice, your heart to be pure and open to His love, your hands to do His work, your feet to walk His road, and your mouth to speak His words to all people that all might call Him 'Lord'.

Dear children, prayer, it is so important! It is as essential to you as water or sun. I tell you, you cannot live without prayer! Certainly, you will crumble up and you will die inside. I do not desire this for any of my children, rather I desire for them to be filled with joy, with peace, with wonderful gifts obtained through prayer. God is waiting to pour out all of His gifts upon you if you would but ask.

Dear children, know that God does not seek for you to accomplish great things. To find favor in God, you do not need to accomplish these tasks. God finds favor in His children when they try. All of your efforts, all of your trials, all of your sufferings, if given to God in the spirit of love and charity, are worth more than any accomplishment, any gift you can give back. Truly, God desires a heart that will continue to come to Him, even in the darkest hour, even in the greatest trials. And so, I tell you, be encouraged and, in times when you feel you are accomplishing nothing, do everything with the fullness of your heart. Even when it seems impossible, even when it seems there is no way, put forth all of your effort, give all that you have to God, for it is not in the accomplishment, but in the road.

Dear children, life truly is a road. It is a journey. God has sent me to accompany you in this time, that I might teach you that which He has already taught you, that which you know, but you forget. I come to remind you and I ask you that you make each day a reminder. Each day, spend several minutes remembering, remembering that God is with you, that He loves you, that you are His, remembering that He has called you apart from all others to be a great example. He has called you in this most tremendous way, in this miraculous way. He has called you especially to be His teachers, to be His followers, to be apostles.

Remember this, dear children. Do not allow yourself to become so absorbed in that which is around you that you forget this simple truth: God Who is love, Who exists from always and to forever, is with you. He loves you. He guides you. He is your strength. He is your courage. He is your very life, for without God, no rain would fall, no sun would shine, the earth would not exist, nor would the heavens be there, the stars would certainly be extinguished, and we would die without His love. His love sustains all of creation, for it is a reflection of His goodness, of His mercy, of His compassion, and His great desire to give all that He is to His precious children.

You know His love for you is great. I have told you. You have seen it in the gifts that He gives to you through His Church, through you, each one of you, through the sacraments which He offers to you, that you might experience the fullness of His goodness, the fullness of His grace, through the way in which He speaks to each of your hearts: individually, uniquely, as He knows each one of you, creating you from the depth of darkness into His light.

Dear children, know that He is with you. It is not in accomplishing great tasks that you succeed, rather it is in doing that which God calls you to do, the tiniest and most trivial of things, the mundane struggles of everyday life, the hardships that you face, the illness, the sorrow, the deaths. These things can be offered, can be sacrificed, can be given to God, and turned from great sorrow into tremendous joy, joy that you cannot know here on earth, but joy given only from the God Whose love for you is so great, that He offers to you His Own life. Jesus came to be the example. He came to be the teacher. His life was filled with joys, was filled with great, great marvels, but also with much suffering, with much, much suffering and death. You, dear children, must follow in the same way. You must die to your own wills, to your own needs, to your own preoccupations, that you might see clearly what God calls you to do.

Know, dear children, that when you put your hearts in the hands of God, when you place yourself fully in the Holy Spirit, He is with you most, most strongly. He is with you in a way you cannot fathom, in a way you will not understand until you join Him in the place He has prepared for you. Take courage in this. Take courage. Take all that I have said into prayer. Remind yourself each day that you are blessed, blessed beyond all of creation, for you are His children and His love for you is unending.

My dear ones, I give to you today my blessing. I pray that each one of you will accept into your heart the great gifts that God will give to you through fervent prayer, through devotion to His Most Sacred Heart, and through a love for His Church and her holy sacraments. Dear ones, may His grace be always with you, may He walk with you always, and may the light of Christ be in your hearts now, and forever.

June 2000

Mary:

My dear little ones, praise be Jesus! I thank you for gathering here today. I thank you for praying as I have asked you to do and continue to ask you to do. Your prayers are most powerful, and many graces pour forth from Heaven when you pray.

Dear little ones, I would like to speak to you today about obedience. Obedience is something that is difficult for my little ones. It is difficult to submit yourself to the will of God. He has given you the freedom to choose in your life. This is a great gift. He has given you the freedom to choose to accept or reject Him, to walk this road or that, to do this thing or another. This is a great gift, for you are apart from creation in your freedom to choose. God has made all things good, and yet the birds have no option but to fly, the sparrows sing, the worms to crawl in the dirt. This is what they were created to do. They can do nothing else. But you are children of God, not just creation, but children!

What parent would force their will upon a child? Rather, you decide to allow your child to grow and to blossom as a flower with all of his natural gifts, talents, and characteristics coming forth, and using all that he has for good. In the same way, God sees you as His little children. He has planted in your hearts the seeds of faith. He has given to you the gifts of the Holy Spirit that they might guide you in your decisions. He has made for you a road to walk that is lit by His love and His goodness and the teachings that He has given to you. He sends His mother to remind you.

Dear little ones, you have been given a choice. You may choose to follow or choose not. Either way, it is your decision. God's hands are always guiding you, moving your hearts, drawing you ever nearer to Him, if you will allow it. Obedience is difficult for many. To obey is not simply to do what is asked of you, but it is to do it with love. It is to do all things for God through submission. To submit oneself to God means to give over to Him your entire will, your entire heart, all that you think and all that you feel, all that you say and all that you do. To be obedient to God, you must be willing to give up your own desires and your own will. How many children have ventured off in their own direction, only to find the wisdom of their parents was the better road!

I tell you this is the way it is with the Father. He knows the roads on which you travel. He sees the sorrows that you face. He goes through them with you, step by step, leading you by the hand. He knows your joys. He celebrates and rejoices with you, and yet He can see what you cannot see: He can see the road before you. As any father leads a child, He leads you. Trust in His wisdom. Trust that His will is the right way, is the only way, for I tell you it is only through God that you will live and find joy. Submit yourselves to Him then. Give to Him your hearts and your wills. Give to Him your families and your homes. Give to Him your jobs, your illnesses, your deaths, your trials, your hardships, your joys. All that you have, all that you have been given, give back to God.

Jesus told a story to His apostles. He said that many, many gifts come from the Father. He described gifts given to three men by a master. To each a share of riches was given. I tell you, you have been given a share of riches as well. One man hid his riches and did nothing, and another went out and multiplied those riches among many that he had much to give back in return. I ask you to examine your life. Look into your hearts. How do you give back to God for what He has given you? How have you been obedient to Him?

You cannot possibly understand the great things God has done for you. I tell you this, again and again, with joy as a mother, for I rejoice, as all of Heaven rejoices, at the mere thought of the grace and mercy of God, and yet never will you come to understand this until you stand before Him. I can speak many words and tell many stories, and none would help you to understand the depth of His love for you. It is only through obedience and prayer that you will come to understand that God's road, His way, is the only way, and it is a way that will lead you to much joy and great peace. God does not desire for you anything that is not good, for He is goodness, and He is love and therefore, can only desire love. You are His children. You are His precious ones. He protects you as a father. He guides you. He walks with you. Your God is not a distant God, but a God Who is with His children.

Dear little ones, will you not submit yourselves to Him? Gratefully ask Him to enter into your heart in a new and most beautiful way. Commit your lives to Him. Consecrate your hearts to Him. Each day, struggle to be ever nearer to Him and know that it is not you who will need to find Him, but it is He Who will find you, lift you up, and gather you into His arms. Dear little ones, praise Him, for He is good. I bless you and I pray that you will accept God in a new way today in your life, submitting to Him, joining your will to His, and asking that He be ever in your heart.

July 2000

Jesus:

My people, I Who Am Love, speak to you now. You are Mine. As I have taken you into My Own heart, I have made you My people. I have called you from all places. I have come to you. I have touched you. I have brought tremendous grace to you, that you would see and know that you are loved above all creation. I have sent to you My mother, for she has been My mouthpiece. She has been My messenger and she has spoken to you that which I have sent her to tell you.

My children, she goes to you as a messenger. I have sent her that you would know that I Am with you, that I shall never leave My people, that My hand works in your lives, that I lead you, that I call you, that I reach into you to bless you, to purify you, to fill you with My Spirit, that you might be filled with love and joy and mercy, for it is these gifts that I extend to you. It is these gifts that pour forth from My heart as blood and water to purify and renew you, as I shall renew the face of the earth. I have sent her to call you. I have sent her to mother you. Heed her words, for they are My Own. Hear her as she calls you, as she brings you to Me through prayer, through obedience, through love and mercy, that which I pour forth into her and into you, for I Am all mercy.

I come to My people for love of them. It is for love of you that I come now. My children, see that I come for you. See that I send to you every grace, every blessing, that you might be enlightened with the truth that I Am the Way, that I Am Love, that it is through Me that you shall be in eternal joy! But without Me, you shall die. Accept the grace that I give to you. Accept the life that I offer you. Listen to My mother. Heed her words, as they are mine. Be led by my Spirit, that I might change you, that I might fill you with every grace, and that you might reach to Me as I have reached to you. Oh, My children, would you not let your Christ embrace you? Come to My heart, that you might know My peace.

Mary:

Dear children, all praise be to God Who has given to you this most precious gift! I have interceded, I have begged before the throne of God that He should give to you this tremendous blessing. As your mother, I am so filled with joy that you have come to know the Lord in a way that perhaps you, and you alone, would know tonight. You do not know what you have received! Praise Him and be filled with His joy! There is nothing for me to say now, for the Master has spoken. May you be blessed, my dear ones. I am with you.

August 2000

Mary:

My dear children, I ask God's blessing upon you. I pray that He might fill you with every goodness and every mercy. I pray that He would give to you all that you need and provide for you as His children, as He has done and will continue to do.

My dear ones, often I have come to you, and I have blessed you with the blessing of the Father, with the words, 'May His peace be with you. May the peace of Christ be with you'. Often, I have told you that the peace of Christ is a peace that you cannot know, you cannot know unless He is within you, living in your very soul, unless He is the center of all of your life and activities. I have blessed you in this way, for I wish that God would send upon you His peace. Truly, when you pray for His peace, when you pray, it is given. He pours forth His peace upon you, immeasurably.

I ask you, dear children, if you have taken into your lives anything that will block the peace that He wishes to give to you from entering into your soul? I tell you, He sends you His peace as His gift. Many times, it is easy to become anxious, or worried, or scared. There are many things in life that are difficult. There are many trials to overcome. There are many sorrows to bear, and yet I tell you that would you just trust God with all that you have, with all that you are, if you would place in His hands your very being, and your family, and your life, and your faith, if you would just place in His hands your weaknesses, your strengths, your sorrows, and your joys, you would know His peace, for it is not that God does not pour His peace upon you in times of distress, but it is that you have not recognized His gift to you.

I ask you to reflect on your lives. See the ways that you have turned from God's peace, that you have instead embraced the anxiety that the world pushes upon you. There is no reason to fear. Christ Himself gave you these words: 'Do not be afraid'. God is with you. He shall be with you even until the end of your life, to the moment of your death, and He will be with you to welcome you into the place He has prepared for you. Do not be afraid. Do not be afraid! Again and again, I echo these words to you, as Jesus Himself has given them to you, has echoed them to you through His Own life and death, for He went to the cross with fearlessness and courage and the beautiful peace that He desires to bring to you.

You, each of you, have your own crosses to bear. You have your road of sorrows. You have your tribulations. Each of you must endure your own deaths: death to self, death to your desires, death to your own will, before you can enter into the life that God gives to you. When you, like Christ, follow the road of sorrows and die, you, like Christ, will be resurrected into His glory, for He desires to give to you a share in His glory, such is His mercy!

Dear children, His peace, it is a gift that He gives to you freely for love of you. He desires to calm your heart. He desires to put peace in your soul. He desires to take from you all of your pain and give you great joy, a silent joy, a joy that will make all things in life an easier load to bear. You know that your road is difficult, for you have been called to be followers of Christ and follow Him you must, through His teachings, through the miracles that He places in the world and in your life, the miracles that you will experience in your own lives, through the joys, through the triumph, and also through the persecution, through the sorrow, through the suffering, through the death. Each of you must follow this road. To follow the Master, you must walk this road. And yet, you are given the promise of resurrection, of ascension into glory, for God deems that you shall participate in His glorious resurrection, not only at the moment of your physical death when He takes you up and offers to you the gift of eternity, but each day, in each moment.

It is a difficult road to walk, but it need not be one filled with fear or mistrust. Rather, it must be filled with the absolute conviction that God, Who is love and Who is mercy, Who is goodness, Who is grace, is with you, that He shall never leave you, that never will He give to you anything but that which is good for your soul, and that which brings you closer to Him. You must be filled with the absolute conviction that your days of sorrow will end, that your hopelessness will end, that your trial will end and you, too, will know unfathomable joy!

I ask you to place your trust in God each day, to give to Him all of your fear. In this way, you open wide your heart to receive His peace. With His peace, you can come to understand His will in your life. You can come to accept the difficult road with love, even to desire that difficult road, for you will see in those trials and in those sufferings the footsteps of Christ, and you, as His people, will desire to walk in His way.

Dear children, open your hearts to God. Allow Him to be present there, that you might experience His perfect peace. I ask that He might send to you His peace, that the peace of Christ, of His sorrows, and death, and resurrection, and glory, might be with you today, and always.

September 2000

Mary:

My dear children, may the grace and the peace of God our Father in Heaven be with you now, and always. May you be blessed. May you always be children of God. Dear little ones, praise and thank Him for the good things He has bestowed upon you, for the greatness that He has shared with you, for the glory, which is His, which always shall belong to Him, but which He shares with you for love of you. Dear little ones, I am glad to be with you this day. As ever, I am glad, for God sends me to bring His message of love and hope, a message of peace and of joy. He sends me as your mother, to gather up His children, to lead them by the hand, to lead them to the Father.

Dear little ones, I ask you this day to commit yourselves to total abandonment to God. Long I have taught you to abandon yourself to Him, to trust fully in Him, and yet it remains difficult for you. I ask you to give all that you are to God without reserving anything for yourselves. Give to Him all that you are, all that you have been, and all that you will be, for He is your Father, and He desires to guide you, to lead you, to be your Lord, to be the center of your own heart. Give yourself. Give your life. Give your family. Give all that you do and all that you are to Him.

The Great Deceiver lies to the world. He leads the world to believe that God is not present, that He is not with you. So often in times of tragedy, in times of sorrow, little children of God ask, "Where is God? Where is He in this? Why does He not assist us?" I tell you truly, it is in those times when it seems that God is far, when it seems that God is not with you, in those times, it is you who do not allow Him to act.

God desires to do great things in the world, to do great things in the hearts and the minds of His children. The separation that exists between you and Heaven is a separation that need not be so great, if only you would give your will to God, if only the world would consecrate themselves, all of His children, to His Most Sacred Heart. I tell you, the joy of Heaven is that it is in giving our will to God, in saying 'yes' at our deaths, in giving our souls to Him, that we are embraced by the Father, that we are accepted and know sorrow no longer, know fear no longer, know pain no longer, but rather we are embraced in the goodness and grace that is our Father.

You who struggle in this earthly life, you find it difficult to abandon yourselves to God. God needs for you to give to Him your will before He can act in your life. He does not wish to force His children to believe, to pray, to act with goodness, charity, or kindness. God desires your will. He desires your gift of self. If the world would turn itself to God, you would see a part of Heaven here on earth. You do not know the power that you have when you pray as a gift of the will. You do not know the things that you can accomplish in God's will, for He gives to you the grace and the power to do many great things, if you would only commit yourselves to His will. This means that you should pray always and in everything, that you should live your lives each day as a prayer, each moment, through service, through love, through the joy that you find in life, in your sufferings and in your sacrifice, in all that you have, in all that you have not.

God desires you to pray in this way, but also, He desires that you would, each day, pray for Him to show you His will. You might pray for many things but, I tell you, if it is not according to His will, it is not good. God alone sees all that there is to see. He knows your very lives as you cannot know. He knows all things. He knows your soul. Many times, you will pray for things and prayers will seem to go unanswered and yet, if you would pray that you would only do the will of God, that you might accept His will and that you might embrace His will with joy, you will see that what you pray for will come about in your lives, for your will will be in line with His, His Who is perfection, His Who is glory.

Dear children, the faith that you have is a gift. You must not forget this. Your faith is a gift given to you by God. Who of you has felt lost? Who has felt alone and abandoned? All of the world will feel such things, and yet, you have been placed by God in a position of great grace, for He has filled you with the gift of faith that when you look for God and you cannot see Him, for you live cloaked in the darkness of the world, you have your faith! You know that He is present. You know that He is with you in your churches, in your sacraments, in the gifts that He gives to you, in the beautiful presence of the Most Holy Eucharist, in those He sends to you, in your praying and in your sleeping, in your living and in your dying. Dear children, your faith is a gift. To live your faith, you must resign your will to God. The difference between faith and a *living* faith is the gift of the will. You must commit yourselves, each day, to the struggles and to the trials that you will face. You must commit yourselves with love. You must decide for God.

I do not mean to say that you have not served Him, and I do not mean to discourage you in any way, for God is most pleased that you have come to gather, to pray together. This is a great thing! It is something that is so pleasing to our Father in Heaven, and it has allowed me to bring such graces as this to many places and in many hearts. God has been so pleased that you have come together as He has asked of you that He has poured forth grace as you cannot understand. Only when you stand before Him in your home that He has prepared for you, will you see the great things accomplished through His will, through your perfect love given when you gift yourself to Him. It is in this way that you are most like God, for truly this is what you strive to do: to be like Jesus Christ Who is the Redeemer, Who is and always shall be our Savior. This is what you must do. You are most like Him when you give yourselves over to Him in prayer.

Dear children, I am pleased that you have continued to heed my call to you, to come together to pray, to hear my words which I bring to you from the Father, for He has sent me, and it is His message that I give. I am pleased that you have sacrificed, that you have given over many of the things that have held you from God's love, many of the things you have chosen over God's love, and I tell you that you will know so much more joy in your lives for the gift you have given to God, the gift of yourself. You have done much changing, together as a group and individually. Many hearts have been converted. Many souls have been taken from darkness and brought into light, the light that is Christ. And yet, I implore you today to continue to move with love and abandonment toward God, for it is only in this way that you will come to know His perfect peace. My desire for you is that you would take my hand that I might lead you, as a mother, always to my Son, that I might lead you through the cross and into His resurrection.

Dear children, be at peace. Know that God is with you. Abandon yourselves to Him. Trust completely in Him. Turn your lives over to Him and you will see miracles, true miracles! God gave the gift of faith to you, as He gave it to many of those who came before and those who are now with Him, those who walked this earth and did great things, who converted many hearts by allowing God to work through them, who healed the sick, who cured the blind, the lame, the diseased, who raised the dead from their graves. They abandoned themselves to God. They placed their trust, their very life, in His hands, and though the road is difficult and though you must walk the road that Jesus walked, a road filled with pain, with thorns, you too, as the Saints of Heaven, will see the resurrection and the glory. May the peace of Christ be with you. I thank you for responding to my call to you.

October 2000

(This night the prayer group met in darkness due to a power outage. Only candles lit the Church.)

Mary:

My dear children, praise God for darkness, for it is only in the darkness that light can be seen and known! Without the dark, you cannot know light. Without sadness, what is joy? Without strife and suffering, what is peace and eternal rest? Dear ones, tonight, illustrated in this most unique way, you have learned that you, the people of God, persevere through all things. You have come before the Lord today to worship Him. You have come before Him to praise Him, to give Him glory, to see Him where He is present with you, in His Church, in His most holy body and blood, in His priest, and in His people.

My dear ones, look now. Though surrounded by darkness, how the cross is illuminated with light! Look, and I tell you, you will be practicing that which is necessary for life, for when you find yourself in darkness in life, you must look to the cross. What I tell you, I have told you many times before. I am not telling you anything that you have not learned from your priests, in the Gospels. Jesus is the Light of the World. He is the One Who brings truth and reason, Who brings joy and peace, Who brings light from darkness!

You, my children, dear children of God, you are as lights in a world of darkness. Each of you, seen through the eyes of Christ, you are a candle. You go and you spread His light. Dear children, remember the words of our savior, 'Who would hide his light beneath a bushel basket?' I encourage you today, I implore you today, I beseech you today: share the light of truth and faith that you have been given with all of the world. Make your lives a living prayer. Make your lives a light! Through your sacrifice, through your service, through all that you do, each day, as mothers and fathers, as teachers, as friends, be a witness to the truth that Christ has revealed to you.

Tonight, you have, through the Most Holy Mass, lived the passion of Christ. You have been at His Last Supper. You have participated in the gift of His body and blood, His soul and divinity, that He gives to His people freely without price. Only for love of them, does He give Himself. You have gone through the darkness, the days in the tomb, waiting in the dark for the joy of Mass, for the joy of the resurrection, for the joy of life in Christ, that which each of you strives to live, that which you are promised by God, Himself, if you choose to walk His road. Dear children, you have been there through the resurrection, through the ascension. You have seen the glory, as Christ was lifted high in the hands of His servant priest, and you have looked upon Him in adoration as once His apostles and His mother did.

Dear little ones, you have participated in a special way tonight, in the great, glorious mystery that is Christ, and I encourage you, and I invite you, and I ask you, to go and to participate in this Holy Mass, this mystery of love, every day, always! You do not know the gift that you have experienced. You do not know how Heaven sings with joy when Christ is made present in the sacrifice upon His altars. Through the darkness, dear ones, there is light. In times of trial and suffering, through the passion and the pain, there is hope and there is joy, there is resurrection and there is life. I encourage you this day, dear ones, to take this message of life into your own hearts and souls, into your homes. Live as a people of God, alive, on fire as candles of light! Live your lives each day for God and you will never, never know darkness, but the Lord Himself shall illuminate your soul with His goodness, His love, and His mercy.

Dear ones, again today I invite you to pray. I thank you for offering your prayers and sacrifices, all that you have done in my name and in my Son's name, for His most perfect, most beautiful passion, for His grace and His mercy, for all of His children. I ask you to continue to pray, to make your lives a prayer. Think, dear ones, of the great joy that is experienced in Heaven when you lift your voices in prayer. The angels rejoice and our Father is pleased, and He is most generous with His mercy.

Dear ones, I invite you to pray, to live every day as a prayer. It is with these words that I ask you to pray more each day. You do not know the power of your prayer! You cannot know the great joys that prayer brings. You cannot know the healing and the peace that will come to this world through prayer, if only my people would pray, if only they would consecrate themselves to the Sacred Heart of our Lord, to my Immaculate Heart, which will be a refuge for you, dear ones, in your darkness.

Dear children, the Father sends me to give you His love, to invite you to be His people, to ask you to come before Him in His most holy, most precious, sacrament, to come before Him and ask for His mercy, for it will be given to you freely and He waits for you there. Do not live a life of darkness but be in the light and the life that is Christ.

Dear children, may His peace be with you. May you be blessed by the Father Eternal, and know that I, your mother, am with you.

November 2000

Mary:

My dear children, I greet you today in the name of Jesus Christ, who was and always is Lord of Lords and King of Kings. Worship and adore Him! Rightly give Him praise, for He is all goodness, and He is our joy. My dear little ones, I thank you for gathering together to pray as I have asked. I thank you for coming before your Lord in the most holy and blessed sacrament of the Eucharist, for so many times I come to comfort and console Him left alone in your churches and in your tabernacles. So many times, the Angels of Heaven come to sing His praises and how filled with joy He is when His children celebrate this great and divine mystery.

Dear little ones, I bless you this day as your mother and I come to ask you to continue in your vocation of prayer. Continue to make sacrifices, dear ones, in your daily lives. So often you find it difficult to sacrifice, to give up things that are passing for the Lord, to make whole your life by making the Lord the center of your life. You find it difficult to fast. You find it difficult to commit yourselves to prayer. And yet, I remind you that many, many times, dear ones, God gives you the grace to see the beauty, the transformation, that takes place in your own hearts and souls when you pray. He has sent me to you and sent many, many gifts to you that you might see the power of prayer. Here, even in your own group, He has sent miracles through prayer that you might know that prayer is the only way. It is the way!

Dear little ones, again I ask you to pray. Go into your homes and into your families. Pray together. Persevere! I know that there are times when it seems that you are not heard and that you are not answered, and yet I tell you, if you knew with what joy the Lord accepts your prayers, you would be so peaceful and so happy, for He accepts your prayers as a beautiful gift. I ask you in this season of preparation, in this season when you look towards the advent of Christ, the coming birth of the Savior, to make sacrifices every day for the conversion of the whole world.

Dear little children, how willing you are to make sacrifices for your families, for your jobs, in day-to-day life, in all the things that God gives you in the world, and yet you find it difficult to sacrifice for Him. I tell you that these things need not be exclusive. They may exist together, for when you sacrifice for your husband or your wife, your child, or your mother, do it in the spirit of love. Do it as you would serve Christ. In this way, you serve your neighbor, and you serve the Lord and glorify His name. When in your workplaces, you are called to make sacrifices. Do so with joy that others might see your joyfulness and they might know Christ through you. When in times of trial and difficulty, when called upon to make difficult decisions and difficult choices, make these sacrifices and make these journeys to the cross with joy and peace. Entrust your souls to God the Father in Heaven, who has sent to you the Eucharistic Christ to be your comfort, to be your salvation. Place your trust fully in the Lord each day. Commit your own heart and soul, your family and all that you are to Him, and trust that He will lead you, He will guide you, He will show you His way, and you will live life filled with His peace.

My dear ones, when you pray, you will become strong in God. You will become as He desires you to be, perfect reflections of His love and His mercy. When you pray and you make sacrifices, you will become the mercy of God. He will pour His compassion upon the world. He will pour His grace upon the world through you. You are His people, and He has called you to this mission. Continue each day, to strive towards mercy and love. Continue to sacrifice and to pray, especially for conversions in the world, for there are so many who do not yet know Jesus as their Lord and it saddens my maternal heart.

Dear ones, I wish to give to the whole world the gift that God has allowed me to give to you, the gift of revealing Jesus Christ to you as He revealed Himself in your Gospels, in your Church, in your sacraments. I come to remind you that He is present. It is for this reason that God sent Him to this earth, that you might know Him truly and intimately as your God, as your friend, as your teacher and your counselor. I tell you that He is the Way, and He is the Light, and I come to show you the way. I come to bring you, His light.

Dear children, the road will become much easier through prayer and sacrifice. I know that it is difficult to understand the merit of sufferings. It is difficult to understand why they are so essential for the health and wealth of your soul, and yet I tell you that without sufferings, without trials, you would not know the peace of God, for it is through sufferings that you are joined to Him most intimately. It is through sufferings that you receive the treasures of Heaven, the true, true joy of the reward of life eternal with Christ. You, dear children, by making yourselves meek and poor, become wealthy, by making yourselves small, you become great, by making yourselves humbled in the Lord, you become His most favored servants.

I ask you, dear children, to renew yourselves in prayer and sacrifice, to renew your commitment to be a servant of God in your daily lives, in all that you do. Heed His word and listen, for He whispers to your hearts. He sends His Holy Spirit to be your guide. He sends His Holy Spirit to give you His wisdom. Pray that He might continue to bless you with these gifts that you would always follow the light, always follow the way, and be, in this way, united with Christ our Redeemer and our King.

Dear little children, I give to you my motherly blessing and I pray that in this season you will contemplate the greatness of God, for He so loved you that He humbled Himself to walk upon this earth, that He humbled Himself to walk with you, that He humbled Himself to walk for you, to die for you, to rise for you and to ascend to the Father, that you too might have a share in His glory. Dear children, I thank you for giving to me the gift of your prayers and sacrifices. Know that I present them to the Father with great joy, and they are accepted with gratitude. My dear ones, may God be with you this day, and always.

December 2000

Mary:

My dear children, praise be to Jesus, born into your hearts this day and always! Praised be He Who is the Lord, Who is God throughout all ages. Praised be the Paraclete, Who is your inspiration and your wisdom, Who is your courage, and Who is your faith. Praised be God the Father, Who is all good things, Who is love. Dear children, I am pleased to be with you again this day. I thank God for giving me the opportunity to come and to speak to you in this way, to share with you the good news that Jesus is alive today as He has ever been, and that He roams among you, that He is within you, that He shares in your lives, that He is in your hearts.

Dear children, Jesus is with you. He is with you on your altars. He is with you in your churches. He is with you in your priests, in your religious. In your brothers and sisters, He is with you. In your parents and spouses, in your friends and children, He is with you. He walks among His people as a Good Shepherd to lead His sheep. Ever He is with you as Consoler, ever as your friend. He comes to heal you, to teach you, to give to you all good things, all that God has designed for you, His children. My dear ones, rejoice always, for Jesus is the greatest gift of the Father. He has been given to you as Redeemer and Salvation, that you shall not perish but shall live forever in the glory that God has designed for you, the glory that belongs to Jesus.

My dear ones, unite with me in prayer always, that all of my children might come to know Him as Lord. Unite with me in prayer, that the entire world may be illumined by His love, might know His great mercy, and might be truly present with Him always in His Churches. So much has been given to you, my children! So many graces poured out upon you! God our Father in Heaven has seen the good things in your hearts. He has seen the way you have changed your hearts and your lives. He has seen you return to prayer, and He has permitted me to come all the longer to you. He continues to let me come, that I might encourage you and guide you in this way, that you might be converted all the more, that you might pray more fervently, that you may be filled with faith that is unshakable. He has seen the love that has grown in your hearts. He has seen you try with all of your heart and all of your soul to return to Him and live life anew in Him. He desires that you continue, continue the journey toward Him. Walk with Him ever closer each day. Be with Him in your Mass. In the tabernacles, visit Him often. In your home, invite Him in. In your families, make Him head.

Dear, dear children, you do not know the gift that you have in Jesus. You do not know the great grace that He is to the world, the grace that the Father pours onto the world for His sacrifice, for the redemption that He has earned for all men. God sends me to you again, and again, to remind you of this great mystery, to remind you of His love. He will continue to send me so long as you will open your hearts and respond with the fullness of your heart. He will continue to send me so long as the world is in need of His mercy.

Dear children, God is marvelous! He does love you so tremendously, so tremendously! He comes to His children, especially now, in a way that is unfathomable. He comes to you to bring you home to Him, to call back the sheep wandering far from the Shepherd. He comes to you as the Child Jesus, to invite you to befriend Him, to invite you to love Him, to invite you to share in His great mercy and in His joy. Dear children, He reaches out to you as ever, for He is love, He is all goodness.

My dear ones, it is my prayer for you that you will continue on the journey of conversion that you have begun. Continue each day to live the cross, for this is what I call you to. This is what Jesus has called you to. I am sent to remind you, that you must live the cross each day. May your lives bear the fruits of the cross. May you suffer patiently and with joy. May you endure all things for God. May you live in His joy and in His peace, and recognize the great blessings He has poured into your lives. All that you have is of God. He has given to you the air that you breathe, the food that you eat, the shelter over your head, the clothes that you wear. All things, both spiritual and temporal, are given to you by God, for in His mercy He provides for His children. He gives to you so many opportunities in your life to serve Him and to serve one another. He desires for you to learn to love in a way that you do not know. He desires for you to learn to love as He loves, freely without restraint, without condition. He desires for you to love one another as He has loved each of you. In this way, you are forever joined to Him in His great mystery of love, for God is love and those who love, live in God.

Dear children, this day, go forth and make a new commitment to love as God loves. This is the next step in the process of conversion through which I have led you. First, you must pray. Prayer is the very first step in conversion, for you cannot be converted to God if you do not know Him, and you cannot know Him if you do not speak to Him, if you do not listen to the words that He whispers in your heart. You must love the Mass and your sacraments. Love your holy Church and participate often in the great gift of the Mass. You must bear your penances and your sufferings quietly, with patience and love, obedience and humility. You must live with grateful hearts and rejoice in the joys God pours into your hearts.

Finally, dear children, you must begin to love one another as God loves. You must truly begin to give completely of yourself, emptying yourselves out, that God may fill you and work through you. Only in this way will you become a perfect vessel of His will. Only in this way will you share in a union with Him so strong, it will be as if in Heaven. Dear ones, God desires to give you a piece of Heaven upon this earth. He desires for you to begin to share in the glory that is His. You may do this by loving, dear ones, loving as He loves, loving with the fullness of your heart, loving all people as He has loved you.

Dear ones, such a simple message this is, and yet how difficult to live! I ask you to never stop trying to live in this way. Never fail and fall and refuse to walk again. Rather continue, when you stumble, to get up and to reach toward the cross, for Jesus shall bend down from the cross, offer His arms to you, and walk in your stead.

Dear ones, your God calls you to Him. He calls you to be His children. It is for this reason that He will continue to send me to you, so long as He permits, so long as it is His will. My dear ones, heed my words, for they are the words of God. I come as a servant of God to remind you that He loves you and desires you alone. Dear children, be filled with joy on this day, and may Christ as a Child enter into your hearts, open up your hearts and your eyes, that you might see Him and love Him anew, and welcome Him into your homes.

May God bless you always. May He fill you with His Spirit and may the peace of Christ, especially in this beautiful season when you welcome Him anew in the world, be with you always.

January 2001

Mary:

My dear children, it is good to be with you this day. I praise God and I thank Him, for He has done great things for His people. Join in my prayers and thank Him Who is holy, for He is all love and all truth. He is all goodness in your lives. He is all that you are and all that you have, and His mercy is without end.

My dear ones, I ask you, my children, to increase in your desire to love as God loves, to be witnesses to all that you have seen, all that you have been taught, witnesses to the true and living person of Christ. My dear ones, what a calling this is, for as the apostles were called to follow, so too, you are called to follow. As they were sent to every corner of the earth, sent to all nations, to Jew and to Gentile, to all people of all tongues, so too, are you sent to teach, to bring the good news, to bring the light of the world that is Christ, to share the wisdom that God has poured forth, the mercies that He has granted you, the blessings you have received. You too are witnesses to that divine providence that is the goodness of God. You are witnesses to the strength of His Church, to the beauty of His love, to the mercy in His sacraments, and the gift upon your altars. You are witnesses to the real, true presence of Christ. You are witnesses to His actions, to the miracles He performs each day as He did when He walked upon the earth. You are witnesses.

Still, He walks among His people. Still, He heals the sick, cures the dying, is friend to the lonely, brings hope where there is none. Still, He is among His people. Though unseen by many, hidden from the eye, still He is with you. He is with you in your tabernacles as a source of life, a refuge, a shelter from the storm. He is with you in the sacraments, in your priests, in all those whom He has placed in your life to be teachers, to guide you in His way. He is with you in your spouse, your brother, your parent, your friend, when they minister to you in times of need, when they bring to you peace in crisis, a peace that is a gift from God. He is with you in your suffering. In your illness, He is there. In your living and in your dying, He is with you. He walks yet among you.

My dear ones, you must witness to this through the way in which you live. You must make your hearts new. You must fill yourself up completely with the joy that is God! Be the wife, the husband, the mother, the father, the teacher, and friend to all people, that you might be Christ for them, that in you Christ might be reflected in this world, that He might teach and heal and save through you. Jesus our Lord, He is the Great Sacrifice. He came that all might have salvation, that all might be redeemed, that all may share in His glory, but He asks you to help Him continue to reach out in the world in a very real way. As He did once before on this earth, He makes you His followers. He commissions you to this task. He asks you to lift up your crosses and follow Him. Dear children, will you not follow our Lord?

God is so pleased with your response to His beautiful messages, messages that I have shared with you: the message of the Gospel and the message of the Mass, that Jesus is real and present with you. You have opened your hearts and renewed yourselves. You have listened to God in a new way. I encourage you to continue to grow ever more, to truly abandon all of your desires, all of your needs, all of yourself to God. Resign your will to Him, dear children. It is only in this way that you will know His perfect joy. Give all that is of yourself to Him and trust Him, for He is a loving father. He is a faithful father. He will not let you be alone, nor will He let you be lost. If you would but abandon yourself to Him, He would walk for you when you are tired, He would pray for you when you do not have the words, He would live for you when you cannot struggle any longer, and you will be given a taste of His glory, of His joy, and His peace.

This is the road that I have attempted to lead you upon, the road to greater holiness, of conversion, of conversion every day. I ask you to continue to walk with one another, helping one another always. Remember that you are teachers for one another. You are to be as Jesus is. You are to become like Jesus in every way. This is what God desires, that the light of Christ might shine most fervently in this world.

Great graces are being poured upon this world. God in His mercy, Who loves His children and desires only good things for them, has given such grace, such blessings. Many hearts return to God these days, and much praising happens in our Father's home, but there is much to do. And so, I ask you to become teachers, to become like Christ in every way. Share through your example, through your fervent prayer, through your steadfast faith, through everything, great and small, whether it is as great as facing death or as small as being sure that you honor all that God asks of you in your personal lives. Do all that for God. Do all things for Him! With the Spirit of His love within you, His great love, you will, through Him and with Him and in Him, change the world! He will change the world. Our Lord will triumph, for He is all things good, and He is all things holy. Come and follow Him. Take up your crosses and follow. The way may be difficult, but the joy is eternal.

My dear ones, I invite you to pray ever more fervently. Pray for those who have no one to pray for them, for they are especially in need. My dear ones, do not forget anyone in your prayer. Pray for all things. Give everything to God in prayer, for it is through prayer that you will grow, and through prayer that you will come to know God more intimately. Listen to His words. Listen to the voice, the voice that speaks within you, for God does speak to each of His children in different ways and leads them, as the Good Shepherd, on the path of holiness. He is the Great Teacher. He is the One Who has taught with such love and such compassion and such goodness, it can never be measured, nor equaled. Yet strive, dear children, to be as He is. Practice every virtue. Do all this for God and I assure you, you will find great favor in His eyes.

My dear ones, I am with you ever as a mother. I lead you and I guide you, as God desires it to be so. I pray for you each day, and I ask that Jesus would fill your heart with His most perfect love that you, truly, might be as He is, and you might bring His light to the world. May His peace ever be with you, and may you know joy!

February 2001

Mary:

My dear children, today, I bless you with my motherly blessing, and I pray that God Who is goodness will be with you always, in all of your endeavors, that He might walk on the road of conversion with you, the road of faith, the road of peace and a road of joy, that He might lead you into His Own heart that there you will find sustenance, that there you will find drink for your thirsty heart. My dear children, know that I come to you as a mother who desires to teach her children all things that they need to grow and to live in happiness and joy. I come to you to tell you that God loves you, that He is with you each day in all that you do, that He has commanded that you love one another as He loves you, and that you serve one another as He has served you. I come and I tell you these things, dear children, that you might have joy in your heart and peace in your lives.

It is only by following the Word of God that you will find peace and joy, for God gave these words to you in His truth, in the Gospels that you have read, in His Scripture, in His Church, and in one another, that you might know Him. He desires, dear children, for you to come to Him as children, to make yourselves small before Him. Lay all that you are before Him. Give to Him your failings and your joys, all that you are. Let Him heal you. Let Him lead you. Let Him bring you into His joy and His goodness.

Dear ones, He is your father, and as your father He desires that you give yourself fully to Him, abandoning all that you have to Him, for truly I tell you, it is only because of His goodness that you have anything at all, for He breathed life into your very body, shaping it in the darkness. He has given you all that you have. He has placed you in the care of your friends and family, that they too might lead you to Him.

This, dear children, is the truth: God Who is love, God Who is your father, He beckons to you always. He calls His children to come, to share in the mystery that is His love, that is His joy! He asks His children to come and participate in this family of God. He sends the mother to speak to the children, that they might not fear the Father, nor turn far from Him, but might be welcomed into His embrace, returning home to Him.

In many ways you are all lost children, for there are things in your lives that trouble you. There are doubts in your heads and in your hearts. There are sorrows that are too great for you to bear alone. There is confusion. There is trial. There are sufferings, and it shall be so until the end of your lives, for this is the cross that you must bear while on earth. And yet, you need not suffer alone, for God the Father reaches out to you, dear children. He calls you by name. He asks you to abandon yourselves to Him, that as a father He might lead you, He might guide you. He sends me to give you these words, that you would be comforted by the fact that you are in the care of loving parents: the Father Who is great, great above all things, and the mother, the mother of Christ, given to you that I might lead you to God. This is my heart's desire, that I might lead you ever closer to Jesus, to God our Father, through the power of the Holy Spirit, for truly, then you will be home in your Father's house, and you will begin to live the joys of Heaven while on earth.

My dear children, do not reject the crosses in your lives, but embrace them with love. Do not reject the sorrows and sufferings. Do not fear the illness and the death, for God shall prevail above all. You are His children and He loves you. He will not abandon you but will give to you every grace and every power, that you might glorify His name eternally and be welcomed as part of His heavenly home. Dear children, what a message of encouragement and joy this is, and I thank God that He has allowed me to bring it to you, for this is the greatest gift, that God comes to you each day through so many things. In your churches, in your tabernacle, through divine messages, through the Holy Scripture, through your friends and your family, each day He is reaching out to you, dear children. Each day, He is calling you, beckoning you, to give to Him all that is His: your own heart, your own soul, your own life.

My dear ones, trust in your Father in Heaven, for He is a God of love and goodness, and He desires for you perfect peace and great joy. Abandon yourselves to Him. Commit yourselves anew to service, to prayer, for these things will bring you closer to Him, enveloping you in His divine heart, making truths known to you that are known not by any who do not wish to love as God loves, who do not wish to unite their will to His own. Pray, dear children, that you will receive all of the graces of God, all of the gifts He desires to give to you. Pray that you will open your hearts to accept these gifts. Pray that you will not turn from Him, but you will embrace your Father who loves you, and rejoice in the goodness that is His.

My dear children, I bless you this day. I pray that God might always be with you, guiding your every step, guiding your every word, guiding your every deed, for He Who is love will triumph over all things and His mercy is without end.

March 2001

Mary:

My dear children, I thank you for gathering this day, for praying as I have asked, for offering up your prayer intentions to God, Who is a father Who accepts your prayers, Who hears your requests, Who answers your prayers. He has taken you into His heart and He has made you His children. Thank Him with grateful hearts, for He has heard your prayers and He has answered you.

My dear children, I invite you this day to love as God loves. I continue to teach you about the love of God. No matter how many words I spoke to you, never could I give to you the depth, the greatness, the joy that God has for you. His love for you is greater than you can imagine! His love, His mercy, it is without measure. I invite you this day to love as He loves. This is what I have been teaching you these many years, all of these virtues: obedience, charity, kindness, mercy, compassion. These things all come from love, a love that is of God.

Dear ones, begin to love anew in this way. Begin to love so fully and so freely that you reserve nothing for yourself. Give completely of yourselves, as God has given completely to you, that truly you might be Christ on this earth, that you might be for others, God, as He works through His people.

Dear ones, it is in this way that God touches the hearts of His children. By pouring a measure of His most Holy Spirit into those children who desire to do His will, who accept Him, who love Him, who will accept with open hearts the grace poured forth from Him into them. He pours forth His Spirit into you, that you might go and speak His word, that others might hear and know Him, that you might walk as He walked, a road filled with sorrows and joys, but one that is ever closer to the Father in Heaven, that you might do as He did: teach, minister, love. Share with the people of God His glory, His love, and His life. I ask you to begin to love anew today, to put aside all that is of yourselves, to relinquish your will to God, and to allow Him to love through you. Only in this way will love fill this world.

So many times, you lament the world. You lament the evil, the wickedness, the sorrows, and the trials. I tell you, my children, it is you who will create the world in which you live, through your love, or your lack of love. Be an example, dear ones, of love, that your example might teach others and that many might come to embrace the love that is Christ. In this way, this world, your lives, your homes, they will be filled with peace, with joy, with unending mercies, and grace. Begin to love anew each day. Begin to love as God loves. Only in this way, will you come to know Him most fully. Only in this way, will you be united fully with Him. Only in this way, can you find shelter and refuge in His Most Sacred Heart.

Dear children, do not turn away the gift that God gives to you, the gift to know Him through His love and mercy. Do not turn away His graces, rather, open your hearts and invite Him to love through you, to give to you every grace that you might glorify Him and in doing so, dear children, you too will come to have a share in His glory.

May God Who is peace and joy, may God Who is greatness and mercy, may God Who is love be ever with you, as I your mother am with you.

April 2001

Mary:

My dear little ones, praised be Jesus risen, and may He bless you now, and always! Praised be God, Creator, Holy Spirit, Holy Advocate! Dear ones, today again, I call you to peace in your homes, in your families. In your daily life, work for peace, work for peace! When you pray, when you live as Jesus has called you to live, with love in your hearts, with forgiveness, with understanding, and with joy and gratitude, you will know the peace that God intends for you, the peace of Christ, that peace which He desires for you to spread among His people.

This world is sorely in need of peace. There is much division. There is much hatred. There is much darkness, but you are able to bring light into the dark because God has given to you every grace necessary to do so. You are as candles to light a flame of love in the hearts of all mankind. I desire for you to work for peace, because it is in peace that you will find joy, gratitude, and total abandonment to God. To live in this peace, you must give your will to God, you must entrust your heart to Him, your own soul. You must give Him your family, all of your cares, all of your needs, all of your blessings. You must give Him your sorrows and your trials, your illness, your death. Give Him all things and allow the Master to care for His creation.

He has loved you as a father always, and He desires to love you still. Each day of your life He calls to you, beckoning for you to come before Him, that He might love you more, that He might love you fully, that He might embrace you in His divine presence. Heed His call! Answer Him! Give Him all that you have that He might fill you with every grace and every joy, that He might make your heart light, and that you might shine as candles in the darkness, the light and the love of Jesus to all of the world.

My dear ones, this is my plan for the world, that I might touch the hearts of my little ones who will spread the love that I pass on to you from the Father, Son, and Holy Spirit to all nations. It is in this way that God has always worked, for He sent His humble Son into the world as a poor man, and it is only through the efforts of those who loved Him that you now know of Him, that you now accept and embrace the Church that He, the Lamb, gave His life for, that you now have a share in the knowledge that Jesus came that you might have life eternal. Through those first founders of the Church, those who shared the message of Christ, the Good News of His death, resurrection, and ascension to the Father, you have been handed down this beautiful faith, the Church of God!

God works through His people always. He calls you again to be as they were, to share the Good News you have received, news that is not new but has been forgotten by the world, that you are loved above all creation, that God Who is mighty is with you, that you have no need to fear, that you may rejoice, for you are His children and He is your Father. He desires for you to turn to Him in all things, to abandon yourself to Him in prayer, to give Him your sinfulness, your selfishness, your hardness, your anger, to give to Him your past and your present, and to entrust in His hands your future, for only He can show you the way.

My dear ones, do as you have been asked by God. Do as you have been asked by Christ, Himself, in the words that He left for you through those first ones who saw and witnessed His miracles and who wrote that you might, too, know the truth. Follow Him. Give to Him all that is His. He has created you and provided everything that you have, that you are, that you ever shall be. Be as joyful as the children of a loving God ought, for if you do not live with joy, you do not spread the love of Christ, Who desires for His children to live joyfully! Live with gratitude, with awe that the Son of God came that you might be saved! Live with love and reverence for all of His people. Live with peace in your heart, a love for His most holy Church, for His Eucharistic body sacrificed, that you might again be in His presence in body and in blood. Reflect always on this great mystery that is Jesus, that is God the Father, and the Holy Spirit Advocate, for they are with you, one God with one people. And they have sent me to tell you.

My dear little ones, know that I am your mother. As always, I guide you and I am with you. I do love you. I lift you up to the Father and bring before Him all of your intentions. May His peace flood your heart, may you know His mercy, and may you always, always remain faithful.

May 2001

Mary:

My dear little ones, peace be with you. May God Who is glory, Who has loved you all the days of your life, be with you. Today, I come to you particularly as your mother. I wish to remind you of my maternal love for you, a love that is without condition, a love that is without end. I wish to remind you that God, our Father, loves you with such profound love, such immeasurable love, you cannot fathom it.

Today, I invite you, dear ones, to begin to love in a new way. Often, I have spoken to you of love, of the love that only God can give to you, the love that is His most perfect gift to you. His love comes to you in many ways. His love is on your altars, in the Holy Sacrifice of the Mass. His love is in your sacraments, in your Church, in the priests who minister to you, in the friends who console you in your time of need. His love is in His Word, the Living Testament of His love. His love is in His gifts, in His graces, in His every mercy, in every blessing that you receive, in every healing, in the softening of every heart, in every conversion, and in everyone who has been given the tremendous gift of faith. These blessings shower forth from the heavens because God's love for you is so great! His love is in this entire world, in every creation, in all of the good things that He has given to you that you might live joyfully.

Tonight, I wish for you to learn to love in this way, to learn to love with a maternal heart, a paternal heart, to love as a sister and a brother, to love as the closest of friends, all people. It is this that Christ called you to, to love all men, regardless of whether they treat you with kindness, regardless of whether they treat you with love. He invited you to love all of those whom you encounter with His love, the love that God has given to you. This, my children find difficult. There is so little love in this world today. The darkness and the pain, the agony and despair of this world, all of it is caused by a lack of love. There is no other reason. All of the hurting, all of the deaths that you encounter, all of your sorrows, they are a product of a lack of love, love for God, love for neighbor, and a love for the dignity and the beauty of life.

This is the great weakness of humanity. It is why we, as the children of God, are a fallen people, for we have chosen not to love. And yet, you are given the opportunity, the grace needed, to love anew each day. You are invited to love as you ought to love, as God loves. I ask you to heed my call to this love. I invite you. It is only in this way, that you will know peace in your lives, in your homes, in your hearts, in your world. It is only in this way, that the darkness shall be quenched, that light shall enter the world, the light that is Christ. It is only in this way, that the pain will end, that the agony will disappear, that despair shall be no more, only when man decides to love.

You are bearers of that love. You are bearers of a great gift. God has given you so much! So many graces! Would you not love for Him, as He has loved you? Bear His love to the world that, others might see and learn. My children have forgotten how to love. They need to be taught, instructed, guided. It is for this reason that the Father pours His Holy Spirit out upon every nation, sending many witnesses, performing many miracles, giving many graces, that my children might once again be filled with peace, with joy and love.

Do, children, choose to love in your every action and in your every word. Do nothing that is contrary to love, for God is love, and when you do not love, you do not stand with God. If you will allow no wickedness, no sinfulness, no evil to reside within you, you will know a union with God that you can only now imagine. You will be perfected in His image as He has always desired for you to be, as He created you to be. This is your choice. You must commit to your choice with the fullness of your heart. You must persevere, even when it is most difficult, even when the trials are great, especially when they seem unbearable. You will find, my little ones, that when you love as God loves, when you accept every grace that He desires to pour into your hearts, when you accept His peace, the difficulties of this life will be lessened, for your sufferings will have great meaning. To suffer without meaning is only to know pain, but to suffer with love, you cannot know the graces, the joys, the mercies, that your suffering will merit. And so, little ones, even in times of trial and in times of joy, love without condition, love without end, love selflessly, love purely, love as God loves. It is in this way that truly, you will emulate Christ, and you will be the disciples He has called you to be.

My dear ones, may He be with you especially this day and always, as my maternal heart blesses you, loves you, and intercedes for you always.

June 2001

Mary:

My dear children, peace be with you. Know that I come to you today bearing the blessings of the Father, the graces that He wishes to give to you. Thank Him and praise Him, for He allows me to come still to speak words of encouragement to you, to teach you how to pray, to teach you to love, to teach you how to follow Him, as He desires you to do.

My dear ones, you are a people filled with faith. You love God. He, your Lord, loves you tremendously. The difficulties that you have are not in your faith, but in the practice of your faith. I have come to teach you how to live your faith more fully, to teach you to live joyfully, to live as God desires for you to live, a holy and peace-filled life. In this way, you are lights in the darkness. You are a shining example to the world of Jesus, of His love, of His mercy. You are filled with faith, my people, and God has seen your faith and responded to you with many blessings, with such grace. Your hearts desire to do as He wills you to do, yet you have not disciplined yourself to do so. I understand that the road is difficult. Know that you do not have to go alone. You do not struggle alone. You do not falter alone. God has brought you together as a people to love and to support one another, to share with one another, and minister to one another. He sends His angels to minister to you, to guard you, to guide you, and He sends His mother to encourage you and bring you hope. My dear ones, place yourself completely in the Father's hands. When your will is weak, pray! Pray that the Holy Spirit would fill you with His strength, with His joy. In this way, it will be God Who works through you, and much more will be accomplished in His name.

This day, I again ask you to commit yourselves anew to God, to the task at hand, becoming His faithful servants, living each day the life of Christ, the crosses, and the joys. Allow your will to be joined to that of the Father. Pray, each day, that He would fill you with His Spirit, to grant you the wisdom, the knowledge, and the courage that you need to live His road. My dear ones, it is not easy, but it is not impossible. God has sent you many signs and many graces. He has given to you many words of encouragement. He has given to you all that you need. Be as children. Trust and obey.

Little ones, the difficulty is in giving up yourselves, that God might be all through you. It is a difficulty, it is a cross, but it is one that brings great grace and great strength in God, for if you can give to God all that is His: your heart, your soul, your mind, your family-everything placed in His care, then, dear ones, you will begin to know the peace and the joy that I have promised to you, that I have spoken about to you for these many years. I am so pleased as your mother that you have responded with the fullness of your hearts and the desire to do as I have asked you to do, as God has asked you to do. You continue to persevere in faith and my maternal heart is filled with joy. Now, I ask you to continue to persevere with your will, to decide for love, to decide to live your faith, to decide for God! It is not an easy choice, but it is a choice that is filled with grace, grace that you cannot imagine!

My dear ones, be encouraged, for God is with you. He hears your prayers, and He answers them. He pours down a multitude of graces upon you. He fills you with His Holy Spirit. Now, He sends His Spirit to you as never before, that you might be filled with His graces and spread those graces around the world. God works through His people. He touches the hearts of His faithful, that they might go and share that message of joy, of love, and of hope, with all of those whom they encounter. It was the same way when my Son was born upon this earth. How few saw Him! How few spoke to Him! How few touched Him or were touched by Him! And yet, all the world knows of Him now, because of those who were faithful. In this same way, I call you to be faithful, to be faithful to the decision to love God, to live as He commands, and in the same way, you will be apostles, you will be leaders, you will be servants, and this is a very, very great blessing! My dear ones, let the world see Jesus in you, that they may be filled with the hope and the joy that you have known.

My little ones, I bless you with my maternal blessing and I remind you that as ever, I am with you, guiding you, leading you, bringing you into the heart of my Son.

July 2001

Mary:

My dear little ones, it is good to be with you again on this day. Praise God, for in His goodness, He gives you many blessings, He grants you many favors, He lifts you up and gives you a share of His glory, He gives you all that He has, all that He is, all because of His love for you. My dear little ones, I come to you today again to invite you to enter into a deeper union with God, our Heavenly Father. His people on earth, separated from Him by sin and death, they live their lives apart from Him, many times because they choose not to see that which is there, that which is true, that which is God. I invite you to begin to look with eyes of faith, to begin to live through these eyes of faith. See that God is with you. See how He blesses you. See how He works in your lives and see the great opportunity He has given to you to serve your brothers and sisters, to live in love and peace and joy, to give back to Him all that you are, that He might glorify you all the greater.

Dear ones, choose to see Him. Choose to walk on His road. So many times, I have come and have asked you, little ones, to respond with the fullness of your hearts, and I am so pleased, for you have learned to pray, you have learned to love, you have learned to serve. Still, as my children I guide you in these ways, for as children, there are many mistakes to be made and many places where you will fall, but as your mother I encourage you. I ask you to take my hand and to again commit yourself to living all that you have been taught, all that you know, to living the way of God. You are to be true apostles, disciples, those who follow in His footsteps. What a great gift this is and what a responsibility, for it is up to you to teach the world of God's love, to teach the world that they are loved, that all people are loved by God, that God desires each one of His children fully and without reservation. It is up to you to show mercy, compassion, love, charity, devotion, faith. These virtues are not known in the world without God, and they will not be known without you if you do not choose to live in this way. Teach the world what is truth, what is right. Teach them, for so many are in the darkness, for there is no one to reach out to them.

Your world and your nation suffer greatly from a disease that is evil, that is sin. Sin blinds the people of God. It takes away their ability to see Him clearly, to enter into a deep union with Him, a union that is constant, without end, and always. Sin takes away the freedom that God gave to you to love, to live joyfully. It takes away your life, your joy, your peace. It takes away every grace and leaves only sadness, sickness, and death. As a mother, I come to invite my children to accept the healing love of God, to accept His healing in the sacraments, through His Church, through one another, through prayer, through service, through the giving of oneself completely to His will. Accept the healing that God brings to the world that you might not suffer in blindness, but that you might truly see. You are called to be the light in this world. It is an illustration much used and yet so true, for the darkness that envelopes this world is great, and yet, the light is greater.

God desires His people. He calls His people to live in union with Him, to truly commune with Him, each day, in every moment. Come into His Churches and find Him there. Look for Him in your tabernacle. Spend precious moments before Him in His presence, loving Him, prayerfully asking that He change you, mold you, shape you into the creation that He has designed you to be. Find Him in one another. Listen. Counsel. Help one another. You are called to this vocation as truly as to any other, for you cannot, cannot exist alone! You need one another just as much as you need your families, for you are an example to each other and to the world. You are support. You are guidance. You are the hand that is outreached to pick up those who have fallen.

Be the hands and the feet of Christ. Gather His people up with love in your hearts. Be merciful, for most of my people do not know true mercy, for they have not accepted the mercy of God and they do not know how to live with mercy in their hearts. See that my children are broken, and they are weak. See that they suffer. They are in need of healing, the healing that God alone can bring, and as truly and as really as Jesus our Lord gave sight to the blind, so too, you, through the power of the Holy Spirit, in the grace of God, will give sight to those who cannot see, who are lost.

And so, I invite you, dear ones, to make yourselves perfect vessels for God, and in doing so, you will, truly, become one with Him, knowing Him, being in His presence, living with Him and through Him always. You must pray. Without prayer you cannot enter into such a union with Him. Without the holy sacraments you will not know Him. Without His body and His blood your faith will wither, and it will die, for He alone gives you sustenance, He alone gives you life, He alone is your strength and your counsel, He alone is your God, your Lord, your Master.

Dear ones, ponder what I have said and keep it in your hearts. Remember in the times that are most frustrating and most difficult, the times when you do not feel the presence of God with you, what I have said and know that truly, He is with you, He is with you always. You will not be abandoned. Seek Him out through service and love, and you will live in His joy. May His peace ever be with you, and may He bless you in all of your ministries. In all of your lives, in the daily things that seem mundane, may He be with you, ever greater.

August 2001

Mary:

My dear children, as ever, praise God, for He is good and has allowed you to come tonight to share in His most Blessed Sacrament, to receive Him in His body, to know Him. Dear ones, what a gift, what a gift you have been given! Do not cease to pray in thanksgiving, for our God gives you all things.

My dear ones, do not be afraid to open your hearts to His grace in your life. How many times in your life you seek Him in prayer! You take to Him your troubles, your sorrows, the little deaths that you must suffer each day in your life, and yet you refuse to give them to Him, to allow Him to bear them as He has borne the sins of the world upon His own back. You hold tight to your troubles, afraid to let go, afraid to let God free you, give you grace, give you peace. Your hearts desire to change, to trust completely and fully in Him, and yet it is difficult for you. My little ones, it is with great joy that I tell you that you need not be afraid! Do not ever fear coming to our Father in Heaven Who is goodness, Who is mercy, Who is forgiveness. Take to Him your burdens, your sinfulness, your sorrows. Give Him all your brokenness, all of your pain, that He might cast into the fires all that is evil and give to you all that is holy.

My dear ones, our God, our Father, loves each of His children with such immense love, with such perfect love! What He desires for you is holiness, a life lived in full communion with Him. You experience this in your Mass when you receive His body, His blood, soul, and divinity. When earnestly you lift your hearts up to

Him that He might fill you with His every grace and, as His body enters into you, He makes you a holy vessel of His love, filling you with His Holy Spirit, cleansing you, purifying you. Seek out the Lord in your life. Do not be afraid to allow Him to come into your heart, to see the darkest recesses, to know your every secret, to know your every wound, your every weakness, for God desires to heal His children.

Each day, He is present in your life. How often I have said this, and I cannot say it enough. God is with His people! He sends His mother. He sends His saints. He sends His earthly messengers, each of you, to teach the world that He is alive, that He is with you, that He is merciful. There is much sadness in the world, there is much pain, but it need not be so. God desires for His children to return to Him with love, return to Him with a desire to live in holiness, to accomplish this through prayer, perseverance, and complete reliance on Him, trusting in Him, placing your will in His care, that He might make it His Own.

My dear ones, you have received so much! You have seen such goodness from the hands of God! He has blessed you each day in your life, that truly every day, you are standing in a miracle! Little ones, do not fail to see with the eyes of a child the miracle that is life around you, the miracle that is the eternal life that your God gives to you freely, without price. Come to Him. Come to Him in His holy sacraments and there find peace and reconciliation, a healing of your wounds, and a changing of your heart as you have never experienced before. Flee to your Father in Heaven, for He is your comfort and your solace. He is mercy and forgiveness. He desires for you only holiness, joy, and peace. My little ones, banish all fear from your hearts. God has not made a fearful people. He desires for you to live in abundant blessings, in abundant grace, but you must open your hearts, change your hearts, set your will upon living in holiness, and pray always that the Holy Spirit might enter into you and make you a perfect vessel of love.

Dear ones, will you open yourself to God completely? When you place all in His hands, when you invite the Holy Spirit to work through you, then, only then, will you fully commune with God in your soul as it was always meant to be. See Him in your life, for He is there. He is waiting for you. Answer His call and seek His mercy.

September 2001

Mary:

My dear little ones, peace be with you. Know that I come to you again as your mother. Know that I come to gather my children in my arms, to teach them about the Father, to gather you. Dear ones, what a difficult time it is in the world, for even in these days you have seen the face of evil in your nation. This is nothing that is new to you. I do not need to tell you that evil exists, that it is real, that evil desires to destroy the kingdom of God, for you know this, you live it each day. What I come to tell you, what God sends me to tell you, is that there is grace without limit in His hands, in His care, in His mercy. He desires to heal His people, to pour His love upon them, to comfort them in their affliction, to take away your sorrows, to make you a people of joy.

My dear ones, if all of my children, everyone in the world heard this message, how then could anyone reject such a gift? God does not ask you for anything more than what He gave, your heart, your soul, your mind. What great gifts these are! He gave them to you, that they might be used for His will, which is always love, which is always goodness, which is always joy. I invite you then, my children, again this day to make yourselves His willing servants, vessels of His love. Open your hearts to Him. Hear Him when He calls you.

The malady of evil will exist in this world, so long as my children do not turn to God with the fullness of their hearts, so long as my children continue in their own ways, the fallen ways which mankind has suffered under for this long time. God sent His Son into this world to be a beacon of light, to be hope in the darkness. It is the same Son, the Christ, Redeemer, and King Who is your salvation, Who is your hope, Who is your joy.

You are called to share Him with all people, to share the gift of faith that you have been given. What a gift! To be so blessed as to be gifted with faith, to be gifted with the faith that God has given you through Jesus, through His sacramental Church, through His body and blood. What a gift! You must share this gift in the way that you live, in the words that you speak, in the way that you pray. Those who come to you looking for God will find Him only if you place yourself entirely in His care. Pray about all things. Find Him in the sacraments and in the Church and, most especially in times of temptation and trial, live a life of perfect humility, obedience, and joy. It is only this joy, this life lived abundantly in Christ, that will prevent evil from overtaking the very children of God. God offers this gift to His children. He offers it through His Son, through the Redeemer, but my children must accept, they must accept the gift.

Dear ones, I ask you, make yourselves bearers of the light of Christ, that all of the people of God might see Him clearly, and that you, in your own times of trial, of temptation, of doubt and struggle, might clearly know Him and might not abandon Him. Your God is a faithful God. He does not abandon His children. He does not leave you. He will not allow evil to overcome you, but you must trust in Him. You must place yourself in His care. You must accept the gifts of faith that He gives, for if you will close your heart to Him, if you do not place your trust in Him, if you do not love as He commands you to love, you will not know joy, but only sadness, despair, and death.

You, dear ones, are the hope for the world, for those who are faithful to God are beacons of hope and joy, beacons of light and grace, and they make this world a joy for me to look upon. I ask you to share this grace with all those who are not as fortunate as you, who do not know God as you have come to know Him; for you, dear children, you have been given much and when you open yourselves to the Spirit of God Who will work with you, through you, and in you, you can accomplish much.

Dear ones, know that I, your mother, am with you in all things. Know that I come to you to always bring you joy, to bring you hope, and to share with you the great grace that is the gift of faith, that gift that God pours forth upon this world in abundance. Share this message, I implore you! Let all the world see you as children of God, that they too might follow that example, the example of Christ, and might be delivered into joy. First you must live this way. Second, you must pray, always. And third, dear ones, you must always live out your faith in the promises you have made in your lives, as mothers and fathers, husbands and wives, teachers and friends, priests, and celibates. Always live your vows. Do these three things, dear ones, and I assure you, you will always know the light and the peace and the grace that God gives to you. Do them not, and you will have much trial.

As any mother, I come to you with a heart filled with hopes for my children, with a heart filled with great desires for my children to know God as I have seen Him, as I have known Him. One day at the moment of your death, you will stand before Him, and you will see with eyes unknown to you. Begin to see Him in this way now through the way that you live each day. Do not be led away, for the prize is great, the treasure worth the struggle, and the grace all consuming. Dear ones, may the peace of Christ be with you, and the gifts of the Holy Spirit be upon you this day, and always.

October 2001

Mary:

My dear children, it is good to be with you tonight, to be given the grace from the Father to speak to you as a mother, to come to teach you, to remind you that God is with you, that He loves you, that He will never leave you, that He desires you to return to Him with the fullness of your hearts.

My dear ones, know that I come to you to be His mouthpiece, to bear His message. He calls to you time and time again. He beckons His children to Him, gathers them around Him, calls His little ones home to Him. Our Father in Heaven is good. He desires for the world to be filled with mercy and joy and peace. He has designed His children to be vessels of His love, to live in service and in joy, to live keeping His commandments, honoring His name, and rejoicing in the blessings He has given them. He has designed His children, each one, to be loved by Him and to love one another.

Dear ones, from many places, in many ages, He has called to you. Through the Scriptures, through the writings of the old prophets, to this present day, He beckons a lost people home to Him. Throughout history, the world has known unrest, disaster, pain, sorrow, and violence. God never intended for it to be so, but by choosing to walk apart from Him, man has chosen to live this way. It grieves my maternal heart, for it does not need to be so. Every day you are given the choice to love, or not. Every day you are given the choice to serve, or to serve yourself. Every day you have the choice to believe, to trust, or to doubt and despise. Dear ones, this is your blessing, and also your cross, for you have such freedom, and yet many of my children do not know how to close their eyes, open their hearts, and trust in God. God designed this world to be a place of joy, to be a place of peace, to be a place of love. Today, you have the choice. You may help it return to such a place, or you might contribute to the desolation that exists now. Choose well, my little ones, and do not choose alone. Invoke the Holy Spirit to come upon you, to dwell in your heart, to live in your lives and to work through you, that His wisdom, that His power, that His glory might be yours, that you might glorify God.

Dear ones, pray always, for it is in prayer that you will be given all graces and all blessings and all strength that you will need to choose well. Do not fear to come to your Father, to reconcile yourself to Him when you fall. God desires His children to come back to Him. He calls to them, and beckons them. Come back to Him with the fullness of your heart, with all of your soul, and lead those around you, those who you have charge of, those whom God, Himself, has placed in your life, lead them back to Him as well, that all of humanity might worship Him, that the world might know peace and joy and the love that God desires to give to all of His children, to spread upon this earth as a fire in the hearts and souls of His little ones.

Dear ones, I assure you, if you follow His law, if you live by His way, if you bind your heart to Him through prayer and the sacraments, truly, you will know peace, you will know joy, and things will be as they were always designed to be. May the peace of Christ, who is our redeemer and king, be as ever, with you.

November 2001

Mary:

My dear little children, I thank you this day for all that you have done to come to know the Baby Jesus, Christ your King, in a new and fuller way. Today, you begin a time of celebration, of preparation for celebrating His coming into this world: God, penetrating time and space to come into the hearts of His children, coming to you, not in grandeur, but as an infant child, as the weakest, the smallest, the most helpless of all creation! During these next weeks, you will recall how God, in His mercy, sent His angel forth to announce the Good News to the world that Jesus, the Redeemer, the Savior, was with His people. What joyful news!

Dear ones, in these next weeks, you will be reminded of the great humility of Christ, how He, God, became the lowest, the smallest, the servant, slave to the desires of men, obedient even until His death. In these next weeks, you will be reminded, dear ones, that God did these things, that He became His creation, because He loves you, because He is merciful, because He is good, because He desired to show His children that which is right, the way to live. It is the example of Christ that you must follow, for He is the teacher. He is the Master.

Dear ones, I ask you, how many of my children during these next weeks will remember these things? Do not forget. Do not be among those who cannot truly see with the eyes of faith because they have no faith, for the gift given to them has been rejected, the grace poured upon them is not with them, for they have chosen another road. Do not forget. Do not become distracted. How much there is to distract my dear ones from prayer, from love of God, and love of neighbor. It is difficult in this world when evils multiply, when trials are great, to remember to love and to live as the Master commands. You are called, dear ones, to remember always that you are the people of God, and as such you must live with dignity, with love, and with mercy.

How many times, dear ones, must you forgive those who hurt you? How many times must you love those who are unlovable? The world will tell you that there are those without worth. The world will tell you that respecting life, that loving life, that life, which is sacred, has no worth. Many will tell you that to think of oneself, to desire the things of the world, to act in one's best interest, is the way to live. You are blessed, for you know otherwise.

Dear ones, what I am telling you is nothing that you do not know. You yourselves, you pray, you beseech God for an end to such evils in this world and in your nation. I call you to remember, to renew in your heart, the commitment to pray that this might be a season of hope and joy for all people, that they might truly believe that God hears prayers and answers them in His divine will, in a beautiful and glorious way.

Dear ones, you are blessed! How blessed you are to be gifted with truth. I ask you as your mother, do not forget to live the truth. May your lives be shining examples of that which you know. God- Father, Son, and Spirit Eternal, is with His people in humility, in His mercy, in His justice, in His peace. He, now as ever, crosses space and time and all things to bring love to His children, reaching

His hands to you, offering you His peace, offering peace to the world. He Who is mighty comes again in humility, as the smallest and the weakest, those without a voice, those most abandoned, those most abused. He Who is mighty and great comes again to you, to be taught by you, to be loved by you.

Who is this person? Who comes to you in this way? It is Jesus, in your brothers and sisters, in the hearts of all people, all of His creation! See with eyes of faith now, that He reigns within you, that He truly is King of the Hearts of all Mankind, and that to serve Him is to serve one another. Therefore, may I impart this message to you, be servants first, masters last. Be teachers and friends and counselors and, above all, pray! In this way, you will begin to live a life of service. In this way, you will find yourself growing closer to God through Jesus, our living Lord. In this way, you will find your prayer renewed and your faith will bloom as a rose before the crown, the throne, and the glory of God.

Remember, little ones, in this season and in these next weeks and always, that Jesus Who is Lord is with you. May He reign always with the Father Almighty through the power of the Holy Spirit, one God forever and ever.

December 2001

(This message was given during a candlelight prayer service on Christmas Day.)

God in His Trinity:

My children, I call you. I make you a new creation unto Me. I fill you with every grace. I grant you every blessing. I know your every word, and every bone, and every hair, and every thought, and every deed. I know you as you do not know yourselves, for I have seen that which might be if you would protect your souls from sinfulness and death, and embrace the light, the light which I bring you.

Children, your Father calls! I beckon you. You are Mine. Be in My presence. See the gift I give you in Myself, that I send my Spirit upon you to heal you of all afflictions, to make you whole, to bind your families to My heart that bleeds for you. See, I send My Spirit to be your advocate, to be your counsel, to be your light, that you might share in that glory that is Mine! See that I send My body to your table to be broken, to be part of you, My people, that I now and always shall be joined unto you: God, one creature, My heart. See now, I send My mother, she, who was ordained from all time to be the one woman clothed in the sun, who comes to bring My peace, and My joy, and My glory, who is My servant. She is My prophet. I speak to you through her. My daughter, she comes to you. She brings My words that you might come to know Me, as I know you. There is nothing hidden from My eyes. There is no pain I do not feel. There is no joy I do not know. Always, I am with you.

Children, accept the gift of My grace that I give to you. Accept this gift now. Fill your hearts with My mercy, for My mercy alone shall sustain you. Fill your hearts with My love, for My love alone, My love alone is all things. Fill your heart with My Word. Become that which I know you to be. Join your hearts to Me and give Me your will. You do not trust enough to give to the Creator that which is My Own, that which first I gave unto you. I am calling.

Dear children, dear precious ones, dear thought of My heart, breath of My life, answer this call. Give yourselves to Me, that I might do great things through you to bring all of My children into the mercy of their Father. Do not, do not leave Me alone. Remain in Me always, for such I created you to be, one in My heart now and forever. Turn your faces unto Me. See My mercy that awaits you. See My forgiveness, My joy, My love, My peace. Let me, your God, free you from the chains of sin and death, and lift you up into that glory that I have created for you. Children, come! Your Father calls.

January 2002

Mary:

My dear ones, how good it is to come among you as your mother, to be given the grace to speak to you the words that the Father gives, that you might hear Him and know Him, that you might serve Him in every facet of your life, that you might serve one another and do as Jesus did upon this earth: give fully and completely from yourself, that others might come to know God through you. Dear ones, as your mother, I come to you always, imploring that you continue to walk toward holiness, that you continue in your journey of prayer and reconciliation, that you continue to find God each day in His Church and in the sacraments. Again, as your mother, I bring you to the Father.

Dear ones, my little ones, continue though the road becomes difficult. Persevere in your faith through all trials and all hardships. Now, dear ones, you must decide to love fully with all of your heart. Reserve nothing for yourselves, for God shall give back to you manyfold what you give.

Dear ones, it is not difficult to hear the words that I speak to you and to understand them. The difficulty is in putting them into action in your life. In the times when you are most frustrated, when you are most angry, when you are most away from God because you have chosen not to see Him, it is in these times that you must recall my words that echo the holy Gospels, that call you into prayer, that call you into the Church, that call you into reconciliation. I cannot tell you, dear ones, how important it is to always, always, place God center in your life, in your activities, and especially in your home.

Dear ones, this is a time of darkness for the family. It is a time when so many families find themselves pulled away from the love of God and lost in materialism, in consumerism, and even in the daily routines of life. My dear ones, as a family you eat together. As a family you play, you cry, you laugh together. Why, dear ones, should you not pray together? This must be first in your home. Let it be the first thing you do when you wake and the last thing you do before you sleep, and may your mind and heart be set on God in every moment in between.

Dear ones, I come to you as a mother and, as your mother, I advise and I counsel you. There is no better advice that I can give to you but to continually search out God, to continue to serve Him through serving one another, and to always be strengthened in His grace through prayer. I ask you especially in this time to pray for families who are dear to my heart, and who I see so lost and so confused in this world. Dear ones, many times I have told you that it is the family that is the fountain, the source, the very seed of faith. Through the family, my littlest ones, my dearest children come to know God. Through their mother's love, through their father's care, through the fellowship and companionship of their siblings, every child comes to see the face of Christ. And so, you see how important it is that every family strive toward holiness, that every family honor and respect one another and grant to each other the dignity that is afforded to them, simply because they are an image and likeness of God.

Dear ones, in this time when there is such abuse, such neglect, such sorrow is in my maternal heart because of these things! Dear ones, will you not pray especially for the families and my littlest children, those who, because their families have chosen not to walk with God, shall not see the face of Christ, shall not know love, shall not know the grace and peace of God? These little ones, these precious ones, I touch with my own hand that they might one day come to the Father, that He might plant in them the faith, and the hope and the joy into their hearts, the faith, hope, and joy that their families, that their mothers and fathers, have neglected.

Dear ones, I do not tell you this that you should have worry or anxiety, for always my message is one of joy and of hope, for in every darkness there is the light, dear ones, and you, you are the light. How many times, how many times do you hear the words of my Son, "You are the light of the world"? Truly, become the light of the world, and especially the light to families! Illuminate the darkness by being an example in your own home, by praying as a family, husband and wife, children, mothers and fathers, praying as a family for all families and all people.

You know that married life, that parenthood, it is a calling, a vocation, and a tremendous blessing that God gives to you, that you might know a part of Him that would be hidden from you without it. Truly, the love of a mother, a father, a husband, and a wife, it is most like the love of God in that it is unending, it is unconditional. Practice these things in your home and do not let the trifles of life interfere with your relationship with God, with your relationship with one another, with your love. Love, as many times I have taught you, means service. It means giving completely of yourself and reserving nothing. Do this, dear ones! Do this and God shall reserve nothing for Himself, but shall pour upon you His every grace, His every peace, His every joy.

Dear ones, as always, I am your mother, and I pray that God would bless you and that the Holy Family, whom you should always ask the intercession of, shall guide you and watch over you always. May the Holy Spirit be upon you and may you live always in peace.

February 2002

Mary:

My dear children, it is good to be among you, to come to you with my motherly blessings, to bring to you the gifts of the Holy Spirit, He Who is sent as Paraclete, to fill you with wisdom, to fill you with knowledge of the truth, to fill you with courage and boldness of spirit, that you might truly witness this love of Christ that you have come to know. Dear ones, just as you live and breathe and laugh together, know that it is Christ Who is life within you! I have come, speaking of Him as teacher, as counselor, as friend and brother, as Lord and master, as healer, as savior, and still, He is many things, so much that there are not enough words in the world to describe His majesty. Today, I desire to speak of Christ as your life, for truly, He is life! He, Who reigned over death, Who through His majesty and glory destroys all evil, He Who, through the giving of His Own life, His Own blood, brought new life into this world, is with you. He dwells among you and in you. He is present! In your church, in your homes, in one another, He works. He changes the hearts of those who love Him and makes you a more perfect creation in Him. He desires for you, His children, to turn all things to Him, to give all that you are to Him that within you, He might work miracles!

Dear ones, if you do not have the life of Christ within you, truly, there is no worse, no more painful, no more horrible thing! If you fill your hearts with self-love and greed, with envy for one another's things, mere possessions, if you live your life in a state of sinfulness and darkness and you reject the light of God, then you cannot have life within you. If you do not find Him in the Eucharist often, as often as possible, if you do not seek Him in the sacraments and in the Church, you will not have His life within you. If you do not pray, each of you and as a family, you will not have His life within you. And so, dear ones, I tell you now, as I have told you many times, you must pray together, for one another, always. You must find Christ as He reigns over you in His Eucharistic love, in His holy Church. You must seek Him in your own hearts and lives by placing Him first, above all else, for none is greater.

Today, I invite you anew to look at the things that are in your life that cloud your vision, that make it impossible to see the light and the life that is within you, impossible to see the will of God. Be single-minded. May your heart and mind always be on God. Be filled with the Holy Spirit that He pours forth upon you to renew you, to make you a new creation unto Him. Live with peace in your heart and in your home, seeking holiness, seeking joy, bearing the light that is Christ's love to the world, that all might know Him through you, and thus, bringing the glory of God into this world.

Dear ones, as your mother, I desire all good things for you, and I truly wish to impart the peace that Christ alone can bring to you. Accept the life that He brings to you. Accept Him as He comes to you in many ways. Renew the baptismal promises that you made to be one with Him, to walk in His light, and to, upon your death, be united in glory with Him. Renounce all things that take you from Him, for truly, He alone is joy, He alone is goodness, He alone is majesty!

Dear ones, as ever I am your mother. I am with you, praying for you, interceding for you, for all my children. Continue to pray and to grow in holiness, that you might be drawn ever closer to our Father in Heaven through Whom all grace is possible.

March 2002

Jesus:

My dear sons and daughters, many times I have sent My mother and she has brought you My words. Today, I, your Christ, Am with you. This, dear ones, this is the time when you bear in your hearts and your minds the memory of My passion and My death and My resurrection. I have come to you today to tell you that I love you, to speak to you about that which you prepare to celebrate.

Recall how I entered Jerusalem. Recall how I was greeted with joy, and yet, not all there would welcome Me. There were many who hated Me. There were many who despised Me. Recall that I came to a place to gather with those brothers whom I had chosen, whom I had traveled with and known for so long, those who, though they first set eyes upon Me from fishing boats and streets, I knew before their birth. Recall that I gathered, that I brought them unto Me, that I broke bread with them and gave them a gift of My soul, the gift that would nourish My Church, My people, to this day and for all days. Recall, dear children, that I gave My own body, that I gave My own blood, not that they would remember Me in symbol but in truth, that I, your God, would be present with you in My body, in My blood, in My agony, and in My glory. Recall that those who gathered there, they could not understand the words that I spoke, the promises that I made to them. They fled in fear. When I was taken to a hill and placed upon a tree, all of My faithful were lost unto Me, and I knew despair. In the garden I prayed. And as they did that night, when I carried my cross, all who were with Me, all whom I loved, fled Me. I bore the stripes of the scourging on My back, each one with love, for you. Though I prayed, "Father, do not make Me undergo such a thing; take this cup from Me", it was not His will. And I, His Son, embraced His will with the fullness of My heart, that you might be saved.

I was mocked. As I, on My cross, looked out among the people there, I did not see their hatred, I did not see the curses, I did not see the insults and the stones that they hurled upon Me, but the love that God placed in them, He and I with our Spirit, that love which poured into them a share of our own life, that which is a reflection of Me. And as I looked out from upon My cross, I did not see only those who had gathered, some to mourn and some to mock, but every heart of every person for all of time.

I beheld you from the cross. I knew you. In My heart I spoke your name as I prayed, "Father, forgive them. They know not what they do". You now, in your lives My children, you turn from Me. You desire not My will, but your own. Do you not see that still I seek, and I see you? I know you. I Am with you. Even now and always I pray, "Father, forgive them, for they know not what they do".

Into the dead I descended, and many, many righteous souls were waiting to greet Me, and every knee bent, for none could stand in the presence of God. Then the dawn, and light! And the glory of My Father came upon Me and again I lived, as I live now in the kingdom I have prepared for you, and upon your altars, and in your tabernacles! And yet, those who knew Me so well, they did not know Me then. They did not recognize Me. Dear ones, My children, do not fail to see Me in your own life. I am waiting. I call to you, again and again, because I love you, because I desire to pour mercy upon you, and give you every grace and fill you with every joy! I, your God, desire to fill you with peace! Would you not accept this gift?

I, in My glory, in the life which is Mine now and always, in the life which is My Father and We in Our Trinity, in that life I come to you, and I Am with you. And each of you, each of you, I Am with you in your agony, and I Am there when all others flee you. I Am there as you break bread and share your meals among friends. I Am there! And as you gather at My table and celebrate the great banquet feast I have given you from My Own heart, I Am there! And when you crucify your own wills that My Father might act in you, and that Our Spirit might act through you, then too, I Am with you. I assure you as your Lord that when you die, when you come and see the glory that I merited for you on that dawning morning, then, I will be there waiting for you. Do not turn down such a gift! I long for you to embrace Me with the fullness of your life and grant to Me that which is My own: your body, your heart, your soul, your mind. Do not be afraid, for I Am with you even to the end of time!

April 2002

Mary:

My dear little ones, peace be with you. Know that as ever, I come to you as mother, as counselor, and advocate. Know that I pray that God would send His Holy Spirit upon you to make you a new creation in Him, to fill you with every grace, to fill you with every joy, to help you grow closer to Him. Dear ones, as your mother, I come to you. As your mother, I ask many things of you, all for your good, for the growth and the nurturing of your holy soul, placed in your bodies by God Himself when He breathed His life into you. Dear ones, my concern is with your soul's eternal happiness and with the glory of God. It is for this reason that so often I ask you to turn your hearts, to turn your minds, to turn your every action, and every word, toward God.

How often in this world, as parents, as friends, as teachers, as a great many things, you turn yourselves to taking care of the needs of your body. You, as good people, prepare a nice home for your children. You set aside good food for them to eat. You clothe them. You give them every good thing. You educate them. And yet, dear ones, there are many in the world today who forget, who forget to remind my dear little ones that they are a good creation of God Who loves them most preciously, Who is their father. This is something that you must do not only for your children, but for all whom you encounter, for the greatest sickness in the world today is that of despair. There are many in this world who suffer for want of food, for want of shelter, for want of friendship and yet I tell you, of all of these horrible things, of all of these sufferings, none is so great as those who have all and yet lose it because they do not have faith in God. How difficult it is for you to see this through the eyes of the world, that many of those who are most successful, as you have defined it on this earth, are most lost.

Despair is a deep sickness of the heart, soul, and mind. It plagues my children as a death, as a darkness that cannot be lifted, except through prayer, except through faith, except through trust. You, dear ones, you must cooperate in the plan of the Divine Physician in that you dispense His Good News to His people, that they might be healed. I ask you to do this each day through the way that you live your lives, through the words that you speak, through the way that you pray, through your own faith in God. How much light could be in the world if my children would but accept the fact that God is with them and loves them and would, in this knowledge, love Him in return.

Dear ones, you know that every mother asks her children to obey their father. It is my role as your mother, as your advocate. So again, I come to you asking you to obey your Father, to love your Father, to give to your Father all that is due to Him. Give your hearts, dear ones, that He might truly fill you with the joy that you have not yet known. Give your lives that not only your temporal needs might be cared for, but those of your spirit as well. Give your families that those children that you have provided every good thing for upon this earth through God's grace, might also have the gift of faith nurtured in their hearts. In your jobs, in your daily lives, in the strangers whom you encounter, dear ones, always be a light of Christ's love. It is the greatest gift that you can give back to the world.

My little ones, I come, and I teach you, and I bring to you the Word of God that you might know Him and understand Him. You cannot know God as He fully and truly is unless you envelop yourself in His holy Church, in His holy sacraments, in His divine will, and in the Holy Bible. The scriptures that you have been given, they are a treasure, for truly you can see with the eyes of those who saw the works of Christ, who knew Him, who walked with Him! God gave to you, through this prayer group, a great grace. He allowed you to see into the lives and hearts of many of those who are now glorified with Him in His heavenly home. For many months, He sent to you the Saints of Heaven, that you might come to see and know Him as God not only for the holy and righteous, but as God for the sinful and sorrowing.

Dear ones, I ask you again to remember the example that was set in their words and in their deeds. Go, dear ones, into your homes with your children and pick up the Scriptures that God gave to you as a gift and read and pray and love God through His words. See the example of His holy ones: of Peter, of Paul, of all of those who witnessed in His name and who, through their holy lives and through their deaths, merited the greatest reward, the pearl of great price.

Do not forget, dear ones, that to minister to your souls is the greatest, most perfect gift that you can give to your children and to your family. Families in this day are so often caught up in the turmoil of this world. How many homes are broken! How many families destroyed? How many marriages suffer? My maternal heart breaks at the thought. Yet, it need not be so, for still, after these many long years, you do not yet understand how powerful your prayer is! You do not yet know what a great gift you have been given. Dear ones, fill your heart with gratitude. Be filled until you sing with joy with the Angels of Heaven, for truly, it will be at the moment of your death that you will see what God has done for you, and you will fall to your knees and cry tears of joy.

Dear ones, my children, I am your mother, and I bring you always to the Father. I lift you up to Him in my prayer, in my worship, in my adoration, and I ask that He continue to pour tremendous grace upon you. How easy it is when you are not with God: in your mind, in your heart, in your faith, in your prayer, in your churches, to lose sight of Him, to let Him become a fleeting and passing thought in the back of your mind. Dear ones, do not allow this to be so, for if God is the center of your heart, if in your homes He is worshiped in His Eucharistic presence, in the sacraments that He has given to you, in His Holy Scripture, and in your lives, you, dear ones, will begin to learn to love as He desires for you to love. You will see each day that your family, your home, all that you are and all that you have, will grow close to God. I tell you, those who have found this way have known great joy and even in their sufferings, they have the peace that only Christ can bring.

My children, again this day I bless you. I ask you to continue to persevere on this journey that you have undertaken in your faith. God is with you! God is with you! God is with you!

May 2002

Mary:

My dear ones, praised be the name of Jesus Christ our Lord, our redeemer, and our king, for He alone can work great things in your hearts. He alone can save and heal you, can bring to you the grace, the mercy, and the peace that you desire in your homes, in your hearts, and in your world. Dear ones, as your mother, I come to you again to lead you to the Son. Always, always, I am a mother calling her children to the Son.

Dear ones, I have been blessed by God that I might come among you, that I might teach you, that I might share with you part of that vision which is mine: the glory of God! He Who has loved you so much as to send His Son to suffer, and to die, and to rise in glory, has sent me, that I might take your hand as a mother and lead you through your sufferings, through death, and into His glory, that which will become yours. God is so good that He sends a mother, for whom could we trust were it not our mothers, to teach and to lead and to, with gentle kindness, instruct, inspire, and change their little ones into that which God desires them to be? And so, I have come, and tonight, again I come.

Dear ones, I tell you, the love of God, it is without limits. It is immeasurable! You do not love a God Who desires to punish His children, Who distances Himself from them, Who desires to seek an earthly revenge upon them for sins, but rather, a God Whose love is so great that, truly each day, many thousands of times, He bleeds again for you on your altar in the breaking of the bread at the consecration. Dear ones, your God is such love that He desires to forgive you, not punish, or chasten you. Your God desires to forgive you with a forgiveness that is not known upon this earth: one that is complete, one that is without condition, one that is both merciful and just.

Turn your hearts to Him in your sinfulness, in that which leads you to die. Examine your hearts and your lives each day. See the places where pride, and pain, and fear pull you from Him. Then, dear ones, find solace in Him through your sacraments, through prayer, through the Eucharist. God gave these things to you, that you might have them as a most precious gift. Immerse yourself in His love by living His commandments and, in this way dear ones, you will see that it will not be difficult to change. What struggles all of humanity has! What fears! Truly, I tell you, never, never was there a time when more people on this earth were lost and afraid, and I, their mother, beseech the Father to send His light that is Christ to all nations. He has chosen to send that light through you!

Dear ones, you know that God has blessed you immeasurably. You know that the faith that you have is a gift. It is a grace. I tell you, how many of the Saints of Heaven who, once living wayward lives, turned toward God and would rather give their very lives, all that they had, all that they could possibly possess, just to have served Him for every moment of their lives! There are many who live many years without Him and find Him before they are called home, and there are many who do not. It is for this reason that my maternal heart aches. I, a mother, as you many are mothers and fathers too, love my children so much that I want all that is good for them. Having participated fully in the banquet feast that is God, in His heavenly kingdom, in all the splendors of Heaven, having seen things eyes cannot comprehend, words cannot describe, nor ears stand to hear but for God's grace, I wish to share this with you because the Father wills it.

You know the strength of love, for you feel that love for your children and your spouses and your friends. You know the strength of love, for when you pray, you feel it too toward those who hurt you, those who cause you pain, those who wish you harm. It is that love which must be your inspiration, that love which is God in His Most Holy Spirit, Who works among you, Who works within you, Who works through you, that must act. Each day, invite God in His Holy Spirit to come into you and make you a new creation, that all that is you might be perfected in Him, and all that is Him might perfect you. In this way, united fully to God, the Holy Spirit will pour forth innumerable graces into you and you, truly, can become the lights of the world!

And so, my children, I invite you to embrace your siblings, those who are your brothers and sisters in Christ. Take them by the hand and lead them, for your mother desires it, and the Father wills it to be so. May the peace of Christ Who is eternal, Who is the one true light, God forever and ever, be with you now and always.

June 2002

Mary:

My dear little ones, peace! May the peace of Christ be with you. Know that I am your mother, that I come to you always as a mother. Know that again this day, I bless you and I thank our Father in Heaven for allowing me to come, for it is such a blessing and such a grace that I can reach my children in this way to instruct them, to share with them the glorious mystery that is God, to grant them the peace that Christ alone brings, to lead them as ever back to Jesus.

Dear ones, you truly are my children, as all the children in the world are my own. Jesus gave the world to me to be a mother to the world, to be children to me, that all might be saved, that through the Immaculate Heart the gate might be opened, and you would see shining ever brightly the Sacred Heart that is my Son. Dear ones, let this be in all things a light, a truth. Dear ones, let the knowledge that you have been given be for you a gateway, a window. Let the great grace you have been given be for you the means to clearly see the Father through the Son, through His mother. Know that I do not come for myself, but for God Who sends me, and I come for no reason but that you might see Him more clearly.

In all things, do this: look for Christ, for the Father's glory, for the work of the Holy Spirit. When you examine your life, see how you are allowing God to act through you, or not. Examine all that you do and all that you are. See the person you are through God's eyes. See the great beauty you possess as His children, as His precious ones, as those created in His own image and called His sons and daughters. See how blessed you are and see the great ability He gives you to do much good in this world, to truly act as His instruments. Our God loves His people so much, His dear children, that He in His great wisdom, in His great power, in His great majesty, fills His church, fills His people, fills even your holy tabernacle with His presence, that you might be strengthened and have a source of life, a window to hope. See, dear children, that God our Father gives to you all things. See His presence in the world and be, dear ones, His hands and feet.

My children, how God, how our majestic Lord, pierces into this world, breaks into this world, into the consciousness of all people, of all races, in all time! See that every person, everyone, is given the tremendous beauty of a soul created as God designed it to be. And see too, how you, when you keep yourself close to God through the sacraments, through the Church, through prayer, through penance, through fasting, see how your soul can become a magnificent reflection of Him, and therefore, be a window, that others might see Him through you.

Dear ones, still you do not know how present God is with you. Still, you cannot see. Know that His Angels surround you, that the Son walks amongst His people in those who would carry Him in body and blood and soul and divinity in His Eucharistic Self. See that, now, after participating in the greatest of sacrifices, He dwells within each of you. He is present here, more present, more real, more truly, than you can see. Know that all of Heaven, all of Heaven prays for you, knows you, rejoices when you turn your faces toward the light of God and see that which is truly there: His love, His unending mercy, His perfect peace.

All my children given to me are precious. And each was born, each one conceived, with a glimmer of the light of God within them, for He breathed His own breath into each child and spoke His name to the newly formed soul, and every soul rejoices in Him. Dear ones, it is you who distance yourself from Him, for as infants, as children, as young ones, who did not rejoice in God and truly, and fully, and really believe that He was present? How many times my children remark that they have grown out of their belief in God. How sad to start life with eyes open, only to blind oneself!

Therefore, dear ones, I tell you this: rejoice in God and always commit to your hearts the words which He spoke to you, "Be as little children," for the little ones, they can clearly see God. Do not allow your lives, your needs, your desires, your difficulties, to cloud your vision, to close the window to the truth that you have on your altar, in your Mass, in the sacraments, in your very selves. Do not do as many would: close off your conscience, close off your soul and let it wither and die, that you might seek physical and material pleasures, pleasures that are passing. Know that I see my children suffering and, as any mother, I go to retrieve them, for many walk blindly toward the great abyss. They do not see the truth, the truth that was with them all along, the truth that they knew at their very conception, but chose to walk away from.

Each of you, my children, has an obligation, truly has a mission to share the light of faith you have been given. There are so many, so many who suffer so because they have not been shown the truth in their life and, though God might speak His name and breathe His life into them, the world has injured them greatly and there is no one, no one who would heal them. Therefore, again, again I beseech you, be instruments of the Father by allowing yourself to be open to His will, even and especially when it is not what you will. In doing so, He might act through you, and your sacrifice, your penance, will make reparation for all of those who, through their fault and through no fault of their own, do not yet know God as you have been blessed to know Him.

See that what you have received is a gift earned and merited only by the sufferings of Christ Himself upon the cross, through His glorious resurrection and ascension, and through the majesty that He is, sitting at the hand of our Father, Creator, and Lord. He has earned for you eternal life. He has merited for you a gift such as this, this tremendous mercy of God, this gift that is your faith. Thank Him, for it is only through Him that you know God and have any hope of salvation. Truly, little ones, God does not forget His chosen people, His dear ones, His true ones, His heart, and His joy. Every child is precious to God, and He desires for everyone to know

Him, truly and really as He is in His Eucharistic Body, in His true presence. You know that He comes to you in many ways. In all parts of the world, He manifests His glory, that all of His children might come to Him. Pray, dear ones, pray that He will continue to pour His mercies upon a willing world, a world that desires Him. Pray that my people might make themselves open to Him, might accept Him, might rejoice in Him, and that the things of this life that distract them might be no more, but rather, all things they do might be for Him.

Dear ones, you know your failings and your faults. You know your trials and difficulties, but you, dear ones, having been blessed by this grace, know too that God desires to forgive His children. God desires to gather His children into His arms. God desires to continue always to love you, to cherish you, to be your ever-present Lord. Remain with Him always, children. Always.

July 2002

Mary:

My dear ones, peace be with you. Know that I, your mother, am with you. Know that I come to you as your mother to bless you. Still God sends me to you, that I might give you His words, those words brought through me that you might know Him, that you might be more fully in His presence, for as always, dear children, He is with you. He beckons to you. He asks you to turn your faces to Him, that His mercy and grace might pour upon you and fill you with every blessing.

Dear ones, how the Holy Spirit acts in your lives when you allow Him to come fully into your heart, to fill you with His gifts, with His power, with His glory! Dear ones, I have, again and again, spoken to you about the great grace of pouring out all things of yourself and letting God pour Himself into you. When you live, when you pray, when you work, when you do all the things necessary in your life to sustain yourself and your families, I ask you to do them through the Holy Spirit. All my children are called to a vocation in God. All my little ones are called to a life lived fully in Him, even those of you who do not see for yourself a place in His plan. I tell you, the smallest of His little ones, the least of His people, can become the greatest, if he were to open Himself completely to the workings of God, and let Him work through each one of you.

Dear ones, I tell you, God is waiting for you! He is waiting for you to allow Him to come into your hearts and to free you from your sinfulness and your deceits, to free you from your sufferings and your pains, to free you from all things but that which is good for your soul. Know that God loves you so much that He desires for you to know perfect joy and perfect peace. Yes, it is possible to have joy even in suffering, for in those who have His Spirit dwelling within them, suffering can become a great joy. These things, they are incomprehensible to the mind of man, and it is for this reason that you must have the Holy Spirit within you, for alone you can do nothing, but in Him, all things are possible!

And so, my dear ones, again I invite you. Each day, each moment, turn your hearts and your minds to God. Invite the Holy Spirit in His majesty to come into you to work in, to clean, to purify your hearts, to truly pass them under the fire of His love, that they may become a new creation and that you, changed through the mercy of God, might become His perfect servant. Each day, open your hearts to Him, give to Him all things, and allow Him to work through you.

My dear ones, you struggle so hard, with such difficulty, to live the words that I have spoken to you, and to live the Gospel truths that alone will bring you joy. I tell you as your mother, it is not difficult to do such things when your heart and your mind are focused always on God. You will find, dear ones, that when God is the center of your life, when the Holy Spirit acts within you and through you, you will in your daily lives, become more fully alive, more fully aware of the gifts God has given you. Rather than turning away from the world, turning away from your families, turning away from the places God sends you to minister to His people, you will embrace them with a new love, with a new joy, a joy that is of God. You will see in your children the face of Christ. You will see in those around you His love, His image. You will see in the world, a majesty that is God, and you will rejoice always in the Lord and be a blessing upon this earth.

Therefore, if you wish, dear ones, to truly begin to love your families, to truly begin to love one another, you must love in the Lord, you must invite Him to love through you. Keep your hearts pure, that He might be in you, dwelling always in your hearts. Do not allow the temptations and sins of this world to distract you from that prize that is great and without price. Rather, live a holy life. Live a life in God, that clearly you might see Him, and fully you might know Him, and truly you might serve Him.

Dear ones, as always, I call you to prayer. Prayer is essential! You must pray, for it is through prayer that you can see your soul clearly. You can see your faults and your failures, and you can see the workings of God. In this way, you will become ever more perfected in Him and become a gift, a holy vessel, a tabernacle of His love, of His mercy, of His joy.

May peace be with you always, as again I invite you to learn to love as God loves, and then to live in His joy. Know that as your mother, I bless you. I pray that the Father Who is great, the Son Who is Redeemer, and the Holy Spirit, forever espoused to the Church, might be with you always.

August 2002

Mary:

My dear little ones, peace be with you. Know that again I gather you together, my children, to love one another and to love

God as you ought to love Him every day, to worship Him and praise Him with your voices, with your song, with your prayer, to love Him through the service of one another, through adoration of His most holy body and His holy blood. Know that again I call you together that I might teach you, that I might instruct you, that I might advise you, that you might grow closer always to Christ.

Dear ones, God Who is in Heaven desires for you to live in His mercy. His joy is without end. His peace, His peace is unfathomable! How many times I have spoken to you these things and how it encourages and lifts your heart up, and yet, you allow the sorrows and privations and the difficulties of life to continue to weigh heavily on your heart. I have called you to a life lived joyfully, a life lived in joyful sacrifice. Joyful sacrifice – something that so few can understand, but how clearly God speaks it to you, that you may know that which He calls you to: to love giving, to love abandonment, to love service, and above all else, to love only Him.

It is the joyful sacrifice, the joy-filled sacrifice, that I speak to you about. These words, how many times they are applied in your lives, for truly, even this night you have celebrated the most joy-filled sacrifice: that of the altar! The joy-filled sacrifice of Christ is the living body of Christ, though broken and crucified, risen in glory, and living, truly living! The joy-filled sacrifice of your own lives, it is your family, your friendships, your husbands and your wives. It is your difficult times, your sicknesses, your sorrows. It is your blessings, for there is no blessing that does not have a price.

Dear children, the blessings of the Lord are worth more than all the gems on this earth, but there is a price to be paid for all things. As followers of my Son, the price you pay is sometimes being scorned, sometimes being abandoned, disbelieved, taunted. The price you pay sometimes is more subtle: loneliness, a feeling of desire for God and yet, the inability to attain His perfect presence. It is a spiritual battle and a spiritual hunger, a joy-filled sacrifice in your prayer, in your heart, in your mind, in your soul, in your homes, in your workplace. In all that you do and in all that you say, you become a joy-filled sacrifice.

This is the way to become that which is given to you each day through the Holy Eucharist, the gift of Christ's presence. Follow in His humble way. He does not come in glory, but in humility. He does not come with grandeur, but simplicity. He does not come as king, but as the weakest, as the smallest, as the most menial. Truly then, I encourage you, each day begin to live this sacrifice joyfully and, in doing so, living the Christian life, following Christ even to the cross. Then you will begin to understand His joy and you will begin to participate in the true beauty that is God.

My dear ones, lift your voices and your hearts to Him with all things and let Him, He Who is mighty, lead you. Be but His servant and the blessings will be great. My dear ones, as your mother I am with you always, and I lead you ever toward holiness.

September 2002

Mary:

My dear children, again it is good to be with you in this way. Praise God, for in His goodness He has poured forth such mercies into this world, that you might come to know Him ever as your Father, ever as your savior, ever as your Lord. Dear ones, I your mother come to you to spread the joy that is Christ, to give to you His words, that you might hear and obey, to give to you His love, that you might immerse yourself in it and love all in return.

Dear ones, I know it is difficult for you to maintain the life that you desire, to live each day, in every situation, at all times. Constantly you are fighting against the nature that is your own, faulted, free of God's will. And yet I tell you, with the Holy Spirit, with the power of God in Jesus Christ, you, dear children, can be perfected in Him and never will His will leave your mind, your heart, your soul. Each month, I speak to you. I bring you these words from Heaven with joy. I am so pleased that you have responded with love, and yet, how many go to their homes and their families and their jobs and forget what I have said, though you desire not to do so.

It is the same problem in the hearts of all. Each of you seeks to know how to live God's will more perfectly. It is the amazing fact of human existence that sometimes, the things we want most to do are the things we do least, and that which we despise, is what we cling to. Therefore, dear children, knowing that it is the faulted nature of man that falls, God gave to you the sacraments to strengthen you, to perfect you, to help you overcome that fallen nature, that humanity, and raise you up to His glory.

I tell you it is not possible to live the will of God each day in your life without His most holy presence within you, body and blood, soul, and divinity. If you do not start your day receiving Him, loving Him in the Eucharist, it is as if you are starting without water or without air. How could you possibly succeed in all that God lays before you that day? If you do not seek Him in the sacrament of reconciliation often, if you do not examine your heart and your soul to see the faults that bind you to the same life each day, a life that you despise, a life of sinfulness, then how can you be perfected with the love that God pours into your soul? How can you accept His mercies? How can you accept His grace if you have not eyes to see it?

Dear ones, for this reason I recommend always, always come to God in the holy Church He has given to you, through its teachings, through your sacraments. This is the difference between failing in your humanity and living in God's perfect grace! This is the difference. Pray! This is the third thing you must do always, in every situation of temptation. In every situation of difficulty, pray! In joys, pray! In sorrows, pray! At all times, make your life a living prayer.

Dear ones, you strive to be what I ask you to be, what God asks you to be, an example of His love in this world. And you, my dear children, you have fully accepted this grace I have brought to you, and none gathered here today desires to live in sinfulness, to live without God's love. The danger for you, dear ones, is not an overt rejection of God, but the simple human action of forgetting! Ask yourselves always, when speaking to your children, when speaking to your spouse, whether at your work, at church, when you are playing and praying: is your mind and your heart on God? If it is not, you will succumb to the faults and failures that will always be your cross until the day that you die. If your heart is on God, then, only then, will your life begin to change, will every single relationship begin to change, will every single person whom God has placed in your life begin to see Him in you.

It is crucial then, dear ones, that you find Him in the sacraments, that you pray often, and pray as a family, spouses, children, mothers, fathers, extended family, friends- all pray, pray together! It is the strengthening, this outpouring of grace that happens in prayer, that will give you eyes to see when you have drifted far from God and the grace to be grateful, to fill your heart with a joyful song always, for God who loves you so much is worthy of all praise.

My dear children, let this message not depress you in your spirit, but encourage you and bring you new hope, for I have seen how my little ones have struggled to live as I have called you to live. And it is my prayer that these words that I have shared with you tonight will lessen your burden, will ease your way, and will show you how to find the way back to the path of the cross.

My dear ones, know that I am your mother and as ever, I love you as a mother loves. It was a great grace that God gave the world to me, that I might mother them, that I might lead them, that I might bring them to my Son. It is in His name that I bless you and that I come, and may He be praised forever and ever.

October 2002

Mary:

My dear little ones, peace again be with you, upon your families, upon your homes, in all that you do, in all that you say. May peace be with you, for in peacefulness you will hear the silent voice of our God Who calls to you. In the angst and turmoil of this world, you cannot hear. In the daily struggles, if not offered to God, you cannot hear. In the trials and the tribulations, even in the joys and celebrations of your life, if you do not turn your ear and heart to God, you cannot hear. You must live in His peace now and forever. I pray that the peace of Christ will be with each one of you this evening and always.

My dear ones, as your mother, again I come to you to call you to the Father. In your families, in your homes, you see how God loves, how He loves so tremendously. God, the Father, leads the home with love. He leads His Church with dignity, with beauty and respect, glorifying His Church every single moment: the times of great joy, the times of tremendous darkness. The Father protects the Church. He cares for it. He Who is life, defends life, defends love. He cares for His family, His children, His Church, and truly no evil shall ever prevail against it, for God in His mercy and wisdom will protect it from all and, in the end, only His holy Church, established in His glory, will stand.

Dear ones, I come as mother, a position given to me by the mercy of God, for He has blessed me so that I might come and speak to you and teach you truly as a mother. I come to gather the children, to bring them into the light. I come to show them the truth that is the Father, the Son, and the Holy Spirit. I come to lead and to teach, to gently admonish when necessary, to show you the way to God, that you children might be gathered together.

You are my children. You are first and always the Father's children. He has created each of you to be brother and sister to one another, to love each other, to defend each other, to protect each other, to pray for each other, to heal each other, to teach each other, to love one another. He has created you for one another, for no man will enter Heaven by his own doing, it is first and always the grace of God in his heart and then the prayers, the help, and the love of others. How many of you would still nourish the faith that is a seed in your heart planted by God were it not for the love of a parent or teacher, one who taught you the right and the truth?

My maternal heart is sad, for so many in the world do not teach my children any longer the truth that God loves them, that He is alive, that He is with them, that He desires their love. How sad it is, for God grants to all people in their lifetime the opportunity to see Him, to know Him, to love Him. There has never been a man, nor will there ever be one, who did not in one moment of his life have the definitive opportunity to grasp at the gift of faith with the fullness of his being and to love God fully. Were it to be not so, then truly God would not be a God of love and mercy, but He is. How many times the light of God penetrates the hearts and souls of my little ones only to be squelched by the darkness around them. You see then, how important it is that you be carriers of my message of truth, that message that is the Gospel message, that you be carriers of the light of Christ, modeling always His love, that others might see through you and Him within you.

The gift of faith, it is truly one of the greatest gifts you have upon this earth, the greatest, second only to the true body of Christ, for when one is in the true presence of God, faith is no longer in question. Were my children everywhere on earth but to open their eyes, see through the veil of darkness and death and into the light of God in a way that they always were meant to, then, truly every man, every woman, every child, would lie flat on the floor in gratitude before God in His Eucharistic body! How blessed are you then, that among all the people of God, He has chosen you to receive the fullness of His truth!

There are so many, so many faiths. God does not divide. It is man who divides, and yet, God loves each of His children without exception, His love is that great. But you, you have been given the fullness of the sacraments, the tremendous gift of the body and blood of Jesus Christ! How blessed are you! How blessed! With every gift there is obligation, there is responsibility, there is the grace, the privilege, the joy of sharing that gift with your brethren.

All of you know, love, are friends with, those who do not share your faith and yet, they too can truly commune in the presence of God through you, would you be but a willing vessel for the Holy Spirit and abandon your own will, your human will, to God, that His will might work through you. Never has a man accomplished great things by his own doing, but it is God in you who accomplishes mighty things.

Through these many years I have taught you. Through this long while you have come and gathered here. Through the messages that I have given, that I have taught, through the saints of Heaven who have come to you, sent by our Father, you have come to see that the definitive change, the moment when one accepts the grace of God, is not brought upon by human ways, but the infinite mercy of God penetrating the heart of His children. It is God first. It is God always. And when you, dear children, in your homes, in your families, in your lives, begin to truly live God first, God always, then, and only then, will the full grace of this gift you have been given, the gift of my words, the gift of your faith, the gift that is the Church, come to realization. Then, and only then, will every knee bend at the name of God, and every tongue utter, "Jesus is Lord"!

My dear ones, pray fervently and pray always, for prayer is your defense and your weapon. Prayer is your strength. It is truly most essential. Pray with your families. Pray without ceasing. Pray always. My dear ones, may that peace that is Christ's love, that is God's Holy Spirit, that is the Father's grace, be with you now and always.

November 2002

Mary:

My dear children, again it is good to be with you this day. Again, I bless you as your mother and pray always that God would draw you nearer to Him, nearer each day in your thoughts, in your words, in your actions. Dear ones, open yourselves to the light that is Christ, to His life in you. God has poured forth a portion of His Spirit upon His people, that there might be a great renewal in His faithful Church, a great renewal among His people, a great renewal in the hearts of each of you! My little ones, God's Spirit works as never before in the world today. How true it is that He is present and alive in this world, as true and as real as you have experienced Him this night when receiving His most holy body and most precious blood.

Dear ones, for so long the world has walked in darkness. As the years have passed, they have forgotten the truth that Christ came to teach, the truth that God our Father in Heaven taught years before Christ walked upon this earth, the truth that has been from the beginning of creation, truly from the beginning of time and before, the truth that is God, always will be God, and will forever more be God, He Who has no beginning and no end, He Who is all things, for all time.

Dear ones, this truth, this precious and beautiful truth, passed on from God Himself through the person of Jesus Christ into the Church in the wisdom of her teaching, in the holiness of her sacraments, is available to you now and always. God sent His Son into this world to be a powerful force for conversion, to be a reminder, to be a true and new covenant with His people, and yet, when Jesus rose, He did not leave you, but He left His holy sign, His holy Church, and His holy body in the holy sacraments.

Dear ones, what a great time this is, for the Spirit works in ways unknown to men. The Spirit works in the hearts of people. He works in the Church glorified. He works in the Church militant and in the Church in Purgatory, that all souls, all souls touched by the love, the grace, the mercy of the Spirit of God will come to know Him, to truly see Him, to experience Him with hearts and eyes unveiled, and truly love Him anew. Dear ones, what a marvelous time this is, for God gifts you in so many ways and gives you every grace that you need to accept His love, to live His way, to live in eternal joy! What a great time this is for the holy Church, for God Who has created this, His bride, shall never let it go asunder, but has led her through many years, through many times, through many struggles. And in this time when you, blessed with such great and powerful leadership, with such holy leadership, have come to see these wonderful awakenings of faith in parishes individually, in the Church as a whole, in individual families, in individual hearts, you will truly come to praise God as never before and thank Him for His glory.

I share these things with you, dear ones, that you might always be encouraged. How often I have said this to you, "Be encouraged!" May you be encouraged. May you live in hope. This is the heart of my message: hope in God, for with no hope in God there is nothing. With no hope in God there is no reason to live, for if you do not trust Him, if you do not hope in Him, and you do not love Him, you shall not have life within you. If you do not seek Him in the Church and in the sacraments, if you do not love Him in the Eucharist, you will not have life within you. If you do not pray, if you do not live truly the call of sacrifice and service, if you do not love others your very best, you will not have life within you. How sad it is that so few in this world truly know what it is to live!

This is why God has sent me. It is why He continues to send me and will continue to send me until the time of His appointed hour has come, the time known not even to myself. Then He will cease to send me here and to all places, for it will no longer be necessary, for the entire world will come to know Him, and so many, so many will fall to their knees in adoration. This is the time spoken of for all time, from all history, from every prophet, in every age, in your sacred Scriptures, and at every pulpit every Sunday since. Dear ones, as your mother, as one who in Heaven sees the exaltation of the Church glorified and the glory of the face of God, I too can say to you, "God has great things in store for His children!" Be faithful to Him. He is faithful to you.

Dear ones, then, never despair. Never have a lack of hope. Never have a lack of love, nor truth. Do not allow yourself to be deceived by the darkness that is a perception in this world, that is a deception of the evil one, for I tell you, there is great light, and there is great hope, and there is marvelous conversion, and there is true awakening. Do not allow yourself to be deceived, to think that all things are bad and that all of creation is truly without God, for this is not so. His voice, His face, His Spirit is echoed in everything He has created, and it glorifies Him. In every child, in every heart, young, old, He is glorified simply in their very existence. This is what it truly means to have a love and a respect for the tremendous gift of life that God gives, to know that every soul, every soul glorifies God by its very existence.

How different those who have faith see the things of this world, and the trials of daily life. How different those who have faith see the Church, the sacraments, your priests, your bishops, all your leaders. How different those who have faith see each of you, when you gather to worship and to pray together. How different the world will look, if you would unveil your eyes and see God's tremendous grace, His tremendous mercy, His great will.

And so be encouraged, but never, dear children, lose your vigilance in prayer. Persevere in prayer. Pray again and always. Never cease to pray, for you cannot pray enough. It is the food for your soul, for it is in prayer that you commune with God, that He speaks His will to you and makes Himself known. Prayer with the sacraments, a love for Mass, and frequent reception of the Holy Eucharist, is the way to come to know God fully. What great gifts He has left for you here on earth. What great gifts He extends to you from Heaven. What great gifts He will extend to the world as He does each and every day. What a tremendous gift to allow me to come this night and speak these words to you, even if it is only to encourage you to persevere one more day, one more hour, one more moment.

Your lives can be filled with joy, even in the midst of terrible suffering. Your lives can be filled with peace even, in the midst of unrest. Your lives can be filled with love even when surrounded by hatred. Turn your hearts, turn your minds, turn your prayer, turn your lives, to God. Always keep God center in your heart and your life, in your homes and your families, in your community, in your church, in the world. In this way, truly, the renewal that is promised, the renewal that occurs each day when many hearts are converted to my Son through the tremendous mercy of God, will come about in your heart as well as the world. May the peace of Christ be with you now and always.

December 2002

Mary:

My dear children, all praise be to Jesus Who truly is, King of Kings and Lord of Lords! As you have gone through this time of celebration in the Church, as you have gone through Advent, looking with eyes of wonder toward the coming of your Emmanuel, the eve of Christmas, when you celebrate in the dimness of the Church the coming of the light, and Christmas Day, when you celebrate the coming of our Lord not in glory, but in humility, in obedience, in perfect love; as you have gone through the great mystery of the birth of Christ incarnate, I, your mother, have been with you. I bless you and praise God! Join your prayers to mine in thanking Him, for truly, He is so great as to give you His Own Son. How tremendous a gift! How tremendous.

As you have gone through the celebrations, as you have come together as a parish, as a community, in your families, as friends, you have, it is my prayer, kept in mind the great gift, the greatest gift, that is Christ. To keep your heart focused on Him, your eyes firmly upon the cross, your mind always on the will of God, that is the greatest gift that comes with faith, the gift that God gives to you on Christmas, the gift of the Son born of a lowly woman, born in humility, born to die for you, the gift of faith to hear and to believe though you do not see, though you were not there. But I was there that night, and I tell you, truly God is great!

Dear ones, it has been the time of celebration, a time of joy, of remembrance of the great gift that is Christ, present now with you always in your soul, always in your church, always in the sacraments, and most especially, in the holy gift of the altar, the eternal gift of God: the body and blood, soul, and divinity of His Own Son. What a tremendous gift to have each day in your life! What a tremendous grace to have in your churches, in your homes, even now in your hearts, as you have participated this evening in the Mass and received Him. Truly, this is a joy that should not be remembered only at Christmastime, but always, each day, each moment. Then you will live with joy in your heart, peace in your homes, peace in your families. Your time of celebration is not through, for though many now are quieted after the Christmas rush, you, my faithful ones, you, my children, you, all those in the world who would hear me, you know there is reason to celebrate, for still, the Christ is with you, still He is the Living Sacrifice, still He is the Eternal Gift, the gift given daily, broken on your altars. Soon you will enter the season of Lent. In this time, you will remember the greatest gift of Christ on earth, the true gift of a man and God in One: His passion, His death, and His resurrection! What a beautiful thing God has created in the celebration of these many mysteries in the Church, for truly in the Church, with the Church, together as the Church, you remember the fullness of the life of Christ and, in doing so, you are pulled closer into our Father's heart.

My dear ones, this evening there are many who celebrate a different thing, for it is the turning of a new year. It is the coming of a new time. Let this day be no different than any other in your life in that this is a day to change your heart. There will be many tonight who will make promises they will not keep, who will celebrate a time that for them holds fear because they do not have faith, who will celebrate the coming year with uncertainly, with doubt, perhaps with sadness and loneliness. This is not what God has for His faithful children. It is not what God desires for you, for you have been gifted. You dear ones, you have been gifted to see that God is alive, that God is with you, that God is ever present. What then should you fear? What then should you doubt? It is a gift offered not only to you, but to the whole world. And this is the reason that God sends me and many messengers, and works many signs, and has given to you even your angels to lead you and the saints of Heaven to pray for you. He desires for His children to see Him though they do not see with eyes of the body, to hear Him though they cannot hear with the ears of the body, to know Him though they could not know Him as I did, one night long ago, when He came upon this earth, Word Incarnate. You have been given these things by God. You have been gifted by Him. You know the truth and have been given every grace.

Now dear ones, you must share this blessing. In your homes, in your families, in every place you are sent, share the truth and the light you have been given freely, without price, for love. Truly, there is no man upon this earth who can say he deserves, through his own works, the great graces that God pours into the hearts of all men. Even I, a simple woman, I cannot believe that God chose me to become a living tabernacle, and yet, that is the measure of God's love! Dear ones, why then should you know this joy when your brothers suffer? Why should you have such faith when they are alone? Why should you have no fear when there is tremendous fear in this world? It is for you to share this gift, to share the grace. In every home, in every domestic church which is the household, it is for the parents to teach and the siblings to help one another. It is the same for you. God your Father in Heaven has sent me, blessed to become your mother through His Word, to teach you. And you, you blessed ones and gifted ones, given a tremendous grace that so many would die to have one moment of, you must share with your brothers and sisters in Christ the truth that is your faith.

Let this, then, be your promise for this new year and always, for every day, for every year, for every moment, for every breath upon this earth that God allows you to have, that you will with a steadfast heart, with the courage of the Holy Spirit, with the commitment and the love and the fidelity that God has shown to you, spread the truth that God loves you tremendously, and that He is alive in this world and is calling His children to Him! Live this joy each day and others will see Christ in you. Pray each day with gratitude and God will continue to bless you. Speak the truth in all that you do, and all will see God's love growing in your heart, multiplying the graces, and bringing the light of Christ, born upon this earth, into the hearts of many.

May the peace of Christ Who is all goodness, Who is all joy, Who is the gift of love be with you now and always.

January 2003

Mary:

My dear children, peace be with you again today as always. May Christ be center of your heart, center of your life, center in your home. Dear ones, with joy I come to you as mother, to bless you, to care for you, to advise you, to intercede on your behalf. As mother, I come to show the way to the Father, to the Son, through the Holy Spirit.

Dear ones, often you have heard me speak about making Christ the center of your heart, the center of your life. Never is it more important than now, when there is such distraction from the faith, when there are many, many things that would pull you out of God's loving presence, not by His will, but by your own, for my children, God is, as ever, with you! Each day, in all that you do, He is present with you. Each day, He waits to guide you, to help you, to lead you, to send His Holy Spirit to teach you, that the road on which you walk will become easier, that your burdens might be lighter. He gives to you His own body, flesh and blood, soul, and divinity, in the Holy Eucharist, the Great Sacrifice. He gives to you your sacraments, that you might be reconciled unto Him and know peace in Him. Do not then, dear children, take such blessings for granted. Do not walk astray from them, but firmly and fastly stick to that which brings you closer to Him, the sacraments, the Eucharist, prayer, and prayer with family.

Dear ones, the family that does not pray together cannot survive, for prayer is most essential. I have said before that you would do better to survive without the sun or the rain, than without prayer. Again, I tell you this. My dear ones, mothers and fathers, you must guide your children from a very young age to know God through prayer, to hear His voice, to love Him, and to desire to serve Him. The family is the cradle of faith. It is the place where God plants the seeds of joy into the hearts of His little ones, for truly, you who are mothers and fathers, you are the face of God to your young ones. You must come together to pray. Celebrate together as you attend the Mass and receive Christ into your bodies, as you receive Him into your homes. Celebrate the great Mass, the holiest of prayers. Do not allow yourselves to become distracted, but know that your God, Who gives you such blessings, calls you to life anew in Him and desires for you to live it joyfully.

My little ones, in your families, let peace rule in the home. Spouses, do not bicker and quarrel among yourselves, for truly there is nothing worth dividing a kingdom of God over. You are an example of the Trinity, husband and wife joined with the Father, like Father, Son, and Spirit: one. Dear ones, you are an example to your children. You are an example of love and of forgiveness, an example of obedience, an example of service, an example of humility. Live each day this way and pray that the Holy Family might intercede on your behalf, for God so loved the family that He placed His Son into a home with an earthly mother and an earthly father, that He too might grow to love God in the way in which your children will come to love Him, through the love of a mother and father.

Children, obey your parents. Speak kindly to them. Always respect and grant dignity to those who have loved you and provided so much for you, for they are an example of God and if you are obedient to your parents, you will be obedient to God. Learn the discipline of humility. Learn the discipline of servitude. Learn the discipline of obedience above all else, and you will not wander far from God.

Let the home be a joy-filled place. Do not allow divisions, do not allow strife, do not allow the tensions of your everyday lives: work, family pressures, your friends, the world about you, to disrupt the peace that Christ gives to His children in the home. May the home become a sacred place where the sanctity of life is celebrated, where the dignity of each one, each individual person, is raised above all else, because you, you my precious ones, are an example, the life, the very breath of God's love.

Dear ones, I speak to you on the family today, as often I have, because families are so in need of prayer, and there is such sadness in families today. In your own nation, in your own community, in your own parish, there is sadness in the homes. There is division. There is strife. There is pain. God did not design the family in this way, but He designed it as an example of love and of truth, of beauty and joy. Begin to live this way in your own homes: husbands caring for their wives as Christ loves the Church, wives bearing fruitfully children, that they might glorify God and love Him and serve Him alone, children obeying their parents and learning to love as they must to grow into the men and women that God desires for them to be. Begin to live this way, each day, that those around you might see the joy in your home, the joy in your family, and the joy that pervades your heart, that they might too desire to live as God desires and they may too, come to know the peace that Christ offers you, the peace that you embrace.

Dear ones, as your mother, again I bless you. I am with you. I am with your families, and I am with this parish. I guide you each day. Heed my words. Heed the words of God. Pray faithfully and live faithfully, for your God is a faithful God and He is with you always. Dear ones, may the peace of Christ be with you this night, and always.

February 2003

Mary:

My dear little ones, peace be with you. Know that again I come to you as mother. Know that again I bless you. I bear to you the peace of Christ. I bring forth from God His blessings, His mercy, and His grace to share with you, that you might come to know Him, love Him, and serve Him ever more in your lives.

Dear ones, how blessed you are that you have the opportunity, each day, to give all that you do to God. Truly, your lives can become a living sacrifice. How easy it is to forget, when we go about the daily things of life, to make God the center. How easy it is to become distracted, to lose your focus on Christ Who truly is the Way, the Truth, and the Life. Dear ones, again then, I remind you. Each day, you have the tremendous opportunity to bless all those God sends into your life, to be a source of grace and mercy on this earth, to glorify the Father by that which you do.

Your lives are a gift from God. Your families, your friends, even your homes: they are blessings provided to you by God. God cares for your every need. He cares for you spiritually, physically. He cares for you in all things. It is to you, dear children, the task given to care for one another. Each of you in your daily lives has the opportunity to serve. Each of you, in going about your daily tasks has the opportunity to glorify God by making your life a living sacrifice.

Dear ones, it is not difficult to live in such a way if you focus completely on Christ. When the cross is the center of your heart, it will be that which you most desire. My dear ones, know that it is Christ Jesus in His glory, Christ Jesus Who is center in your heart, center in your life, center in your mind, Who will accomplish great things in you. You need not do anything but trust in Him, place your cares in Him, give all to Him, for He has given you much.

Dear ones, to become the living sacrifice, this is the way to most emulate Christ Who loves you so dearly that He gives to you, each day, His body, His blood, His soul, His divinity. On your altars, in His Eucharistic love, He has given to you Himself, the true Living

Sacrifice. When you truly begin to serve Him through serving those around you, when you begin to serve Him by making Him the center of your heart, when you begin to serve Him by, each day, living for Him, through Him, and in Him, then, and only then, will you understand the true grace, the true mercy, the true glory, that is His Eucharistic body.

Dear ones, what blessings you have been given, that your God cares for you so much, is so great, that He gives to you His Own self. Dear ones, would you not do the same in return by giving all that you are to Him, by giving your all to Him? Truly, I tell you, as your mother, the Holy Spirit Who is great, the Holy Spirit Who is great, the Holy Spirit Who is great, will work many miracles through you, if you will open your hearts, open your minds, and truly place God first, always first!

Dear ones, it is as your mother that I bless you. Know that this day and always, I am with you, interceding before God for all of you. I carry your intentions to Him. I place you at the foot of the cross. Always you are in my heart. Always you are in my heart! May the peace of Christ Who is eternally King of the World, King of the Universe, King of the Hearts of all Mankind, be with you now, and always.

March 2003

Mary:

My dear children, praised be Jesus! Thank God and bless Him, for what good things He has done for us this day and always. God Who is ever faithful to us provides all things, that we might be filled with His love, filled with His joy, filled with His Spirit. Now, you gathered here, having shared in the great mystery of the holy Mass, having participated in the gift of the Eucharist, you now, as I once was, become Christ-bearers, truly holding Christ in the depths of your heart, in the fullness of your bodies. You have become living tabernacles. You have become a sign to all people. Dear ones, what a gift and what a grace, that those who might see you will see Christ within you, both in the way you act, in the words you say, in the faith that you have, and in your own corporal bodies, for truly you are united, one people, under the same God, in Christ.

Dear ones, what a gift God has given us in Himself, for He is Father to children. He is the One Who guides us, Who teaches us, Whose wisdom is greater than all things. He is Son and Redeemer and Healer and Teacher. He comes in His body and blood, soul, and divinity, to fill His people, that we might have strength in Him and in Him alone. He comes in His Spirit to be the great advocate, the great teacher, the great minister to all people. He sends His Spirit upon His Church, upon His priests, upon His faithful, that they might minister to one another, teach one another of His holy love, love each other with the love of God and, in doing so, bring the beatific vision of Heaven to this earth. In some part, each day, you are able to see God as He is in one another.

Dear ones, do not forget that God, Who loves you so much that He came to this earth and became man that you might know Him as a man, that you might know Him as a divine person and a human soul, loves you so much that still He comes to you! Daily, He is on your altars and in your churches. Daily, He is in your homes and among your family. Daily, you have the opportunity to serve Him, to love Him fully, to give all that you have to Him. In doing so, dear children, you will be most blessed, for giving all to God, giving all that you have to Him, all that you are to Him, all that you ever shall be to Him, truly it is the road to sainthood. You have come to know through those whom God has sent to you that the way to become a holy person of God is not to be perfected in your own will but perfected in God's will. To abandon yourself completely to Him, to give to Him all that you are, that is the greatest gift that you can give to yourselves, to your families, to the world. When you become for Him a vessel of His Spirit, when you empty yourself of all that is of you, then, dear ones, God can do marvelous things through you.

I urge you and encourage you this day, to again commit your hearts to being fully in love with Christ. Fill yourselves with His Word. Absorb the Mass, the sacraments, the great life that He breathes into your soul in each meeting, in each encounter. Live each day the faith that you profess so devoutly when you pray. Live the faith that God gave to you as a gift, that you might gift others with the example of that faith.

Dear ones, do not become discouraged or distracted. Do not become so absorbed in your problems, in your troubles, and in your sorrows, that you fail to see the road that is ahead of you. It is easy to become lost. It is easy to become distracted, for there are such trials in life and such difficulties, and yet, he who has true faith, who sees the love of God, who knows how God works in the hearts of His children, can look past the storms, can weather them out, can see the glory that waits on the other side of the passion.

Dear ones, just as Christ Himself walked the road of passion, just as He, He Who is greater than all things, first had to suffer, had to die, before the resurrection, before the ascension, so too must you die to yourselves and to your own lives, giving up all that is yours, all that you are, all that you have in your mind that God might work through you. It is a great sacrifice, for the mind of man does not desire to give up that which he wants, but rather to seek out his own pleasures. It is the state of the nature of man, and it is the reason why man continues to sin even with such good news, even with such grace, even with such blessings. But you must not think that there is no hope, for other than your sinful nature, you are an image of God! He created you as He is, perfect! He created you to love, to shine His light, His joy, His beauty, His grace, to be carriers of light into a dark world. Other than the sinfulness, which you must not embrace, but you must fight against each day, praying for conversion, other than this you are as Christ was and always will be. It is the intention of God, it is the will of God, that you return to such a state, that again man and God might be united in one: Creator and creature, Father and son, always united in love.

It is for this reason He sends His mother to call you, to teach you, to show you the way. It is simple, dear ones. Place your hands in God's. Place your arms around God. Place your eyes upon God as a child with a father or mother. Trustingly, let Him embrace you. Trustingly, let Him fill you. Trustingly, let Him free you, that you might again become that which He knows you to be, a people always united in Him. Cling to nothing in this world. Cling to nothing in your lives. Cling to the cross and embrace it, for it is through the cross that you will receive eternal life.

Dear ones, know, as your mother, I am with you now, and always. I intercede always before God on your behalf and pray that He may fill you with His unending peace.

April 2003

Mary:

My dear little children, alleluia! Christ is risen! You are celebrating the season of Easter, the season of hope and of joy, a season filled with the goodness of God's merciful love, of His greatest gift. Dear ones, what a joyful time it is for the Church. What a time of celebration, for passing through the passion you came upon Easter morning and, as the first disciples discovered, you found Christ risen in your churches, in your homes, in your hearts.

Dear ones, what a joyful time in Heaven, to remember the great gift of God, a tremendous gift, the greatest gift: the resurrection, that gave to us the promise of eternal life! Without His resurrection there would be no life for us, for He died that we might have life abundantly. We who are in Heaven, who share in His glory, the glory that God promised from age to age, from Abraham to a humble maiden in a small town many years ago, to you, that glory that became alive on Easter lives with you. Dear ones, be then, a joyful people, for God created you to be joyful! If you do not have joy in your hearts, if you do not see the resurrection in your lives, in your faith, in the service that you offer to others, if you do not begin to live life anew, how can others see Christ in you?

Dear ones, truly as it was those many years ago, Christ is alive and walks among you, but as many of His followers could not see and then did not believe, much of the world is living in a state where they do not see that Christ lives, nor do they believe that there is a God of hope and mercy, a God of justice and strength, a God of love and joy Who has given them such a precious gift. Much of the world is still living the passion. Much of the world is lost in the desert. Much of the world is seeking Christ and cannot find him, for there are few who will truly bring Him into this world, living through them.

Dear ones, you, as the first apostles, have been told the good news: He lives! He is with you! You have the choice, for you, as they in those first days, cannot see Him with your eyes, you cannot feel Him with your hands, you cannot hear His voice, and yet, you must decide if you believe His words are true. If you believe, then you must understand that when He said, "Lo, I am with you, even until the ends of time," that was truth, spoken from the master of truth, and that, truly, as real as He was in the room in which He appeared, He is real among you. He is with you. He is with you in body and blood, in soul, and divinity, in His humanity and His divinity, perfected beyond all things, for He was truly and will always be God-Made-Man, the Godhead and the Humble Servant. He lives! He is with you! I come to tell you this good news, to remind you of this, for what a joyful season it is. How can you not have hope in your hearts when reflecting on this?

Dear ones, dear precious children, I am your mother. I come to you to encourage you, to teach you, to show you the way to Christ. I tell you now, look to Him, the most precious of gifts. Look to Him through His passion, through the gift of His Own body, through His death and into His resurrection. Look to Him in glory, for He is there. He waits to come into your hearts, into your lives, into your homes anew. He waits to resurrect your families, to renew your marriages, to renew your parenting, to renew your friendships, to renew every vocation that you have taken into your lives, that all may become a glory for Him. He waits to heal you. As God healed His broken body and made it whole again, made it new, so too does Christ desire to transfigure you, both in body and in spirit. He waits for you. He waits to direct you as He directed His first apostles to go among all nations and make disciples therein. He waits for you, to whisper His will into your hearts, to teach you the way to love as He loved, to teach you the way to come to Him in eternal joy.

Find Him in your lives, dear ones, for He is with you. He lives! What a joyful thing! What a joyful day! May the peace of Christ, Who is our risen Lord, be with you now, and always.

May 2003

Mary:

My dear children, as always it is good to be with you. I come again and always as your mother with the love of the Father, with the blessings of the Holy Spirit, to offer you the salvation of the Son. Dear ones, you who have been called by God. You know Him. You know of His goodness and His grace. You see how He blesses you in your daily lives. Your families, your homes, and all that you have, you have been given through His goodness. He provides for you the most basics, the necessities of life. He gives to you this earth on which you live, the air which you breathe, the food which sustains you, but more important than these things that care for your temporal being are the spiritual gifts He offers to you. The greatest gift, the gift of His body, blood, soul, and divinity, offered to you on your altars, is available to you always. You have partaken of it this night and, in doing so, have become truly one in God, one people.

Dear ones, God cares for your every need. He gives to you all good things. He provides for you, that you might provide for one another, love one another as He has loved you, and serve each other. God in His goodness does not abandon His people, for even when you walk wayward, even in times when you have not decided for Him, even in times when you have chosen a death over life, true life with Him, He has not abandoned you. In the same way, dear ones, I ask you not to abandon your fellow brothers and sisters, those among you, in your homes and families, in your communities, in your workplace, in the city in which you live, even those of you in times most dark, even you who sometimes are lost, do not abandon each other. Do not leave one another alone on your Christian Walk.

Every person has struggles and trials, difficulties in the faith life. There is none among you who always feels the presence of God with them, for there is none who is without sin. It is not that God abandons them, but that you close your eyes to His presence. Just as God has provided for you all that you need, all that you need to know Him, to love Him, and to serve Him, provide for those around you when they are in darkness, when they are in despair, when they seek to know God and cannot see Him. In your communities, be a light of hope, be a beacon of faith. Share your faith with your family. Encourage one another. Pray together. Live together in harmony. Love one another as Christ has commanded you, that in the dark times, in the times of hopelessness when you have, through your faults, given yourself over to a lack of love, then perhaps, there will be a Christian brother or sister there to lift you up and to show you the face of Christ. This is your mission: to evangelize to all people, to teach them of the love of God, not only through words, but more importantly, through your faith, through your prayer, through that which you do, and the way that you treat people.

Dear ones, how many of you can think of a person that you know that is so close to God, that loves God so much, that they radiate the light of Christ? These people, they are a great grace in the world. They have chosen to be the face of Christ. They do not do it because they are better, because they have less struggle, because they do not have temptation, but those who chose to live this way, they do it because God gives them the grace to, and they accept that grace and live it each day. And so, I invite you, dear children, as I offer to you this grace, the grace to look upon your altar and see with eyes of faith and to live that faith in an extraordinary manner. I invite you to take this mission into your soul and to make it your daily pledge, your daily vow before God, to live as He commanded, to be as He is, to lead others to Him, that when you stand before Him, many will stand with you.

Dear ones, together as a community of faith you can lead each other to hope, to love, and to life. Even in times of sadness, even in times of trial, most especially in the darkest hour, God is with you. He is with you now, as He always has been. He will never leave you, nor abandon you, but will remain always in your hearts, if you allow Him to be. Dear ones, what a gift and what a grace! Celebrate your faith then, this day and all days, for God is good!

It is as a mother that I bless you, and as a mother I love you, I guide you, and I pray for you. Do not cease to pray, for through prayer you will become that which God knows you to be, truly His children, His disciples, His apostles.

June 2003

Mary:

My dear children, peace be with you now and always. Again, thank God for His blessings and goodness, for because He loves you so much, He has allowed me to come to you, to speak to you, to lead you and to guide you once again. It is a pleasure for me to come to you, that I might show you to the way to Christ.

Dear ones, it is because of God's goodness and mercy, it is because of His faithfulness and steadfast love that you have all that you are, all that you have, all that you ever will become. God, Who knows your hearts as you do not know them yourselves, leads you when you invite Him into your heart through the power of the Holy Spirit. He guides your every action and your every word if you would but let Him. He guides your families, your lives, all that you do, all that you are. It is in this way that God made saints of mere men, for it is not through your own grace, it is not through your own power, that you will become as He is, but through Him Who created you, making you a new creation in His love.

Dear ones, God Who is all powerful, God Who is all mercy, God Who is all goodness desires to make you as He is, perfect in love, perfect in joy, perfect in all things. To do this, you must abandon your will to Him and entrust all things to Him. You must give to Him that which is most difficult to give: your thoughts, your desires, your hopes, your fears. Give to Him all things. Do not merely say the words but mean what you say. Jesus, I trust in you! A heart that truly trusts, that is filled with love for God and total surrender to Him, will fear nothing, for when all is given, trust that He will carry upon His own back all that you need, all of your sinfulness, all of your sorrows.

Dear ones, God created you. He created each one of you. Individually He knows you. He knows your hearts. He knows your soul. He knows your mind. He understands, dear ones, your fears. He rejoices in your joys. God, Who is all, calls you back to Him, calls you to reconciliation in Him, to the Eucharistic love that is offered each day, to you. Seek Him then, and find Him there, always in prayer, always in the Eucharist, always in reconciliation. In this way, dear ones, you will prepare your hearts through prayer to see Him as He truly is, glorified on this earth in that which was mere bread and wine. Then, when you receive Him, your heart will be filled with joy, filled with goodness. You will be as He is, an example of all good things, and a light in the darkness around you.

Dear ones, always, always, always love one another as He has loved you! In this way, others who are lukewarm in their faith will see you with your family in your peace filled homes, your lives that are a model of Christ, and they will believe. Christ once said to man, "I will make you fishers of men", and again, He says this to you. You all, all the people of God, are called to be fishers of men. Through your example, through your words, through your prayer, you will win souls for Christ through the power of the Holy Spirit, but you must be willing to accept this, and you must be willing to give to God all that first was His, your very lives, all that you have, all that you shall be. How difficult it is to turn to God and to, with the trust of a child, ask Him to lead you and to follow His direction! How many saints and holy persons took many years of struggling to come to that place where they truly understood that it was only through following God that they would become leaders.

Dear ones, in this same way you have struggled through many years, and I have come to you and spoken words of encouragement to you. And again, I speak to you, and again I remind you that God loves you. He will not abandon you. He will not let you alone, but will walk with you every step, every day of your life. Do not fear, then, to turn yourselves over to God, to trust in His mercy, to love Him by serving one another. Do not fear anything, for fear is not of God but rather peace, joy, and a love for one another.

Dear ones, as your mother, ever I am with you. I pray for you and intercede for you before our Father's throne. I ask Him to bless you, to bless your lives, and to make you a holy creation in Him, to lead you in the path of holiness. This parish is dear to my heart, for it is named for me, and I lead this parish, this community, and the faithful gathered here, together and individually. I will continue always to be your intercessor, to guide you, to show you the way to Christ. I ask you now to commit anew to doing this for one another.

May the peace of Christ be with you today, and always. May your lives be a reflection of His love, may your homes be filled with joy and love for God, and may the world look to you and see His goodness.

July 2003

Mary:

My dear ones, peace be with you. Know that I come to you as mother, as advocate, and always as intercessor. Again, I say to you that I love you and I am with you, that I lead you closer to the Father, through the Son.

Dear ones, I rejoice with you this day as you gather here in this new building dedicated to me. Know that I wrap my arms around this parish and the community gathered here. You are most dear to my heart, mine, and my Son's. We are united, the Immaculate Heart and Sacred Heart, one heart in the eyes of God. God sees the love of mother and Son, and He honors that love by allowing me to come to bring you His light, to give you His grace, to share with you the joy of Christ. In the same way, dear ones, you are united together, each of you, as a parish community, as a prayer community, in your families. You are united. You stand together or you fall together.

Many times, I have taught you that God calls you to a life of service, and even greater than that, He calls you to a full commitment of your heart and will to Him, to His work. Dear ones, what a great joy it is to be as an apostle, going and spreading the light of Christ, and yet how many people look to spread God's love to faraway places when it is needed most desperately in their homes, in their community, among their brothers and sisters in Christ. I want to remind you again today, of this first responsibility to those whom God has placed in your life, to lead them in the way of Christ, to teach them of His love.

United with the Sacred Heart of my Son, my prayers for you are great, and daily I intercede before God that He would continue to bless this place abundantly. And oh, how He has responded to my prayer, and to the prayers you too have offered here! I desire for this to become a place of great holiness, of great love, of strong faith. I desire for each of you, each one, all of your families, all who you know, to come to love Christ in a greater way every moment of your lives. It is not a difficult task when one commits their heart completely to God, gives to Him all that they are and all that they have. It is not a difficult task when you give to God that which first is His, your very life.

Dear ones, pray always! Again, I say this to you, for the words that I speak to you will come to pass, truly, if you continue to embrace prayer. This will become a place of holiness and tremendous grace, as you gathered here will become carriers of this grace. I desire for you to share my message, the message that is the Gospel message, that Christ is life and truth and the only way to the Father. What a joy in the hearts of those who have not yet seen His mercy in their life, for they are blinded and need the light to open their eyes anew, that they may become a new creation in Him. You are called, each of you, in your own vocations, to be bearers of that light, to shine forth brightly and illumine the darkness that is sin and death and sorrow. When you, as a community and individually, begin to love as Christ loves, then, oh, what miracles you would see!

Dear ones, I ask you again this day to embrace my message of conversion, to embrace my message of peace, and to embrace my message of service to one another. Learn to love as God desires you to love, for only then can you understand how it is that God loves you, how perfectly, how mercifully, how justly, how eternally.

Dear ones, as you mother, again I am with you and always I shall be. I bless you in the name of the Father, Son, and Holy Spirit. May the peace of Christ be with you now and always.

August 2003

Mary:

My dear children, today again I come through the grace of God, for He has gifted me to come among you, to speak to you in this way, to praise and to worship Him with you, that together, you and I might lift our voices to Him and give Him the glory and praise that He alone is deserving of.

Dear ones, how blessed you are, for God has given to you all the things necessary to grow in faith each day, to love Him more each day, to serve one another in perfect harmony as His children. To you, He has given the greatest of gifts. He has given His Own body, His Own blood, His Own soul, and divinity, for each time you partake of the sacrament of the altar, then, and only then, are you in full communion with Him. Those who do not come to Him in the Eucharist are lacking the life within them that He promises, and a great grace that will make the crosses that you must bear in your lives easier and make your load light.

Dear ones, you have been gifted with great teachers, with great leaders among you, who show you the truths of the Gospel, who lead you in times when you, perhaps on your own, would falter from the grace of God, who come to you to teach you and speak words of wisdom and counsel, both your priests and those who pastor you, and also friends who are brought into your life that you might know God and see Him through His creation around Him.

Dear ones, you have been given the sacraments, especially the sacrament of reconciliation. In this great sacrament you come before God and you are exposed fully in the most beautiful and most intimate sense, for God sees you as you truly are, and He knows that which you can become in His grace. What a beautiful sacrament this is and how neglected in the Church today. My children fear to come before Him. They do not know that God is One Who loves to give mercies as water flowing forth from His Own heart. They do not understand that His love is without bounds. That He comes to them and desires them. They do not understand that forgiveness is given to all who seek it and that to become one with God is to reconcile in Him, in this holy sacrament.

You have been given the great gift of a mother. From His cross, Christ gave to the whole world a mother, a heavenly mother, to intercede before God for you, for your intentions, and all of your needs, for all of the world until the end of days. And do I intercede for you!

Dear ones, know that I am with you now, as I have been these many years. Still, you are blessed by my coming and echoing to you the words of the Gospels, the words that you have known since you were children, that you heard at the knee of your parents, and yet still are striving to live each day. The lessons are simple. They are the love of God and the grace of God that you need to be complete, to know joy, to know peace. It is only when you begin to truly implement the Gospel message in your life each day, in your homes, in your hearts, in your community, that you will come to understand the peace that God desires to give to all who would accept Him, all who would love Him, all who would serve Him. This is what I desire for you, dear ones, to bring you into the light of Christ, to bring you from darkness into light, to bring you from despair into joy. I pray that God would bring healing upon you, that He might within you do great things, that you might do great things for others through Him.

Dear ones, it is as a mother, as always, I come to you and so it is as a mother that I advise you. Again, I call you to prayer. Always pray, for in prayer you are communing with God, and you are able to hear His voice speak clearly in your heart. Do not cease to pray as a family, for families suffer greatly and it is prayer that is the remedy for this suffering. Pray as a family. Participate in the Mass with joy. Receive the sacraments, especially the sacrament of the altar, with great fervor in your heart, that God might do great things in your heart, and that through you the light of Christ might be known to all. May the peace of Christ be with you this day, and always, as I pray God blesses you now and until the end of your days.

September 2003

Mary:

My dear children, again it is good to be with you. Still, I come to you as mother and advocate. The Lord sends me to call you to Him. He loves you so much that He sends His mother, that you might not walk in darkness but be filled with the light. Praise be to God!

Dear ones, how many times I have spoken to you, and these messages that I give to you, you try diligently to work at, to put into your lives each day. Still, I call you to this same message, to gather together and to pray as a family, both in your church family and in your families at home. Again, I give you this message. Seek Christ in the sacraments, in the most blessed and high sacrament of the altar, in reconciliation with Him, in union with the Church, and then you will know the fullness of grace. Fast. Give up things that draw you far from God. Live a life of simplicity with your faith firmly planted in the Gospel truth that is Jesus Christ. It is only in this way that you will continue to grow ever closer to the Father and continue to walk the path that He has designed for you.

Dear ones, ever as a mother I continue to come. I continue to exhort you to prayer, and again I say to you, pray with a new vigor and a new fullness in your heart. Pray, always! Dear ones, my desire for you is peace, peace in your homes, peace in your lives, peace in this world. It is only through prayer, through a simple, humble obedience to the Scripture, through a love for the Church and devotion to the sacraments, that peace will be obtained. How often, dear ones, I have seen you try, try with the fullness of your being, to live these messages and how pleased I am, for I have come to you with love in my heart, with the love of God to share with you, and it is my pleasure to give to you the graces that God allows me to bring, even these very words.

Dear ones, do not lose hope in times of trial. Do not be distracted by the things of life that pull you away from the truth that is Christ. May Christ be the center of your heart and your life each day. When you do all you are called to do, do all things for

God. In serving your families, in loving one another, in your teaching, in your listening, in your friendship, in your service, in your living, in your dying, in all things, make Christ center. It is only in this way that you will come to understand how suffering is joy, and how God, Who has done great things for you, is with you in the most real way, in the most true way, always. For, it is in practicing the Gospel truths, in living your faith each day, that the sacrifice of the altar will once again become for you a renewal of Calvary, will become for you, truly a joy beyond joys. It is through living the Gospel truths that you will look with eyes of faith upon your altars and see the Christ, He Who came once as a humble child, Who was scorned and mocked, Who was nailed to a cross, Who suffered, died, and was resurrected in the glory of God, now seated at His right hand, Father and Son, with the Holy Spirit still leading, still guiding, still loving you, always!

See with the eyes of faith, children. See with the eyes of faith. I invite you to a renewal in your lives, a renewal in your homes, a renewal in your hearts. Seek the Holy Spirit, for He is with you. He guides you if you allow Him to speak to your heart, to teach you to love as God loves.

May the peace of Christ be with you this day and always. As I am mother to you, I pray God bless you and lead you always to a life filled with His peace.

October 2003

Mary:

My dear children, peace be with you again today and always. Let us praise God and thank Him for gifting us all with the grace of salvation that we might share in the eternal life that is His. Dear ones, again I come to you as mother. Again, I say to you, I am so pleased to be able to come, to speak to you about Christ, to lead you to the light that He is that your lives might be changed, that your hearts may be changed, that those around you might be changed because of His glory.

Dear ones, what a precious gift you are given each day. God Who is so great has given to you all that you need to see Him clearly in your hearts. He has poured every grace upon you. Through the waters of baptism, He has washed away your inequity and brought you into a wholeness with Him, a fullness in His life. Through the gift of His Holy Spirit, He has poured upon you every grace, every gift, that you might speak His words to all people, be an example of His goodness and His mercy, live His compassion and His love, and be truly the body of Christ as families, as a church, as one people in one God.

Dear ones, through all of the sacramental gifts He has given you, most especially through the gift of the Eucharist, He is with you. He blesses your every day and your every night. He is there waiting, waiting for you to seek Him out, that you might be reconciled unto Him and begin your life anew. That is why, dear children, I call you again and again to the sacraments, to reconciliation, to frequent Eucharist, to Mass whenever possible, the greatest of prayers. That is why I ask you to pray together and in your families.

Dear ones, God desires to give you all things. He Who merited salvation through His own death and resurrection still desires your hearts. Continue then, the work that you have started in your lives and in your homes. Continue to persevere in goodness, to live your faith according to the Gospel truths, to live truly as the hands and feet of Christ. Do not bear ill will against one another in your hearts but embrace forgiveness. Do not live preoccupied with the distractions of your life but let Christ be the center of your heart. Do not live with worries or cares for tomorrow but rejoice in what God has given today. It is only in this way that you can become a people of God and know the peace that I have promised you, the peace that Christ alone can bring.

Our God is so good that He sends a servant to you, His people, to speak His words to you as clearly and as truly as He spoke them Himself upon this earth. God is so good that He raised me up, as He will raise each of you up, to His glory, if only you seek His love, His forgiveness, and take up your cross to follow Him. God is so good that He does not lose His children. No matter how far you walk, He is there waiting for you to turn to Him that He might embrace you and catch you as you come near to the precipice.

Dear ones, how then, can you have any cares at all? How then, can you have anything but joy in your hearts? You know that God is steadfast, and He is faithful. You know that He Who is, and always has been, will continue on forever. Infinitely His love is with you. Infinitely His mercy is upon you. Infinitely His graces are yours if you will seek them, if you will live in His love.

Dear ones, embrace your crosses with joy, for it is through the cross that you have received salvation and eternal life. It is through the crosses of your own life that you, joined with the meriting grace of our Savior, will become, truly, the creature that God desires for you to be, one in Him in His perfect image. Embrace your crosses. Let this be your daily struggle. Each day, suffer joyfully. Each day, love more. In this way, dear ones, my coming here among you will not be in vain but will be a great testament to those who will look to you to show them where Christ is. My coming to you will be a great sign to those who see you and know you, and those who are converted by your example, through the glory of God, will thank you when with you in paradise, when they see His glorious face.

Dear ones, it is a heavy responsibility that I ask of you, but a great gift that God gives. How wonderful He is! How blessed the servant, how great the master! May the peace of Christ be with you now and always. Amen.

November 2003

Mary:

My dear children, peace be with you. May your hearts be glad as you are about to enter into a time of preparation, when you remember the great gift of the Son, the Redeemer, the One Who was chosen for all eternity, the One Who was given to you as a baby, the One Who grew, and taught, and healed, and loved, and died for you, the One Who ascended to the Father after He was resurrected in glory. Prepare your hearts then, in this moment. Be prepared to accept your faith, your life, your blessings, and your crosses, with a new joy as you begin a new season of hope.

Dear ones, again as your mother, I call you to prayer. It is difficult in the hectic day that you live to find solace in your heart, to find peace, if you do not pray. You must begin your days with prayer and end your day with prayer and live prayer each moment in between. If you do not truly begin to accept and embrace prayer, you will not have peace within your heart, and though you might find yourselves going about good deeds throughout the day, you will not find the deep longing, the deep fulfillment, of that grace in your heart that is God.

Dear ones, it is through prayer that you, each day, come into the presence of God. He speaks to your heart. His Spirit guides you. The Son renews you with waters of mercy and life. It is through prayer, through that intimate relationship with your creator, that you will truly become that which God desires for you to be, a people apart, a people who as lights in the darkness are images of His love. Again and again, I call you to prayer, for it is a great grace. It gives your heart strength. It gives you courage through the Holy Spirit. It is a great gift to pray for others that all of your brothers and sisters in Christ might be blessed.

Dear ones, also this day I call you to accept the gift of Christ Jesus into your hearts, minds, homes, and lives, again. It is a time of preparation, a time of true anticipation, a time of joy as you prepare for the fullness of the grace that God gives you, for the fullness of all things, for He for Whom all things were created, Christ Jesus. Dear ones, do not then forget to be a joyful people, for a people awaiting a messiah, a people awaiting the coming of a king, rejoice! Their hearts do not hang in desperation. Their eyes are not downcast. They do not feel despair, but alas, they dance, they rejoice, they praise He Who is coming.

Dear ones, God promised a messiah to the world and sent Him in the humility of a child. Again, make your hearts humble, that you might truly see how God acts in your life each day. To see His workings, to see the action of His Spirit, you must see with the eyes of a child. Let go then, of all of the things that you seem to know and let God lead you to true knowledge, to true joy, to true wisdom, that wisdom, that grace, that gift of hope in Him that can only be obtained by truly abandoning your heart to Him, giving to Him all that He gave to you. Dear ones, what a gift this is for you, for when you abandon your heart to God, when you love Him and embrace Him and rejoice in His presence, then, dear ones, do you have a glimpse of Heaven.

My little ones, as your mother I lead you. As your mother I pray for you. As your mother I rejoice with my Church, with my people, with those who are committed to my Son and, therefore, who are alive with His glory. I rejoice in anticipation, for all of Heaven sings in joy and all of Heaven celebrates with you. Let your hearts be joyful. Let your homes reflect the coming of a king. Let all that you do be focused on He alone, for He alone is all things.

My dear ones, I bless you this day in His name, He Who created you that you might be loved, He Who redeemed you for that love, and He Who in Spirit leads you, that you might truly learn to love one another.

December 2003

Mary:

My dear little ones, peace be with you this day as I rejoice with you, as I love you and come to you as a mother. Know that still now, I speak to you, as I have spoken to you these many years. Still now, I rejoice with you. Still now, I look with anticipation to this great feast day that you celebrate. Still now, in Heaven the Angels rejoice and share in the great prayer of the Eucharist.

Dear ones, see that you look with anticipation to the remembrance of the coming of the Christ Child. As you reflect this Christmas, with your families and loved ones on this great event, this greatest gift given by the Father in Heaven, see, dear ones, see how the Lord has worked such great things even to this day, that the miracle that was Jesus, the miracle of the Christ, continues now to this day, for Christ was born as an infant, an infant destined to die for sins, His birth necessary only for His death, for through Him salvation was gained for all people if they so choose it. See as you reflect, as you look upon the nativity scene, the Christ Child swaddled in the same linens in which His body was lain. See as you reflect upon that manger, that as the infant Christ is pressed against the wood, so too His flesh was pressed to the cross, that you might know salvation. See as you reflect on those who came to worship Him, your brothers and sisters in Christ, that even today throughout the entire world, all people come to Him bringing their gifts, the things that they offer in their homes, in their hearts, through their prayer, in their daily lives, through their works and their faith. See that He Who once was proclaimed the Infant King and Savior of Judea and the world, is still today from your altar proclaimed King, as He comes to you in His body and blood. See, dear ones, that no longer does He lay against the wood of a creche, no longer does He lay against the wood of the cross. Now He is comforted. He is cradled in the wood that is this church, in the gold that surrounds Him in the tabernacle where He is worshiped now, as once He was worshiped a long time ago. See that the same Christ Who came then is the same Christ with you now. See that you do not look in anticipation for the coming of a king. See that now at this moment, He is with you, for He truly is forever and ever, Alpha and Omega.

He came to give God the glory that once was His before the beginning of time. He came and was born to die that you might know salvation and that you, with Him, might share in the gift of eternity, of absolute love, of mercy, of joy. Without Him, without the gift of salvation, without His presence in the tabernacles of His Church throughout the world, there would be no light, there would be no love, there would be no joy. All of creation would simply cease to exist, for He alone sustains you, He alone sustains the life that He once created and gave to you. And so, my children, when gathered with your family, when in your Christmas prayer, when celebrating the coming of a child, celebrate now the gift of a king Who is with His people, the lowliest and the greatest, now, and forever.

My dear ones, I am your mother, and as a mother I come always to exhort you to choose salvation. It was a gift merited through Christ alone offered to the entire world, to every person, for God loves each soul He creates with a love that cannot be measured, and it is His greatest desire that each soul might return to Him, return to the sanctifying grace given to them in the baptism, the baptism that is only possible through the death and life of Christ. Therefore, dear ones, choose salvation! Choose to live as I have instructed you, for my words are not my own, but those that God has given to me to share with you. Choose to live for Christ, for once He lived for you and still, He lives for you. Once He died for all, and still His death has a power that can be toppled by no one, that no king on earth shall match, that nothing, not the gates of Hell, shall prevail against. He is our true King. He is the Messiah. He is with us. Praise God and thank Him for such a gift, for His love is without measure, His mercy is great, and He is with you.

January 2004

Mary:

My dear ones, peace be with you. Today again, I am here with you as your mother. Today again, I come to you joyfully, thanking God for the gift, the grace, to come to you and to speak to you His words, that you might know Him, that He might be present in your daily lives, in your families, in your hearts. I have given to you such grace from the Father, for He has sent me to love you, to show you He is Lord. Today again, I bring you grace and a gift from the Father, for today, I shall bless you only and speak no more words to you, for the Master comes to you and I am His servant.

God in His Trinity:

People of Mine, My mother has implored from Me this gift for you. It is through her intercession that you receive My presence in this tremendous way this night! She, on bended knee before Me in My Trinity, brings you, your prayers, your needs, all things, that she might obtain for you grace without measure.

Dear children, I have come, for you have invited Me here into your hearts, and you have seen with the eyes of faith that I was present here with you all this night, that I am present here with you always, that here upon My altar you will find Me. Creation of My heart, I Am with you yet. I remain with My people who have invited Me to come into their hearts and their lives and to know them, for truly, I have known you. I have known you since first I breathed life into your soul.

My daughter, Mary, mother to the Savior, servant of the Creator, spouse of the Holy Spirit, speaks to you My words, that you might hear and believe and know that I Am! My people, take into your hearts My words, that they might be etched upon your soul: I Am, and I love you! I call you home to Me. It is for My love of you that My heart is burst open, and grace and mercy pour forth. I will renew the face of the earth! There will be a time of endless joy. My mercy is a gift to all who will accept it, who will embrace it, who will be merciful!

You are living in a time without mercy. You are living in an age without love, save for a few. This is why I have sent her. This is why she implores Me to come to you this night, to tell you that I Am! Search your hearts for love and mercy, for mercy is given to those who seek it, and love is the design, the reason, the purpose of all things, and is all that I Am! Hear My words, My people. I Am with you.

February 2004

Mary:

My dear children, peace be with you. Know that again tonight, I am here as your mother, that I bless you, that I exhort you to prayer, for in prayer you come into the presence of God. I thank you for having offered many prayers at my request. I ask you to continue to pray always, for it is through prayer that many hearts will be changed, and many will come to know the mercy and love that God offers to them.

Dear ones, again, I am with you as you are about to enter into the time of remembrance, remembrance of the greatest gift that God has given, the life of His Own Son. Recall, dear ones, how often I have said to you how God loves you so much, He has given His life, He has spilt His blood. He has given to you every grace, that you might one day live with Him in Paradise. What a blessing!

During this time of preparation, when you bring to mind the great sacrifice that Christ our redeemer freely chose that you might have life, when in this time you recall the great grace of the sacrament where Christ again is alive and with you, and again, gives to you His body and blood, rejoice! Rejoice and thank God, for it is through His grace, through His tremendous mercy, that we are all saved from certain death through the giving of one life! Dear ones, during these times remember the sacrifice and let it live again in your lives when you give of your own heart, your own time, your own wealth, your own gifts, to others. Live the sacrifice of Calvary each day. When you meet the cross, embrace it, for it is life for you.

How great God is, that the death of one is life for all! How great the gift! Let this be a time when you recommit yourselves to sacrificial love, to the love that God has for each one of you. You become as Christ is when you love with all your strength, when you love without condition, when you love for nothing for yourself, but all for God, for His glory, in His way. Sacrificial love is the perfect state of the human soul. It is God. He is love, He is mercy, He is compassion, and every reflection of these things in the human heart is an imprint of the face of God. Therefore, dear ones, embrace the cross in your own life. Embrace your sufferings and sorrows. Embrace sacrificial love and begin to truly understand the gift of the cross.

Dear ones, you know that I am with you and that I love you. You know that I come always to advise you and to guide you to my Son, our Lord. You know that, again and again, I call you to Him, always to Him, for it is only through God that you will come to know peace. It is only through God that you will come to know joy. It is only through God that you will live. What a grace, dear ones! May your hearts be unburdened and rejoice in the love of God always. May the peace of Christ be with you this day, and always.

March 2004

Mary:

My dear children, peace be with you again this day, as I come to you as your mother and bless you. Know that I pray with you, and I thank you for praying for my intentions and for the holy Church. Now you are in the season of Lent when you call to mind the sufferings of Christ. In these days when you approach Good Friday, recall how our Lord suffered for you, how His love alone, His love alone made salvation possible.

This is a time of great contemplation. It should be a time of prayer in your families, of joyful anticipation in your heart as you look forward to a day, a day that many in the world would consider dark, the day that your beloved Lord, died. And yet, for you, it is a day of hope and gladness, for on that day, He took it upon Himself your sin, that you might be made a new creation in God, and that He might rise, that you too might rise and live again. Today then, I call you to resurrection as well as contemplation. I ask you to resurrect in your heart, prayer, fasting, conversion, each day. Resurrect in your homes, prayer. Gather your children and pray. In your parish, resurrect the love and faithfulness that you show one another because you are brothers and sisters in Christ. Let these things become a new life for you this day.

You have these many years, tried so hard to do that which I have asked of you, and yet I ask more, as always, for you never will be complete in your journey until you are perfected in the image of God. It is for this reason that He gives to you your very lives, that you truly might become one with Him. Also, dear children, in your lives, be an example of His joyful patience, of His holy obedience, that those around you sent into your life by our Father in Heaven might see and believe through you. It is through His people that God speaks in this world, through His faithful ones that the Holy Spirit comes into the world and renews the world. And so, again I ask you, be perfect, be obedient in all things, that others might see in you a joy filled and peaceful heart and desire that which you possess, a deep faith in Christ that cannot be shaken. Know that He is with you, and as you enter into the great mystery of His dying and His rising, so too, die to those things that have kept you from Him.

How easy it is to become distracted. Often, I have spoken to you about the things of your lives, good things given by our Father, distracting you from placing Jesus in the center of your heart. I urge you to care for your families, to love your friends and your coworkers, by being an example of His love, to be focused on your daily vocation, whether it be a parent or spouse or child, but also and always to keep Christ at the center of your heart and to do all of these good things because you love Him, because His love comes forth through you.

Therefore, dear ones, I ask of you again today that which I have called you to many times: prayer, conversion, peace, and love. Without these things there can be no joy. Without these things there is nothing, for this is what God is. This is His mercy. This is the truth.

Dear ones, live in that truth, that it might fill you completely and change your very heart. I am with you now as always. I guide you as a mother and I pray that, each day, you might recommit your heart and your life to our Lord, that He might do with you what He wishes and use you to bring others to Him. May the peace of Christ be with you always, and may His mercy shine forth in your life.

April 2004

Mary:

My dear ones, peace be with you. What a pleasure it is for me to be with you again this day. Thank God and praise Him, for He Who is the Holy of Holies, Who is all things, has made this gift, this grace, possible. Alleluia! Christ is risen! God is so good that He became for us the Savior. He became for us the Word Made Flesh. He became for us the Lamb, the Paschal Sacrifice, that salvation might be gained for all who choose to love Him, who choose to accept this grace. Praise God for what good things He has done!

Little ones, again today, I come to you as mother. Again today, I come to comfort and encourage you, to help you to walk the journey of faith which many of you started, many of you began with the smallest of steps, with lukewarm hearts. Many of you have come to know Christ, truly, in the sacraments, as you have not before. Through these words God has sent me to bring you, I have shared with you the grace that is our Lord in the Eucharist. How blessed is the Church, that God sends to her His body, blood, soul, and divinity to become the perfect sacrifice, offered from morning to night, each day in all places. How blessed are we that He Who is Creator, that He Who is King, that He Who is Lord, came and dwelt among us as a child! How blessed are we that He came to save us, that through His beautiful passion, through His glorious death, through each suffering, He redeemed all of mankind!

Dear ones, when you truly understand what this gift is, what this grace is, your homes, your lives, your families, will reflect the glory that is God. When you truly understand what you receive in the Eucharist, your face will shine as the sun. When you truly embrace the love that He brings, that He offers to you, and begin to love one another as God loves you, your lives will be a model of perfect charity.

Dear ones, as your mother I pray that in your homes you might embrace prayer, embrace the sacraments, love the Mass, and be obedient to the Church. As your mother, I pray that you might help those little ones entrusted to your care grow in loving faith, to know God and serve Him each day. As your mother, I pray that husbands and wives might glorify God through their love for one another and, in their daily lives, bring each closer to the perfection, the perfection that is God, for truly your marriages, they are a representation of that love that exists between God and His people, Christ and the Church, Father, Son and Spirit.

How blessed we are that we have been given so much by our God, Whose love is without measure. Truly, then, as His children, we are called to give all that we have to Him, for first He gave those things to us. That is why, dear children, I ask you and implore you to embrace a life of prayer in your families, to embrace a life of devoted love for the Holy Eucharist, to embrace reconciliation and every gift of the Church God offers to you.

There is no man while on earth who is perfect the way God is perfect. Only Christ, who is the Paschal Lamb, who was the perfect sacrifice, is perfect. And I was blessed, blessed by God, to be born, conceived without sin, that I might be truly the Ark of the Covenant. This new covenant, Christ, He is offering to each of you the ability to become saints while upon this earth. He desires for you to love perfectly. This is what my desire is, for I wish for every heart to glorify Him, I wish for every mind to know He is Lord, and for every knee to bend at His name. Only then will I be satisfied. Only then should you be satisfied.

Go, then, in your daily lives, and perfect yourself in Christ. Through the sacraments, through your faith, through the trials that He blesses you with, and, dear ones, as He sent His first disciples to evangelize and to teach through their word and example, so too must you become great evangelizers. This is a world without peace. It is a world without mercy, save for a few. I ask you, dear ones, to embrace mercy, to live mercy, and then you shall receive mercy.

My little ones, I thank you for having responded to all that I have asked of you. And I implore you again to embrace this life in Christ that I offer, that He sends me to give to you, that first the Gospels taught you and now I remind you. My little ones, peace be in your hearts, for you rejoice now in this Easter season. Remember always the great gift that God gave through His suffering Son, our redeemer, and the glorious resurrection. May His peace be with you now and always, and may your families become a model of love.

May 2004

Mary:

My dear children, peace be with you this day and always. Again, I come to you as your mother. Again, I thank our Father in Heaven for permitting me to come, for it is only because of His great love for you and His tremendous mercy that I am permitted to come into this world to share messages of hope, joy, encouragement, and faith, to lead my little ones by the hand back to the Father in Heaven.

My dear ones, daily in your lives, you encounter Christ. Daily, you see the souls He has placed into your homes and your hearts, those whom you must care for as Christ cares for His people. Daily, you are given opportunities to serve one another, to serve the Church, to serve in your families, your children, your spouses, your friends. Daily, God gives you so many chances to truly become sanctified in His love, in His holiness, in His grace. Many times, dear ones, when you see these opportunities in your lives, you do not recognize them for that which they are, chances to grow in holiness. Because man's heart often turns from God, God gives to His precious ones so many opportunities to accept quiet sufferings, to live joyfully the cross. In this way, my little ones, and only in this way, can you be fully united to Christ and perfected, more like Christ each day, less fallen as human beings are.

Dear ones, I ask and encourage you then, each day in every opportunity God puts into your life, through every person whom you meet, through every service that you extend to your brothers and sisters, do all things for God! Do all for love of Him, and praise and thank Him for the tremendous opportunity He has given you to suffer, to sacrifice, to truly know how to love. Dear ones, without these opportunities in your lives, without these small sufferings, you could not possibly overcome the trials, the temptations, the sorrows that would grieve your heart, for it is in these opportunities that God plants in you grace, grace without measure, grace to overcome and to persevere in all things, grace to live the life you have been called to live.

Therefore, dear ones, again I call you. I call you to pick up your crosses and follow the way of Christ with joy. Follow His path. Follow in His footsteps. Live as He does, with perfect love, with perfect mercy, with perfect compassion, with absolute forgiveness, and joy. Then, dear ones, you will become a people of God that is a joyful people. You will become a people of hope. Now, especially in your nation, there is no hope. Many struggle and suffer greatly because they do not understand how present God is. They do not know that He calls, calls them home. They do not know that He is there if they but turn their hearts towards Him and away from the many temptations that this world offers.

My little ones, because our Father is so good, He does not desire to lose even one, but despairs in the knowledge that they may become lost and, therefore, sends me. I come to deliver to you hope, and I ask you to embrace this message of hope and to live it each day so that, dear ones, always you might be examples of hope and teach those around you, those who like you are so loved by God, and perhaps have not been gifted with the many graces, with the many gifts, that you have. Teach them that God is present, that God loves them, that God is calling them to Himself.

Dear ones, what a tremendous, tremendous honor and what a responsibility! How God is so good to allow His people to participate in the mystery of salvation, we will never understand! Dear ones, what a gift, what a gift you can offer through your lives, lived in perfect service, embracing all those whom God sends to you in Christian love. Dear ones, go then, and do all that I have asked. And be mindful always to pray, pray about all things, giving all to God. It is in prayer that you will be strengthened. It is in prayer as a community that you will be strengthened. It is in prayer in your homes and in your families that you will be strengthened. For, dear ones, the Holy Spirit works in this world now. The Holy Spirit works in your hearts. He desires to open a floodgate of mercy, a floodgate of grace if you but ask, if you would live according to His Word.

Dear ones, He sends me to speak this to you, that you might know that you are loved, that you might know that He is Lord. May the peace of Christ be with you and may He bless you in all of your services.

June 2004

Mary:

My dear little ones, peace be with you! Again today, I come to you as your mother. Again today, I call you to thanksgiving and gratitude, for God has blessed you without measure. He has given to you the fullness of His gifts. He has given to you every grace, even His Own body and blood, that you might be sustained, that He might fill you and free you through His mercy, through His grace, through His goodness. Therefore, my people, be joyful and filled with love.

You must, dear ones, love always as He calls you to love, to love one another as He loves you. Truly, so few human hearts can understand what a gift the love of God is. So few truly understand what it is to love, for God, Who is love, He is truly in the hearts and minds, the souls, and bodies, of each one of His children who loves without condition, who loves with mercy, who loves with compassion, who loves in peace. When you love, dear ones, in perfect love, you experience God in a way that is enviable even to the Angels.

Dear ones, my children, I have called you this long time to learn to love in this way, for you are His chosen creation. God Who is so mighty that He set apart the world, the earth upon which you live, to be His own blessed place throughout all of the universe, God Who chose you, His creation, to be children above all other creations, He loves you and calls you to love. What a blessed thing it is for us, dear ones, we who have become His children. What a blessed thing to be loved as He does.

These many years, I have spoken to you and asked you to pray, to pray always, taking all things to prayer, and it must be so, for truly the darkness in the world will surely dampen your heart, the light of Christ within you, if you do not pray. Through prayer, God gives to you every grace. He hears your every thought and word. He speaks to you in prayer, and it is in prayer that you will discern His will for you, as a community, as families, as individuals, and as the holy Church. Dear ones, I have spoken to you about sacrificial love and obedience, and I ask you from this day forward to take all I have said and begin to live it anew. Truly, learn to sacrifice with the heart, to give to God all that is His, for He first gave you His sacrifice, the greatest sacrifice.

Dear ones, always I come to you as your mother and lead you. Always I come to you joyfully, for God our Father is so good, He has permitted me to come and to speak to you these words, that you might be encouraged and not know despair, but only joy. Therefore, dear ones, it is in this same spirit of joy, in this same hope, that you will begin to live mercy, that I again ask you to continue to pray always for one another, to love one another as Christ loves you, and to sacrifice with your heart, in your soul, for the good of those around you. It is in this mystical participation with the redemption of Christ, the redemption that He alone can merit for all mankind, that you are purified and perfected. This, my dear ones, this has always been my prayer for you. May the peace of Christ fill your hearts and may His joy live always within you, your families, and in His holy Church.

July 2004

Mary:

My dear children, again today I am so pleased to come to you, to bring to you the message of our Father in Heaven, to bring to you words of encouragement, words of trust, words of love, words of discipline, to be for you, truly, a mother.

Dear ones, God Who is so great has blessed you. He has counted the days of your life. He knows the deepest parts of your heart. He knows your soul, the very fabric of your being, for He created you from nothing. Dear ones, He breathed His life into you, that you might live to worship Him, to adore Him, to serve Him in serving those around you. Dear ones, this is at the heart of my message, service through sacrificial love. How often I have spoken to you and called you to a new love. I call you again to a new love, a love that is the love of Christ. Dear ones, God's love for you is so great that He sent His Son to walk, to teach, to serve, to heal, to die, to rise, to ascend to glory, that you might know God as He knows you, for He created you and thus He knows you even better than you know yourselves.

How often my little ones, who struggle so in their prayer life, see Him as a faceless person, a deity that they cannot reach, One Who hears their prayers at a distance, yet perhaps, is not real and present in the moment, in their life, in the trials of day to day. And yet, He sent His Son, that He might be made flesh, that He might touch His people, embrace His people, know His people, laugh, and cry with His people, that you might see God for Who He is: love, tremendous love! Joy! Peace! Forgiveness and justice! For you, He desires all good things. He calls to you. He asks you to follow in His footsteps, for He has laid the road bare for you. He has cleared away every thorn and every snare by walking the journey to the cross. Therefore, dear ones, how simple, yet how difficult, to pick up your cross and follow.

You, dear ones, are truly as lambs. It was no accident that Christ Jesus chose to speak in parables, to call Himself the Good Shepherd, for you are as lambs tended by One Who cares for you in all things. He shall not let you be lost. He shall not let you dash your foot upon a stone. If one wanders, He will go and seek you and find you, for He has done so today in this Church. Dear ones, the Great Shepherd sends me to call to His lambs. The Great Shepherd sends me to lead you back to the flock. This is why I have come, to call you back to a true understanding of Who it is that God is, and whom He desires you to be.

Sacrificial love, it is something that is inseparable from God, for it is the Spirit of God. Sacrificial love. Jesus gave His life freely and with love and still, this day and every day until the end of time, He gives His body and blood, soul, and divinity to His people, that they might be one with Him. He was not content to walk among His people, to teach, to minister, and to heal, but He desired to become one with His people. And therefore, He has given to you the Eucharist, the great sign, the only sign. Dear ones, in times when there is great darkness across the world, it will be the only light. It is the only light.

Therefore, how blessed you are, for each of you today has partaken in the greatest mystery, the greatest gift. Each of you has received into your being, God. Like me, once a tabernacle, you too are a tabernacle for His spirit, for His body. I ask you then always, my little ones, as your mother who loves you and desires for you to grow close to your Father, to always conduct yourselves as such.

Little ones, so many things I could teach you, and so many things I have given to you through the grace of God alone. It is He Who sends me. It is He Who gives me the words to speak to you, for it is He alone Who is truly master of all things, Who sees into each one of your hearts, and knows you perfectly. The words I speak, I give to you because He knows your hearts. He knows your desires. He knows your needs. He cares for each one of you as a precious lamb. He Himself became the Lamb that was slaughtered, that you might be free.

Rejoice, then, in God Who is all good things and Whose gift of sacrificial love, that gift that you must live each day, truly has freed you and saved you, and will be that which allows you to join Him in His glory forever.

August 2004

Mary:

My dear children, peace be with you. Praise God, for again this day He sends me to you, that I might share with you His message of hope, peace, and joy. Dear ones, know that as your mother, I come. I care for my children and love them and desire for them to be drawn ever nearer to the Father. It is for this reason that I teach you, that I speak to you, that I encourage you, that you might know that God has called you unto Him, to be His as He has always designed you to be, for the moment He first breathed life into man, God designed you to be children. You are not mere creation, but children of a father Who loves you so much. He designed you to love as He loves, and this is what He calls you to do.

Dear ones, God made you free to love. He gave you the opportunity to choose to love Him and love one another as He has commanded. Humanity chose to walk apart from Him, and the consequence of sin was death. And yet, the love of our Father is so great that He sent His Own Son, that He might come to save through death all children, for in dying, He destroyed death and opened the gates of eternal life and, once again, restored man to the friendship of God.

Dear ones, it is then, through sacrifice, that salvation, that every grace, that glory, is attained. Again, I ask you to make your lives a sacrifice, to live each day striving to that love that God calls you to, that sacrificial gift of yourself for your brother and sister in Christ. Then, dear ones, then all people will see Christ as He still exists in this world, in His people, in His Churches, in the great gift of the Holy Eucharist.

Dear ones, how can I tell you how blessed you are, for truly God is with you! Each time you celebrate the great sacrifice of the Mass you receive Him in His fullness, you receive the Way, the Truth, the Life that has been restored for you through Christ's sacrificial death and His resurrection. How blessed are we, that God loves us so much that He calls us to Himself, that He calls us back when we wander, that He makes us a new creation in Him. How blessed are we, then, to have one another to be an example, for from the first days, Christ called brothers in the Lord to serve Him, sisters too, and those who followed Him were commissioned and sent out to teach all nations of His goodness. It is because of them, the workings of the Holy Spirit through them, that you are privileged to know Christ this day. This is how God has always designed faith, that one might show another, and that freely all might choose to love.

God designed His people to be children, and so He does not force His will upon you, but rather, allows you through your love, through your desires, through your gifts and talents and graces that He has bestowed upon you, to multiply His grace, to multiply His peace, to multiply His love. What an awesome and tremendous responsibility, then, it is to truly believe, for belief is a gift given by our Father in Heaven. It is a gift! If you believe, then you must live as you believe each day, each moment, in all ways. If you believe that Jesus Christ came to die, that you might have life and have it abundantly, then, dear ones, you must live life abundantly!

The abundance of God is peace. It is joy. It is a love for prayer and the Mass and the holy sacraments. It is a love for your children, your spouses, your parents, your friends, and those who do harm to you. It is a love that the world cannot know, except for Christ's presence here upon this earth in His people and in the Eucharist. It is a love that is perfect. And, dear ones, truly, when you begin to embrace that love and live abundantly in His grace, then, dear ones, His kingdom will be made manifest upon this earth, and you shall see the dawning of a new age. Therefore, dear children, again let my words be an encouragement to you. Let my counsel be for you, truly, words to live each day by and, greater yet, let my words inspire you to begin to love now.

Dear ones, as always, I am a mother, and I care for you in all things. I am greatly concerned with the welfare of your souls, but also for your temporal needs and, therefore, I thank you for bringing to me your prayer requests, and again, I remind you that I take all of your intentions to our Father in Heaven and ask Him to continue to bless you as He has blessed you all these years. My dear ones, know that I am with you, and I wish the peace of Christ upon you, for that is my prayer for you, that all of His children might embrace the sacrificial love of Christ and become a reflection of Him. Dear ones, may His peace be with you now and always.

September 2004

Mary:

My dear children, peace be with you. Again, it is good to be with you this day as we celebrate, the Church on earth and the Church in Heaven, together at this joyful Mass, praying for those who are in need of prayer, those souls who are in a time of purification. I ask you to remember them and to do penance for them, for the one Church composed of many is great, and God gives to you your brothers and sisters to pray for you, to lead you.

Dear ones, I am pleased to be with you. As a mother, I have come to you to speak to you words of encouragement, to give to you strength and solace, to give to you all that you need to turn your faces toward the light of Christ. Truly, He has sent me because He is so near to you, because His love is for you is so great that He sends His mother, that you might see Him clearly.

Dear ones, God has been present in the lives and the hearts of his people since your very beginnings, and yet so many times His people have chosen to walk far from Him. They have failed to see the grace that is about them. They have failed to see His presence, to recognize His true presence. They have failed to understand that He calls, that He is present. This is why He has sent me, to tell you and to show you through my workings here and the words I have given to you, that He is present here, and present in your lives.

When first He sent me, dear ones, to you, I came with a message: "God exists! God loves you!" This, dear ones, is that which I wish to impart to you tonight. God exists and He loves you! He sends me, His mother, as a messenger, with His words to you to call you back to Him, to call you to a new life in Him, to truly call His holy Church into a renewal, a time of grace, a time of grace that cannot be imagined!

Dear ones, what a joyful thing it is for me to announce to you that God truly, truly loves you, that He would give to you His body and His blood, His soul, His divinity, every grace and every gift, every sacrament and every help, that you might not be lost, that you might not choose to turn your faces from Him, but that you might embrace Him as a father and He embrace you as His children. What an annunciation of joy, something that you, dear ones, have been told again and again, and yet, it has not taken root in your heart. You have not believed with the fullness of faith that can move a mountain. And so, dear ones, again I say to you, God exists, and He loves you!

Take, then, to Him, all things in your hearts. Take to Him your sufferings, your sorrows, your pains, your sins, the barest parts of your heart, that which makes you the person He created you to be, and that which makes you faulted from that person. Take to Him all things, for He created you first and He knows you as you do not know yourself, for He knows that which you might become through prayer, through the sacraments, through a steadfast life persevering in faith and trust in Him. Of all the things I have asked of you, perhaps this is what you have had the most difficulty with, trusting in God's mercy, trusting in His providence, trusting in grace. For a heart that trusts, knows no fear. A heart that trusts is filled with joy. A heart that trusts does not look to tomorrow but looks to the present moment and sees God there. The heart that is trusting lives life in peace.

I have often said to you, "May the peace of Christ be with you, the peace that Christ alone can bring". Truly, that peace exists. It is real and it is yours if you choose it, but you must choose! You must choose to accept the grace God offers to you. You must choose to live a life in Him. You must choose faith, in your families, in your marriages, in your workplace, in your parish, in your community. You must choose it! God offers to you every grace. He has sent me to teach you, to call you back to the truth that you have known and have not lived. He calls you to a life in Him because He has designed you for joy. He has created you for peace. He has loved you in all things and loves you still.

Therefore, dear ones, again, I call you and beseech you as a mother to her children, to truly open your hearts, open your minds, open your eyes, and see that which God has placed in your life. See His presence. See His love. See the mercy and the forgiveness that is yours, if you choose it. It is not a road that is without thorns. It is, in fact, the road that is most difficult. So few, dear ones, so few truly come to understand how to love as God desires you to love while on this earth. If you, dear ones, through opening your hearts and praying, and fasting, and sacrificing, and truly living sacrificial love, if you really learn to love as God loves, then you would die of joy, for you would see Heaven upon the earth and your heart would be renewed in Him!

This is my prayer for you, a true renewal of your hearts, of my children, of the world, that they might see God and worship Him. I, dear ones, I pray that the day will come soon that every knee shall bend, and every lip profess that Jesus Christ has redeemed us all. What a great day that will be! And that day will come, for God has said, "I will renew the face of the earth", and He shall. Your choice is to live in this moment. You may live with Him, in Him, and for Him, through the Holy Spirit, or you will live apart from Him. The choice is yours, dear ones, and I come to call you to God. I come to call you to the life that is most difficult, but the greatest of joys, the life that can be confusing, but is the source of wisdom, the life that can truly be the only way to peace.

So long, dear ones, I have been with you and God has given to me so much to speak to you of. I have taught you truly how to pray with your hearts. I have taught you to see Christ in the Eucharist, for He alone sustains the world there and were it not for His presence, truly, the sun would refuse to shine, and the rains would not fall. What a wondrous thing, then, to think that He is with you in this moment. I have come to teach you obedience, to teach you discipline, to teach you to fast, to do penances, and to become sacrificial love, because in doing so you become Christ on this earth. That, dear ones, that is what He has commissioned His people to do from the moment that He came to this earth and walked among you, and taught, and preached, and died, and rose, and ascended to the Father in Heaven, sending His Holy Spirit not only upon those gathered in that time and in that place, but on all generations to come, that His Spirit, the Spirit of God, might work every day until the end of time upon this earth for the salvation of souls and the glory of God. Praise Him, for what a grace! What a gift!

Dear children, as your mother I am filled with hope then, because I see how in your lives you have come to embrace prayer, you have come to love the sacraments, you have come to accept much of what I have spoken to you of, and truly, it is with a hopeful and joy filled heart that I know you will persevere in this path. Dear ones, the time for my coming to you in this way is brief. Know that I come always to be with you, that I am present in your life, that I am present in your hearts, and that at a time that my voice will be silent, still I will be with you.

Dear ones, persevere in that which I have taught you. Embrace the love that God offers to you, for it is your salvation. Live each day for God. Place Him at the center of your hearts, of your marriages, of your families, of your vocations and ministries, and do all for Him, for it is in this way, dear ones, that you can become an instrument of His will, and as you pray, "Thy kingdom come, thy will be done," it shall. May the peace of Christ be with you this day, and always.

October 2004

Mary:

My dear little ones, again I say peace to you. May peace fill your hearts and your minds and your souls, that you might live each day in Christ's peace. He alone can give you true peace. He alone can deliver the world into peace. Therefore, my little ones, do not seek peace and joy in things that are not of God. Rather, seek your peace, your joy, your love, your fullness of being, in God alone. It is in Him that you will find the answers to all things and only in Him that, truly, truly you will come to understand that peace that I have told you about these many years.

My dear little ones, how good it is again to be with you, to be able to come and to bring my words of encouragement that you might truly begin to live your faith with joy filled hearts. This is that which I have asked of you, that you pray, that you love, that you serve, and that you live with Jesus at the center of your heart, for only in this way will you truly understand the grace that God extends to you, the gift that is Himself.

My little ones, how many words I have spoken and how many messages I have brought, and yet, were I given the opportunity to speak to you but one thing, it would be this: love God through serving others! This is the heart of the life of Christ upon this earth. It is for this reason that He came, and taught, and healed, and loved. Glorify God by loving His creatures. Embrace His people and you will be loving Him. This is the Christian life, this is the gift of the Church, this is the heart of the sacraments and of the Mass, sacrificial love!

God loves His people so much that He sent me to you, that I might remind you of this, for so many have forgotten how loved they are. So many do not understand that God, God Who created them and knows the ever most secrets of their hearts, the littlest and the greatest, that same God, reaches out to them and implores them to love! Therefore, dear children, God Who has sent me to you, God Who loves you so much that He sent His Own Son to live, and to preach, and to die, and to rise for you, God Who is present today in your lives, as truly and as really as He has ever been present, sends me to tell you that He loves you and implores you to love.

My little ones, when you begin to love as God loves, when you embrace this message of love and become the message of love, letting every fiber of your being and your soul be filled with love, then, dear ones, you will see the face of Christ in one another, and never again will you know loneliness, or sadness, or darkness, or despair, for even in the midst of every danger and every trial and every sorrow, there is God! He first suffered for you. He first died for you. Will you not, dear ones, die to yourselves and become sacrificial love, that you might live for Him?

My little ones, this is the heart, the true heart, of my message. It is for this reason that I have taught you to pray, that I have taught you to come together in a community to form prayer groups, to support one another, to love one another. It is for this reason I have called you to the sacraments, for you cannot live without them. It is for this reason, I have called you to the Church, to the priesthood, to support of one another, to love for one another, and I call again and again and again.

My little ones, when you pray with the fullness of your heart, your voices rise to Heaven as beautiful songs of joy. You cannot see that which God sees and you do not know that which He knows. Therefore, I beg you, hear the voice of a mother who loves you with the fullness of my being. Trust God, for He has your days numbered and He knows your every thought. Trust Him, for His love for you is so great that He stops at nothing to call you unto Him. Trust Him, for He is with you even when you turn yourself from Him and seek to hide yourselves, for as it is written, there is no place you can go to escape Him, for if you shall rise to the highest of heavens or sink to Sheol, there He is. My little ones, He wishes for me to remind you that He loves you and that He desires for you to love one another. It is a choice that must be made each day, in every moment. You must love, little ones, or you will not understand all that I have come to teach you.

Dear children, again I wish to bless you with my motherly blessing. I thank you for responding with open hearts to that which I have asked of you, to embrace prayer. I thank you for coming together and offering so many masses, so many rosaries, for my intentions. What grace God pours forth upon the world when His children pray! How much more grace He has to offer if you would continue to pray.

I thank you, dear ones, for dedicating your lives, and your hearts, and your families, and your marriages, and your vocations, and everything to me and to the Sacred Heart of Christ, for together, His Sacred Heart, king of the hearts of all mankind, and my Immaculate Heart, shall reign. Yes, dear ones, God has spoken to you. He has touched your lives and sent His Spirit to this place to make it holy. It is for you to live this gift with the fullness of your lives.

See, then, with hope on the horizon, God's promises will be fulfilled. He shall renew the face of the earth and give to every heart a measure of grace so great, so great that the world has never known such grace! He desires for His children to accept Him, to love Him, to serve Him, to be with Him. He invites you, dear ones. He calls you. He sends your mother to you to call you home to Him. Therefore, accept this great gift. You do not know, you do not know the greatness of what you have received. Glorify God with all that you do. Praise Him in your hearts, and in your lives, and through your prayer, and through your works, and live, live as He has commanded.

My dear little ones, I bless you in His name. I ask that God our Father in Heaven will always be merciful to you and just, and fill you with every grace, for I know that He shall. And I ask my Son each day, interceding on your behalf, to fill you with love for one another, for He alone was the greatest example of love, and He upon the cross, and through His resurrection, and His glorious ascension, defined for all mankind for all time, what love must be. And I ask the Holy Spirit, eternal spouse of the Church, friend and advocate to all the faithful, to be in your hearts, and in your minds, and in your souls, that you might be pierced with the knowledge that God is love, and that you might be moved to live that love. As always, dear ones, may the peace of Christ be with you this day, and always.

November 2004

God in His Trinity:

My children, long I have sent My handmaid to you. Long I have given to you My words through her. From age to age, I call My children to Myself, for I created you to be known by Me, to be loved, to serve one another as I have commanded you.

My children, truly I have called you. I have known each of you. I Am with you. It is I Who works in this world to bring light where there is darkness, from the moment of creation to this present moment. It is I Who brings forth new life, that I might create out of love. It is I Who provides for your every need, Who gives to you a share of My Own heart, that you might know eternal life. It is I Who come, Who walk among My people. It is I Who came, that all of My little ones might prophesy, and speak, and preach, and heal, and announce to the world that I exist. It is I Who come to you now, Who created the stars of the heavens, the water, the earth upon which you sit, and the tree upon which I died for you. It is I Who loves so much that I took on the form of My creation to become as you are, not satisfied with simply making you an image as I Am, of love.

Dear ones, I Am love! I Am mercy! I Am joy! And when you, My faithful children, embrace mercy and joy, and become forgiveness and love, then, only then, do you become that which I always meant for you to be.

My dear creatures, how blessed are you that above all else, I raised you up and made you as I Am, that forever you shall be with Me. I Am your God, and you are chosen people. To the world, I call now. To the world, I invite My children home. To all people, I give innumerable graces, but you must choose grace, for first I gave you freedom.

I wish for you to love Me. To love. I desired children to love. I created you each, knowing every sin, and every fault, and every failure, and yet I loved you, and love you to the end of time! This is the love you must live. There is nothing that remains, for I have created everything. Nothing existed but love, as I Am. All of creation will cease to be, but My love, but you, My children, whom I created to be with Me eternally. There is nothing, nothing that is worth the price of separating yourselves from Me. Do not abandon Me, children, for never have I abandoned you. From the exile of your forebearers, to the coming of your Messiah, to this present moment, and My return to you in glory, I Am with you! I Am a God of mercy, and justice, and love, and you must become mercy, justice, and love.

Long I have sent My servant to you. Long have I sent her with My words, that she might speak to you that which you must know to turn your hearts, and your minds, and your wills, to Me. Heed that which she has taught you and live it, for I Am the author of your days. I know you. I know your failures, and yet, I love you and offer you every grace necessary for salvation, for this is why I sent her and sent those who now are with Me in glory to speak to you. Yes, to you, you whom I have gathered here, you whom I have called by name, you who know Me now. I have sent them to show you that it is not through your works, or your words, or your thoughts, or your being, or any breath that you take, that you will glorify Me, but it is I Who will lift you up, grace and bless you, and pour My Spirit upon you, that I might be glorified! Do nothing but turn your hearts to Me, and I will complete you. Do not be afraid. Fear is not of Me.

My children, hear My words as you have never heard them before. Hear now that I speak to you as real, and as true, and as present, as I Am in the sacrifice of the altar, in My Eucharistic body, offered up for you, that you might know salvation. See how I call you. See how, again, and always, I invite you. I shall not leave My people. Do not depart from Me.

My little ones, above all else know this, you are loved above all creation. You have been given that which nothing else, none of My creation, has been given, My Own breath of life, My Own Spirit. Yes, I send my Spirit upon you to make you a new creation in Me. I am calling to you, My children. The world will hear My voice. Respond with love. Fill your hearts with the Spirit that I pour down upon you and accept the grace, the gift that I offer you: salvation, and eternal union with Me.

The Yearly Lessons from Heaven

October 2005

Mary:

My dear little ones, how great is our God that again He permits me to come to you this day, that after this long while, as you have gone on in your Christian journey, as you have walked each day with His Spirit, as you have come to live my messages ever more fully, here again, I am with you. My dear little ones, how blessed are we, His creation, that together we gather as a family in front of His eucharistic table, that we all, His children in Heaven, His children on earth, and those who will come to know Him in Purgatory, can be united in the one great Church that is the Body of Christ. My little ones, you who are gathered here, I am so pleased to be with you this night. Much time has passed for you. It may seem as though an eternity has gone by, and yet, a blink of the eye of God has passed and here again, I am with you, though never did I leave you.

My dear little ones, our Father sent me so many years to speak to you of His love. Never would I come, for any reason, other than to tell you of His tremendous love, His great mercy, the forgiveness that He holds out to you, the grace that He offers you. Too, I come as mother, and it warms my heart to come to my children, to be with them, present in this way. Your Father in Heaven spoke many words to you through me. Your Father called you to a new love, to a new walk, to live your faith fully each day in every moment, in every word, in every deed. Through my messages, He called you to embrace your faith, to truly pick up your crosses and live them with joy, for in suffering, my little ones, you will find peace, and strength, and wisdom, and courage. Our Father in Heaven sent me to speak to you of the tremendous gift that you have been given in the sacraments, the grace that awaits you in His body and blood, the grace of sacramental confession, the grace of small sacrifices and obedience that you might become disciplined in love. He sent to you those in Heaven to be witnesses to His glory that you might, for but a moment, see His shining face and be filled with joy. Still, He is so good that He allows me to come to you again tonight, to my daughter who has received these messages and those who have gathered here to share in this day with her. Still, He allows me to come because He has not forgotten His children, but loves you each unto your death and forever, for He created you to eternally be with Him. I ask you, my little ones, to search your heart, this night and always, to see how you have responded to what He has asked of you and to increase ten-thousand-fold your efforts, for never can you walk too close to Him.

My little ones, I thank you for hearing my words, for coming and truly loving one another, your Father in Heaven, and me, so much that you would share this night, this tremendous glory, this gift of God, with one another and with me. As your mother, again and always, I implore you to pray, to become a prayer, to make your lives a prayer that each day the sufferings that you bear will be eased, the joys will be multiplied, and God our Father in Heaven might make you a witness to His mercy, to His grace and to His love. Dear ones, I thank you for your steadfast commitment, for promising your hearts to our Father in Heaven and, each day, living that promise. Through your baptism you became one in Him. Through His body and blood, you are one flesh with Him. Through this community of faith, you are one in mind and one in heart with Him. Hold fast to the gifts He gives you. Seek His love and it is there. Know His mercy is great, and He is a father who loves His children until the end of time.

My little ones, I thank you again for coming this evening to offer your hearts and your lives in prayer, and again I implore you to live, truly live, these messages I have given you from the Father in

Heaven, that your life might abound in grace and, one day, you might find yourself home with Him.

October 2006

Mary:

Dear ones, great and merciful is God the Father Almighty, Who allows me to come to you again this day, to speak to you, to bless you, to pray with you, to bring to you every grace that you might be filled with Him and His Holy Spirit. Praise His name and glorify Him, for He alone is the source of all good things. He gives to you your life, the breath that you breathe to live in His love, the food that sustains you: His eucharistic body. He alone is goodness and provides for all things. He fills you up. He is your light. He is your health, your wellness, your home, your family, your true father. He is all things. Though concealed from your sight, He is with you. He is here at this present moment. He sends His mother to bless you, to comfort you, to console you, to show to you a glimpse of Heaven that you might be filled with light that is unquenchable, light that is within you always that no darkness might frighten you, that your soul might rejoice in all things both sorrowful and joyful. God is with you!

My dear ones, as your mother, I rejoice this day, for I have been allowed to come to you again, and to truly admonish you, and ask you to pray, to pray, to pray! My little ones, you do not know how important it is to pray! It is as a mother with love that I come to my children, that I beg my children, to make their lives a living prayer. Never has it been more important. Never, dear ones, have I asked you for anything less than the fullness of your being. Again, I ask you to lift your whole heart, to lift your soul, to lift the fullness of your being to the Father in prayer. Pray with your words. Pray with your songs. Pray with your thoughts. Pray with your actions. Pray in serving one another. Pray in receiving His body and blood.

Pray in ministering, in participating in the beautiful sacrament that He has given to you to be, truly, a gateway to salvation, for no man can live if he does not have the body and blood, soul, and divinity of Christ within him.

No one, dear ones, can understand the depth of God's love until they see His face upon their death. No one can understand the truth that He desires to reveal to you until they are with Him in the heavenly home He has prepared. No one can understand how He calls to you, beckons to you, begs you, dear children, to love Him, to serve Him, to be one with Him, intimately connected, creator and creature, one being. Dear ones, He created you a part of Him. He breathed into you His own life that you might live as He lives, with an immortal soul, created like the One who had no beginning and no end.

Dear ones, I beg you then, to make your lives an example and a witness to your faith. It is prayer that will give to you the strength and the grace that you need to be living witnesses, to be a testament to truth, to be a testament to the good news that Jesus is Lord, that He has ransomed you from death and lifted you to the Father, upon the cross. Dear ones, pray then. Pray always in your families. Gather together and pray. Teach little ones the Scripture. Teach them to pray, that from the moment they are able to speak, the name of Christ might be on their lips. Pray! Pray for those who are in Purgatory, who are being cleansed, awaiting the time when they will be united with the Father in the perfect kingdom He has created. Pray! Pray for those who do not yet know my Son, who are so dark, who are so desolate, who cannot see that the light of Christ is before them would they but lift their eyes, lift their hearts, and reach out their hands to Him. Pray for the sick, for those who suffer under bodily weakness, for those whose illness drains upon their heart, and their mind, and their soul, that they might be strengthened with the knowledge that Jesus Christ is teacher, and healer, and the giver of every grace, that He brings healing to the hearts of those who seek Him, and that they might know peace. Pray for my young ones, those who have no one to instruct them in the faith. Pray for those who have no one to pray for them at all, especially those who have died.

My little ones, prayer is the first step to a relationship with God and so I call you, again today, for a renewed love of prayer. Also, my dear ones, I call you to serve. Prayer and service! It is the message I have given you again and again, month after month, year after year, for it is essential. Jesus, in His divine love upon the cross, saved all men, ransomed you from darkness and death. Truly, little ones, His salvation, His love, the redemption, is complete and it is perfect; but, little ones, you still are human with human nature, and given to falling into temptation and sin. Even with the redemptive love of Christ, even with the sacraments He has given you to sustain you, even with the Mass, the greatest prayer, still you are tempted, still you will fall.

And so, dear ones, I ask you to serve one another by ministering to one another. Reach out to those who are hard-hearted. Reach out to those who are suffering. Reach out to those who live without Christ and show them, through your works, through your words, that Jesus loves them and desires to bring them home. Serve your community. Let all who see you know that you love Him by the actions, by the words, by the look upon your face when you mention His name. Dear ones, serve in your homes, serve in your workplaces, serve in your parishes, serve your country. Serve God always, for everything can be lifted up and made into a prayer, if done for the love of God! Prayer and service! Prayer and service! I cannot tell you, dear ones, how much joy you will know if you truly learn to pray with your heart and serve with love.

Before, dear ones, you heard me speak about sacrificial love. Again, I bring you to that word: sacrificial. For Jesus, the Great Sacrifice, the one who breaks Himself upon the altar, Who pours out His blood that you might be saved, calls you to sacrifice with Him. Join your sacrifices to His, His most perfect sacrifice, that little ones all the world over might truly merit such grace as the world has never known. Yes, little ones, it is possible! The world is at a time where grace, and peace, and love, and service, and prayer is most sorely needed. It is to you- dear ones, I commission you- it is to you that I give this task, to all those who would hear my voice and heed my call, the call of the Father in Heaven. Pray! Serve! Love! Live in faith, for truly, where one heart is faithful, there God is! Where there are two, there He rejoices! Where there are three, all of Heaven rejoices and, where there are many, the world can be changed. The course of human events can be changed.

The future, the past, it is all one in God, and God desires for you to love. That is why He sent His Son. That is why He created you, to love you, to love each of you individually, for He has known you since He created your soul. Since He placed it upon you and burned an image of His face into your heart, He has known you. He knows you now and will know you always until you are united with Him in glory. Dear ones, then, how can you resist Him? How could you turn your faces from Him? How could you ever forget that He is God? Let your hearts rejoice. May they be filled with peace, always. Never shed a tear, for God is great and He shall overcome all things: sickness, death, desperation, desolation, and all evil. Truly, place your faith in Him; it is well-founded. Place your trust in Him. You will not be abandoned. Place your lives in His care and He will lead you, for He has known you always, and desires only for you to know Him, and to love Him as He loves you.

My little ones, as always, I am your mother and I offer myself to you as protectress and intercessor. Do not fear to bring to God all things. Know that I pray for you, that I pray with you, that I worship with you, that I partake in God's goodness with you and, with you, rejoice in the salvation that was earned for us by Jesus Christ the Lord, now and forever. Amen.

October 2007

Mary:

My dear children, peace be with you this night. I am so thankful that again, the Lord allows me to come to you and to speak to you in this place that is holy, this place that is most dear to my heart. Dear ones, again as your mother, I come to you. Again this night, I beseech you and implore you to make God center in your life. My little ones, God bestowed upon you such a grace, a grace to hear my voice, to hear my words which are words He has given me to give to you. He gave to you the grace to hear, to hear that which others have not heard. He gave you the grace to understand that the truth lies in His holy word, in the Gospels, in the teachings of the Church, and that which He has imprinted upon your very heart.

My dear ones, you know, truly, that God is with you. How many times I have echoed that message to you! How many times I have told you God is with you and He loves you! It is for this purpose that still, God allows me to come into this place and to, truly as your mother, remind you that He is with you. The world has forgotten Him. Many are far from Him. Yet, He is so good, and He is so merciful, that He continues to break forth into this world like the dawn of a new day to bring peace, and mercy, and joy, and hope to His people, people scattered about, yet one in Him.

My dear ones, again this night, I ask for your prayers, for truly, it is with prayer that you will change to face of the earth. It is only through prayer that peace can be obtained. It is only through prayer that love can be lived each day. It is only through prayer that you can commit to God and keep your vow to Him to follow His way, for God loves you so much that He takes your very heart and molds it, and shapes it, and changes it, not into what you were, but into that which you might become in Him. Dear ones, as your mother, there is nothing else I can ask from you but this: continue to give your heart to God.

You have begun the journey of conversion. These many years, you have followed my words and you have implemented them in your families. You have prayed, you have sacrificed, you have fasted, you have converted, and yet I ask for more. More always, dear ones, for that is your mission upon this earth: to be perfected in Christ Jesus, to each day take on Christ like a cloak to protect you, to really and truly be with you, to fill you, to free you. Therefore, dear ones, I ask God today and always to truly envelop you in His love, to embrace you, to make you one, one amongst each other and one in Him, for that is what you are called to be, one people in one God.

Christ sends me, the Father sends me, the power of the Holy Spirit sends me that I might be a messenger to you and witness to you of the glory of God. It is His glory that He desires to share with you. It is His transforming love that He desires to give you. You must open your hearts, open your eyes, open your ears, open your lives to Him. It is that simple, dear ones, and that difficult! You must abandon your natural self. You must give up all within you that keeps you from Him and embrace the cross. In doing so, then you will find joy, then you will find peace, then, and only then, will you be fulfilled, for you are a creature, created by the Father to be completed by Him. There is nothing in this world that will complete you but His love.

My children, as your mother, again I remind you, it is only when you place God as the center of your lives, at the center of your home, at the center of your heart, that you will truly know Him and become Christ to one another. In doing so, you will bring light to the earth and where darkness once was, light shall prevail. God, God who is mighty, will do great things through you if you let Him use you as His vessel, in His way, in His time.

Dear ones, I thank you for gathering in such great numbers this day, for being committed to my messages and, most of all, for going to the Holy Mass, frequenting the sacraments, and making prayer the most important part of your day. In this way, you will be sanctified, and a mother's most ardent desire will be satisfied. My dear ones, may the peace of Christ be with you today and always. I offer to you my motherly blessing, and you are before the Father in my prayer always.

October 2008

Mary:

My dear little ones, peace be with you this day and always. Again, I come to you as mother with a thankful heart. I praise God for the opportunity to speak to my children, to implore my children to pray and to love as my Son has taught you. My dear little ones, know how much I love you. I have come to you these many years and spoken words of encouragement to you. I have recalled you to the Gospel truths that you have always known, and yet forgotten. My little ones, again I say to you, be true to your faith in God. Do not abandon my Son, as much of the world has abandoned Him. Rather, cling to Him, for He is your truth and He is your salvation.

My dear little ones, for these many years, I have spoken of many things. I have brought to you such grace, such grace, it is immeasurable! The Father is most generous, and He is so merciful! My little ones, still I come to you, still He permits me to speak to you because, still my little ones, He desires for you to enter into a deeper love with Him, to love Him with the fullness of your being, to make Him truly the center of your heart, the center of your life. My little ones, it is a mother's wish, it is my prayer, that you would truly make Him, Jesus our savior, the center of your life, for when you do, my dear children, you will become a light that cannot be quenched, a light that will illuminate the world. All darkness will be dispelled and there will be no need for my children to suffer as they suffer so now. They suffer from a lack of faith. They suffer because they do not know my Son. Dear ones, help me to teach them of His love, to show them through all that you do, through the person who you are, through the faith that you have in your heart that He is Lord forever. He comes not only for you, not only for those who call Him, "Lord", but for all people, such is His desire to save His children. Our good shepherd comes to call His lambs, dear ones, to speak to you truth, that you might hear truth. Harken and listen to Him!

My little ones, you truly have been a blessing to me. You have been a joy in my heart, for so many of you have embraced my message, have spoken truth, have placed Jesus on the altar of your heart and have loved Him, have loved Him with the fullness of your being. My little ones, still and always I say, more. More, my little ones! For truly, the life to which you are called is one of total union with God. It is only then, only then, my little ones, that you will know peace in your lives and in your world, and it is only then, only then that you will feel the fruit of prayer, the fruit of faith, the fruit of every sacrament and every gift blossom in your hearts, in your homes, in your church, in your life, in your world. Dear ones, I implore you as a mother, heed my words and turn your hearts to Him Who desires to save the lost, Who is the only light, Who is all salvation and truth, and desires to bring you into union with Him.

My little ones, I praise God, for it is through His mercy that He has permitted me to speak to you again this night, and I pray that He will allow me to come again, as I have spoken. Dear ones, truly, respond with love in the fullness of your hearts, that Christ might see in you a perfect sacrifice like His own. Truly, is that not what we are called to do, my little one, but to become the image of Christ? Therefore, offer yourselves to the Father unceasingly as a sacrifice in union with the sacrifice of Christ. In that way, you are made perfect in Him, and God receives you as a great gift before His immortal throne.

My dear ones, that is my request, that is my prayer. Truly, I am with you. In the days when you feel far from God, there I am, imploring you, asking and beseeching you, to pray, to trust in Him, to place your faith in Him Who will not abandon you, Who will not deceive you, Who will not leave you, but shall seek the one and leave all else for the save of he who is lost. My dear little ones, peace, peace be in your hearts and your homes, and know that a mother's love is with you this day and always.

October 2009

Mary:

Dear Children, how I am pleased to be with you, to gather with you this day, to offer praise to the Father in Heaven, to worship the Son Who came, Word Made Flesh, and dwelt among you, and to be one with the Holy Spirit Who inspires you to live a life worthy of the blood of Christ. Dear ones, as your mother, I grieve for the sorrow, and the sickness, and the sadness, and the sin in this world. Many years I have spoken to you through the grace of God. I have come to you, my little ones, to lead you on a better road, the road that leads to Heaven. My little ones, again this day as always, I beg you to embrace the love that Christ offers to you, the love that He gives to you, the love that you must share with one another.

My little ones, it is a time of darkness. Sin, sin is not the way to life. My little ones are lost, and they cannot find their way to God. You, my little children, must embrace the Gospel message and live with the fullness of your being the love of God. You must be obedient, my children, to His law, for if you keep His commands, you will know joy. You must love one another with sacrificial love. You must teach one another through your humility, in your littleness. My little ones, I do not call you to accomplish great things in this world, to go out and win many converts, to go and to baptize the world, but rather, in each day, in the place where God has put you, to witness to those who need to see the love of Christ in you, for it is only in this way, my little ones, that you, my lights in this world, the light of God, might shine more brightly and fill the world with the illumination of the Holy Spirit.

My little children, long I have come to you. Again and again, I come as mother and will come so long as God permits me, and yet I say to you, many have heard my voice, but few, few, my little ones, have loved my Son as He must be loved. Therefore, my little children, go before Him always in His eucharistic Self and worship and adore Him, offer to Him every praise, and make reparation for the grave injustices committed against Him. My little ones, in this way also, I do not ask for great deeds, only the simple gift of your contrite and love-filled hearts. Give yourselves completely to God that He might do great things in you, and that when you permit the Spirit to fill you, He might do great things through you, that this world might no longer know sadness, grief, sin, sorrow, and death, but might be resurrected into a new glory, the glory that exists through, with, and in, our Father in Heaven, only because of His love, only because of His justice, only because of His mercy.

My little ones, I commend you to the care of the Holy Spirit Who guides the Church, guides the people of God, and will guide each of you each day in your life, as you are converted to my Son. May the peace of Christ be with you today and always.

October 2010

Mary:

My children, peace be with you. I ask you this day to be at peace and to listen, for it is not I, but my Son, who desires to address you.

Jesus:

People of My heart, I have sent to you My mother, that she might give you My words. I have sent her to this place that she might speak to you truth, the truth that I am! My people, today I come, that again you might hear My voice and know that I am! How she has implored you to heed her call, the way of life, for there are but two ways: the way of life and the way of death. How many of you, My little ones, will choose life? My people, I who come to offer to you salvation say now, "Choose life!"

My children, My brothers, My sisters, you whom I walked among, you whom, before I became incarnate, I knew as creator, you whom I have known from always, are the beloved of My heart and I call you back to Me. It is the only way. How long, My little ones, must I call? So many of you have turned your hearts to Me. So many have opened their hearts and their lives to Me, and yet, if but one is lost, it is too many. Look with eyes anew. See as you have not seen before. Examine your heart. What do you find? There are but two ways. I am calling you. I am calling you to embrace My life, the life that pours forth through Me in abundance, perfect joy! How, My little ones, can you desire anything else?

I am your Christ! For love of you, I poured Myself out. In the Eternal Now, I pour Myself out yet. Come to me. Hear Me! Heed Me! For your sake, I sent My mother. For your sake, I come again. For your sake, I am present here, but more so, every time you meet Me as I give you My body and My blood. Do you perceive Me? Do you see Me? I see you. Come to Me. I am calling. There are but two ways. Choose life and I will grant it in abundance! That is My vow. That is My covenant. That is My word that is alive. That is the only way. I offer you peace, peace beyond your comprehension. Come! Follow!

October 2011

Mary:

My dear little ones, praise and thank God, for it is because of His great goodness that He permits me to speak to you in this way. Dear children, it is with a mother's heart that I approach you this day. Little ones, do you know how great our God is? Do you know the heights and the depths of His love? Can you see, my little children, how desperately He wants His little ones to come to Him, to place their trust in Him in all of their cares, to rely on Him alone.

My little ones, it is a time when many say, “destruction,” and yet I say to you, “peace!” It is a time when many say, “despair,” and yet I say to you, “Hope!” It is a time when many say, “All is lost,” and yet I say to you, “There is all to be gained in Christ Jesus the Lord,” for just as the darkness is greatest, the indomitable light of God shines forth. Just as His justice is most deserved, His mercy breaks through and penetrates the darkness that my children have chosen. I speak to you today of mercy. Our God who is love, desires to grant mercy to this world. My children must choose mercy!

Little ones, you who come and gather here have heard my voice these long years. You have read the words that I have been permitted to grant to you. You have put into practice the same message that I bring, which is no new message, but the message of Scripture, the message of the Church, the Bride of Christ, the message that God has spoken to you through the prophets for all time: “Repent, for the kingdom of God is at hand!” These words were spoken in the desert before the coming of the Christ, cried out by the Baptizer to those who would heed them, fulfilled in the person of Christ, truly God made man. What a thing! What an impossible thing, and yet in the mercy of God, part of His plan from the first moments of creation.

You do not see as God sees. You experience this life as a chain of successive events. You cannot see how everything is in the Present Now before our creator. In this Present Now, He sees the first act of creation and the last triumph of His Son. In this Present Now, He sees every soul He has ever brought into this world and every soul that ever shall be. In this Present Now, He sees your every action, your every choice, your every “yes,” your every “no,” and He desires still to grant mercy. How, my little ones, can my children say, “no”?

You who gather here know that I have called these many years with this same message: Come, the Father waits, His arms are open, He desires you. He wants to free you from the slavery which you have entered into by your own accord. You have bound yourself in chains. He desires to free you. You have closed your hearts and blinded your eyes. He desires to free you. It is through the grace of the sacraments that you will see Him clearly, that you can toss off the chains that bind you, that you will no longer be blind and deaf and mute, but you will see, and hear, and speak, and witness, and prophesy. All of creation waits in eager anticipation for the revelation of the sons of God. When my people, when my children, will you come to be the sons of God?

It is a mother who pleads with you who comes today, a mother who asks this out of great love, and because I can see that which you cannot see. I see the face of Christ always, in all things, at all times! Can you imagine? Can you imagine the grace, the gift? This is a gift not reserved for me, most blessed and favored by God, but to you, most precious to the Father, dearest creation, joy of His heart. For if there was but one, one, He would have come, and died, and sacrificed, and rose, and ascended, and begun this most beautiful and glorious church for one, and there are many! How great and abundant is the love of our God, that it pours forth into life in this world without measure! The souls, the innumerable souls He has created, each unique, each distinct, each eternal, and designed to be with Him forever in the most intimate union, a bond that is indestructible, except for your choice to sin! Nothing can separate you from the love of Christ, but you.

My little ones, you who have embraced the message I have given to you, who have attempted to live it in your daily life, you who have- through the messages I have given and, more so, through the Scripture, through the Mass, through the sacraments- enriched your marriages, and your homes, and your families, and your lives, and grown in faith and holiness, and become a person set apart for God; you must witness this joy! The world says, “All is destruction,” and I say, “It is time for my people to reclaim their place as children of the Father.” The world says, “There will be no peace,” and I say, “Peace is possible if you choose peace.” The world says, “God is dead,” and I say to you that He lives more so than you live, than anything lives, in a life that you cannot comprehend! You do not know what life is! You cannot see as I see, and I desire to give to you a glimpse of the joy that I experience in the Present Now.

My dear children, do not think that I come to you severely, or to admonish you, or to condemn. Rather, I come to exhort you to embrace and renew your commitment to holiness, because it is holiness that will win the world for Christ. You are not alone. We would certainly fail without the grace of God. No man without His grace, without the sanctification He offers to us, no man could do His will, so great and so unfathomable is the mind of God. And yet, He gives to you all that you need to accomplish what He asks, not great acts, not tremendous martyrdoms, but simply to give, to serve, to love, to die to self, and to be a witness in your life where He has placed you, each day.

My children, renew your commitment to prayer. In your families, in your homes, make prayer the center of your family life. Let my Son be seen and known by your children. Come, partake of the gift of the sacraments. Receive the body He freely offers you. Reconcile yourselves to God. Then you will see holy families and, in the family where holiness is, there will be tremendous love, and where there is love, there is God. You see, my little ones, that is the mystery. God has the power to come with flashing lights and peels of thunder, with fires roaring, and yet, He comes in a whisper. He comes in each home, in each marriage, and by lighting each family on fire with love, each heart on fire with love, He will set the world ablaze. My little ones, be merciful as your God is merciful, and love one another as He loves you.

October 2012

Mary:

My children, it is good for you to come, to offer your prayers for my intentions. Thank God for the tremendous gift that He provides to you this night and always, for in all places and in many times, He sends me, and many, to speak to His children and bring them home to Him. He has sent me these many years to you and, year after year, I speak the same message because there is but one message to speak. I have obtained for you that He, Himself, ought to speak to you this night. Be still.

Jesus:

My children, I am your sovereign Lord. I, your Jesus, speak. Through My servant I come, she who is My mother, as she intercedes on behalf of you all. Through this one whom I have chosen, who allows Me to come and to speak to you in her voice, I come. In greater measure, in greater power, in greater glory, in the Church and her sacraments, I come. In My eucharistic self that lives in you at this moment, I come.

You, you among you here, who have received Me even this day, do you know that My heart beats in you? You, among you, who have come before those whom I have ordained on this earth, who stand in My stead in the confessional, to be reconciled unto Me, do you know that it is I, I Who spoke, I Who absolved, I Who made peace where there was sin and death? How many of you, this week, this month, this year, sought Me in the stillness of a church before My body exposed, before a tabernacle in which I reposed? Do you not know yet that there I was with you? You do not see, you cannot. In these small ways, I break into the world to seek you. You cannot comprehend what I do to come to you in these ways. You cannot imagine what it was for Me to come to reside in you. You do not know what your God has done.

It is not through your fault that you do not know. It is not because of your sins. Simply because you are not as I am, you do not see My face as I am. Even, even if man had never walked from My grace, still My creature could not comprehend My majesty. How perfect, then, My ways, that I should deign to come unto you, as one of you, that I took upon Myself human flesh and a human soul that, forever, for always, in every age, I and you would be one.

Think! Imagine! Can you comprehend it? How does this not fill you with indescribable joy?

My people, I speak out to you, this day, in this little way, through this little servant, that you might see that there is nothing that I would not do to reach you. What I accomplished on the cross is perfected in you. Each time that you suffer, each burden you bear, each trial you face, you suffer in Me. What a blessed gift I give! Do not now, then, dear children, think on My most glorious Passion. Do not see the nails and the crown and the scourging. Do not see the cross, but see what is now and ever shall be, your Jesus, alive, resurrected! All authority in Heaven and earth is mine, and I come to you.

Hear Me, My people! Hear Me! In every age, I call. I send My mother. I send saints. I send prophets. I send My priests. I send religious. I send My popes. I send My teachers. I send the small, the lowly, the sick, the ill, the imprisoned, the sorrowing, the grieving, the widow, the orphan, those most destitute, because they are Me! I walk among you where they are. This is a world filled with Christ, if you but have the eyes to see.

Therefore, My beloved, be at peace. Be in indescribable joy. In every sorrow, in everything, in all that comes to pass, know that there is nothing I would not do to reach you. You need only lift your face, raise your hand, speak My name. My arms are extended waiting to embrace you, My people. My hand reaches to grasp yours. All who hear these words, in this room and those who shall hear them in times to come, hear Me. Remember. Know this, that no matter what may happen in your daily lives, no matter what trial you might face, no matter what adversity I permit to come to you, there is nothing, nothing that can separate you from Me.

You have the choice. You may live in Me, and suffer in Me, and love in Me, and have My peace and My joy, or you may choose a way apart, which is only death. There is nothing else at the end of that road. It has always been that way and it will be until I come again in glory. And so, you see clearly, as did those first whom I called to be My apostles, there are two ways, and the choice is yours. I beckon to you, I call to you, I ask you, to take My hand and to follow. Pick up your cross, no matter how great, and follow, for as you are crucified in Me, so too shall you rise in Me, so too shall you have a share of My glory, and then, then when all things have passed, then you will see Me as I am.

October 2013

Jesus:

My people, it is I who come to you tonight, your Lord, for it has been My way to send My mother, she who first came to you and spoke My word in her way, her gentle mothering way. She first came to you because I sent her. I sent her to call a wayward people. I sent her to call a people who were apart from Me, as only a mother can. My people, she, the precursor, the one who came before, the one whom I sent, has spoken to you and taught you and led you. Her presence has blessed you. Now, it is I who come, for she leads the way to My heart in all things. It is My desire to speak to you, for I have sent her yet, so few have heeded her call. So few have come, have approached the fount of living water, the ocean of mercy that is My heart. So few have heeded the call of a mother. How, children, can you not respond to a mother?

Many of you, many who have come to know Me, to seek Me, many of you have turned to Me in trust and it is good that you should do so, for only I, your God, can ransom you. There is darkness to be sure, but I offer light. There is trial and deprivation. There is ruin, but I offer salvation and hope and life. My people, I invite you, turn your hearts, turn your hearts to Me! There is nowhere else you will find rest. There is nowhere else you will find love as you were always meant to know love.

My people, it is not enough to hear My words. It is not enough to think on them. You must live them! You must live them, for how will My children see the light if you do not bear it in yourself? You, you whom I have called here, to you I entrust My light, My word, My message of life. You, you many who come before Me now in this place where I am present as I am present nowhere else, in this place where I reside body, blood, soul, divinity, all that I am that I wish to give to you, take the love, take the light I desire for My people and bear it brightly. How My children are discouraged! How My people need My love!

My children, know this: I choose to come because I will not cease to seek your hearts. I am the lover that comes to the beloved time and time again. I knock on the door of your heart. I seek you in the dark places. I have come down from glory to die for you, to rise for you, to open the gates of paradise! Choose life, My people!

Children, let your hearts not be troubled, for My words are stern and yet, they are words of hope and grace, for I know the love in your hearts will compel you to carry this light to others, that you might be true witnesses of the Gospel message I have given to you in My word and My deeds. Come then. Follow Me. Give yourself to Me completely, and I shall do great wonders. Permit Me to work in you. Be joined to Me, united in your sufferings to My cross, and you will know great peace and tremendous joy, and this world that has chosen darkness will be converted, will choose light, will choose goodness, and hope, and joy, and love, because first they have seen it in you. Know that I am with you in all things, and I bless you always.

October 2014

Jesus:

Dear people of God, My people, it is I, your Lord, who come to you tonight. Long I sent My mother to you. Long I sent her to speak to you, for she was My ambassador. It was not by her power that she came, but she was sent to deliver a message to My children who are far from Me, who had walked into darkness. I send My mother to many places because she speaks My word, the word that I give to her, the word that is My Father's word. She, who first bore Me from her womb, who bore the Eternal Word in Flesh, bears My word still. She was appointed as the Woman of Revelation. She is the Woman, the one who is the mother of all peoples, the one whom the Devil, the Serpent, goes and makes war against, and against her descendants.

Do you recognize, children, that she has been mother to the Church? Is this a stumbling block for you? Do you see that I have told you in Scripture that it would be so? Is it not fitting then, dear children, that I ought to send her again, as she first became the tabernacle holding the Living Word made flesh? Again, she became the tabernacle of the Word, bearing My spoken word to My people of this generation.

My word speaks to all people. It lives and moves and breathes. When you hear my word proclaimed, you hear Me speak to you, to each of you. When, on the pages of Holy Scripture, you read, "Who do you say that I am?", it is not to men years ago that I speak, but to you. My mother came. She was My prophet. She spoke the message I desired to give to you because of My great and tremendous love for you. Now I come. I come as King to reclaim My rightful place on the throne of your heart. Long has this world worshipped idols. Children, it is time to let go of your idols. It is time to smash your idols!

Why is it, My little ones, that you who see and know and understand my word, cannot believe that I love each of you, each one, uniquely, personally, with unbridled love? You cannot conceive of the love I bear for you. You know with your heads, but you do not know with your hearts. You learn much about Me, but speak to Me little. You read, but you do not understand. You seek, but you do not find because you do not look where I can be found. The hearts of My children are broken and they seek the pleasures of this world, but they will never satisfy, for you were made for Me and you will never know satisfaction until you rest in Me.

I come as King. I come as One Triumphant. Do you fear? Do you have anxieties? Why? I have won! The victory is mine. I, I Am! Are you lonely? Do you seek love? I am the fount of love, crucified for you, My flesh torn and broken for your sake. Do you look for beauty? I am beauty. I will give to you every desire of your heart. You do not know what your desires ought to be. Smash your idols! The time has come. What is in the center of your heart? What have you placed on that altar? What has your fear made you cling to, My little ones, as a child who will not let go of a security blanket for fear of being lost, when he is safely cradled in his father's arms? How can you be lost if you come to Me, the fount of life itself?

I am the only way, the only way to life, the life that you are longing for and yearning for, the life that I desire to bear in your soul, that streams of living water might quench your thirst and you might never know thirst again! How is this possible? You doubt. You say, "But Lord, but Lord, my cross is too heavy. My burden is too great." No, for never was there a cross as heavy as mine, nor a burden greater than mine, and when you call upon My name, I live in you. No longer do you bear your cross, no longer do you bear your burden. I bear your cross as I did on Calvary and will do so until the end of the ages.

Do you see that you were made to worship, you were made for adoration, and you will never know peace until you bend the knee, and clear your hearts of all things passing, and enthrone Me there, for when I am enthroned and sitting upon my rightful place, no storm, no persecution, no trial, no death, no pain will be great enough to separate you from Me, and you will welcome these things in My name and for My name's sake, and you will become saints? My Church needs saints! Will you become saints?

The choice is only yours. I am giving to you every grace necessary. Choose to become a light to this world, for whenever My church is persecuted, whenever she is scourged and she is beaten and she is bloodied, whenever she walks through the cross and dies as she must, because where the bridegroom is, the bride will follow, there I am with My grace, and My power, and My majesty, and My mercy, and I am waiting for you!

You are My church; you, each one of you. I speak not to peoples long ago. I speak not to peoples far from here. I speak to you in this present moment, and every act from my hand, and every grace, and every gift, and all My power, has been given for your sake, and I bore each one of your sins and I knew you by name. Still, I know you. Permit Me to carry your cross. Join Me. Let Me be your God, and you will be My people.

October 2015

God in His Trinity:

My dear people, I come to you this day to speak to you Truth, a truth that the world has long since forgotten, a truth they do not desire to hear, a truth they have turned their faces from, the one thing needed by every human heart. I come to speak to you today the truth of My love, the love that I have for each of you. Over these years, I have come with many messages, spoken to you of the gifts that I have for you, the gifts of grace that are waiting for those who respond to My invitation. At some times, you have heard Me admonish. At other times, you have heard Me encourage. My children, still I am calling, and I desire to remind you that you are loved!

As I see you gathered here, as I read your souls as the pages on a book, and see your hearts as through glass- yes, nothing is hidden from My eyes- I see hearts who have come to Me from many places, all broken, and it is the same when I survey the world. Every heart I see is a broken heart. How much pain have you endured? How much sorrow? How many injuries? How weak have you become under the weight of you own sin? Do you look for reprieve? Do you look for rest? Are you weary of the burdens of this life? Do you cry out for something else? Do you sense in the depths of your soul that this is not as it was always meant to be? That is the image of My love there, for there is no heart that has not been impressed with My love.

If you lived in the misery of this world, without the image of My love in your soul, you would not know that you were in misery. You would not seek to look up to find something greater. You would not raise your eyes to Heaven to say, "Father, where have you gone?" It is a mark of your fidelity that you seek me, that you cry out for something else and rebel against the present darkness in which you live, the present misery that oppresses you, for you were created to be so much more. You were each created to be sons and daughters of the King of Heaven! That is the gift I offer you, that is the truth I speak to you. You are loved beyond your wildest imaginings with a passionate, intimate, love!

Does this surprise you? Do you look to your own failings, and faults, and sins, and think, "How, Lord, could I possibly do your will or accept your love, as weak as I am?" Do you not yet know that My power is perfected in weakness, for where you are weak, I am strong. Where you are broken, I will heal. I heal! Where you are lost, I will find you. Where you grieve, I will give you joy. Where you sorrow, I will bring peace. Where you despair, I will bring hope. Where you die, I will bring life eternal. Nothing is incomprehensible to Me, save one thing: the simple choice to reject what I offer. It is, itself, the mark of a creation so lost that it cannot see that which it desires most.

I made you rational minds, and you seek irrationality. I made you stewards of love, and you desire hate. I made you for Me, and you turn from Me. My people, do not turn from Me any longer. Rather, take one step toward Me, one step. To some of you gathered here, this will be a simple matter. For others, it will be very difficult, for each of your hearts is broken in different places and each of you need healing in different ways, but I, Who am the Divine Physician, bring healing to all, and I know your hearts as you do not know yourselves.

Therefore, little ones, step toward Me. Make a motion. Move toward Me. Think of Me. Breathe a sigh of desire toward Me. All that I need to work in you is one moment where you give your will to Me. That is the depth, and the breadth, and the width, and the height of the love and the mercy I extend to you. I require no great penances. I require no great offerings. I require no great works, simply a moment where you give to Me your will, and I will act! One step is all that is required, and I will give you grace, and if you will grasp that grace and hold fast to Me, I will hold you as you take a second step and a third and a fourth, until you are walking on the road that leads to Me.

Reach out to Me then. Permit Me to save you. Permit Me to love you, to bring you out of the misery and brokenness in which you live, and create a new life in you, a new heart, a new soul, a beautiful and precious, infinitely precious, creation of My own heart. Each of you is infinitely precious. For each of you, I give My all. Respond to Me in love and let Me hold you fast to My heart.

October 2016

Jesus:

My people, see how it is I, your Lord, Who comes to you this night. Again and again, I tell you that I sent My mother to you first, she who is precursor and prophet of My word, she who was sent into this world to call you back to a life in Me, to a life in union with My holy will. See that it is I, Myself, that come this night, for so great is My love for you, so great My desire to save you from your present sin, that I come, I.

My little ones, I have given this grace to the world because My church, My people, are in need of conversion. They have forgotten My love. They do not know their value, their tremendous worth. The Adversary has sown seeds of division and despair, where I desire unity and hope. He has sown seeds of hatred and anger, where I desire love and forgiveness. He has told you every deceit about who you are. Why can you not hear the word of your Lord crying out to you from the silence of your own heart, speaking to you, "You are loved for all ages"?

Truly, I come bearing this message. See how I am present here even now in the tabernacle before you. You come to hear My word. You come to experience My presence and it is good, for I have called each of you here. Yet, I desire to give My full self to you each day as My Body is broken again upon your altars and, in My eucharistic presence, that great sacrifice that I made is present again.

You come seeking My word, and yet I call you. Gather in your families. Read Scripture. Hear My Living Word spoken to you in this present moment. You look to find Me, but you fail to see because you do not look rightly. I have always been here in the tabernacle waiting for you. Come, then, My beloved! Sit with Me. Be in My presence. Let Me tend to the garden of your soul. Let Me plant in that garden seeds of joy. Let Me give you living water that you might never thirst again!

Many years I sent My mother to this group. I sent My saints of Heaven that you might see that holiness is attainable, not through your own will and ability, but through My will, My fiat, and My unimaginable power, and still, the fear, the fear that you have in your hearts! Do you not know I am capable of destroying even death? Children, let go of your chains! I spoke to you and told you it was time to smash your idols. Again, I spoke to you and said that it was a time for healing. This year, on this day, on this third message, I say, you have smashed your idols, you desire to be healed, but you will not let go of the shattered pieces or hand Me your heart for healing. I am the Gentle Physician. Come! Are you broken? Let Me heal you. Are any of you ill? Let Me strengthen you. Do you know despair and brokenness? Let Me fill you with grace. I am not deaf to your cries, nor am I blind to your struggles. Yes, you here gathered, many have suffered terrible, terrible trials since last you heard My voice and yet, how great is My providence. How I love!

You are here but a brief instant. In this time that I wish to purify you, and refine you as gold tested in fire, will you submit to that purification? Will you let Me burn, with the fire of My love, all impurities from you, and create in you a clean heart? Come sit with Me. Be present with Me. Let Me speak healing and peace to your soul, for all power in Heaven and earth, beneath the earth, in all created space, in every place, is Mine. I am the only One that can save you, give you peace and give you unimaginable joy!

Receive Me. Be with Me. Let Me love you, My children, weak, and damaged, and broken as you are. Give to Me your shattered idols. Give to Me the chains that have been broken. Hand over the fullness of your being, and I will breathe My life into you and, in this way, in this darkness, I will renew My Church. The Adversary, who for so long has wreaked havoc on My church, and My people, will have power no longer, for all that it takes to deprive him of his power is your consent to My will.

October 2017

Mary:

My dear ones, peace be with you. It has been some time since I have spoken with you, for my Son deigned to choose to speak with you these last years. Again, this year, He sends me. Do recall that He has called you over many years. Yes, my little ones, He has called to you. First, He spoke a message, "Smash your idols! Give them to God." Then He spoke a message, "Let go," for even once you had smashed your idols, still you held onto the broken pieces, clinging to them as if they could save you, or help you at all. Now this night, He sends me, again to come to you as a mother, for who could turn away from the voice of a mother? Is it not true that when no one on earth can prevail upon you, your own mother has power? And so, He sends me to tell you this third part of His message that He has shared with you over the past three years.

First, He asked you to smash the idols, then to give up the pieces of the broken idols. Now, He asks you to embrace the True God, the One God, the God alone Who can bring you joy, and peace, and happiness, and the fulfillment of every desire you have.

Little ones, the world has forgotten my Son. They do not know of His great love. They do not know what He has done for them. Everywhere there is darkness and the Evil One desires to blot out the name of my Son, and so He sends me as a great mercy to the world, to announce to the world His great love and desire for unity with His people, desire to be one with His people.

Throughout the ages, God has made many covenants with His chosen ones, you, my children, and each time He was faithful to each and every covenant. Faithfully, He walked by His people and only when they turned their faces from Him and began to worship false idols, did they find malcontent, misery, desolation, and despair; and yet, little ones, still, even now, my children fall into this same trap, this snare laid by the Enemy so cunning. You cannot have joy apart from God.

These are the steps to conversion. This is the way to live faith fully. First, you must make a place on the altar of your heart for God, for I tell you, every man worships some god. Not every man worships the God, our God, the only God, the One Who is and was and ever shall be with all power, and all majesty. Every man has a god on the altar of his heart, and when they are false gods, they make promises of happiness, and there is no happiness, only sorrow, and promises of peace, and there is only disharmony and disunity, promises of joy and there is only despair, for all false gods will fail and be shown for what they are: chaff, weeds, not the True Vine, not the Living Water Who desires to fill you with grace beyond your imagining.

So, you must make space on the altar of your heart for God, and it is for this reason that I ask you, again this day, to be aware of the false idols that are placed there, for even good and holy things can become idols when they take the center of our time, our hearts, our love. Then you must give them to God. Have done with them children! Have done with them! Give the smashed pieces to God. Let Him take them from you. Release the grip of your hands upon them. They do you no good. Now, now having heard those messages, you are ready. You have an open space in the center of your heart, on the altar that is there. Whom will you enthrone?

I invite you, even as a mother I beseech you, to enthrone the One Christ in your heart. He who even now in eternity bears the wounds that He took upon His flesh for your sake, that you might never forget what He has done for you. It was not necessary that He bring His woundedness into His glory, but it was a choice that He made, such that He appeared to His apostles transfigured, yet still in His glorified, resurrected body, bearing the very wounds that are the source of His glory and your salvation. And on the day when you stand before Him in His kingdom, He will be a king, resplendent, and bejeweled, and crowned, enthroned, and broken in the flesh bearing the marks of His scourging and a terrible death, because it is these very pains that are His glory and yours. You are called to be the image of Christ. How do you enthrone Him in your hearts? You must love as He loves, because you must become what He is. You must become a new creation, resurrected into a new life, for that is what comes after you have done with your idols and cast the pieces away: resurrection, a new life in Christ! You must make Him center of your heart by keeping Him always at the center of your mind. In everything you do, may He be worshipped.

This is not to say that at every moment of every day you need to speak audible prayers. On the contrary, God desires you to live your vocations fully. It would be impossible for you who are husbands and wives, and mothers and fathers, sisters, brothers, employees, to pray in this way. No, you are called to a different kind of prayer, a living prayer. Yes, pray your Rosary, for it a most powerful prayer. Yes, above all else, come and receive Him in the Mass. You must, must receive His eucharistic flesh to know the fullness of His grace. You would sooner do better without water or the sun than without His Body and Blood to feed and nourish you.

Yes, pray from the heart mentally, vocally, in groups, alone, in your families, with your spouse, but also, transform your every action into prayer. How are you to do this? Every action that is dedicated to the service of God, that looks not to self, but to other, that seeks to bring souls to Heaven, is prayer, and when you do this in union with the suffering of the Christ, remembering His glorified wounds, lifting your own wounds, your own scars, your own traumas, to Him, then, dear ones, your breathing, your living, your sleeping, and your waking will be transformed into prayer and will be made holy, for this in the end is what God is requesting. This is what He desires, a holy people, and that must start with holiness in your own soul, holy marriages, holy families, holy parishes, holy communities, and a holy world.

This is how God desires to work. He could come in His glory and His power and illuminate the darkness so that no man could deny His existence, but, my little ones, how much more beautiful that you, having faith without sight, trusting Him without certain knowledge, would carry a tiny light, each one of you a simple flame in the darkness, to illuminate the place God has placed you. Imagine the glorious light of millions of souls reflecting the light of God, the light of Christ in their own homes, families, and communities!

Do you not see this is how God always works, since the very first covenant with Adam in the Garden, when He commanded man to go forth, and be fruitful, and be multiplied, and fill the earth and subdue it, and be servants first, and stewards first, living in peace, and in harmony, and in joy? That covenant, like many that followed, was broken, but that did not stop the Lord from fulfilling the glorious plan of the Incarnation. Think, think on it children! How greatly you are loved that God Himself came to you as flesh and blood that could be beaten, and broken, and die for you. What love! And so, you must become as He is. You must die each day to self and live for other. You must bear your wounds as Christ bears His and transform them into a source of glory, glory for God and your eventual glory in the kingdom of Heaven, by using these wounds, these sorrows, these pains, and these sufferings, to serve the people of God, to grow in compassion, to grow in mercy, to grow in love.

My little ones, I come as a witness to you. My Son, Jesus, has spoken to you of these things, but I, with truly human eyes, have seen these things. My eyes, even at this moment, behold the glory of God. Perhaps you can relate better to me, as I was as you are, a simple woman living in the place that God planted me, with family, with friends, with joys, and with sorrows. And yet now, I come to you after these many years of speaking to you, and say again, there is nothing on earth that compares to the glory that awaits those who love God with all of their hearts, all of their minds, all of their soul, and all of their strength. You cannot conceive of what is waiting for you in our Father's kingdom. And so, reflect even now on the Gospel that you heard this very night as you received the body and blood of the Lord Christ into your hearts and into your flesh, and were, despite your inability to see, transformed already into a new creation, for it is not possible to receive Him and remain as you were.

What is the Kingdom of Heaven? How are you to find it? Yes, it is a prepared place, prepared by my Son for you from the beginning of time, from the beginning of ages, but also it is a secret place in the heart of every man where there is an altar. Whom will you enthrone on that altar? Will it be the Kingdom of Heaven or the kingdom of this world? The choice is yours. It is only yours. God can send me year, after year, after year, to speak the same message to you, but it is you who must choose, and He will respect the freedom of your choice. He desires relationship with you. He desires to love you, to comfort you, to encourage you, and to be your God, to be in covenant with you. Receive Him, then, dear ones, and know that you are receiving more than you could ever hope for, much more than we deserve, all things, when you receive Him.

Be good stewards of this tiny Kingdom of Heaven that resides within your own soul and bring it unstained and cleaned to the moment of your judgment, when the time comes when you will stand before my Son, and you will see upon His flesh the wounds He bears that were yours, and you will see your own flesh transformed and glorified because He first bore your pains.

Be faithful, my little ones. Do not be discouraged or dismayed. Do not walk apart from Him. Love! Love God and love all those you encounter, and know that, as your mother, I will be with you, ever your advocate and intercessor.

October 2018

Mary:

My dear children, peace be with you today. You gather here in this place because you seek the presence of God. You come to receive a message from Heaven because you are searching after God. You gather in this church and in your home parishes because you desire the grace of God. Little ones, in all of your searching and seeking, in all of your chasing, you feel you must approach the Father, you must find Him. You do not understand that it is God Who has drawn you to Himself. You cannot comprehend how God desires to come to you in your brokenness. You do not understand how in each and every moment of your life, God is present, waiting for your response, waiting for you to give your entire heart to Him that He might do great wonders.

What joy there is in this word, for those who are seeking after God, those who are chasing the Lord, those who are running to find Him, so often get discouraged because they look about and they cannot not see Him. What joy there is in this word, that you do not see Him because He has been beside you, above you, beneath you, below you, and within you, always. He drew you to Himself. He called you to this place, this night, to receive a message from Heaven. He called you to this parish, each and every Sunday, and into your own parishes, to receive His grace.

You run and you seek, and you look for Him in the things of the world. In power, in prestige, in worldly wealth, you seek and yet you do not find what you look for. In the happiness this world has to offer you, you find only despair, for what your heart seeks is the peace and the joy only Christ can give you.

Little ones, He wishes to meet you in your brokenness. Precisely in the center of the storm in your lives is where you will meet Christ. Precisely on the cross, your cross, is where you will meet the Christ. Each and every one of you has a burden you are carrying, each and every one a brokenness, each and every one a wound. It is there that Christ desires to come, to transform, to renew, to heal, to re-create! He desires to make you a new creation in Him. How easily you will let go of the things that are easy, uncomplicated, and happy. How hard you hold onto your hurt, and your wounds, and your brokenness, as if any effort on your part can heal these things or give you peace. Give this brokenness to God. He is the only one Who can give you the peace you are searching after.

There is much fear in the world, much fear amongst my people. Fear is the enemy of peace. Fear is the mark of the evil one who desires to sow in you distance from God, rebellion from God, despair, and a lack of faith. Peace trusts as a child. Peace says, "Yes, God. I want your all!" Peace knows that God, in His infinite goodness and wisdom, in His tremendous compassion and mercy, will run to you as a father to a child to heal, and save you. In this way you obtain the peace of Heaven, a peace that can never be interrupted by anything on this earth, a peace that cannot be broken or stolen, a peace that can never be taken from you. No one can deny you the peace of the Living Christ in your heart, but you must choose this peace and this healing. You must choose.

Little ones, I do not doubt your sincere intention to live the peace of Christ and the love of Christ. Where you are lacking is in your ability to let go of the things to which you hold fast that keep you far from Him. Over these years, my Son has deigned to speak to you at times, and when He has done so through my messenger, His messenger, He has spoken to you of smashing idols. Still, you stubbornly pick up all of the little pieces and reassemble them. I do not chastise you, little ones, but come to you as a mother who can look into the hearts of each of her children, knowing each so uniquely, so individually, and see not only the gifts, and the talents, and the beauty, but also the weaknesses and the struggles. As any mother, I come to my children, I encourage my children, I support my children, and I extol my children to greater virtue, that they might have the joy that their hearts desire. Stop building yourselves these small idols. They are as nothing compared to the One, True, and Living God. They cannot bring you peace, and they cannot bring you happiness that you long for.

What are these idols that you build? Every time you make of yourself a god, every time you put your needs before the needs of your brothers and sisters, every time you fear living your faith to the fullest, every time you deny Christ by denying the truth of His teachings, every time you cave to the pressures and desires of the world instead of living the virtue God desires for you, every time you raise your voice in anger, every time you turn away from one who is rejected and abandoned, every time you fail to speak truth where there is a lack of truth, every time you speak when you ought not, you are building of yourself a small idol. It is you, yourselves, that become the idol.

Often I have said to you over many years, that on the altar of the heart of every man there is a god. Let it be the One, True, Living God! No other god will satisfy. If you make of yourself a god, you will be disappointed. That life can only lead to greater brokenness and greater fear, and I desire for you great peace, the peace that surpasses all human understanding, that is rooted in the perfect trust of God the Father who wants nothing more than to love you exactly as you are. My children, I call you to virtue not that you might earn or merit the grace of God, but in response to the amazing, miraculous, and incomprehensible gift of His love and mercy. Never can you merit the gift He has given. You need not. It is given freely to you. Simply open your hands and receive Him and know that He is God.

My little ones, as I come and speak to you these many years, and I speak to you of the path to Christ, how easy it is to think of the world as those out far from you and yourselves who are, in your minds, exempted from the message that I bring. Tonight, this message I speak not to those out "far from God," some place in your imagination, but to you, in this moment, who hear my words! Whether you hear these words in this church or at another time, God has brought them to you. Through whatever means you are hearing them in this moment, God has called you to this moment of conversion and grace. Hear me then, little ones, as I say: now is the time to give your heart entirely to God, that you might live and know His joy! There is no other reason. God has no need of your love. He has no need of your worship. He desires to love and to inspire you with joy that leads to worship. Receive your God.

Tomorrow, when you wake, you will for the most part have forgotten the words I have spoken. You will open your eyes to each of your individual lives, and you will begin to go about the life in the place God has planted you. This is human nature, and it is not wrong that you ought to live where you have been placed, for that is the vocation you are called to. You need not do great things in the name of God, but the small things, the things He is asking. However, my little ones, I do ask that you do not forget these words. I do ask that as you open your eyes to greet the sunlight of the new day, think first of God. Let Him be your first thought and your last thought. In this way, you will come, each day more and more, to remember God. Yes, little ones, my children struggle so that they cannot even remember the God that even in this moment, places the air within their lungs. When you begin your day thinking of God and His goodness, when you end your day with this thought, my words will be alive for you and you will have a growing gratitude in your heart for the graces and the crosses. Gratitude is the seed of worship, worship is the seed of adoration, and adoration is the work of the saints.

Dear little ones, I impart to you my motherly blessing. I ask you as your mother, who loves you and wants all good things for you, to hear with open ears and an open heart. Be opened! Let the Holy Spirit fill and free you, unbind you from the chains that fetter you, and give you peace and life in Christ.

October 2019

Mary:

My dear little ones, peace today, I bring to you. I come as mother to bless you, to encourage you, and to comfort you. I come to remind you of the call that first I gave so many years ago through my chosen servant. So many gathered here today have not been with me since the beginning, since first I came to this place at the direction of our Father in Heaven because He saw the seeds of faith in the hearts of His people and desired for them to be renewed. Throughout the world my children have lost faith. They have been broken by the hardships and dangers of this world. The adversary desires to snatch them from the hands of Holy Mother Church and from the hands of freedom, love, truth, and life. Everywhere the Father sends me, He sends me with one message, one truth. He sends me to call His children back to Him to be renewed in spirit, to be renewed in faith, to come to know His face and worship Him rightly.

Little ones, from the beginning I have spoken this one message to you, in different ways, in different circumstances, but always the same one truth: the Father in Heaven, Whose love you cannot comprehend, desires to be one with you. You do not yet understand, as you one day will, the purpose of this life. As I survey my children, I see so many hearts gone astray because they seek happiness and joy in places that cannot bring these things. Within your heart is the desire to know the face of God, to know the One Who made you and for Whom you are made, and yet, you continue to seek this joy apart from Him! The world will only know peace and true joy when they return to the Father. Our Father in Heaven sent me because He is a good and merciful God. He does not desire to judge and condemn, but to save, to stretch forth His hand of salvation to all people that would simply turn to Him in trust. What father among you would do less for your children? What mother would not incessantly encourage and even, at times, cajole her children into right behavior, for we do this as mothers and fathers because we desire the happiness that we know is possible for our young ones when they live rightly and in truth. How much more does your Father in Heaven desire to give you these things?

Little ones, you who have not heard the full story of my messages, you who perhaps for the first time are acknowledging that God is real, and present, and exists in this world, and has broken through time, and space, and distance, to reach you in this present moment, to you I say: Come! To you, I beckon. Perhaps you think not of our Lord? Perhaps the busyness and the tasks of daily life have kept you from coming to God? Perhaps you come, but your heart is not present when you worship, for you are distracted by the things of life, and you come because it is your duty rather than your joy? It pleases me that you are here for duty's sake, because obedience itself is a virtue. Yet, greater it is that you should come to the Lord for joy and for love of Him alone, desiring nothing for yourself, but only to give glory to God Who made you and knows you as you do not even know yourselves, but come! Come as you are in this moment, where you are in your life. Those who have not known that God is real, and alive, and working, and moving in this world, come and follow! I invite you as surely as Jesus, on the banks of Galilee, invited His first apostles to come and follow.

Come! I invite you into a new life. You cannot go back. You cannot live the way that you once did, for in this present moment, God has chosen to speak to you, to give to you His great love and His tremendous mercy, to show you that there is hope and a new dawn coming when the world cries, "blackness and despair," that there is life when the world cries "death," that the adversary for once and for all was defeated on Calvary and shall not rise against the Victorious One, the Lamb of God who is slain upon the altars of the earth to take away the sins of the world, He who took into His flesh every sin and every transgression, that you may be washed clean and made white like the snow, and that in the twinkling of an eye, in one splendid moment, through the grace of the sacraments, God reconciles you to Himself and you are made a new creation, your heart transfused with the very blood of Christ, your body animated by the Spirit of God! It is your Father that has made this way for you. In a place, in a time, where there was no path forward for humanity, God took upon himself the task of the salvation of the world, for it was the only way forward. So great is His love that He, Himself, took upon, the pain that was yours, His shoulders, His back, His flesh. He became the Paschal Lamb that you might live and be saved. This Father runs to meet you. This Father chases you as the Hound of Heaven. At every moment of your life, He is seeking you.

The adversary lies to the people of God. He hides in half-truths and in outright falsehoods. He has told the people of God that God is dead, that He does not exist, that He does not love, that He is not present. This is an outright lie! He has told the people of God that they are unworthy, that they are unable, that they are incapable of coming to live the joy and the life that Christ desires for them. This is a partial falsehood. It is true, on your own, left to your own devices, you cannot live the tremendous life of joy that God desires to give you, but you have not been left alone. You have not been abandoned or orphaned. You are not a people cast aside, but a beloved people, a chosen people, sons and daughters of the Most High King, Who is and always will be on His throne. You cannot obtain anything on your own, but with the grace of God you can attain the heights of sanctity beyond your imagining, and with it, the joy and the inheritance that is due to you. I struggle to comprehend how it is that my people, who are offered a treasure greater than all that is in the world, still fail to simply outstretch their hands and receive.

My people, my children, from His cross Christ made me mother of all mankind. I now reign as Queen of Heaven and Queen of the Angels, but my greatest joy is to come to you and minister to you that you might hear the truth as surely and as real as His first disciples did, and that you might come to embrace and live it with your whole being. Choose love, little ones! It is really that simple. It is in choosing love and living love that you will find the face of Christ. The deep longing in your heart to see the face of God will be satisfied in the love that you give and receive from God; and then, one day, at the appointed hour, you will hear Him Who loves you above all else say to you, "Come, now." No longer will it be I who beckons, but He himself who says: "Come! Receive what has been promised to you. Receive what has been prepared for you and gaze upon my countenance that you may see Me, face to face." My little ones, rejoice in the fact that there is so great a God and honor Him, each day in every moment, that your life itself might become prayer.

October 2020

Mary:

My dear children, I come bearing the peace of Christ, the peace of my Son given to you freely, purchased for you through the price of His blood, on a cross on Calvary. I come to offer you joy and freedom from the darkness that threatens to envelop the world: a darkness of materialism and greed, a darkness of sin and death.

My little ones, you cannot imagine how precious you are to God our Father! You do not know how great a price He would pay, and has paid, for your salvation. You see the cross, but you cannot understand the tremendous suffering of Christ that He willingly took upon His own flesh, and spirit, and mind, and heart, that in a mystical way your suffering might be perfected in Him and given tremendous value. Suffering is a cruelty beyond measure if it has no value, and it is you alone amongst all creation, together with the Angels, who can spiritually understand, and know, and see, the plan of God. It is for you a gift, to know the things of God that He has revealed in the person of Christ Jesus, and it is to you given the gift of suffering. No man desires pain and it has no purpose if it is not formative and transforming, for no man who suffers ever remains as he is, but all are changed and transfigured; and it is to you, little ones, the decision about what that transfiguration will look like and what it shall produce in you. For truly, I tell you that it will be to one end or another: to a perfection and a glory beyond your imagining, or to a grief and a loss beyond your comprehension.

Now in this world, all cry "fear!" All are lost, and lonely, and isolated, and afraid, so afraid! My children, why? Why fear when you have such a God who loves you? No, you do not understand, you cannot, but you are not alone in your struggles! Look to the cross, for there you see the measure of the love of God poured out for the world. There you see, viscerally, the price paid that you might be redeemed, for He has called you by name and you are His. Do not think that you are so far from Heaven, little ones, for you are surrounded by so great a cloud of witnesses who do not simply watch you in your struggle and in your trial, but actively participate each day, at every moment, in the working out in your flesh that which is lacking in the sufferings of Christ, which is your participation: the gift of your will. These hallowed and holy ones, these saints of Heaven, these who now behold the face of God, reveal to you the face of Christ. It is in them, in these holy and blessed saints, that you find your help, an army of God ready and waiting to assist you at every moment, and not only these blessed and holy ones, but those who in purgation are even now praying for you, even now offering their sufferings for your sake, helpless as they are for themselves, your brothers and sisters who are in need of your prayer, for you are one holy church.

Holy, set apart for God, not pretentious, not prideful, not better, but set apart. In your brokenness, in your faults, in your failures, in your sinfulness offered up to Him and sanctified, you are one. What greater gift can you give to these poor souls than your prayers, these who wait even now and work toward seeing Him in beatitude, these holy souls, precious to God, who, though they suffer and struggle, would never for a moment return to this earthly dwelling, for they are assured of salvation, assured of forever in Christ. No, it is you, you church here militant, you church working, praying, suffering, loving, it is you who are the hands and feet of Christ in a very real way; if you are to encounter the face of Christ on this earth, it will be only in your brother and sister and the holy sacraments He has left to be your strength and your power. He has given you an authoritative church with the power to bless and to heal. He has given you the sacraments that you might be renewed and strengthened. He knows how you have faulted; He knows your sinfulness. He loves you exactly as you are, always, but He desires so much more for you than this present life you know!

You cannot understand the value of each gift you make, given out of the will, for the kingdom of God. You cannot understand. It would do no good for me to continue to try to explain, for you can see no more than an infant can see and know of the workings of his mother and father, and if an earthly mother and father work for the good of a child, how much more does your Father in Heaven Who is perfect in every way, work for your good? How much more does He love you? How much more does He desire you? He has made you good and beautiful, a wonderous creation. He has ensouled you from the first moment of your conception and has known you, and will know you, for always.

When this world cries out in fear and darkness, respond with love, and peace, and joy! What is there to fear? Do you not know that death is gain and life is gain when lived for Christ? How many holy saints must write to you and speak to you of such things? I ask you, little ones, to take this into your heart, to truly begin to live it, not with the knowledge that comes from the mind, but with the firm will of one who, without reservation, determinedly perseveres, perseveres in truth, and goodness, and beauty. When this world is afraid of that which can destroy the body, I say to you little ones, have no fear! Your God is with you. Seek to work toward the good of your souls. Turn away from the lies of this world that tell you that you have no value. Turn away from the sinfulness of mankind that strips you of your dignity and robs you of your peace. Turn away from those who wish to destroy you, and break you, and turn to the one who was broken for you, whose flesh was laid open and arms outstretched wide as he was crucified for you, because only He who knew what once was, what was given up, what was lost and stripped from you. Only He could freely choose to offer Himself as a holy sacrifice, to purchase back a greater glory than that which was lost.

That is your destiny, a greatness beyond your imagining, a union with God your Father in Heaven that is perfect where you will experience love that you cannot even now comprehend, that you cannot begin to understand. Begin now to turn in love to one another, to encourage one another, to be strength for one another, and to remind one another of the inexorable value of each human person, especially those most reviled by the world, who are my chosen children, my sons and daughters, given to me by Christ Himself as He took His final breaths. You who are my children, I will defend you as my own and I will love you with the love of Christ which even in the perfection and sanctity that is proper to the saints of Heaven, pales in comparison to the love of Christ, which is extraordinary!

I will love you and walk with you. You do not need to do anything except turn your face toward me and extend your hand, that I may take your hand and lead you. I shall do this through those God places in your life to walk with you. I shall be an instrument in your healing. Permit me, little ones, to enter into your heart to clean up, as a good mother does in the home and hearts of her children, to wash away the dirt, and the stains, and the pain, and the grief, and the scars, the scars that are even now on your flesh. Let me wash you clean with the living water that is Christ. Be free, for who can stand against Him? Even the Demons of Hell flee at the sound of my voice, not because of any power or grace that is mine, but because of the love of God that lives in me and in every saintly soul, because of the beauty of the grace of the Holy Spirit Who is even now moving in His Church, and cleansing His Church, and cleansing His people. I your mother come with strength, given to me by God through no power of my own, but through the authority of the Most High God to tell you, be free in Christ, receive the freedom of Christ, and permit Him to love you, for you are so loved.

My little ones, pray in union with the holy souls now in Heaven and making their way to Heaven, suffering, and waiting, anticipating the beatific vision that, please God, will one day be yours. Unite your prayers with the Church Universal for the salvation of souls and the renewal of the faith of the earth, that the Holy Spirit may come with power and glory, with the mercy of God, purchased by the blood of Christ, and open wide the floodgates of His love to transform the face of the earth. May the peace of this same Christ be with you, as I give to you my promise of prayer, advocacy, and protection. Amen.

October 2021

Mary:

My dear children, peace be with you. I greet you today as a mother. I bless you and I thank you for gathering here in such great number to hear the words, the words that God has desired for me to speak to you, a call to conversion, a call to love, a call to peace. My dear children, you live in a time and an age when your world is always changing; there is always something to be afraid of. I tell you that God is not changing. God does not change. He is the Eternal Now. In Him and through Him all things were made. For Christ Jesus, all of creation came into being. In an instant, everything that you know, was!

You cannot comprehend the mind of God. You do not know the permanence, the perfection, the omniscience, the beauty, and the glory of the mind of God. You cannot comprehend how great His plan is for all of the created world. And so, He sends me, my children, all of these years to you, because I too once walked upon this earth, and I understood and knew suffering as you do. I felt the pains of the brokenness of this world and the brokenness of life. I grieved, I suffered loss, I struggled, I sorrowed, and yet it was faith in my God, faith in the living God, the God of Abraham, Isaac, and Jacob, that sustained me and helped me bear the crosses that are present in every life of a believer. And then, to be standing, watching, at the foot of the cross, as I saw my Son, His body pierced and flayed, broken for the salvation of all mankind, to be there at that moment, to suffer such pain in my heart, but to see the glory, the glory that awaited Him, and myself, and you, and all who believe. What words, what words can explain? You cannot understand what God has in store for you!

And so, He sends me, little ones, into this world of darkness and constant change. If it is not this busyness, it is another. If it is not this fear, it is another. Constantly you are being told that all is unwell, and all is unrest. And while truly there is great darkness in the world, a darkness that spreads through the souls of mankind like a plague, worse than any plague or pandemic that you can know, I tell you there is reason for great joy!

Are you living joy, my little ones? Do you have joy in your heart each day, the joy that comes from knowing the risen Christ, He who is Victor over the devil, He who is Victor over death itself? What can befall you in this world that He cannot have victory over, that He has not already been victorious over? Why are you so afraid? You live in a prison of fear. That is exactly where the adversary wishes for you to be, because when you are afraid, you are turned away from God, for there is no fear in Him, and fear comes not from Him.

He has called you to trust like little children; to trust. How is it that a little child trusts? A little one looks with great expectation to his father for all good things. When afraid, he runs, yes, runs to the arms of his mother, knowing that she will protect, and guide, and teach. Are you running, children, to my arms that I might protect you, and guide you, and teach you? Are you running trustingly to the Father? That is the only thing that matters, for in this present age the sufferings are great, but every suffering and every sorrow that you know is the opportunity to be one with Christ, to join your sufferings to His passion and, in doing so, make up that which is lacking in His sufferings: your cooperation, your participation. The beauty of a soul that suffers with patience, with the understanding that God is still God above the heavens, and that He is unchanged, that soul shines in this dark world and is a beacon of light for others who are so in need.

You, you all come here tonight for the same reason, because you are seeking. You know in your hearts that there is more than what you see in this world. Yes, there are glimpses of the divine here given to you in beauty so that you might know the One who is beautiful, but there is so much ugliness, and death, and suffering! You know that you have been created for more than this, and God will take all of this ugliness, and all of this suffering, and all of the death, and He will turn it into something glorious, just as the cross was the greatest glory! In the moment when my maternal heart wept and pained for the suffering of my Son, the greatest act in all of creation was occurring, that singular moment of time, when Jesus gave up His soul to the heavens, when He went to the Father. All of creation shuddered! The skies were rent open! Every angelic host in being, more numerous than you can imagine, more numerous than the stars, shook! Those who chose God shook with joy; those who opposed Him shook, with deep and tremendous awe at the Son of God! And yet, mankind saw it not. Men went about their day working, and trading, and talking, and laughing, and eating, and drinking, and saw it not. Imagine!

You, you who gather here, when you gather and you go to the Holy Mass, when you participate in this great act of worship, when you receive the body and blood, soul and divinity, of your Lord and Savior Jesus Christ, your souls are rent and torn open, and the brokenness that is inside is exposed, exposed to the fulness of

His glory and healed! You do not see. You do not feel. You go about your day eating, and drinking, and working, and praying. If you but could see with the eyes of Heaven. Joy! Your joy would be everlasting! Just as blind Bartimaeus called out to Christ, so you must call out to Him and ask Him to give you eyes to see, to see His face as He truly is, to see Him in His glory. You will not experience great manifestations or miracles each and every time you utter this prayer, but truly I say to you, there will not be a moment that God does not reveal His face to you. You must only look and know how to see it.

If you desire to see, to have eyes to see, look to the face of your oppressed neighbor. Look to the face of the poor. Look to the face of the one who is grieving and sorrowing. Find the suffering Christ there and love Him. If this world turns to love, the light will be unstoppable. The choice belongs to you, my little ones. God is unchanging. The same God who was, is, and ever will be and is present with you now. You must choose. You may choose joy, and faith, and trust, or you can choose fear, the constancy of change, and the irrational busyness of your modern life. There are two roads, and one is the way to life and the other leads to death, and you must choose.

I am with you, guiding you and leading you. I have ever been with you, and I pray God permits me to continue to be with you, that I might lead you, and guide you, and teach you, and instruct you, and be the arms of the mother to whom you run when you are afraid, for I tell you this, the smallest and lowliest saint in Heaven is something so glorious and so beautiful that all of Hell shudders at the thought! Be at peace, little ones, and know that you are loved, so very loved, so precious, for you have such a great redeemer. Amen.

October 2022

(On this date, elementary students from the parish school and their families were present.)

Mary:

My children, It is good to be with you this day to speak words of hope and encouragement to you, to speak the message that the Father has given to the world through the person of His Son, through Jesus Christ, God made Flesh, the One Who came to the world, that He might become man and be as you are, that He might endure all of the things that you have endured and know your sufferings as you have suffered, that He might teach and heal, that He might show you the way to worship the Father, all these things that He might save and redeem you, that you might be in friendship with God and live a life of holiness in Him.

Dear ones, I come to speak a message of peace, and hope, and love to you. I come to encourage your families in these times of trial and desperation. The world struggles in darkness far from God because they do not acknowledge Him as Lord and Savior. They do not know the greatness of His love. How often my children feel oppressed, cast down. How often the enemy has done his work well and has sown seeds of division and strife, where God desires unity and peace. How often my little ones believe the lie that they are not valued, that they have no worth, and that they are identified with and defined by their sin. I tell you this is not so. God Who is love itself, Who is the essence of life, the beginning of all things and creator of everything that you know, sends me to tell you, sends me, a simple handmaiden, one who is unworthy of the gift of the Incarnate God growing within my womb, but who, for reasons known to the mind of God alone, was chosen, was blessed, was called, that I might reveal to you these words in this moment, and again reveal to you Love Itself, Who is the Christ! I was chosen, I was called, for love of you. And you too, my children, are chosen and you are called.

God has set you apart for Himself. God desires to love you as you have not been loved before. God desires to be with you, to intimately know you, to guide you and to love you, to encourage you, to build you up into something that you cannot even now imagine yourself to be. It is false that God desires to oppress you or inflict upon you rules and guidelines that separate you from Him. Do you know your worth, my children? Do you know your value? Truly, you are worth the life of God's Own Son. You are worth the life of my Son, poured out for you on Calvary, that you might, through His blood, be saved and recreated. And as surely as He left the tomb on Easter morn resurrected and transfigured, so too are you resurrected in the baptismal waters of grace and made into a new creation, and every time you fall and return to Him and are reconciled to Him in the sacraments, then, dear children, you are born again, and you live anew. You are transfigured as surely as the Lord appeared bedazzled on the mountain in front of His apostles. You are transfigured when you receive His body and His blood, and His life shines within you. When you pray, when you turn to Him in your desperation, and in your pain, and in your suffering, He makes you new. He will make all things new.

I speak to my young ones, to those who are young in the eyes of the world but wise in the eyes of God, now. My children, littlest ones, know that you have a God in Heaven that loves you above all things. You cannot imagine how much you are loved, and there is nothing that you can do that can make your Father in Heaven stop loving you. As you grow in wisdom and in age, as you experience the trials of life and the love of your families, hold your faith. Hold on to your faith. It has been given to you as a gift, first and always, by God Who loves you, and by your families who have brought you to faith, who have committed themselves to teaching you that you are precious, and you are dear, and your value is without estimation. Hold that faith tightly, for everything in this world that is dominated by the powers of Hell will seek to destroy it with great severity, with ruthlessness unyielding.

And yet, God Who is Christ, Messiah, has won the victory! And He Who is now seated at the right hand of the Father, is no adversary of the Evil One. No. The Evil One goes to make war against His children because he has been crushed, for God took this humble servant, one who was chosen, myself, for reasons I cannot yet comprehend even in the sight of God, and has permitted me through my work in this world, in many places and at many times, to crush the head of the serpent, to place my heal upon his head, that his power might be restricted and that he might not act any longer against my children with such viciousness and such deceit. I come as a mother to point out the enemy, that you might recognize him as he is, but more so, to point out Christ. Do not take your eyes off Christ. He is victorious in all things, and He loves you with an unfathomable love!

Little children, as you hear and reflect on these words, pray simply. You do not need to be wise in the ways of the world. You do not need to be wise in faith to turn to God with simple trust. I tell you, in this room now there are simple ones, little children, whose faith is greater than those who have reached an esteemed age. Pray, my children. Speak to God plainly. Tell Him your joys and your sorrows and trust Him to love you where you are. He will not abandon you. He will not forsake you. He will guide you each day of your life until He brings you to Heaven to be with Him in eternity. That is His plan for you. That is His design for you. It is for that reason He sends me to speak this message to you, not to the world, not to the masses, to you, you who are present here in this room at this moment.

I speak this to you because God has known you. He has heard you. He sees the struggles of your family. He sees how you are parenting your children. He sees how you are attempting to obey your parents even when it is most difficult, little ones. He sees the families that are gathered here today, and He blesses you. For one He would have come, He would have come to Calvary to suffer and to die, and for one, He sends me today. That is the measure of His love. He will never stop seeking His children. You do not have to go far to find Him. Simply turn your heart to Him. Pray with simple words asking for His help and He will be present to you, and there is no power in Hell that will stand against it, because God's love is greater than all things. My children, be at peace. Let peace reign in your marriages, in your families, in this parish, in this community, and in the world.

October 2023

Mary:

My dear children, peace! Peace, I say to you! How many years I have come promising you peace, peace that Christ alone can bring, the peace that is beyond your understanding, the peace that pervades all things, the peace that overcomes all darkness, the peace that fills your souls and makes you new, the peace that you cannot understand. You cannot grasp the peace of Christ that I offer to you, the peace that God desires to give to you. In the time when the world has no peace, I say again to you, peace! Be at peace.

My little ones, I have called you here throughout these years to hear my words, words that are given to me by the Father to give to you. I have no message of my own. There is nothing that I wish to say. Everything that I give to you, has been given to me by the Father. Everything I give to you, all of the graces, all of the gifts, everything I have within me, belongs to the Father, proceeds from the Father, and is given to you because of the love of the Father. It is the Father Who calls you. It is the Father Who beckons to you. It is the Father Who extends peace to you. It is the Father Who sends me to tell you that you are loved.

You are beloved children, children of the Most High God. You are His people, and He is your God. How faithful He is! Never has He abandoned you. Never will He leave you. Never will He turn from you, my people, my children. My dear ones, respond with the fullness of your heart to the life that Christ desires to give you. The peace of Christ, the peace of Christ can fill your homes, and your hearts, and your lives. It can fill this world through the peace that each of you embrace and live. You are the bearers of the peace of

Christ. It is to you the task is given. It is to you that the challenge is given. Embrace the peace of Christ and be peacemakers, for the world is sorely in need of peace. And in these days, I tell you, God desires to pour upon you a portion of His Spirit so great, so tremendous, that I tremble at the thought! God desires to give you the perfect peace that is His, to make you peacemakers in this world. You say, "What can I do? I am but one man." You are united. Your prayers, together with the prayers of all men of good will throughout this earth, the prayers of the Saints in Heaven, the Holy Souls in purgation, they are a resounding symphony of grace, and goodness, and love! You do not know the power of your prayer. Therefore, do not cease to pray! Do not cease to pray and to embrace a life of prayer.

I have come to call you to live anew. I have shown you a new way to live in your homes and in your families, to live your lives, to live in relationship with the Father. I have come to give you a new way, a new way that was revealed first in the person of Christ, always in Christ, but which I now as a mother come and extol you to, as every good mother does for her children. Christ is the revelation of the mercy and the love of God. He is and always will be, all that you need. In Him, is your joy and your salvation. In Him, is your healing, oh broken people, oh ill ones, oh sorrowing children, oh suffering ones! In Him, is your healing. Turn, then, with open hearts to Christ. Give Him all that you are, for first He gave it to you. You belong to Him. What a blessed thing that is! He takes care of His possessions. He has given me the opportunity to come in this miraculous way to many places, over many years, because His people have wandered far, and God desires His people to return. Return to your Father.

Dear ones, there is a Father of love Who waits for you. There is a Father Who desires to give to you all that you need. The sufferings of this life are great, and you experience much pain, but I tell you, could you but see the joys and the grace of Heaven, all of your sorrows and sufferings would fade in the light, the perfect light, of the goodness of our God! He knows you, each of you. He calls you each by name to be His cherished one, His beloved. Hear and answer Him! Embrace the peace He desires for you. Live as Christ lived, as He lives yet in each of your hearts, and give to one another that same love that He extends to you, that same mercy you have known. The way is simple, but it is not easy. You must turn to prayer to strengthen you for the task to which you have been called and the mission that is yours. You, my little apostles of love and mercy, go into this world of darkness and peacelessness, and bring the light of Christ Jesus, the light that surpasses all understanding, that overcomes all darkness, and that has victory even over the grave.

My little ones, turn back then. Turn back and return to your Father in Heaven. Turn back to prayer. Turn back to those things I have called you to, that you have forgotten to live. Go to the Word of God. See Him. Know Him. Love Him. Abandon yourself to Him in trust. Be His little children and let Him be your God.

Made in the USA
Middletown, DE
26 December 2024